BUDGET MANAGEMENT

A Reader in Local Government Financial Management

BUDGET MANAGEMENT

A Reader in Local Government Financial Management

The *Public Budgeting Laboratory* consists of the *Workbook, Instructor's Manual, Data Sourcebook,* and *Budget Management: A Reader in Local Government Financial Management.*

Edited by

Jack Rabin

Associate Professor and Chair
Graduate Program for Administrators
Rider College
Lawrenceville, New Jersey

W. Bartley Hildreth

Assistant Professor of Finance and Public Administration
Graduate School of Management
Kent State University
Kent, Ohio

Gerald J. Miller

Assistant Professor
Department of Political Science
University of Kansas
Lawrence, Kansas

published by Carl Vinson Institute of Government University of Georgia

BUDGET MANAGEMENT: A READER IN LOCAL GOVERNMENT FINANCIAL MANAGEMENT

Editorial coordination: Emily Honigberg, Rebecca McCarthy

Editorial assistance: Elinid Apostolik, Gail Karwoski, Dorothy Paul, Inge Whittle

Graphic production: Reid McCallister

Typesetting: Debra Peters, Angela Fegley

Institute publications editor: Ann Blum

Library of Congress Cataloging in Publication Data
Main entry under title:

Budget management.

1. Local budgets—Addresses, essays, lectures. 2. Local budgets—United States—Addresses, essays, lectures. I. Rabin, Jack, 1945- . II. Hildreth, W. Bartley, 1949- . III. Miller, Gerald.

HJ9111.B82 1983 352.1'2 83-10799
ISBN 0-89854-090-9

Foreword

Budget Management provides a comprehensive collection of articles on topics relating to budget development and budget execution, by authors from academic, public sector, and business environments. It is one component of the *Public Budgeting Laboratory*, a simulation that gives participants experience in local government budgeting. *Laboratory* participants learn how to analyze data relevant to budget decisions, including revenue forecasting, expenditure estimation, and budget balancing.

The *Laboratory* is a result of a collaborative effort begun by the authors while they were associated with the Vinson Institute. It includes four volumes—the student workbook, the data supplement, the instructor's manual, and this reader.

Besides meshing with the *Laboratory* simulation, *Budget Management* can be used alone, as a source book for people involved in local government budget decisions and for public administration students and instructors.

Robert E. Crew, Jr.
Director
Carl Vinson Institute of Government

Contents

UNIT II: BUDGET EXECUTION 145

Preface

This collection of essays deals with local government budget management. Designed as a basic source on the development and execution of the annual budget, it addresses the needs of three target user groups.

The first target group consists of participants in the *Public Budgeting Laboratory* simulation (also published at the University of Georgia). As an experiential learning exercise in budget making, the *Public Budgeting Laboratory* guides participants in the development of a city budget and the structuring of a budget analysis. In teaching the lab, we found that participants needed ready access to additional materials. This reader fills the void in information.

A second user group is the ever-increasing number of budget participants in local government who want to become more familiar with skills and perspectives of budget management. Whether the interested person is a police chief, fire fighter, social worker, budget officer, or assistant city manager in charge of collective bargaining, the budget and its management are critical. This reader covers the basics of budgeting.

Finally, the book addresses the needs of public administration students and instructors. For so long the only materials available for classroom use have been very technical manuals or, at the opposite extreme, highly theoretical and conceptual approaches to public budgeting. Lately, however, the term "financial management" has been adopted more frequently as the label for the course in MPA programs focusing on the budget. Along with a recasting of course titles, instructors have faced the need to structure lectures and discussions with more substantive material on local government budget management. This has meant that instructors have had to either refine already acquired budget-related skills or acquire such perspectives for the first time. This reader strikes a balance of sorts in allowing the person reviewing the material to gain an understanding of the various elements of budget management while retaining an orientation to practice. The authors believe it can help student and instructor alike.

As we see it, *Budget Management* divides roughly into two divisions: budget development and budget execution. Our overview essay links the readings and the two major units. Unit I focuses on budget development, opening with two readings designed to help define budgeting and the budget process (including the use of zero-base budgeting). Then, the unit turns to a review of the budget's setting, revenues, and expenditures. Unit II reviews budget execution, including management options (e.g., cash and debt management), controls (i.e., accounting), reporting practices, and accountability devices (i.e., auditing). Combined, the book's two units introduce the reader to the variety of skills, perspectives, and concepts critical to budget management.

Jack Rabin
W. Bartley Hildreth
Gerald J. Miller

Overview

Once a year every local government adopts the most important possible statement about its purpose or existence. The statement is a *budget* and it includes decisions concerning the allocation of community resources to meet goals of civic improvement. The effort to decide on these goals and execute the resulting policies represents *budget management*. The readings in the following sections attempt to describe and apply available techniques for making and implementing the civic will. Thus, we divide the readings into two logical units—the development of a budget and its execution.

What concerns us is a full understanding of relationships within and between budget formulation and execution. Budget participants, as the accompanying readings suggest, must devote attention to questions involving budget development such as the following:

1. How is budgeting defined and what is the budget process?
2. What preconditions, or settings, structure budgetmaking?
3. What are the various types of revenues and how are they projected?
4. How does one analyze expenditures for services, compensation costs, and capital outlays?

and those involving budget execution, including these:

5. What are the financial operations and policies that can help maintain the soundness of one year's budget and improve financial opportunities for future years?
6. How can management controls—the accounting system—meet the needs of decisionmakers?
7. What purpose does financial reporting serve?
8. How can evaluation and auditing be of use to managers?

These questions serve to illustrate the range and scope of issues facing budget makers. Each question frames the discussion contained in this collection of readings. Thus, Unit I of the readings focuses on budget development and its four subdivisions—definition, setting, revenues, and expenditures. Unit II of the readings reviews the budget execution process, again using four subdivisions—operations, controls, reporting, and auditing.

Unit I

Budget Development

1 Introduction

Budget management describes orderly decision making and execution. The first half of the budgeting process—development—covers decisions about what community resources are allocated to meet what goals of civic improvement. How do budgets meet these goals? The type of budget dictates how the budget works. For purposes here, the definition of the budget and the type used determine much in the process of allocating dollars to one activity or another.

This unit examines the development of a local government's annual budget. Fundamentally, this examination requires defining a budget and showing how budgeting can differ among governments. We first look at the budget-making setting and directly at constraints imposed by mandates; then at budgeting in an era of scarcity; and finally, at questions concerning the government's financial condition.

Local governments must adopt balanced budgets. Attention generally focuses quickly on the simplistic balancing equation of local government budgeting: "projected revenues equal authorized expenditures." To deal with the left side of the equation, a section of the following readings examines typical revenue sources—including federal grants that are declining somewhat in emphasis and user charges and service fees that are increasingly emphasized by economists and decisionmakers alike. A second selection covers growing revenue projections. A final reading discusses expenditure analysis, including the identification of the costs and benefits of services, methods of analyzing the costs of compensation, and problems in planning and scheduling the payment for large capital outlay purchases.

Definition

What is a budget? A "budget," according to Arthur Mendonsa, can be viewed as a spending plan for a particular period of time, usually 12 months. The spending planning, however, may follow simple or circuitous routes, according to Mendonsa, across the various types of budgets.

What do all of these budget types really signify? Probably the type of budget dictates the city government's philosophy regarding civic management. According to Allen Schick, a budget orients managers to the types of questions—the decisions—on which they need to concentrate. He states,

> A *planning orientation* focuses on the broadest range of issues: What are the long-range goals and policies of the government and how are these related to particular expenditure choices? What criteria should be used in appraising the requests of the agencies? Which programs should be initiated or terminated, and which expanded or curtailed? *A management orientation* deals with less fundamental issues: What is the best way to organize for the accomplishment of a prescribed task? Which of several staffing alternatives achieves the most effective relationship between the central and field offices? Of the various grants and projects proposed, which should be approved? *A control orientation* deals with a relatively narrow range of concerns: How can

> agencies be held to the expenditure ceilings established by the legislature and chief executive? What reporting procedures should be used to enforce propriety in expenditures? What limits should be placed on agency spending for personnel and equipment?[1]

As Schick suggests, form does dictate function.

Completion of the budget by a target date normally is ensured because such calendars are imposed legally. For management purposes, then, governments find it useful to follow a ritualized process that includes steps and responsibilities. Mendonsa presents linkages among and between the various budget steps. Furthermore, he indicates how a set of forms can help in presenting necessary data.

In addition to the three basic types of budgets, one reform (zero-base budgeting or ZBB) has gained recognition as one of some utility. This budget type, according to Sydney Duncombe ("Zero-Base Budgeting") is "a budget system in which each department or agency develops a series of requests for differing levels of services and then arranges these requests in priority order." Zero-base budgeting garnered attention following its use by the state of Georgia, the city of Wilmington, Delaware, and the U.S. government. While the process does not actually live up to its name in practice, by forcing one to plan a budget from zero, ZBB does foster identification of programs and subdivisions and relevant performance and cost data for use in comparing services both within and between program units. To elaborate on this, Duncombe offers a basic review of how ZBB can be used in small local governments with step-by-step instruction using a hypothetical department.

Setting

Public budget making occurs within an often-ungenerous environment. A section of the readings that follow explores three broad characteristics of the budget actors' surroundings—legal mandates, economic uncertainty, and the structure of resources and constraints that one calls a government's financial condition.

Fundamentally, local government budgeting operates in a complex web of legal requirements, or mandates, from both the federal and state governments. The cost of adhering to such mandates can be quite expensive. At the federal level, formal orders, such as court orders, and voluntary arrangements, or contracts—the so-called "red tape" of grant administration—help tie local government spending patterns to the federal government's policy decisions. Mandates also come from the state government because local governments are creatures of states. Therefore, states have large stakes in the affairs of their local governments.

What is the magnitude of these mandates? Why are concerns raised? Consider the statement by the National Association of Counties:

> Investigators in ten local jurisdictions, for example, found that each was expected to comply with a minimum of 1,000 federal and state mandates; even if all conditions of aid are excluded, each jurisdiction must comply with the 500 mandates . . . . In fact, local governments are spending more and more time trying to cope with the administrative chaos resulting from combined federal and state mandates. Sometimes, these requirements are inconsistent and unrealistic. The Maryland state requirement that hot water in health care facilities be no less than 110 degrees F. is complicated by a federal requirement that the water can be no more than 110 degrees F. County hospitals are therefore forced to install sophisticated and costly equipment to maintain a constant temperature for federal and state compliance.

Further examples illustrate state interest. State law, for example, might dictate a specific date by which the city council must adopt the local budget. Furthermore, laws can specify that particular budget formats and accounting systems will be used. The taxing power of local government also operates under limits—perhaps permitting adoption of a sales tax only upon the approval of citizens in a local referendum. Moreover, the basic right of a jurisdiction to exist often rests on the provision of particular services. For example, states incorporate municipalities, in part, to have major responsibility for maintaining public safety. Thus, police and fire services are fundamental to the municipalities' existence.

The National Association of Counties report, reprinted here, explores the critical role of mandates local officials face. The report includes guides for determining the fiscal impact of mandated costs. If utilized, such techniques can force actors in the government's budget process to identify the amount of expenditures mandated by the state and/or federal government and amounts controllable by local officials.

Local governments face compelling problems in matching needs to resources, especially at times of economic uncertainty. In such situations, services or programs have to be reduced or taxes have to be raised, or both. Citizens, however, generally express disapproval of the idea of new taxes. In fact, some commentators feel "tax revolts," such as California's Proposition 13, are not just a passing fad. Managers must cope with demands to reduce or limit government activities—the concept of cutback management. Of course, budget makers have little chance of getting federal and state mandates lifted. Thus, attention turns to doing more with less. Charles Levine, an authority on cutback management in government, addresses the issue. He defines cutback management as

> managing organizational change toward lower levels of resource consumption and organizational activity. Cutting back an organization involves making hard decisions about who will be let go, what programs will be scaled down or terminated, and what clients will be asked to make sacrifices.

He also attempts to outline the sources of resistance and problems one encounters as one manages fiscally stressed governments.

A local government's financial condition rests upon the interplay of many factors, including past budget decisions, economic uncertainty, resource scarcity, taxpayer revolts, and legal mandates, many of which subtly escape the attention of decision makers until unexpected fiscal stress rivets attention and creates unwanted surprises. To help monitor a government's financial condition, fiscal indicators have evolved. These indicators help one track changes in the social, economic, and financial characteristics of the governmental unit. A selection from the Governmental Finance Research Center offers a review of purposes, uses, and examples of fiscal indicators. According to this selection, fiscal indicators fall into three broad categories:

> *external influences*, including local demands and resources, the national and regional economy and intergovernmental issues;
> *organizational practices* and policies in issues management; and
> *internal financial characteristics*, such as revenue, expenditures, debt, unfunded liabilities reserves, and condition of capital assets.

Budget makers can employ such indicators to help uncover favorable or unfavorable trends deserving further analysis.

Revenues

A budget links projected revenues with expected expenditures. In arriving at projected revenues, a budget maker must first understand each individual source. Such knowledge results only from a study of each revenue item's legal basis and the manner in which it must be collected. General comments can be presented here since local governments generally use variations of the same revenue types. Mendonsa explores basic features of major revenue sources, particularly the property tax, and other "charges levied against values." His catalog of nontax charges is a veritable cookbook of possibilities.

Local governments have received large amounts of intergovernmental revenue—federal and state grants and shared revenues, such as general revenue sharing—in the past two decades or so. Changes in this aspect of intergovernmental finance are likely, but not to the point of elimination of all federal aid programs. Managers continue to pay attention to how such funds can both be acquired and managed. To help, the Governmental Finance Research Center examines ways federal grants can, and do, have an impact on local government. While advantageous in some respects—increased revenues can be acquired without local tax increases—such funding arrangements have unique problems. The use of federal grants also leads to distortions of local spending priorities as federal initiatives and priorities displace them.

While federal funding may have declined, locally imposed user fees appear to be used increasingly. These fees are direct charges for services provided. For example, citizens may pay a fee for the use of public swimming pools and tennis courts, and a city's garbage collection service can be financed through direct charges for services rendered, not out of a general levy.

One reason for the growth of this revenue source is its equity: the user fee follows directly the ability-to-pay principle underlying taxes—one may accept or refuse the service and pay accordingly. Supporters of user fees argue that charges and fees can reduce the cost of government services. Critics suggest, in part, that user fees place public services out of reach of the poor and economically distressed segments of the population. Likewise, many government services are, simply, "priceless." Paul Downing outlines the economic justification for user charges and service fees and assesses the future of this category of revenues.

In preparing a budget, collections under all current and any new proposed revenue sources must be projected. How can this be accomplished? Charles Liner provides some answers. In this pacesetting article, Liner elaborates two basic projection methods: time series and trend-line analysis. Each technique can be employed in even the smallest unit of government.

Expenditures

Governmental entities provide direct services to citizens (e.g., line activities, such as fire protection and snow removal) and perform activities to support the line agencies (e.g., staff activities, such as personnel and computer services). Each service component expends money, but the exact costs and benefits defy easy measurement. Because of these problems, performance improvement efforts face enormous difficulties in government.

New and expanded services present special difficulties for the budget maker. For example, are all service expansions worthwhile? If not, how can managers differentiate among and between service alternatives? Analysis could help. Research on the costs and benefits of projects can help guide the preferences of policymakers and prevent arbitrary service changes. Perceived or artificial political pressure may be weighed against study of the actual problems and gains from service improvement. "Evaluating Public Expenditures" offers guidelines, as employed in Massachusetts, for public expenditure analysis, emphasizing ways to determine calculated project costs and benefits.

If analysis and management of the costs and benefits of additional services come only with great difficulty, measurement of improvements in current services—especially through productivity program evaluation—faces intractable problems. For example, public sector performance budgeting, which relies upon measures of productivity, never has been implemented satisfactorily by local governments. A difficult and frustrating offshoot of private sector cost accounting, this type of productivity evaluation requires personnel skills, large amounts of calculative detail, and much analytical time, creating tremendous pressure to withstand its use. Nevertheless, progress may come through trial and error, as indicated in a report issued by the state of Rhode Island. Measurement efforts do promote a clearer understanding of the city's program and services, and "the process of improving services relies heavily on effective evaluation of existing services."

Salaries and employee benefits account for an estimated 60 to 75 percent of most local governments' annual operating expenditures. Unfortunately, many governments have little idea of their total compensation costs. This lack of information complicates both budgeting and collective bargaining. Marvin Friedman presents an exercise showing how to "cost out" compensation agreements. If costs are known and understood by both management and union, bargaining can begin on a firmer financial basis, resulting in settlements tied to their full costs. In terms of budgeting, such compensation calculators give managers and citizens alike an accurate picture of the full cost of government services.

Another major problem area for government managers is budgeting for costly, long-life capital improvements such as new fire trucks and waste treatment facilities. Typically, these expenditures are impossible to fund out of one year's revenue collections, especially in small local governments. Most governments seek external funding either from debt issues or federal or state aid, a complex procedure of both planning and purchasing. In order to deal with these capital item purchases and their funding in a more orderly fashion, a specialized budget process has evolved called capital budgeting. The capital budget helps one systematically plan and schedule the purchase of expensive, physical improvements that will serve the community for several years. John Vogt outlines procedures employed in this budgeting procedure. He shows how the capital budget process can be integrated with the annual operating budget, and he outlines methods for constructing the various parts of a capital budget.

Following a matching of resources with expenditure needs through the budget process, the local government must formally adopt the budget as a guide for the upcoming fiscal year. Typically, the chief executive—the mayor or manager—presents the proposed budget to the legislative body—the council—which has the responsibility to approve the budget plan officially, either with or without modification. Once formally adopted, budgeted expenditures and planned revenue serve as the basis for decisions within the fiscal year. While service provisions reflect the actual end result of the budget preparation and adoption phase, other financial efforts continue throughout the year.

Note

1. Allen Schick, "The Road to PPB: The Stages of Budget Reform," *Public Administration Review* 26 (December 1966): 251.

Definition

2 Budgeting

Arthur A. Mendonsa

What is a budget?
What are the three types of budgets?
What principles should guide the budget program for a small town?
What are the steps in the preparation and adoption of a budget?
How is a budget entered to the accounts?

What Is a Budget?

A budget is a plan for spending the money of an enterprise. It designates the purposes for which money will be spent and it designates the amount of money which will be spent for each purpose. A budget also contains a schedule showing the amount that will be available to spend. This schedule shows the sources from which money will be received and the estimated amount of money which will be received from each source.

A simple budget is illustrated at the top of the next column. Note that this budget is divided into two parts. The first part shows the estimated revenue that will be received during the year. The second part shows how this money will be spent. Note that the amount of money which has been budgeted for expenditures exactly equals the amount of the estimated revenue.

Budget for 19 __
Nowhere, Georgia

Revenue Estimate 19 __		
Source	**Estimated Amount**	
Tax on Real Property	$50,000	
Total Estimated Revenue		$50,000
Budgeted for Expenditures		
Department	**Budget**	
A Department	$10,000	
B Department	15,000	
C Department	25,000	
Total Expenditure Budget		$50,000

The Three Types of Budgets

A budget can take one of three forms: it can be a line-item budget; it can be a program budget; or it can be a performance budget. The three forms differ in the way in which each allocates money for expenditures.

A Line-Item Budget

A line-item budget is one which allocates money for expenditures to specific items or objects of cost without reference to the programs or the departments which these costs will serve. This type of budget lists expenditures by such cost categories as labor, contractual services, commodities, and furniture and equipment. The expenditure portion of a line-item budget is illustrated on page 12.

The principal advantage of a line-item budget is that it is easy to prepare. However, this form of

Reprinted from Simplified Financial Management in Local Government *(Athens, Ga.: University of Georgia Institute of Government, Institute of Community and Area Development, and Center for Continuing Education, 1969).*

Budget for 19___
Nowhere, Georgia

Expenditure Budget

Item	Budget
Personal Services	$25,000
Contractual Services	5,000
Supplies and Materials	5,000
Other Items	5,000
Capital Outlay	10,000
Total	50,000

budget tells very little about the activities or functions of the organization it serves. For example, it shows the amount of money that has been budgeted for personnel, but it does not show the nature of the services which these personnel staff. This characteristic of the line-item budget limits its usefulness as a device for giving direction and purpose to public service programs.

A Program Budget

A program budget is one which allocates money to the functions or activities of an organization rather than to specific items of cost. A municipal budget of this type lists expenditures by such cost categories as public safety, streets and traffic, and sanitation. The expenditures portion of a program budget would be in a form much like that which follows:

Budget for 19___
Nowhere, Georgia

Expenditure Budget

Program	Budget
Public Safety	$25,000
Streets and Traffic	10,000
Sanitation Services	5,000
Leisure-Time Services	10,000
Total Budget	$50,000

The program budget described above can be presented in more detail to show the departments or activities involved in each program category. Thus:

Program	Expenditure Budget
Public Safety	
Police Protection	$15,000
Fire Protection	10,000
Total Public Safety	$25,000
Streets and Traffic	
Street Maintenance	$ 8,000
Traffic Engineering	2,000
Total Streets and Traffic	$10,000

Few, if any, budgets are prepared exclusively on a program basis. Instead, program costs are usually broken into line-items. When prepared on this basis, our program budget might take the following form:

Budget for 19___
Nowhere, Georgia

Expenditure Budget

Program		Budget
Public Safety		
Police Protection		
Personal Services	$10,000	
Contractual Services	2,000	
Supplies and Materials	2,000	
Capital Outlay	1,000	
Total Police		$ 15,000
Fire Protection		
Personal Services	$ 7,000	
Contractual Services	2,000	
Supplies and Materials	1,000	
Total Fire		$10,000
Total Public Safety		$25,000
Streets and Traffic		
Street Maintenance		
Personal Services	$ 4,000	
Contractual Services	1,000	
Supplies and Materials	2,000	
Capital Outlay	1,000	
Total Street Maintenance		$8,000
Traffic Engineering		
Personal Services	$ 1,000	
Contractual Services	500	
Supplies and Materials	500	
Total Traffic Engineering		$ 2,000
Total Streets and Traffic		$10,000
Sanitation Services		
Refuse Collection		
Personal Services	$ 3,000	
Contractual Services	500	
Supplies and Materials	500	
Capital Outlay	1,000	
Total Refuse Collection		$ 5,000
Total Sanitation Services		$ 5,000
Leisure-Time Services		
Recreation		
Personal Services	$ 3,000	
Contractual Services	500	
Supplies and Materials	500	
Capital Outlay	1,000	
Total Recreation		$ 5,000
Libraries		
Personal Services	$ 3,000	
Contractual Services	500	
Supplies and Materials	1,500	
Total Libraries		$ 5,000
Total Leisure-Time Services		$10,000
Total Expenditure Budget		$50,000

The principal advantage of a program budget is that it shows the functions for which money will be spent and the emphasis which the budgeting authority places on these functions. The disadvantage in this kind of budget is that it does not show the level of service that will be produced by the functions for which money has been allocated. This characteristic weakens its value as a tool for managing the quantity and quality of public service programs.

A Performance Budget

A performance budget is one which allots money to various activities or programs of an organization and at the same time describes the work load or work output which will be produced with this money. A performance budget for the refuse collection activity shown in the program budget illustrated would be in a form similar to the following:

Budget for 19___
Nowhere, Georgia

Expenditure Budget

Refuse Collection	**Budget**
Personal Services	$3,000
Contractual Services	500
Supplies and Materials	500
Capital Outlay	1,000
Total	$5,000

Performance Statistics

Residential Collections
Dwellings - 1 pickup per week: 1,000
Tons of refuse collected per year: 375
Cost of collections per ton: $8.00
Cost per dwelling pickup per year: $3.00
Total annual cost: $3,000

Commercial Collections
Commercial stops - 2 pickups per week: 100
Tons of refuse collected per year: 250
Cost of collections per ton: $8.00
Cost per stop per year: $20
Total annual cost: $2,000

The principal advantage in using the performance type budget is that it shows both the activities of local government and the service levels of these activities. Thus it can be a useful tool for regulating in a positive way both the quantity and quality of public activities. This characteristic makes the performance type of budget the most useful of the three types mentioned. However, of the three types, the performance budget is the most difficult to prepare. There are three reasons for this. First, it is difficult to define the units by which the work of a department or activity can be measured. Second, even when the work units can be defined, it may not be easy to establish a system which will supply a reliable measure of the work outputs. Third, it requires much thought and study to establish acceptable service levels for various activities. These problems can be resolved, but it will take time and study.

Preparing a Budget for a Small Town

In the preceding paragraphs, we have defined a budget, and we have identified and described the three types of budgets. We will next turn to a discussion of the steps involved in preparing and adopting a budget for small town governments.

As we have stated, a budget is a spending plan for an enterprise. A small town operates through funds. Each of these funds represents a separate enterprise. Therefore, a budget should be prepared for each fund. Since the principal fund used by a town is the General Fund, the discussion which follows will relate primarily to the procedures used to prepare a General Fund Budget. However, the principles and procedures discussed will apply equally well to other funds.

Some Principles That Should Guide a Budget Program

The budget programs for a small town should meet certain minimum standards if they are to be of any real value. These can be summarized as follows:

1. The budget which is adopted should be a balanced budget. By this we mean that the amount of money allocated by the budget to various expenditures should be equal to the amount of revenue which the town expects to receive during the fiscal year which the budget will serve. The reason for this standard is obvious. A town which budgets to spend more money than it expects to receive has, in effect, committed itself to operate with a deficit. This may be acceptable practice in the case of the federal budget, but it can seldom, if ever, be justified in the case of the budget for a small town.
2. A town should not deliberately overestimate the amount of money which it expects to receive when it is preparing the revenue estimates for the budget. At the same time, the town should not deliberately understate the expenditures which it proposes to make in the new budget year. Unfortunately, both of these

are sometimes done to conceal the fact that the town is operating with a deficit. By the time the deception is discovered, a town can be deeply in debt.

3. When a budget is adopted it should be followed. If a town ignores the budget after it is adopted, nothing was gained by adopting it in the first place.
4. If a budget is to be of any value to a town, it should be adopted before the beginning of the fiscal year which it will serve. If this is not done, then the budget has no real value.
5. After a budget is adopted, suitable measures should be taken to insure that money is spent only for authorized purposes and only within the amounts authorized. Such measures should include the use of an allotment system, the use of purchasing controls, the use of monthly income and expense statements, and the use of a sound system of budgetary accounts.

Steps in Preparation and Adoption of a Budget

The procedure for preparing and adopting a budget in a small town can be divided into five steps.

1. Prepare and adopt a budget calendar.
2. Prepare revenue estimates for the budget.
3. Prepare the proposed spending budget.
4. Prepare the proposed budget and present it to council.
5. Adopt the budget and enter it to the accounts.

In the paragraphs which follow we will discuss each of these steps.

Prepare and Adopt a Budget Calendar

The preparation of a budget is not something that should be done on an informal "back of the envelope" basis. The preparation of the budget should be planned in advance. Each step in the preparation process should be identified. A time schedule for completing each step should be established and the persons responsible for performing each step should be designated. The budget preparation plan should be formalized in a document called a "budget calendar." This calendar should list each step in the budget preparation activity; it should list the dates by which each step is to be completed; and it should assign responsibility for each step. A typical budget calendar is illustrated in Figure 1.

We should note three things about the calendar . . . . First, it allots four months to prepare and adopt the budget. This may be too little time for some towns and too much for others. There is no fixed rule about time. The point to remember is that sufficient time must be provided to complete the preparation of the budget on or before the first day of the fiscal year which it is to serve.

Second, the calendar assigns certain responsibilities to a Budget Officer. Most small towns will not have a Budget Officer as such. Instead, the duties usually assigned to this office will be performed either by the City Clerk or by the Finance Director, if there is one. In such cases, the title of the officer who is performing the duties of a Budget Officer should be substituted where the title of Budget Officer is listed in the calendar.

Third, the calendar lists most of the steps involved in the preparation and adoption of a budget. However, it can be expanded to include other steps, or it can be condensed by omitting steps. These are decisions which must be resolved by each town. In resolving them, it should be remembered that the calendar's primary purpose is to present a detailed plan for preparing a budget. It should show what must be done, when it must be done, and who must do it. The more detailed this plan is, the less likely it is that there will be confusion about what must be done.

Prepare Revenue Estimates for the Budget

As we have noted earlier, a budget contains an estimate of the amount of money which will be received during the budget year. The amount of money that will be budgeted to spend will be determined by the amount of this estimate. The objective should be to produce an estimate which will be reasonably close to the actual cash revenue collections for the budget year. Therefore, the preparation of the revenue estimates should be undertaken with care. Remember that spending will be carried out on the basis of these estimates. If they are lower than the actual amount of cash revenues collected, there is no problem—assuming, of course, that spending during the year does not exceed the estimates. However, if actual cash revenue collections for the year are lower than the estimates, then a problem is created, since the town will spend more money than it will collect.

Some towns go to great lengths to insure that cash revenues will not be overestimated. In some cases, a town will adopt a policy by which the revenue estimates for the new budget year cannot exceed the actual amount of cash revenue collected during the preceding budget year. This is a con-

Figure 1: *Budget Calendar*

Nowhere, Georgia

When Due	Budget Preparation Activity	Who Is Responsible
September 1	Budget preparation forms are printed and ready for distribution.	Budget Officer
September 15	Budget information for current year and for prior years is posted to forms for each department and activity.	Budget Officer
September 15	Budget request forms are distributed to Department Heads.	Budget Officer or Chief Executive
October 1	Revenue estimates for the next budget year are completed.	Town Finance Officer or Budget Officer
October 15	Budget request forms are returned to Budget Officer showing budget requests for next budget year.	Department Heads
November 15	a. Budget requests are summarized.	a. Budget Officer
	b. Requests are analyzed and adjusted.	b. Budget Officer
	c. Proposed expenditure plan is assembled.	c. Budget Officer or Chief Executive
	d. Proposed revenue program is prepared.	d. Budget Officer or Chief Executive
November 22	Proposed budget for next budget year is submitted to the Town Council	Budget Officer or Chief Executive
December 15	Town Council's review of the proposed budget is completed. Revisions are made to the budget.	Town Council and Budget Officer
December 31	The budget is adopted. The Appropriation ordinance and the Revenue ordinance are adopted.	Town Council
January 1	Monthly or quarterly allotment schedules for departments are prepared. Budget accounts are created. The adopted budget is entered to these accounts.	Budget Officer, Town Finance Officer

servative but effective policy, since it almost guarantees that the estimates will be less than the actual collections for the new year. Of course, this policy must be tempered to recognize unexpected, one-time revenue collections. Otherwise, the estimates for the new year can be overly optimistic.

In preparing revenue estimates, a town is concerned with two categories of revenue sources: current sources of revenue and new sources of revenue. Collection estimates cannot be prepared on the same basis for each category. In the case of current sources of revenue, the estimator is usually dealing with known quantities. However, in the case of new sources of revenue, the estimator is dealing with unknown quantities. We will first discuss each of these problems, and then we will illustrate the forms which can be used to prepare revenue estimates.

Estimating Revenues from Current Revenue Sources: Current revenue sources are sources from which the town is currently obtaining its revenue. Most of these sources will have been in use for several years; therefore, the town has past collection experience to use in estimating the amount of revenue these sources will produce in the new budget year. If the town has compiled a collective experience record then the estimating process will be more or less routine. All that will be required in this case is to determine the collection trends on the basis of past experience and then project them forward. If the collection trends show that revenues from a given source have been increasing at the rate of 2 percent or 3 percent each year, then the estimate for the new year should be some 2 or 3 percent higher than the collections for the current year. If, on the other hand, collection experience records show that the collections from a particular source have been decreasing at the rate of 2 or 3 percent per year, then the revenue estimate for this source should be some 2 or 3 percent lower than the amount collected for the current year.

We can show how to make a revenue estimate for a current revenue source by using an example. Let us assume that we have a collection experience record for dog licenses which looks something like this:

	Collected 1st Quarter	Collected 2nd Quarter	Collected 3rd Quarter	Collected 4th Quarter	Collected For Year
1960	$100	$150	$150	$100	$500
1961	120	170	160	110	560
1962	125	175	165	115	580
1963	135	175	165	115	590
1964	130	170	165	120	585

On the basis of this collection experience record, we can estimate, with some degree of certainty, that revenue collections from dog licenses in the new budget year will total $585. We can make our calculation by visual examination. We might break it down by quarters as follows:

	1st Quarter	2nd Quarter	3rd Quarter	4th Quarter	For Year
New Budget Year	$130	$170	$165	$120	$585

The above example is a rather simple one. Yet the process used to arrive at the estimate can apply equally to any revenue sources for which we had developed a collection experience record.

Estimating revenue from current sources is made more difficult if a collection experience record has not been maintained. In this case, we must search the accounts in the Revenue Ledger and compile such a record. If accounts have been maintained for each minor source of revenue over a period of years, compiling such a record, while time-consuming, will be relatively easy. However, if the practice had been to account for revenues only by major source, then we must use these figures to make our revenue estimate. In this case, our estimates will not be as precise since we cannot determine which sources account for the fluctuation in the collections from each major source. However, if we are conservative, our estimate will still be reasonably valid.

One source of current revenue which can cause difficulty in preparing a revenue estimate is the tax on property. All of a tax levy will not be collected within the same year that it is made. Consequently, the expected collections from a tax levy must be calculated on the basis of past experience. A problem arises because the amount of the tax levy can fluctuate from year to year. Consequently, we must calculate collection trends on a different base each year. For example, one year the levy may total $100,000. The next year it may be increased to $120,000. The next year it could conceivably be lowered to $90,000. Fortunately, the problem is not too difficult to solve. Usually the ratio of the portion of the levy collected to the total levy is uniform from year to year. Thus, we can calculate this ratio for several years, then average it, and then use the average ratio to estimate the amount of revenue which we can expect to collect from the tax levy. For example, our calculations may show that, over the years, the town has averaged collecting 93 percent of a tax levy in the same year the levy was made. Therefore, to make the estimate of the revenue which we will obtain from the tax levy in the new year, we have only to multiply the levy by 93 percent. Our estimate will be the answer we obtain from this calculation.

Estimating Revenue from New Sources of Revenue: A town may find that it is necessary to create new sources of revenue to obtain the money which it needs to finance its budget. If this is the case, some means must be found to estimate how much revenue these new sources will produce. The means used to make these estimates will be determined by the nature of the new sources. Finding a suitable method on which to develop these estimates may be extremely difficult and in fact may not be possible with the resources available to the town. When this problem occurs, the town should consider using a consultant to help it make these estimates.

A form can be used to compile the revenue estimates for the new year. Figure 2 illustrates a Budget Revenue Estimate form that can be used for this purpose. Note that the form shown in Figure 2 lists both major and minor sources of revenue. Also note that columns are provided to list actual revenue collections by source for each of the two preceding budget years. Columns are also provided to record revenue collections for the current year, to record the date of the estimate, and to estimate the amount of the collections which will be received for the balance of the year.

Prepare the Proposed Spending Budget

To prepare a proposed spending budget for the General Fund, the items for which money will be spent must be identified and then the amount of money needed for each item must be calculated. The items of expense are the "raw materials" which the fund must purchase to produce public services and facilities. These include labor, services, and commodities. The amount of money which will be

Figure 2: *Budget Preparation–A Form for Preparing Estimates for the Budget*

BUDGET 19 ___ FUND: ___

Revenue Source	Actual Collections 19___	Actual Collections 19___	Current Year's Revenue: Collections to___	Current Year's Revenue: Estimated Collections Balance Of Year	Current Year's Revenue: Total Estimated Collections This Year	Estimated Collections New Budget	Collections Estimate Approved By Council
General Property Tax							
Real Property:							
Current Levy							
Prior Levies							
Personal Property:							
Current Levy							
Prior Levies							
Intangible Tax:							
Current Levy							
Prior Levies							
Public Utilities:							
Current Levy							
Prior Levies							
Total Property Tax							
Penalties and Interest							
Delinquent Tax							
License and Permits							
Business Licenses							
Beverage Licenses							
Parking Meters							
Building Permits							
Other Licenses and Permits							
Total License and Permits							
Other							

needed for each item is calculated on the basis of service level requirement, the operating procedures used to supply various services, and other factors. The proposed spending budget for the General Fund is usually prepared by the Chief Executive or his designated representative. To prepare the proposed budget for the General Fund, he must calculate the budget needs for two categories of expense: departmental expenses and non-departmental expenses. The basis for making the calculations for each of these categories is discussed below.

Calculating Departmental Budget Needs: The functions of the General Fund of a town are usually performed through operating units called departments. Thus, when preparing the budget for the General Fund, the money which will be needed to operate each department must be calculated. This calculation is usually made by each department and then submitted to the chief executive in the form of a request. To make this calculation, the cost trends for each item of expense within a department are analyzed and then projected forward into the new budget year. These trends are adjusted for such cost factors as price increases, program changes, salary increases, and normal fluctuations in expenditures for equipment and other capital outlay items.

The budget for a department may provide for four classes of expenses as follows:

1. *Personal Services Costs.* These are the costs for salaries, wages, and employee benefits. The money that will be needed for this category of expense is calculated by adding together the annual salaries of all of the employees within a department. To this total there must be added the money that will be needed for overtime, for salary increases, for employee benefits, and for new employees.
2. *Contractual Services Costs.* These are costs for such items as utility services, legal services, subscriptions, dues, and maintenance contracts. The money that will be needed for this group of expenses is calculated on the basis of the cost of these items in prior years, with adjustments for price increases and additions to service.
3. *Commodities Costs.* These are costs for supplies and materials such as paper, water pipe, gravel, pencils, food, clothing, medicine, and vehicle maintenance supplies. The money that will be needed for this group of expenses is calculated on the basis of the cost for these items in prior years, with adjustments for price increases, and changes in program requirements.
4. *Capital Outlay Costs.* These are costs for furniture and equipment and perhaps for capital improvements, although in most very small towns capital improvements will probably be budgeted as non-departmental expenses. The money needed for furniture and equipment is calculated on the basis of the unit prices for the furniture or equipment which the department proposes to purchase.

The preparation of a proposed spending budget for a department can be made easier if preprinted budget preparation forms are used. Some of the forms which can be used are listed and discussed below.

1. *Budget Expenditure Request Form.* This form can be used to show the details of a department's budget request. It can also be used to help in calculating the amount of money which will be needed in the new budget year for various departmental expense items. An expenditure request form is illustrated in Figure 3. Note that this form is divided into two parts: a summary section and a details section. The summary section lists the major expense categories. The details section lists the expense items which make up each major expense category. Also note that the form shown contains seven columns. The first two columns are used to record the actual expenditures during each of the two preceding budget years for each item of expense. The third column is used to list the amount of money which has been budgeted in the current budget year for each item of expense. The fourth column lists the estimated amount of money which will be spent for each item of expense during the current budget year. The fifth column is used to record the amount of money requested in the new budget year for each item of expense. The sixth column records the difference between the amount of money requested for the new budget year and the amount of money budgeted in the current budget year for each item of expense. The seventh column shows the amount of money which has been allocated to each item of expense for the new budget year. Before this form is given to a department to prepare its budget request, the Budget Officer should fill in the information for the first four columns. This information is obtained from the expenditure accounts for the General Fund.
2. *A Personal Services Cost Explanation Form.* This form is used to show the basis for a department's request for funds to pay personal services costs in the new year. An example of such a form is illustrated in Figure 4. The form in Figure 4 breaks down the cost of personal services into five categories: Current Salaries, Salary Increases, Overtime, Social Security, and New Employees. Space is provided on the lower part of the form to explain the changes, if any, between the amount of the request for the new budget and the amount provided in the current year's budget for these expenses.
3. *Salary Increase Request Form.* This form is used to list the salary increases requested for the employees within a department. A form which can be used for this purpose is illustrated in Figure 5.

Figure 3: *Budget Preparation–A Form for Preparing a Department's Budget Request for Expenditures*

Budget 19__ Activity Title and Account Number: ______ Department: ____________ Fund:

Title	Actual Expenditures 19__	Actual Expenditures 19__	Current Budget	Estimated Expenditure Current Year	Budget Request: Requested	Budget Request: Increase over Current Budget	Amount Approved
Personal Services	$	$	$	$	$	$	$
Contractual Services							
Commodities							
Capital Outlay - (furniture and equipment)							
Total Budget Request	$	$	$	$	$	$	$
Salaries and Wages							
Salary Increases							
Social Security							
Overtime							
Total Personal Services	$	$	$	$	$	$	$
Utility Services							
Communication - Telephone, Telegraph, Postage							
Transportation							
Advertising							
Insurance							
Rentals							
Dues, Subscriptions							
Professional Fees							
Contract Maintenance - Buildings and Improvements							
Contract Maintenance - Machinery and Equipment							
Other Contractual Services							
Total Contractual Services	$	$	$	$	$	$	$
Printing and Office Supplies							
Clothing and Personal Supplies							
Food							
Housekeeping Supplies							
Materials for Buildings and Improvements							
Motor Fuels and Lubricants							
Repair Parts for Equipment							
Tools							
Other Commodities							
Total Commodities	$	$	$	$	$	$	$
Office Furniture and Equipment							
Vehicular Equipment							
Other Equipment							
Total Capital Outlay	$	$	$	$	$	$	$
Total	$	$	$	$	$	$	$

Figure 4: *Budget Preparation—A Form for Preparing a Summary of a Department's Budget Request for Personal Services.*

Budget 19 ____ **Activity Name and Number:** ____________________ **Department:** ________

ITEM	Actual 19 ___	Actual 19 ___	Estimated Expenditures This Year	Budget Request	Increase or Decrease from This Year	Amount Approved
Current Salaries						
Salary Increases						
Overtime						
Social Security						
New Employees						
Total						

Comments:

Current Salaries:

Salary Increases:

Overtime:

New Employees:

Figure 5: *Budget Preparation—A Form for Preparing a Department's Budget Request for Salary Increases*

Budget 19____ **Activity Name and Number:** ____________________ **Department:** ________

Employee Name	Position Title	Pay Range	Current Annual Salary	Annual Amount of Last Salary Increase	Date of Last Salary Increase	Amount of Salary Increase Requested	Cost This Year	Amount of Salary Increase Approved
Total			______	______		______	______	______

4. *Overtime Request Form.* This form is used to request funds to pay overtime expenses in the new budget year. Figure 6 illustrates a form which can be used for this purpose. Note that the form shown in Figure 6 provides space to explain why overtime funds are being requested. Overtime can be a costly item. If not properly regulated, it can be used as a means of supplementing salaries. For these reasons, all requests for overtime should be justified on the basis of actual need.
5. *Additional Personnel Request Form.* This form is used to request additional personnel for a department. Figure 7 illustrates a form which can be used for this purpose. Note that the form shown in Figure 7 provides space to explain the reason for requesting additional personnel.
6. *Capital Outlay Request Form.* These forms are used to request funds for such capital outlay items as furniture, equipment, land, and buildings and other improvements. For budget purposes, requests for capital outlay funds should be divided into two groups: requests for furniture and equipment and requests for land, and for buildings and other improvements. Since the information needed to justify capital outlay requests for each of these groups will be different, special request forms should be designed for each group. Figure 8 illustrates a form which can be used to request funds for furniture and equipment. Figure 9 illustrates a form which can be used to request funds for land and for buildings and other improvements.

Calculating Non-Departmental Budget Needs: The General Fund will have certain general expenses which are not part of the expenses of any of the departments. These general expenses are called non-departmental expenses. They include such items as bond redemption costs, capital outlays for public improvements, and contributions. The costs for many of the non-departmental expenses are fixed by law, by contract, and by policy. Consequently, the procedure used to develop a proposed budget for these costs often involves little more than transferring the appropriate figure of record to the budget request form. For example, the budget requirement for bond redemption expenses can be obtained from the Bond Register; or the budget requirement for a contribution can be obtained from a contract. Of course, certain of the non-departmental costs must be calculated. For example, this must be done for capital improvement costs. Figure 9 illustrates a form which can be used to calculate the cost of a requested capital improvement.

A pre-printed form can be used to advantage in preparing the budget requests for non-departmental costs. This form is similar in design to the one used for making departmental budget requests. However, the items of expense listed on this form will be different from the items of expense used for departments. A form which can be used to prepare budget requests for non-departmental expenses is illustrated in Figure 10. Note that this form contains a summary section and a detail section. Also note that it contains seven columns which are used in the same manner as those shown on the budget request form for departments.

Prepare the Proposed Budget and Present It to Council

When the revenue estimates have been completed and the budget requests for departmental expenses and non-departmental expenses have been processed, a proposed budget document must be assembled by the Chief Executive for presentation to the Council. This document should be organized as follows:

Budget Message
Budget Summary
Detailed Budget Requests

Budget Message: The budget message should describe the significant features of the proposed budget. It should identify the differences between the proposed budget and the current budget and explain the reasons for these differences. It should discuss any new programs which the proposed budget contains. It should identify public needs which could not be met in the proposed budget because funds were not available. It should propose additional revenue sources and explain the need for these new sources.

Budget Summary: The proposed budget document should contain a summary of the proposed budget showing estimated revenues by major source and showing requested expenditures summarized by department and activity. The budget summary may also contain a detailed schedule by departments of the capital outlays for which funds have been requested. Figure 11 illustrates a General Fund budget summary for a budget totaling $100,000.

Detailed Budget Requests: Budget details

Figure 6: *Budget Preparation—A Form for Preparing a Department's Budget Request for Overtime Expenditures*

Budget 19___ **Activity Name and Number: ____________________** **Department: ______**

Item	Amount Requested	Amount Approved
Hours of Overtime:		
Cost of Overtime:		

Reason Overtime Needed:

Figure 7: *Budget Preparation—A Form for Preparing a Department's Budget Request for Additional Personnel*

Budget 19___ **Activity Name and Number: ____________________** **Department: ______________**

			Cost This Budget Year				
Position	Number Requested	Pay Range	Annual Salary Cost	Salary	Social Security	Total	Amount Approved

Why requested:

Figure 8: *Budget Preparation–A Form for Preparing a Department's Budget Request for Furniture and Equipment*

Budget 19__ **Activity Name and Number:** ______________ **Department:** ______________

Furniture or Equipment Requested:

Reason Requested:

__ To replace obsolete item
__ To replace worn-out item
__ To serve (new) or (expanded) program
__ Other (Explain)

Cost Calculations:

Estimated cost of item requested	______________
Cost of attachments if any	______________
Installation cost if any	______________
Total Estimated Cost	
Less: Trade-in if any	______________
Total Budget Request	
Budget Amount Approved	______________

Trade-in Item. Explain reason for trade-in proposed.

Figure 9: *Budget Preparation–A Form for Preparing a Department's Budget Request for a Capital Improvement*

Budget 19__ **Acitivity Name and Number:** ______________ **Department:** ______________

Project Title, Description, and Justification:

Cost Estimate

1. Land Acquisition	$	______________
2. Engineering		______________
3. Construction		______________
4. Other - Specify ________		______________
5. Contingency		______________
Total		

Source of Funds

1. Current Revenues	$	______________
2. Bond Funds		______________
3. Federal Grant		______________
4. State Grant		______________
5. Other - Specify ________		______________
Total		

Budget Amount Approved: ______________

Figure 10: *Budget Preparation—A Form for Preparing the Budget Request for Non-Departmental Expenses*

Budget 19____ Non-Departmental Expenditures **Fund**

Object Account **Title**	**Actual Expenditures 19___**	**Actual Expenditures 19___**	**Current Budget**	**Estimated Expenditures Current Year**	**Budget Request** **Request**	**Increase Over Current Budget**	**Amount Approved**
Other Charges							
Capital Outlay (Capital Improvements)							
Bond Redemption							
Total Budget Request							
Interest on Short-term Notes							
Judgments							
Pension Contributions							
Workers' Compensation							
Contributions to Other Funds							
Contributions							
Other							
Total Other Charges							
Buildings							
Fixed Equipment							
Other Improvements							
Land							
Total Capital Outlay (Capital Improvements)							
Sinking Fund Payments							
Bond Redemption							
Bond Interest							
Other Bond Costs							
Total Bond Redemption							

should follow the budget summary. The budget details should be arranged in the following order:

1. *Estimated Revenue Section:* This section should show revenue estimates by both major and minor source. For comparison purposes, collections for at least two preceding budget years should be shown. In addition, collection trends for the current budget year should be shown. Figure 12 illustrates a form which can be used for the estimated revenue section of the budget.
2. *Budget Requests for Departments:* The budget request for each department should be broken down by major object code. Each department's budget should be introduced with a brief statement describing the function or functions of the department. This statement should also describe the important features of the department's budget request. Some communities may require that a schedule of capital outlay items requested by the department be included. A personnel schedule may also be desired. Figure 13 illustrates a form for presenting a department's budget request. Note that this form includes space to show employment information for the department. Figure 14 illustrates a form which can be used to introduce a department's

Figure 11: *Nowhere, Georgia*

Budget Summary - General Fund
19__

Revenue Source	Estimated Revenue	
Taxes	$50,000	
Licenses and Permits	25,000	
Fines, Forfeits, Penalties	5,000	
Various Others	20,000	
Total Revenues		$100,000

Departments	Requested Spending Budget	
Chief Executive	$ 4,000	
Legislative	6,000	
Finance	5,000	
Police	30,000	
Fire	5,000	
Streets	20,000	
Sanitation	20,000	
Debt Retirement	5,000	
Other	5,000	
Total Expenditures		$100,000

budget request. Figure 15 illustrates a form which can be used to list a department's budget requests for furniture and equipment.

3. *Budget Requests for Non-Departmental Expenses:* These are expenses which are not charged against departments, but instead are general expenses of a fund. Included in this category are–
   Bond Redemption
   Judgments and Losses
   Contributions to Other Funds
   Other Contributions

   Figure 16 illustrates a form which can be used to present the budget request for non-departmental expenses. A budget section should also be included to show the details of a bond redemption schedule. Figure 17 illustrates a form which can be used for this purpose.

4. *Budget Requests for Capital Improvements:* Capital improvements are capital outlays made for land, and for buildings and other improvements. Unlike capital outlays for furniture and equipment, the budget request for capital improvements should not be included in departmental budgets but should be shown in a separate section. There are two reasons for this. First, many capital improvements will be financed with money obtained from the sale of bonds. As such, they represent expenses of a Bond Fund. Second, several budget years may be required to complete a capital improvement. This involves account procedures which are somewhat different from account procedures for other departmental costs. One way to budget for capital improvements is to create a Capital Improvement Fund and budget separately for it. The budget section for this fund should list each project under consideration that is scheduled to begin in the budget year and show the source of funds for the project. Figure 18 shows a suggested form for the capital improvement budget.

Figure 12: *Proposed Budget Document–A Form for Presenting Revenue Estimates*

Budget 19__ **Fund:** ____________________

			Current Year			
Revenue Item	**Actual 19__**	**Actual 19__**	**Actual 19__**	**Estimate For Balance of Year**	**Estimated Total**	**Estimate for Budget**

Figure 13: *Proposed Budget Document—A Form for Presenting a Department's Budget Request*

Budget 19.

Budget 19___ **Department __________**

Major Object	Actual 19___	Actual 19___	Estimated Current Year	Budget Request	Budget Approved
Personal Services					
Contractual Services					
Commodities					
Other Charges					
Capital Outlay					
Total					

Personnel Schedule

Position Title	Salary Range	Last Budget Year No.	Current Budget Year No.	Requested Proposed Budget No.	Budget Current Year $	Budget Request $	Budget Approved $

Figure 14: *Proposed Budget Document—A Form for Presenting a Department's Program Statement*

Budget 19___ **Department __________**

Department's Functions

Program Objectives for Coming Year:

Budget Comments: This part can be used to explain significant increases in the requested budget over the current year's budget.

Figure 15: *Proposed Budget Document—A Form for Presenting a Department's Budget Request for Furniture and Equipment*

Furniture and Equipment Schedule

Budget 19___ **Department ____________________**

Furniture or Equipment Item	Number Requested	Funds Requested	Funds Approved

Figure 16: *Proposed Budget Document—A Form for Presenting Budget Request for Non-Departmental Expenditures*

Budget 19___ **Non-Departmental Expenses**

Item	Actual 19__	Actual 19__	Current Budget Amount	Budget Request	Budget Approved
Other Charges					
Contributions - Capital Improvement Fund					
Bond Redemption					
Total					

Figure 17: *Proposed Budget Document—A Form for Presenting the Budget Request for Bond Redemption Expenditures*

Budget 19___ Bond Redemption

Type of Obligation	Bonds Outstanding	Interest Outstanding	Mature Bonds Payable	Mature Interest Payable	Bond Balance Outstanding	Interest Balance Outstanding

Figure 18: *Proposed Budget Document—A Form for Presenting a Proposed Capital Improvements Budget*

Budget 19___ Capital Improvements Budget

Project Description	Source of Funds					Total Cost	Funds Authorized
	Current Revenue	G.O. Bonds	Assessments	Federal Grants	Other Grants		

Adopt the Budget and Enter It to the Accounts

After the Council has reviewed the proposed budget and made such changes as it finds appropriate, the budget is ready to be adopted. At this time two actions are taken. First, a revenue ordinance is adopted. This ordinance sets the tax levy and the millage rate to be imposed and imposes charges for other sources of revenue. Second, a budget ordinance is adopted. This ordinance, in effect, appropriates funds to the various categories of expenditures described in the budget.

Conclusion

The small town which decides to begin budgeting for the first time should start with a simple budget. As the town gains experience in working with the budget, it can expand and refine its budget as the needs of the community dictate.

3 Zero-Base Budgeting

Sydney Duncombe

What Is Zero-Base Budgeting?

The phrase zero-base budgeting has been used so many different ways by newspapers and news magazines that it is essential to begin with a brief explanation of what it is and how it was developed. Zero-base budgeting is a budget system in which each department or agency develops a series of requests for differing levels of services and then arranges these requests in priority order. Zero-base budgeting is often pictured in the press as examining agency budget requests from the ground up (or from a zero base) and this is one part of a pure zero-base budget system—but not the most essential part of the system.

How Did Zero-Base Budgeting Get Started?

The current system of zero-base budgeting was developed by a large business, Texas Instruments, in 1970 at a time when cut-backs in costs were necessary. Peter Pyhrr of Texas Instruments described the new budget process in a November 1970 issue of the *Harvard Business Review.*[1] The article was read by the newly elected governor of Georgia and Peter Pyhrr left Texas Instruments to help install zero-base budgeting for Governor Jimmy Carter. It was used to develop the governor's budget for 1972-73 and was further described by Peter Pyhrr in a book, *Zero-Base Budgeting,* published in 1973.[2] Subsequently, forms of zero-base budgeting have been used in New Jersey, Texas, Louisiana, Idaho, and other states and by the United States government after Carter's election as President.[3] In the past few years a number of cities have adopted zero-base budgeting, including Wilmington (Delaware) and Garland (Texas).[4] Although there is much variation in zero-base budget systems, the key ideas are still those developed by Peter Pyhrr first at Texas Instruments and then for the state of Georgia.

What Are the Key Elements in Zero-Base Budgeting?

Zero-base budgeting is a budget procedure with a series of steps which can be used to cut budgets (or increase budgets). The four basic steps are:[5]

1. Identify "decision units."

   A decision unit is a program or organizational unit for which budgets are prepared. For example, the Parks and Recreation Department could be a decision unit. Or you could say the parks program and the recreation programs are two separate decision units within the Parks and Recreation Department. It is up to you to decide what you want to consider decision units. The process of identifying what a decision unit is will be described in more detail in the next section.
2. Development of two or more "decision

Reprinted from Zero Base Budgeting for Idaho Cities *(Moscow, Idaho: University of Idaho, Bureau of Public Affairs Research, June 1978). This project was made possible through a grant by the Higher Education Act of 1965, Title I-A Community Service and Continuing Education, U.S. Office of Education, administered by the Idaho State Postsecondary Education Commission. The views presented are solely those of the author.*

packages" for each decision unit.

A decision package is like the information on packages of frozen vegetables you might buy at the supermarket. The package will describe what you are buying (i.e., frozen peas), will describe the product briefly, tell how much is being purchased (i.e., 6 oz.), and give you the price. A zero-base budget package also tells you what you are buying (i.e., a recreation program), will briefly describe what is being purchased, tell you how much of a program is included in the package, and tell you the price. For example, a city parks and recreation department might have the following five decision packages for their recreation program, designated A through E.

		COST
A.	A minimum level recreation program providing for just a summer youth sports program in the city parks. This program will provide for softball, baseball, and other sports for approximately 2,000 school aged children from June 15th through August 15th.	$15,000
B.	The present swimming recreation program. This decision package provides swimming instruction for an estimated 500 school age children in the city pool and the development of a swimming team.	$ 4,000
C.	A new adult sports program. This decision package would staff a baseball, softball, and other sports program for about 1,000 adults.	$ 7,000
D.	A new program for story telling and games for pre-school children. This decision package would provide for a program for an estimated 400 pre-school children each morning from 8 a.m. to noon at city parks during July and August.	$ 6,000
E.	A new program of winter sports. This program would provide for a basketball and cross-country skiing program for an estimated 500 adults from December through March.	$10,000
		$42,000

The five decision packages, A through E, just described total $42,000 and would be the total amount requested for recreation by the Parks and Recreation Department. The first package would be a minimum level package which would result in a substantial cut in the department's current budget. The first two packages add up to the level of service the department will provide during the current year. Packages C, D, and E are new programs.

3. The ranking of decision packages in order of priority.

Each program manager should rank in priority his or her own decision packages. If the city has a person responsible for the recreation program, that person should rank the five decision packages (A through E, described above) in priority order. The Director of Parks and Recreation should then come up with his or her own ranking of both the recreation and the parks decision packages. The total recommended by the Parks and Recreation Director would be the department budget request.

4. Preparing the operating budget and appropriations.

Just as a customer in a store goes around a supermarket and picks up this can and that package for a week's grocery shopping, the chief executive and legislative body in a government using zero-base budgeting can pick and choose what they wish the government to fund. For example, in some small cities, the budget is generally prepared by the city council with the advice and assistance of the mayor and city clerk and finance officer. The city council could look at ten decision packages from the Department of Parks and Recreation and decide which of the ten they wish to fund. The city council could, of course, decide to fund none of the ten packages and zero out the agency. The city council would be more likely to fund the decision packages ranked most highly by the Department of Parks and Recreation, but they would not have to do so. The city council could develop new decision packages (such as a senior citizen recreation program) if they wished. The city council would be like the customer in a supermarket with a grocery cart who goes around and picks up various packages and cans at different prices until his or her budget is exhausted or needs have been met. After the city budget has been prepared and a public hearing has been held on it, the city council has an appropriation ordinance written which specifies not only the amount appropriated from each fund for each department but may specify what decision packages are included in the amount.

What Can a City Gain from Using Zero-Base Budgeting?

The city department directors and others who prepare city agency budget requests find that zero-base budgeting takes additional time. They are able to rank in priority order their requests, however, and can hope that if the city council cuts their requests they will cut the lower priority decision packages. They are also protected (to some extent) from very arbitrary city council decisions such as cutting $20,000 out of a city agency's program and expecting the agency to continue to provide the same level of services. A city council using a zero-base budget process would realize that a $20,000 reduction in a city budget would certainly affect programs.

The main advantage of zero-base budgeting is to the city council. Line item budgets currently used by most cities describe the number of employees, cost of salaries, wages and personnel benefits, and the various amounts of supplies, equipment, and other non-personnel items to be purchased. They do not describe what the city is getting in program for its dollars. The usual line item budget does not provide the city council with alternatives from which to pick and choose the type of programs they want city departments to have. For example, a line item budget on recreation may list a number of summer recreation staff salaries and a number of non-personnel items. However, the city council would probably not know what would happen if they cut some of these items. Zero-base budgeting lets the city council know what happens to programs if they make cuts in agency requests. Knowing this the council should be able to make more intelligent decisions on how far to cut agency requests and which decision packages to eliminate.

Can a Zero-Base Budget Be Used to Reduce the Current Spending Level of a City?

If it became necessary for a city to trim its budget below its current spending rate, zero-base budgeting could be very helpful to the city council in making these reductions as rational and painless as possible. To make this possible, the city budget instructions must specify that each city agency must have a minimum level decision package for each decision unit. This package should be pegged about 60-90 percent of what the department is currently spending and the effect of the package should be described. In our recreation program example, the minimum level decision package which the department gave highest priority was the summer youth sports program. If the city council had to reduce city spending below the current level, it could fund the summer recreation program but eliminate the current summer swimming instruction program. The costs and program effect of such a decision would be shown by the zero-base budget system, and the city council would not have to make reductions in line items without knowing the effect on program.

Can a Zero-Base Budget System Be Used to Increase Current Spending of a City?

If a city council wants to increase the current spending of a city, a zero-base budget system can be used for this purpose. A zero-base budget enables a city council to pick and choose which program improvements and new programs they wish to fund.

Does a City Have to Establish a Full Scale Zero-Base Budget System to Gain the Benefits of Zero-Base Budgeting?

A city does not, of course, have to have a full zero-base budget system in all departments to gain some of the benefits of a zero-base budget system. It is probably better for a city to go into zero-base budgeting slowly and experiment with zero-base budgeting for one or two departments before deciding whether they want to do it for the entire city budget. [The next section] will show you how to install zero-base budgeting in one or two departments. A city does not have to have a budget system with all the elements of zero-base budgeting. There are some excellent state and local modified zero-base budget systems which leave out one or more elements of a full system. Some of the modifications will be described here.

Is Zero-Base Budgeting the Best Budget System for My City?

This [selection] cannot answer this question for you. It can provide information helpful to you in making your own decision.

Developing a Zero-Base Budget for a Single City Department

One of the best means of testing out the feasibility of zero-base budgeting for your city is to develop a zero-base budget for one city department. Once your line item budget for your city is prepared, it should take you no more than three to four hours to prepare a zero-base budget for a department in which there is only a single major program. The zero-base budget for that department would be only about one to two pages in length and would give you a good idea of what a zero-base budget looks like. The city council could review this budget and determine whether they would like you to expand this budget in future years to include other departments. *Do not rush into zero-base budgeting too quickly.* For most cities, it is better to try out zero-base budgeting on one or two departments one year, before trying to install this new budget system for the entire city.

In this [section], we will try to go step by step through the process you would take in preparing a zero-base budget for a single department. A police department will be chosen for illustration since almost every city has a police department or some law enforcement official.

Step 1. Identification of Decision Units

A decision unit is a program or organizational unit for which budgets are prepared. This means that you determine what you want as a decision unit for your police department.

In one large city, you might list the following programs as being sufficiently important for a decision unit to be developed for each:

1. Patrol
2. Investigation
3. Juvenile
4. Dispatching and communications
5. Administration and other

In another large city, traffic control might be a program separate from patrol and records might also be a separate program. If you do adopt a policy of having more than one decision unit for your police department you need to:

1. develop a separate series of decision packages for each decision unit.
2. be able to account separately for the costs of each decision unit. This means you must separate the cost of patrol, investigation, juvenile, etc.

For a small- or medium-sized city, it is probably impractical to have more than one decision unit for the Police Department. The city council probably would not gain great additional benefits from considering separate budgets for investigation and juvenile work, and the costs of the additional paperwork would outweigh the benefits. In this chapter, we will assume that the police department of our city is a single decision unit.

Step 2. Developing Decision Packages

Your first decision is to determine whether you wish to develop a minimum level decision package. The minimum level is a level below the current operating level and is usually about 60-90 percent of current costs. It is the level below which it would be very impractical to cut the budget. If budgets were to be cut below this level the consequences should be so serious that it would be almost better to abolish the entire department. The advantage of developing a minimum level package is that it gives you a fall-back position if it is absolutely essential to make substantial reductions in department budgets. The disadvantage in developing a minimum level package is that it may cause great anxiety and concern on the part of the police chief and his or her staff and it could possibly cause police turnover. If you do decide to develop a minimum level package you should allow the police chief to describe (or assist you in describing) the consequences of cutting the budget to the minimum level. A minimum level package might look like the one at the top of page 34.

Your second decision (if you decide to have a minimum level) is to determine how many decision packages you need to go from the minimum level to the current services level. The current services level is the level at which you could provide exactly the same level of services in the next fiscal year that you are providing this year. To compute the current services level you need to:

1. Determine the cost of the current staff next year with whatever cost of living salary increases they will receive.

DECISION UNIT: Junctionville Police Department

DECISION PACKAGE: 1 (of 7)

1. BENEFITS THAT WILL RESULT FROM DECISION PACKAGE
   This package provides minimal police protection for Junctionville . . . . It permits employment of five patrol officers sufficient for a three shift, 7 days a week coverage of the city by one patrol officer with some extra time. It permits only 16 hours a day, seven days a week dispatching service. It does not provide for an investigator, a juvenile officer, or more than minimal administrative services. It would not give adequate police protection to the city if more than one patrol officer is needed at a particular time. It would leave 8 hours a day uncovered for dispatching. This is the bare minimal police protection that this city can afford to have.

2. RESULTS OF NOT APPROVING THE DECISION PACKAGE
   There would be no city police and very serious law enforcement problems would occur in this city.

COST OF DECISION PACKAGE	
Salaries and Wages	$161,020
Personnel Benefits	37,729
Supplies	8,930
Contractual Services	8,890
Capital Outlay	6,200
TOTAL	$222,769

2. Determine the cost of the same amount of personnel benefits, supplies, contractual services, and capital outlay for this staff next year as you received this year. This means you will need to make price and rate adjustments in your current year expenditures. If gasoline prices are going up about 10 percent next year, for example, you would need to increase your budget for gasoline from $10,000 to $11,000 to buy the same number of gallons next year as this year.
3. Determine whether there has been a significant increase or decrease in workload from this year to the next and make adjustment for it. If the city population will increase about 5 percent from this year to the next, you probably need about a 5 percent increase in staff to provide the same level of police protection. Thus, with a staff of 20 you have a case for including an additional person in your budget as part of the current services level. For the typical city, however, workload would probably not increase sufficiently in one year to justify an additional staff person to meet this increase.
4. Eliminate one-time expenditures from the current year cost base and budget separately for these items in the future. Most cities will not have this problem and an adjustment will not need to be made. However, one city might have a policy of normally replacing one police car a year and may have had windfall revenues last year and replaced five police cars. An adjustment needs to be made in that case to include just one car a year in the current service budget.

If you do not need to consider additional workload in calculating the current services level, I would suggest just one decision package to carry you from the minimum level to the current services level. If you have had enough increase in workload so this is a factor, I would suggest two decision packages: (1) to provide enough (when added to the minimum level package) to provide for your current staffing level next year and (2) to provide a sufficient additional amount to meet increased workload. The following examples assume there has been a sufficient increase in workload in Junctionville so an additional patrol officer is necessary for the current services level.

DECISION UNIT: Junctionville Police Department

DECISION PACKAGE: 2 (of 7)

1. BENEFITS THAT WILL RESULT FROM DECISION PACKAGE
   This package provides for two additional patrol officers and two additional dispatchers which (with decision unit 1) would provide the same staff as currently employed. This does not provide for a separate investigator and juvenile officer and provides only for the current level of records and other supporting services. This package would provide 24 hour a day, seven day a week dispatching service, the current level of record services and coverage of the city by two patrol officers for part of the day and one patrol officer for the remainder of day. The package would not result in quite as good patrol coverage as at present because we esti-

mate a 10 percent increase in city population this year and we are not adding additional patrol staff.

2. RESULTS OF NOT APPROVING THE DECISION PACKAGE
   The city would be left with a minimal type of police coverage and only 16 hours a day dispatching.

COST OF DECISION PACKAGE	
Salaries and Wages	$ 43,048
Personnel Benefits	10,679
Supplies	1,740
Contractual Services	1,640
Capital Outlay	0
TOTAL	$ 57,107

Man Years–4

DECISION UNIT: Junctionville Police Department

DECISION PACKAGE: 3 (of 7)

1. BENEFITS THAT WILL RESULT FROM DECISION PACKAGE
   This package will provide an additional patrol officer to provide additional coverage needed because of an estimated 10 percent increase in city population. With this package the city can adequately expand police coverage as the city grows.

2. RESULTS OF NOT APPROVING THE DECISION PACKAGE
   The city would have the same staff as at present but would not provide as good police service as is now provided. The city would not be able to expand police service as the city grows.

COST OF DECISION PACKAGE	
Salaries and Wages	$ 12,256
Personnel Benefits	2,972
Supplies	710
Contractual Services	1,180
Capital Outlay	0
TOTAL	$ 17,118

Man Years–1

Your third problem is to develop one or more decision packages for improved services, new programs or major items of capital equipment that are not part of normal replacement schedules. You could decide not to request funds for new or improved services and have no decision package beyond the current services level. You could lump all improvements beyond the current services level in one decision package. A better policy would be to use a separate decision package for each type of new program, improved service, or major capital item. The following examples illustrate decision packages developed for distinctly different purposes:

DECISION UNIT: Junctionville Police Department

DECISION PACKAGE: 4 (of 7)

1. BENEFITS THAT WILL RESULT FROM DECISION PACKAGE
   This package provides for two additional police officers which would (with decision units 1, 2 and 3) allow a 24 hour a day, 7 day a week coverage with two patrol officers.

2, RESULTS OF NOT APPROVING THE DECISION PACKAGE
   The city would be left with coverage of one patrol officer for part of each day.

COST OF DECISION PACKAGE	
Salaries and Wages	$ 24,512
Personnel Benefits	5,945
Supplies	1,420
Contractual Services	2,360
Capital Outlay	5,500
TOTAL	$ 39,737

Man Years–2

DECISION UNIT: Junctionville Police Department

DECISION PACKAGE 5 (of 7)

1. BENEFITS THAT WILL RESULT FROM DECISION PACKAGE
   This package would permit the city to hire a full-time investigator. This would provide professional investigation and greatly reduce the time required by sergeants for investigation, thus freeing them for more supervision and patrol.

2. RESULTS OF NOT APPROVING THE DECISION PACKAGE
   The city would return to its current practice of having the day and evening sergeants continue to do most of the investigation.

COST OF DECISION PACKAGE	
Salaries and Wages	$ 14,468
Personnel Benefits	3,346
Supplies	1,050
Contractual Services	1,180
Capital Outlay	6,050
TOTAL	$ 26,094

Man Years–1

DECISION UNIT: Junctionville Police Department

DECISION PACKAGE: 6 (of 7)

1. BENEFITS THAT WILL RESULT FROM DECISION PACKAGE
   This package would permit the city to hire a juvenile officer who would specialize in cases of juvenile offenses, child abuse, and other juvenile problems. It would relieve some of the time of police officers hand-

ling these cases. The juvenile officer would also do some patrol work.

2. RESULTS OF NOT APPROVING THE DECISION PACKAGE
The city would return to its current practice of having police officers (who are not well trained in juvenile work) handling juvenile problems and offenses as they have time.

COST OF DECISION PACKAGE	
Salaries and Wages	$ 13,868
Personnel Benefits	3,245
Supplies	750
Contractual Services	1,180
Capital Outlay	550
TOTAL	$ 19,593

Man Years–1

DECISION UNIT: Junctionville Police Department

DECISION PACKAGE: 7 (of 7)

1. BENEFITS THAT WILL RESULT FROM DECISION PACKAGE
This package would permit the purchase of radar speed detection equipment to be installed in one patrol car. This would provide a much more accurate record of the speed of cars than is now possible and a better means of apprehending those speeding within the city during the past year as speeding has become an increasing problem.

2. RESULTS OF NOT APPROVING THE DECISION PACKAGE
Less accurate means of identifying speeding cars would be continued.

COST OF DECISION PACKAGE	
Salaries and Wages	$ 0
Personnel Benefits	0
Supplies	0
Contractual Services	100
Capital Outlay	2,500
TOTAL	$ 2,600

Man Years–0

The number of decision packages developed for any particular decision unit will generally vary from two to ten. The fact that there are seven decision packages in the preceding illustration does not imply that there should be seven decision packages for a zero-base budget of all city departments. It is possible that a few city agencies may have only two decision packages: a minimum level package and a package to bring the agency up to the current services level. The format used to picture the decision packages need not follow the format shown in the illustrations.

Step 3. Costing Decision Packages

Each decision package must have an accurate estimate of its cost. The estimate may be a single amount or it may be broken into four to six categories as shown in the Junctionville Police Department decision packages. It will usually not be necessary to show in the budget document a very detailed estimate of the cost of each decision package.

To compute the cost of each decision package, you should begin by determining the cost of salaries and wages. If the decision package contains personnel now on the payroll, you would estimate what these persons would be paid in the budget year and include this amount in the package. If the decision package contains a new position (such as the investigator in the Junctionville illustration) then the package should contain the estimated salary cost of the new position for the next year. For example, if the starting salary was $10,000 and the department wanted to hire the investigator on January 1, after three months of the fiscal year had elapsed, a salary cost of $7,500 would be placed in the decision package. The decision package for the new position should also include the following costs:

1. Personnel Benefits. You need to calculate the amount of each personnel benefit for each employee in the package. Some of the personnel benefits a city might include are:
   a. Social Security
   b. retirement
   c. workers' compensation
   d. insurance
   e. other employee benefits
2. Supplies. You need to estimate the cost of the supplies the employee or employees included in the decision package will use during the coming year. This can be made by making an estimate for each type of supplies such as office supplies, gasoline for patrol cars, etc. An averaging process can be used in making estimates. For example, if you have 10 police officers using vehicles this year with gas, oil, and other automotive supplies running $2,000 per officer per year, then your estimate for next year's cost would be $2,200 per officer. A decision package with an additional police officer should include $2,200 for automotive supplies next year.
3. Contractual services and other costs. This may include printing and binding, insurance, travel and meetings expense, dues,

telephone and communications, heat, light, and utilities, etc. You may need to estimate the cost of each contractual and other cost separately. Some costs may not increase as the number of personnel increases. For example, rental of teletype equipment may be the same regardless of whether a police department has 10 or 20 officers. Some costs (such as false arrest insurance) may increase proportionately with staff increases. Other costs (such as training costs) may be associated primarily with the employment of new personnel. Computing the cost of contractual services associated with each new position is important since it will tend to assure that when new positions are added the right amount of contractual and other costs will be added to provide for the new employee.

4. Capital outlay. This may include a desk, chair, a file, and other equipment for each new position. Some new positions (such as patrol officers) may include specialized equipment such as a gun and, perhaps, a patrol car.

There will be some decision packages that do not seem to include personnel costs. For example, a decision package may be established to:

1. Purchase a large, new item of equipment
2. Purchase land and develop a park
3. Construct a new building
4. Replace vehicular equipment at a greater than normal rate. (For example, it is normal to replace them at 50,000 miles. This new policy might require a separate decision package.)

It is important, however, to carefully think through all the ramifications of a decision package with new capital outlay. The new park will require maintenance and this will probably involve personnel services. A new building will require janitorial services, supplies, and other costs. Thus, some packages which seem not to include personnel costs really do require personnel costs, associated personnel benefits, supplies, and other non-capital equipment costs. A very important principle of zero-base budgeting is that all associated costs are put in the decision package.

Step 4. Ranking Decision Packages

Placing the decision packages of a decision unit in priority order is a much faster process than developing or costing the decision packages. First priority should be the minimum level package since you have said this is the irreducible package—the package below which it would be very impractical to cut the budget. Next in priority will probably be the packages that bring you up to the current services level, since these include personnel now on the payroll. However, you may feel that a new position or some new equipment is so important that it ranks ahead of packages containing existing personnel.

Lowest in the priority scale will undoubtedly be new positions that are needed (but not essential for your operation) and new equipment you could do without. The priority order of each package is of great importance since the last package (or packages) in your priority listing may have little chance of being funded by the city council. You may be asked to develop a table similar to Table 1 (for the Junctionville Police Department) to list your priorities and show the cost and cumulative cost of each decision package.

Table 1: *Illustration of Ranking of Decision Packages*

Decision Unit	Decision Package Number	Cost of Package	Cumulative Cost
Junctionville Police Department	1	$222,769	$222,769
	2	57,107	279,876
	3	17,118	296,994
	4	39,737	336,731
	5	26,094	362,825
	6	19,593	382,418
	7	2,600	385,018
		$385,018	

Summary

Developing a zero-base budget for one city department is an excellent way of testing the feasibility of zero-base budgeting for your entire city. This [selection] describes how a zero-base budget system can be developed for a single department using one specific zero-base budget system. Under other systems, different procedures might be used.

Notes

1. Peter A. Phyrr, "Zero-Based Budgeting," *Harvard Business Review* (November-December, 1970) pp. 111-21.
2. ________. *Zero-Base Budgeting* (New York: John Wiley and Sons, 1973) has a particularly good description of developing and ranking decision packages.
3. For a current study of zero-base budgeting in state government, see Allen Schick and Robert Keith, *Zero-Base Budgeting* (Washington: Library of Congress, 1976).
4. One of the best articles on city zero-base budgeting may be found in David W. Singleton, Bruce A. Smith, and James R. Cleaveland, "Zero-Based Budgeting in Wilmington, Delaware," *Government Finance* (August 1976), pp. 20-29.
5. The four basic steps have been taken (with some changes in wording) from Peter A. Phyrr, "The Zero-Base Approach to Government Budgeting," *Public Administration Review* (January-February 1977), p. 2.

4 Living with Mandates
A Guide for Elected Officials

Introduction

This [article], designed for elected officials and their staff, presents highlights from a report entitled *Federal and State Mandating on Local Governments: An Exploration of Issues and Impacts.* That study took a comprehensive look at the effects of federal and state mandating on the activities and finances of local governments. In summarizing its major results, we hope to establish a reference for the officials of local government who must deal with these mandates. The [article] identifies the salient research findings, reviews the classification system developed for mandates and surveys the general policies available to control mandates.

Most importantly, the information is aimed at helping county officials determine the costs of future requirements. If change is to occur in the practice of federal and state mandating, that is, if local officials want to be reimbursed by mandating governments or if they are concerned about easing the economic burden, it will primarily depend on each county's commitment to document the cost impacts on its resources and programs. Having this information, county officials can more effectively communicate local concerns to state and federal officials and the public in general.

Reprinted from Living with Mandates: A Guide for Elected Officials *(Washington, D.C.: National Association of Counties Research, Inc., 1980). Funded by Financial Management Capacity Sharing Program, Office of Policy Development and Research, U.S. Department of Housing and Urban Development.*

Recognizing that "mandating" is a critical and highly political issue, keep in mind the following questions when reading this [article].

What percent of the budget is made up of mandated expenditures?

To what extent does the local government general fund, or in other words, the local taxpayer, bear the costs of mandates?

Are important local services being pushed aside to pay for mandated activities?

Has the avalanche of paperwork and procedural requirements involved in accepting federal and state grants become frustrating and time-consuming for your staff?

Do local pressures "force" you to seek and accept federal and state assistance?

If a mandate were removed, would your jurisdiction continue the program or procedure? If so, would it be at the same level?

Does your jurisdiction seek reimbursement for certain mandated costs?

Whom does the public hold accountable for local actions, if as much as 80 percent of a county budget is mandated by the state and federal government?

Summary

Mandates are not new to local government, but an increasing number of local officials believe that mandates erode local decision-making power and shrink already limited revenues. Why have federal and state mandates emerged recently as such a critical issue if higher levels of government have traditionally told local units what to do and how to do it?

Fundamentally, it is due to the rapid growth over the last two decades in the quantity, scope and costs of mandates imposed on local governments. Some of this is a result of the substantial increase during the last two decades in direct federal grants to localities to deal with domestic problems and to achieve regulatory goals. State governments have also contributed to the growth by increasing their requirements fourfold since 1966.

Today, local governments are the recipients of an increasingly large number of combined federal and state mandates. Investigators in ten local jurisdictions, for example, found that each was expected to comply with a minimum of 1,000 federal and state mandates; even if all conditions of aid are excluded, each jurisdiction must comply with the 500 mandates.[1]

In fact, local governments are spending more and more time trying to cope with the administrative chaos resulting from combined federal and state mandates. Sometimes, these requirements are inconsistent and unrealistic. The Maryland state requirement that hot water in health care facilities be no less than 110°F is complicated by a federal requirement that the water can be no more than 110°F. County hospitals are therefore forced to install sophisticated and costly equipment to maintain a constant temperature for federal and state compliance.

In Illinois, the state requires underground coal mine operators to control highly combustible coal dust by spraying water or calcium chloride in the mine. Yet the federal requirement orders limestone dust to be applied rather than water.

With more and more frequency, local governments are asking, "Who is going to pay?" This is to be expected in light of the current fiscal pressures at the local level—restricted revenues, sustained inflation and increased demand for services—which spur the search for fiscal relief.

Local officials feel one obvious solution to their dilemma is to have the federal and state governments pay for the costs of their mandates, particularly since almost half of the mandates studied introduced entirely new activities to local governments.

But even when accompanied by some fiscal assistance, a substantial portion of mandated activities are paid for by local funds. Localities must displace locally determined needs or increase taxes or fees. Either way, mandates have clearly added to the costs of local government.

In a national survey conducted by the Advisory Commission on Intergovernmental Relations, county officials listed judicial mandates, local share of general assistance costs, solid waste standards, and police being required to provide service and general assistance as the four mandated functions having the most significant fiscal impact.[2]

Accountability

Mandating also raises important concerns about accountability and local discretion. In today's complex intergovernmental setting, where many local actions are taken as a result of federal and state directives, accountability becomes difficult to identify and understand.[3] Local decision-makers are increasingly unable to directly determine their activities or have the control necessary to manage complicated local problems. Study findings indicate that procedural requirements make up 81 percent of existing mandates. Thus, officials must "live" with general rules and bend them as best they can to apply to their jurisdiction.

Certainly the mandate issue can stir the passions of those on all sides of the issue, but the fact remains that many federal and state requirements are designed to protect people and the environment and to promote important social goals. The major question is *how* to get something done rather than *what to do.*

Although little can be done about past mandates, something can be done about those of the future. Actually, local officials are in a particularly strong position to initiate change. As noted earlier, prior to any discussion with higher levels of governments, local governments must be able to provide information on the costs and institutional impacts of a mandate.

This [article offers] an action plan for elected officials in coping with the mandate issue:

- It supports the conventional wisdom that mandating is extensive and alters local government activities.
- It substantiates that mandates have added to the costs of local government.
- It provides a workable method to assess the costs/impacts of *new* mandates for possible reimbursement.
- It provides information to help you lobby for change.

Mandates, A Hot Topic

Although some local governments would like

to ignore mandates, the fact remains that state and federal mandates have had a great impact on what local governments do and how they do it. Many mandates have accomplished their purpose (for the better in many instances) and are indeed altering local government's activities and priorities.

Nearly half of the mandates studied have caused local governments to enter such nontraditional areas of activity as environmental protection, community development, worker safety and equal rights. Moreover, project findings concluded that many of the activities required by state or federal mandates have now been "internalized" by local governments—that is, the local government would continue to operate many programs or follow the procedures even if the mandate were removed. This is true for about two-thirds of the mandates studied.

On the other hand, less than half of the mandates are fully complied with, and some are not complied with at all. This data reinforces the view that mandated activities do not, at least initially, represent local priorities.[4]

What Are Mandates?

To most local officials, a mandate is whatever the state or federal government tells them they must do or must not do.

More precisely, this [article] defines a mandate to be "any responsibility, action or procedure that is imposed by one sphere of government on another through constitutional, legislative, administrative, executive or judicial action as a direct order or that is required as a condition-of-aid."[5]

It must be noted however, that opinions still vary concerning what should be included in the definition; some feel the term should be reserved strictly for those requirements which are imposed as direct orders. Regardless of which definition is used, one thing is clear: the number of state and federal mandates is large and rapidly growing.

There are two types of mandates: those that are requirements of other levels of government (e.g., direct orders and conditions of aid) and those that are constraints. The latter category tells a local government what it may *not* do. Some constraints deal with the type of taxes a jurisdiction may levy or the rates at which it may set taxes; others deal with the amount of money a jurisdiction may spend and set limits on how it may be spent.

Direct orders arise from the legal authority of the state or federal government to require a local government to do something; on the other hand, conditions of aid can only be imposed on a local government if it receives financial aid from another level of government. Because most jurisdictions need and seek as much help as they can find, there is little practical difference between the two types.

Appendix 1 lists the various types of mandates and gives examples of each.

There is a second important distinction among mandates: some are directed at only one function, department or program (a "specific" mandate); others cut across various traditional functions (a "crosscutting" mandate). A specific mandate might be one that requires a local government school lunch program to conform to certain nutritional standards.

Crosscutting mandates include the federal law that forbids discrimination in employment, and federal laws requiring assessment of the environmental impact of new construction projects.

The distinction between the two types is significant, because recently the growth in mandating has been primarily in the number of crosscutting requirements, those which impose substantial compliance costs on both mandatory and nonmandatory programs.

"A public works department, for instance, is no longer responsible only for building a new building, but it is responsible for making sure that minority contractors have an opportunity to bid, for making sure that the plans meet handicapped access requirements, for seeing that the people displaced by the new building are moved and treated in accordance with mandates on relocation, that the environmental impact assessment is completed, that the department hires and trains minority people, that its inspectors monitor all OSHA requirements on the job, etc."[6]

The Problems with Mandates

In the view of local decision-makers, not all mandates are equally worthwhile. Few would argue with mandates requiring governments to protect the rights of persons dislocated by urban renewal or to protect the health of citizens by cleaning up air and water. But many people question whether it is really necessary to specify the height of a doorknob from the floor, to require that all dogs in cities be counted once a year, or to specify the terms and conditions of local public employment. While many local officials are irritated simply by the number of mandates they are expected to follow, this irritation is compounded by those requirements which seem especially inappropriate.

The Cost Factor

With even the most valid and beneficial mandates,

there is the problem of cost and who should bear it. For example, many mandates order a local government to follow specific procedures, such as keeping certain types of records and filing reports, but do not provide any help in meeting the added expenses. In the jurisdictions studied, a substantial number of mandated activities are paid for by local general funds. Approximately 40 percent of all mandate costs and nearly 75 percent of direct-order state mandates are financed either completely or partially by local governments.

In Trenton, New Jersey, officials, with the help of project investigators, identified 1,100 mandates. When costs were gathered on 87 out of the possible 1,100 mandates, [they] amounted to more than 10 percent of the budget.

In the case of crosscutting mandates, which are the fastest growing and among the most expensive, nearly 80 percent were paid for either partially or fully by local funds. To meet these costs, a local jurisdiction must either reduce money available to meet locally determined needs, or impose a greater tax burden on residents and businesses.

One example of how mandates have driven up costs can be witnessed in Nassau County, New York. The county's elected executive recently denounced the state's compulsory binding arbitration law, reporting that it had driven up county police district taxes over 100 percent since 1971. He went on to note that ". . . decisions about matters that affect the fiscal health and stability of the community should be left to locally elected officials, who must answer for their decisions, and not left to arbitrators who can walk away from the fiscal consequences of their decisions."[7]

The study also revealed that state and federal mandates have different impacts. Although more of the costs of state mandates are funded locally than are the costs of federal mandates, state mandates appear to be more closely related to the priorities of local governments. Local officials claim they would spend less on federally mandated activities if the federal mandates were withdrawn than they would on state mandated activities if the state mandates were withdrawn. These findings are partially explained by the fact that federal mandates have introduced new kinds of activities more often than state mandates.

The problem of who should bear the costs of complying with mandates has become especially serious in recent years as the costs of providing even the most basic governmental services have risen and the resources available to many local governments have remained constant or even declined.

The Political Factor

The costs of mandating are not only financial, but political-institutional as well.

This fact turns the spotlight on a basic tension that has always existed between the various levels of government in our federal system: who has the authority to direct the actions of other levels of government? No matter how justified some mandates are, the cumulative effect of these impositions is a serious reduction in local autonomy and an increased dependence on state and federal governments.

This also raises the question of the degree to which the intergovernmental system needs uniform standards in order to operate. As noted earlier, the proliferation of standards, even those that are beneficial, can become confusing. For example, there are 150 different federal citizen participation requirements.

To many local governments, the large number of state and federal mandates seems unnecessary because in many instances they were already meeting the mandate's objectives through local efforts. Similarly, local officials are frustrated by the inflexibility of the many requirements. There is little or no room for adjustments or policy changes at the local level.

Despite these problems and costs, most mandates are enacted for worthwhile purposes, although further investigation is needed to determine whether or not extensive mandating is the most effective means to achieve the benefits intended. The present challenge, however, is to reduce some of the problems inherent in mandating. The remainder of this [article] addresses how this may be accomplished.

How Much Do Your Mandates Cost?

Why should a jurisdiction take the time and effort to determine the costs of a mandated program or procedure?

If county officials want to be reimbursed by mandating governments or if they request the mandating governments to exercise restraint in imposing economic burdens, then the costs of these requirements must be determined. Specifically, the information will be useful in preparing fiscal notes, acquiring accurate cost figures to be presented to the mandating government for possible reimbursement and examining the effects of mandates on budget allocations, since most budgets are not organized to show expenditures by mandated or nonmandated activities.

Knowledge of the exact costs of required programs will have long-term benefits: helping officials to effectively lobby for changes at the state and federal level, determining how limited funds can be applied to nonmandatory programs and determining if a mandate is, in fact, the best way to achieve a desired goal.

Who on the staff should be designated to perform this function?

Someone who is thoroughly familiar with the workings of the departments within the jurisdiction is the best choice, since he or she will be required to make estimates and judgments and exercise a great deal of discretion. The chief administrative officer or chief financial officer is the most likely person to fulfill this responsibility.

What are the constraints involved?

Determining the costs of existing mandates is an expensive and time-consuming task. The large number of mandates to identify and measure and the lack of readily available data are the major problems most jurisdictions encounter. This precludes examination of every mandate.

How then should a jurisdiction proceed?

Precise cost measurement should concentrate on *new* mandates because data can be gathered as it becomes available. However, the jurisdiction may want to examine mandates that are particularly important or costly to the county.

Given the problems in measuring the costs of existing mandates, don't expect to accomplish this with a great deal of precision.

Monitoring of a particular mandate should be continued for one year. The information should then be complete enough to be included in budget presentations for the following year.

A recommended procedure for assessing the fiscal impacts of mandates is outlined in Appendix 2. It includes a basic and manageable model designed to be self-administered by local governments. (Recommended for new mandates.)

Notes

1. States, cities and counties included in the mandate research–New Jersey: Somerset County, City of Trenton; North Carolina: Guilford County, City of Winston-Salem; Wisconsin: Dane County, City of Milwaukee; Washington: Thurston County, City of Olympia; California: Orange County, City of San Bernardino.
2. Advisory Commission on Intergovernmental Relations, *State Mandating of Local Expenditures,* Commission Report A-67 (Washington, D.C., July 1978), p. 61.
3. Catherine H. Lovell, et al., *Federal and State Mandating on Local Governments: An Exploration of Issues and Impacts* (Riverside, Calif.: Graduate School of Administration, University of California/Riverside, 1979), p. 17.
4. *Ibid.*
5. *Ibid.*, p. 32.
6. *Ibid.*, p. 25.
7. Francis T. Purcell, county executive, Nassau County, N.Y., news release, Sept. 17, 1979.

Appendix 1: Types of Federal and State Mandates

- Requirements
  - Program Mandates
    - Basic Program
    - Program Quality
    - Program Quantity
  - Procedural Mandates
    - Reporting
    - Performance
    - Fiscal
    - Personnel
    - Planning/Evaluation
    - Record Keeping
- Constraint Mandates
  - Revenue Base
  - Revenue Rate
  - Expenditure Limits
- Method of Imposition
  - Direct Order
  - Condition of Aid
- Application
  - Specific (vertical)
  - Crosscutting (horizontal)

Examples of Mandates

Program mandates specify something a jurisdiction or one or more of its agencies or departments is required to do or produce. It must be an end product or objective of some service or function.
The different program mandates are:

Basic Program Mandates impose an action, responsibility or goal but do not specify quality or quantity of the program.
Examples:

- All jurisdictions must have a job training program.
- All participants must, to receive [training] funds, submit a plan for teenage job training.

Program Quality Mandates specify the conditions and characteristics of a *given unit* of some product or service, or of some entity or person to which this product or service is delivered.
Examples:
- Lunches provided under a school lunch program *must have sufficient and balanced nutrition.*
- Each student receiving a lunch under a school nutrition program *will receive the minimum recommended allowance for the following list of minerals and vitamins.*

Program Quantity Mandates specify the *number of times* a product or service must be produced or *the number of people or objects* to which the product or service is extended.
Examples:
- School lunch program must be available to *all children below the age of 13* in the school district.
- *Jurisdictions with X percent of their students from low-income families* qualify for the school nutrition program.

Procedural Mandates regulate the way in which a jurisdiction or one of its agencies produces products or services. They are classified as reporting, performance, fiscal, personnel, planning and evaluation, and record keeping.

Reporting Mandates require a local jurisdiction to submit various types of reports, such as results of evaluation studies or documentation of eligibility.

Performance Mandates are nonfiscal mandates which are assumed to facilitate a goal.
Example:
- A drug abuse treatment center must have a career planning person.

Fiscal Mandates direct the manner in which fiscal resources must be organized, accounted for or reported upon.
Example:
- Audits, specified accounting procedure.

Personnel Mandates specify procedures for recruitment, types of qualifications that can be required or fringe benefits that must be provided, etc.

Planning and Evaluation Mandates require that activities be coordinated with an overall plan, either of the agency or jurisdiction.
Example:
- Programs for housing construction assistance must be consistent with local subdivision regulations.

Constraint Mandates are requirements that limit the amount and type of local resources or limit the amount of money that can be spent.

Revenue Base Mandates limit the kinds of fiscal resources that a jurisdiction can use to finance public service.
Example:
- User fees cannot be used to finance library expenses.

Revenue Rate Mandates limit the amount of a particular revenue base.
Example:
- The property tax rate for municipal services cannot exceed the rate of $2 for every $100 of assessed valuation.

Expenditure Limits Mandates limit how or what portion of locally generated resources are spent.
Example:
- No more than 10 percent of the budget for a program may be used for personnel.

Instructions to the Chief Administrative or Financial Officer for Forms I, II, and III, pages 46-51

Instructions to the Chief Administrative or Financial Officer for Forms I, II and III

These forms were made as general as possible so that they could be used by jurisdictions of every variety. They may be modified by adding, omitting or modifying questions. The time period for which data is to be collected is one year. Usually this will mean the fiscal year following the imposition of the mandate.

Before beginning to collect the data required on these forms, it is important that each mandate be identified properly by type.

The following data should be monitored:

Expenditure

Don't forget to include indirect expenditures if they are necessary in order to achieve compliance, for example, an increased workload for the accounting department due to a new financial reporting requirement in the Health Department.

Cost

Find out what expenditures were being made for any similar activity or activities before the mandate was imposed. This provides an estimate of *prior expenditure.* For example, if a mandate requires a $50,000 expenditure for program X, and your government was already spending $20,000 on a program similar to X, then the "prior costs" would actually be $20,000.

An attempt should be made to estimate expenditures if the mandate were to be withdrawn. This is the *present preferred cost.* For example, if a program costing $30,000/year were continued at the same level after the mandate was withdrawn, then the $30,000 would not be considered a cost which resulted from the mandate.

Compliance

Review reports, budgets, etc., to determine the degree to which the government has complied with the requirements of the mandate. Accurate reporting on the level of compliance is necessary in applying for proper reimbursement. In the case of condition-of-aid mandates, compliance may be monitored by the government supplying the grant.

Funding

Identify the source of funding (general fund, grant, etc.) in order to understand more clearly the financing of mandated activities.

Displacement

Determine what other projects or programs have been displaced or cut in order to pay for newly mandated ones. This will be a difficult task; nevertheless, it will enable you to include some of the more tangible effects of mandates in the final cost analysis.

Private Sector

Note the effects of a new mandate on the private sector. New fees and/or requirements by the local government will show in part how much of a mandate's cost is being shifted, and how much is being absorbed by the government.

Other important factors:

Constraint Mandates

Determine the amount of revenue loss due directly to the mandate. Also attempt to estimate how much revenue would increase if the mandate were dropped. This is the *present preferred revenue.*

Expense Caps

Determine what reduction in expense has been caused directly by the mandate, i.e., what was being spent compared to imposed limitations. Also find out how much this expenditure would rise if the limitations were removed. This is the *present preferred expenditure.*

Fiscal Impact Model

Form I: *Program and Procedural Mandates*

Expenditure Considerations

1. What was the total expenditure on the program mandate for the first year after its imposition?
   a. direct labor
   b. supplies and other expendable inputs
   c. indirect labor
   d. indirect production
   e. general overhead
   f. building occupancy
   g. equipment depreciation

   Direct labor ________hrs.
   Direct labor expenditure $ ________
   Total "other than direct labor" expenditure (total of b through g) $ ____________
   Grand total expenditure $________

Cost Considerations

Prior Cost

2a. Did the mandate replace or partially replace a prior activity?
YES_____ **NO**_____ If not, then the prior cost of the mandate is equal to the expenditure on it (Question 1).

2b. Give the increase in expenditure due to the mandate. $ _________

2c. If there was a decrease in expenditure due to the mandate, give the dollar amount of the decrease. $ _________

3a. Have there been substantial expenditures due to disruption, delay, interference with another program or department, etc., as a result of meeting the mandate? (Note: List only those expenditures not included in Question 2.)
YES_____ **NO**_____

3b. Give a complete list of types of expenditures and the amount spent on each.

TYPE	**AMOUNT**

Form I *(continued)*

Displacement

8a. Does local financing of the mandated service diminish jurisdiction funds available for non-mandated services?
YES ____ **NO** ____

8b. Were funds for other services cut in order to satisfy this mandate?
YES ____ **NO** ____

8c. By how much? Provide an expenditure figure, if possible. Expenditure cut $ ________

8d. Were there cuts in services?
YES ____ **NO** ____

9a. If jurisdiction funds were spent on this mandate, was a local revenue source increased to offset the expenditure?
YES ____ **NO** ____

9b. What was the increase in revenues? Amount of increase $ ________

Private Sector Considerations

10a. Were costs shifted to private citizens or firms as a result of complying with the mandate (e.g., cost of filling out forms, fees, permits)?
YES ____ **NO** ____

10b. List completely the types of costs shifted.

Shifted costs:

____

____

____

____

____

____

Form I *(continued)*

Present Preferred Cost

4a. To the extent it is possible, determine the answer to the question: "If the mandate were discontinued, would the presently mandated activity be reduced?" Check below.
YES _____ **NO** _____

4b. Circle the appropriate intervals of reduction of service: 0-10% 11-25% 26-50% 51-75% 76-90% 91-100%

4c. How much would the jurisdiction continue to spend on this activity? $________

Compliance Considerations

5a. In your opinion, how well is the mandate being performed? Check appropriate space:
______ Not at all
______ Minimally
______ Substantially
______ Completely

5b. What percent of complete compliance does the above represent?______ %

5c. Are the requirements specified by this mandate exceeded?
YES _____ **NO** _____

5d. How much in excess? State the percent by which this mandate is exceeded._____%

Funding Considerations

6. What are the sources of funding for the mandate? Check appropriately.
General fund ________
Special fund ________
User fees ________
Grant ________
Other (specify) ________

7a. Is reimbursement by the mandating level of government complete, partial, or not at all?
Complete ________ Partial ________ Not at all ________

7b. If partial, give the level of reimbursement. _____%

7c. Specify the type of reimbursement provided by the mandating level (e.g., grant, shared tax).

____

____

____

____

Form II. *Revenue Constraints*

Lost Revenue

1. To the best of your ability, try to provide an estimate of the loss in revenue due to this constraint.
   Estimate of revenue loss $ ________

Present Preferred Revenue

2a. If the mandate were lifted, would revenue rise?
YES_____ **NO**_____

2b. By how much? $ ________

Funding and Reimbursement

3a. Were other revenue sources tapped to make up for the loss (or potential loss) in revenue caused by this mandate?
YES _____ **NO** _____

3b. Specify which revenue sources were tapped.

____

____

____

3c. Was the jurisdiction reimbursed by the mandating level of government for the loss, if any, in revenue, due to the mandate?
YES _____ **NO** _____

3d. Give dollar amount of reimbursement. Reimbursement $________

Form III: *Expenditure Caps*

Reduction in Expenditure

1. List any services that were cut as a result of the mandate. Also list the amount by which they were cut and the reduction in expenditure on them. Be as specific as possible. If the reduction in expenditure is spread over the jurisdiction, specify this.

Functional area where cut was made	% of Functional Area Budget Cut
______________________	__________
______________________	__________
______________________	__________

Present Preferred Expenditure

2a. If the mandated expenditure cap was lifted, would expenditures rise?
YES ____ **NO** ____

2b. By how much? $

Reimbursement Formula

The following reimbursement formula assumes that there is presently neither funding nor reimbursement by the mandating government. These can simply be subtracted from the amount of reimbursement calculated by the formula.

For program and procedural mandates, the most general form of the reimbursement formula is:

$$\text{Reimbursement} = \left\{ \begin{array}{l} \text{Prior Cost*} \\ \text{or} \\ \text{Expenditure–Present Preferred Cost} \end{array} \right\} - \text{Reduction for Overcompliance}$$

For program and procedural mandates, the specific form of the reimbursement formula differs slightly depending upon whether it is calculated on the basis of prior cost or on the basis of present preferred cost. Both forms, however, are based upon the following two assumptions:

1. The mandating government wishes to reimburse *totally* for all prior cost (or present preferred cost) reported.
2. The mandating government does not wish to reimburse for *any* overcompliance of the mandate. In words, the formula is as follows:

$$\text{Reimbursement} = \left\{ \begin{matrix} \text{Prior Cost} \\ \text{or} \\ \text{Expenditure} - \left(\text{Present Preferred Cost}\right) \end{matrix} \right\} - \left(\text{Expenditure} - \left[\frac{\text{Expenditure} \times 100\%}{100\% + (\text{Overcompliance})\%} \right] \right)$$

Expressed in terms of the questions in Form I, the formula is:

$$\text{Reimbursement} = \left\{ \begin{matrix} 2b. + 3b. \\ \text{or} \\ 1. - 4c. \end{matrix} \right\} - \left(1. - \left[\frac{1. \times 100\%}{100\% + (5d.)\%} \right] \right)$$

*The term "prior cost" may be confusing. It is defined as the amount by which the jurisdiction has increased its expenditure in order to comply with the mandate. "Present preferred cost," on the other hand, is defined as the amount *to which* the jurisdiction would reduce its expenditure if the mandate were removed.

For revenue constraint mandates, the most general form of the reimbursement formula is simply:

$$\text{Reimbursement} = \left\{ \begin{matrix} \text{Lost Revenue} \\ \text{or} \\ \text{Present Preferred Revenue} \end{matrix} \right\}$$

We assume that the mandating government wishes to reimburse the local government totally for all lost revenue (or present preferred revenue). The specific form of the formula, expressed in terms of the questions on Form II is:

$$\text{Reimbursement} = \left\{ \begin{matrix} 1. \\ \text{or} \\ 2b. \end{matrix} \right\}$$

Bibliography

Advisory Commission on Intergovernmental Relations. Federal Assistance Monitoring Project. "Final Report to the President." Washington, D.C., October 1978.

———. *Summary and Concluding Observations–The Intergovernmental Grant System: An Assessment and Proposed Policies,* Commission Report A-62, Washington, D.C., June 1978.

———. *State Mandating of Local Expenditures,* Commission Report A-67. Washington, D.C., July 1978.

Commission on Federal Paperwork. *Final Summary Report.* Washington, D.C., October 1977.

———. *Impact of Federal Paperwork on State and Local Governments.* The Academy for Contemporary Problems, Columbus, Ohio, 1977.

Conder, Sonny. *Local Government Expenditures: Do State Mandates Make a Difference?* Institute for Policy Studies, Portland State University, December 1978.

Cuciti, Peggy. *Federal Constraints on State and Local Government Actions.* Office of Intergovernmental Relations, Congressional Budget Office, Washington, D.C., January 1979.

Gabler, L. Richard. "State and Federal Mandates." Paper presented at National Conference on Taxation and Finance Issues of Local Government, County Supervisors Association of California, National Association of Counties Research, Inc., Biltmore Hotel, Los Angeles, California, September 18-19, 1978.

Kaufman, Herbert. *Red Tape.* Washington, D.C.: The Brookings Institute, 1977.

Lewis, Carol W. *State Mandates: Responsibility and Accountability in Massachusetts.* Massachusetts League of Cities and Towns, 1978.

Lilly, W. and J.C. Miller. "The New Social Regulation." *The Public Interest,* Spring 1977.

Lovell, Catherine, et al. *Federal and State Mandating on Local Governments: An Exploration of Issues and Impacts.* Graduate School of Administration, University of California. Riverside, June 1979.

McLaughlin, Catherine and Marilee Wertlake. "An Analysis of State Mandated Services: Case Study–Iowa County." Madison, Wisconsin: Bureau of Local Fiscal Information and Analysis, Wisconsin Department of Revenue, October 1976.

Minge, David. "Law as a Determinant of Resource Allocation by Local Government." *National Tax Journal,* Vol. XXX, No. 4, December 1977.

Schunhoff, John F. and Terry Campbell. "Intergovernmental Finance and Design: Impacts of Mandate Systems." Paper presented at the 1978 Annual Conference of the American Society for Public Administration, Phoenix, Arizona, 1978.

State of Florida. *State Mandates in Florida.* Tallahassee, Florida: Florida Advisory Council on Intergovernmental Relations, March 1978.

Teaford, Jon. "City Versus State: The Struggle for Legal Ascendancy." *American Journal of Legal History* 17 (January 1973), 51-65.

Tobin, Charles and Catherine Lovell. "The Effects of State and Federal Mandates on Local Government." Prepared for the Commission on Government Reform, Task Force on Mandated Expenditures, October 1978.

Zimmerman, Joseph F. "State-Local Relations: The State Mandate Irritant." *National Civic Review,* Vol. 65, No. 11, December 1976.

5 Cutback Management in an Era of Scarcity
Hard Questions for Hard Times

Charles H. Levine

We are entering a new era of public budgeting, personnel and program management. It is an era dominated by resource scarcity. It will be a period of hard times for government managers that will require them to manage cutbacks, tradeoffs, reallocations, organizational contractions, program terminations, sacrifice, and the unfreezing and freeing up of grants and privileges that have come to be regarded as unnegotiable rights, entitlements, and contracts. It will be a period desperately in need of the development of a methodology for what I call "cutback management."[1]

The challenge of *scarcity* and public sector *contraction* to the viability of our political and administrative systems should be obvious: growth slowdowns, zero growth, and absolute declines—at least in some sectors, communities, regions, and organizations—will increase the probability of rancorous conflict, decrease the prospects for innovation by consensus, and complicate the processes for building and maintaining support for administrative systems and democratic processes. In this potentially turbulent environment, the dominant management imperatives will likely involve a search for new ways of maintaining *credibility, civility,* and *consensus;* that is, in an era of scarcity, we will need new solutions to problems of how to manage public organizations and maintain the viability of democratic processes.

Reprinted from Intergovernmental Personnel Notes *(January/February 1979), published by the U.S. Office of Personnel Management. An earlier version of the article was presented as an address to the American Association for Budget and Program Analysis, Washington, D.C., November, 1978.*

Why Cutbacks?

The most familiar cause of cuts is *problem depletion;* cuts occur when a problem is solved, alleviated, brought under control, or when the demand that it be solved diminishes. Perhaps the best example of problem depletion has been the effect of demographic changes on the education system. Because our population has aged, schools have been forced to close or curtail activities considerably.

Recent experiments with sunset legislation (where programs are brought under review usually three to five years after their initiation) are aimed at attuning public funding to problem depletion rather than to an agency's survival needs.

A second familiar cause of cuts in public budgets stems from the *erosion of the economic base* of some of our cities and states. The litany of problems in our older cities and in the northeast in general over the past twenty years underlines the agony of managing decline: the growth of dependent populations, the suburbanization of business and industry, and the shifts in economic activity to the sunbelt from the frostbelt have put some areas in the impossible position of needing to do more but being forced by declining tax bases to do less. The well-publicized fiscal problems of New York City and Cleveland and the retrenchment of their bureaucracies represent just the most advanced cases of a widespread national problem.

The third type of cause for cutbacks is *inflation.* The cost of government has risen rapidly over the past ten years—at least doubling in most cases—and has really taken off over the last five years.

Because of its service nature, most government costs are incurred by personnel. In an environment of leveling or declining economic growth, something has to give. This means that in order to make any appreciable savings, cuts must be made in personnel and subsequently in the services government agencies offer.

Taxpayer revolt, a fourth cause of cutbacks, has surfaced recently along with much speculation—mostly tied to Proposition 13—about its cause. These explanations usually include reference to the difficulty of tracing the well-being of individual taxpayers to specific government services, the desire of voters to alleviate the impact of inflation on their personal disposable incomes, the backlash of taxpayers against the salary increases of unionized public workers and the services offered to the poor and minorities, and the cumbersomeness of financing local services through the mechanism of the property tax.

A fifth cause of cutback—*limits to growth*—directly or indirectly overarches the others. Our dependence on depletable resources and foreign energy sources has created a severe imbalance between exports and imports, and it is not clear whether we will be able to find substitutes or additional sources of energy by the end of this century. We can also anticipate a further slowing down in the rate of economic growth, at least for the next decade or two.

What Is Cutback Management? Why Is It Different?

Cutback management means managing organizational change toward lower levels of resource consumption and organizational activity. Cutting back an organization involves making hard decisions about who will be let go, what programs will be scaled down or terminated, and what clients will be asked to make sacrifices.

These are tough problems that are compounded by four aspects of resource scarcity. First, behavioral scientists have demonstrated that change is most easily accomplished when the people affected have something to gain, but under conditions of austerity the acceptance of change will be unlikely because the rewards required to gain cooperation and build consensus will be unavailable.

Second, public organizations are confronted with norms, civil service procedures, veterans' preferences, affirmative action commitments, and collective bargaining agreements which constrain the ability of management to target cuts.

Third, organizational contraction produces some serious morale and job satisfaction problems which makes it difficult to increase productivity to make up for the cuts.

Fourth, cutbacks reduce the enjoyment of working and managing in an organization because nearly everyone is forced into a position of having to do with less.

A declining organization confronts its management with several unique problems. The first problem I call "*The Paradox of Irreducible Wholes.*" This problem refers to the fact that an organization cannot be reduced piece-by-piece by simply reversing the sequence of activities and resources by which it was built. The "lumpiness" of public organizations stems from the growth process in which critical masses of expertise, political support, facilities and equipment, and resources are assembled. Taking a living thing like an organization apart is no easy matter; a cut may reverberate throughout a whole organization in a way no one could predict by just analyzing its growth and pattern of development.

The second problem is "*The Management Science Paradox.*" This problem is caused by the way public organizations invest in and use their data systems and analytic capacity. When organizations have slack resources, they often develop elaborate management information systems, policy analysis capabilities, and hardware and software systems. But, when resources abound, this capacity is rarely used because public agencies usually prefer to spend slack resources building and maintaining political constituencies. In a decline situation, on the other hand, maintaining and using this analytic capacity often becomes impossible for a number of reasons including political pressures. Therefore, in brief, the management science paradox means that when you have analytic capacity you do not need it; when you need it, you do not have it and *cannot* use it anyway.

The third problem is "*The Tooth Fairy Syndrome.*"[2] In the initial stages of contractions few people are willing to believe that the talk of cuts is for real or that the cuts will be permanent. The initial prevailing attitude in the organization will usually be optimistic; i.e., that the decline is temporary and the cuts will be restored soon by someone—in some cases as remote as the tooth fairy. Under these conditions, management's credibility suffers and resistance, cynicism, and sarcasm tend to dominate responses to calls for voluntary budget cutting. The preferred tactical response for nearly everyone is to delay taking action while waiting for someone else to volunteer cuts or for a bailout from a third party.

The fourth problem is *"The Participation Paradox."* The field of organization development teaches that the best way to manage change is to encourage the maximum amount of participation by all affected parties. But a rational cutback process will require that some people and programs be asked to take greater cuts than others. By encouraging participation, management also encourages protective behavior by those most likely to hurt the most. The participation paradox confronts management with a nearly insoluble problem: How does one single out units for large sacrifices which have people participating in the cut process? The usual answer is to avoid deadlocks or rancorous conflict and allocate cuts across the board.

"The Forgotten Deal Paradox" is the fifth problem. Ideally an organization or unit should be able to plan cuts and attrition on a multi-year basis. Such an optimum arrangement would allow an organization to plan its cuts so that six months, two years, or further on it will be allowed to fill *some* vacancies, replace some equipment, or restore some services when needed. In the private sector it is possible to make bargains for restoring some cuts later on knowing that they will likely be honored by the management team in the future. This kind of arrangement is much less likely in the public sector because the top management team usually lacks the continuity required to make and keep bargains with a long time frame.

The sixth problem is *"The Productivity Paradox."* Briefly stated, when dealing with productivity, it takes money to save money. Productivity requires up front costs incurred by training and equipment expenses. Under conditions of austerity, it is very difficult to find and justify funds to invest in productivity improvement, especially if these funds can only be made available by laying off employees or failing to fill vacancies.

These six problems are illustrative of the difficulty involved in managing cutbacks. They tend to force management to rethink the process of organizational development and growth; and they force managers to make new kinds of strategic choices in the face of perplexing uncertainty.

What Strategies?

At the present stage of our knowledge about cutback management, strategies are easier to describe than prescribe. So at this point, we need to be satisfied to raise appropriate questions and hope that later their answers can help managers cope with austerity. A proper start, therefore, is to investigate the major steps in the cutback process. that is, the strategic choices that an organization must make about confronting, planning, targeting, and distributing cuts.

Resist or smooth cuts?

When confronting possible cuts, managers and political leaders will have to choose between resisting these cuts or smoothing them out by limiting their impact on the organization's most important functions, procedures, and long-term capacity. Since no organization accedes to cuts with enthusiasm, some initial resistance is likely. But resistance is risky because "stonewalling" financial stress may ultimately force the need to make cataclysmic cuts like massive layoffs; missed paydays; defaults on loans, bonds, and notes; and the selling off of physical facilities and equipment. Therefore sometime, usually quite early in the planning process, an organization's or government's leadership will have to make the choice between struggling to resist cuts or struggling to minimize the negative effects.

Deep gouge or small decrements?

This choice is affected by The Forgotten Deal Paradox; that is, the utility of taking deep cuts initially in order to rebuild the organization later is limited by the risk that the resources needed to build back capacity later will not be available. The alternative strategy is to take the cuts year-by-year in small decrements to minimize their impact in the hope that public support for the agency will increase and the cuts will stop.

The deep gouge strategy tends to make the most rational *management* strategy, but the small decrement strategy *may* make the only rational *political* strategy.

Share the pain or target the cuts?

Sharing the pain of cuts by allocating them across-the-board to all units may minimize pain, help to maintain morale, and build a good team spirit in the organization; but it is not responsible management. Not every unit in an organization or every agency in a government contributes equally to the goals, purposes, and basic functions of that organization or government.

If an austerity situation gets bad enough, some leadership will emerge to identify and rank priorities and allocate cuts to units based on them. These hard choices will be accompanied by intense debates over such matters as the importance of different services, the method of ranking priorities, and the difficulty of maintaining excellence in an organization when it is declining.

Efficiency or equity?

Perhaps the most difficult strategic choice to make in the cutback process involves the tradeoff between efficiency and equity. This dilemma stems from both the cost of delivering services to different populations and the composition of the public workforce.

The most dependent parts of our population—minorities, the poor, the handicapped, and the aged—are often the most costly to serve. Blind cost cutting calculated on narrow productivity criteria could do grave harm to them. The dilemma is also compounded by the recent rise in minority public employment and the salience of seniority criteria in laying off public employees; last-in, first-out criteria for layoffs usually means that minorities and women will be differentially hurt—*irrespective of their productivity*.

Since there will always be a tendency to allocate cuts disproportionately to the politically weak, and productivity criteria *could* be used to disguise such an intent, we can expect cutbacks to spark much litigation as they become more widespread. The outcome of this litigation will, of course, greatly constrain, but never completely eclipse, managerial and political discretion over the locus and extent of cuts.

Directions for Future Research

To begin to answer these hard questions, a commitment must be made to develop a research program on the management of fiscally stressed public organizations. We know almost nothing about what works best under different kinds of cutback conditions. So, the first thing we need to develop is a baseline inventory of tools and techniques for managing cutbacks along with case studies of their application. With this information we can begin to sort out methods for scaling down public organizations and make some judgments about their appropriations to solve cutback problems of different types of severity.

Second, we need to find methods for solving the credibility, civility, and consensus problems that plague organizations and government during periods of large scale cutbacks. We need to invent and perfect democratic processes for allocating cuts which will make cuts effective yet equitable.

Third, we need to devote a great deal of thought to the ethical dimensions of cutbacks. We need to ask, for example, what the ethical responsibility of an organization is to its terminated employees and decoupled clients.

Finally, we need to understand how cuts affect public expectations and support for government, i.e., whether expectations about government performance will be lowered and tolerance for poor services will be increased. If the post World War II era has been until recently characterized by rising expectations and optimism about an active public sector's ability to solve public problems, will this new era produce a downward spiral of expectations and a pessimism about the efficacy of government to help create a better society? On a similar, but more narrow note, how long and to what depths will Americans tolerate the effects of reduced public services on their lives? In other words, if support for government services swings back and forth like a pendulum, how poor will services have to become before support for their improvement begins to build?

These are some hard questions we need to worry about. These, I predict, will be some of the dominant issues of public management in the decade ahead.

Notes

1. For another explication of this theme see Charles H. Levine, "Organization Decline and Cutback Management," *Public Administration Review* (July/August, 1978), pp. 316-25.
2. I credit Robert W. Wilson of Montgomery County (Maryland) Government for first labeling this phenomenon for me.

6 Measuring Governmental Financial Condition

The ability of local governments to control their financial destiny can be undermined by eroding tax bases, mandated programs, costly employee contracts, growing retirement burdens, continued cost inflation and inelastic revenue structures. State and federal grant programs have been increased to fill fiscal gaps, but they carry with them the uncertainties of increased dependency on resources beyond local government control.

Another concern of many local governments is the growing taxpayer resistance to increased local taxes—dramatized by the adoption of Proposition 13 in California. While inflation chips away at the buying power of the tax dollar, local ability to raise additional tax revenue to pay for public services is being severely constrained.

Are local governments heading for financial difficulty? There is little doubt that the financial problems faced by a number of jurisdictions can be called fiscal crises. However, the situation confronting many others is less extreme. This selection is intended to provide insights into the indicators local officials can use to assess their government's fiscal condition. Two cautionary notes before proceeding:

1. Analysis of fiscal condition is an art, not a science. Assessment requires an understanding and analysis of the factors unique to the community. Furthermore, poor financial management practices may hide or obscure certain elements relating to fiscal condition.
2. Indicators provide information on fiscal condition. They do not offer guidance or solutions to solving fiscal problems.

A Definition

There can be various definitions of a governmental financial emergency, but the touchstone is where a unit is running out of cash and cannot quickly raise more. This is the definition adopted by the Advisory Commission on Intergovernmental Relations (ACIR), which defines a financial emergency as an inability to perform existing levels of service, including meeting payrolls, paying current bills or paying debt service.

Such a definition is a starting point for the analysis. However, for many purposes, it is too restrictive and, to some degree, artificial. Where the likelihood of default is low, the jurisdiction is presumed to be in good condition. A financially strong government can exist in the context of a weak or even disintegrating local economy or society. But the long-term prospects for such a situation continuing are not bright—at least as long as the government is subject to the desires of its citizens and reliant upon their resources. Ultimately, the measure of fiscal condition, if it is to have analytical and predictive value, must deal with more general circumstances relating to the destiny of the governmental unit. While default on debt payments is a sure sign of fiscal distress, concentrating an analysis

---

Reprinted from Elements of Financial Management 5 *(Washington, D.C.: Government Finance Research Center, Municipal Finance Officer's Association, May 1980).*

on this single event may provide too narrow a focus.

The ability of local governments to continue to provide needed services under a variety of fiscal and economic circumstances is a more important concern from a resource and policy-making standpoint. A recent report by Sanford Groves, of the International City Management Association, defined good fiscal condition as having the ability to:

- Maintain existing service levels;
- Fund normal demands for additional service;
- Withstand local and regional economic trauma; and
- Meet demands of natural growth and change.

This broader definition appears more useful for policy makers than the simple default test. Obviously, the two definitions are related, but default is such a remote possibility in most communities that using it as a guidepost for analysis is inadequate.

Several other problems must also be overcome in implementing the broader definition. There are few standards against which municipal finances can be measured. While state laws and municipal charters frequently establish legal limits on debt levels and tax rates, such limits are prescriptive in nature and have not been determined through empirical research on the causes of fiscal stress.

Because valid standards have been lacking, researchers generally have had to resort to comparisons among local governments as a means of identifying those likely to experience fiscal distress. Under this approach, governments that vary widely in the wrong direction from the mean or median for their group are considered fiscally distressed, while others are deemed healthy. The validity of such comparative analysis is questionable in some cases because of differences in local government populations, services provided, legal requirements and financial information reporting techniques.

Despite the lack of theory and the paucity of data, analysts tend to agree that good fiscal health depends on two interrelated conditions:

- A strong economy that produces sufficient revenue to meet the cost of public services, while simultaneously providing private employment and income that reduces the need for some public expenditures; and
- Sound resource and fiscal management that minimizes waste, provides the information needed to make sound fiscal choices, and avoids the spending of more revenue than can be raised dependably.

Practical Problems

Beyond the basic issues relating to definition, officials attempting to analyze their local government's fiscal condition may encounter certain of the procedural problems listed below:

- Fiscal stringency is seldom a singular event, such as a default on a bond. Usually it is a matter of degree—both in the necessity of making choices among alternative courses of action and in the severity of their consequences. Fiscal stress can be managed successfully for many years, if circumstances permit. Or, it can be brought on by a relatively major and dramatic occurrence, such as the sudden loss of a major taxpayer or, as in the case of New York City, the closing off of some other heavily relied upon source of cash.
- There are few standards against which municipal government can be compared with confidence.
- It is not easy to compare one local government to another because of differences which exist in populations, services provided and legal requirements.
- It is difficult to measure factors external to the local government itself—such as political, economic and social forces—which have a strong influence.
- The problems which create fiscal difficulties seldom emerge overnight. Rather, they develop slowly, thus making potential difficulties less obvious.
- The information needed to assess problems is not usually readily available in a usable format.

Research to Develop Indicators

Approaches to fiscal indicators fall into two general categories. In the first category are those analyses that seek to further the development of the theory of fiscal condition analysis and to draw general conclusions based on a group of sample cities. The second category worries less about developing theory and concentrates on intuitively appealing measures of variables that common sense tells us are important to fiscal condition.

A Touche Ross-First National Bank of Boston study, entitled *Urban Fiscal Stress: A Comparative Analysis of Sixty-Six U.S. Cities,* falls into the first category. The study defines fiscal distress in terms of expenditures, taxation and debt per capita and correlates these variables with various socioeconomic, demographic and structural factors. It found that fiscal distress is not the inevitable result of a weakening economy. The study concluded that good management can forestall, at least for a time, the fiscal decline of a local government even in the face of the economic decline of its community. Conversely, poor management can create fiscal difficulties for an otherwise economically healthy local government. The report also concluded that "fiscal stability between the demand for public services and financial resources appears to be within the grasp of most cities."

Terry Nichols Clark of the University of Chicago has also examined the problem of developing measures of urban fiscal strain. Among the indicators identified by this study are short- and long-term debt, revenue and flow-of-funds measures. Sources of fiscal strain include intergovernmental relations, municipal employees, the poor, loss of jobs, nonpoor residents and fiscal management procedures. Policy choices available to local officials to avoid or ameliorate stress are one product of the analysis.

Philip Dearborn of the Center for Municipal and Metropolitan Research has compiled a series of reports describing elements of municipal fiscal analyses that present methods of identifying municipalities that are on the brink of financial emergency. Operating statement and balance sheet analysis is used to evaluate a municipality's financial condition. Various budget performance indices are developed to explain changes in financial condition. Welfare-related expenditures and tax and debt burden data provide measures of budget flexibility used in evaluating a municipality's ability to deal with a financial emergency.

The Urban Institute, in its draft report entitled *Urban Fiscal Monitoring,* has also developed a guide and reference for better fiscal monitoring. It considers the following factors in arriving at measures of fiscal stress:

- Indicators of economic condition and their impact on fiscal condition;
- Long-term fiscal measures such as local tax and revenue capacity;
- Short-term factors, including operating deficits and surpluses, net cash position and liquidity;
- Dependence on federal and state aid;
- Long-term and short-term debt; and
- The amount of outstanding pension obligations.

Recently, the Government Finance Research Center of the Municipal Finance Officers Association (MFOA), in conjunction with the congressional Joint Economic Committee, completed a survey of the current fiscal trends and conditions of U.S. cities. . . . In all, more than 300 cities of various sizes responded, giving detailed information about their fiscal 1978 and 1979 budgeted and actual results, as well as what they anticipated their results would be for fiscal 1980. These data, when tabulated, will give a most up-to-date picture of financial performance and conditions.

(For further review of recent efforts to develop fiscal indicators, see the bulletin *Municipal Fiscal Indicators* prepared by J. Richard Aronson for the Urban Consortium.)

Assisting Local Officials

The International City Management Association (ICMA) [has completed] a series of practical handbooks that managers of local governments can use to assess their fiscal condition. The handbooks present detailed measures in three broad categories of variables:

- External influences, including local demands and resources, the national and regional economy and intergovernmental issues;
- Organizational practices and policies in issues management; and
- Internal financial characteristics, such as revenue, expenditures, debt, unfunded liabilities reserves, and condition of capital assets.

Local officials are presented with information on collecting data, methods of calculating data and interpreting the results.

A volume recently published by the Municipal Finance Officers Association entitled *Is Your City Heading For Financial Difficulty?: A Guidebook for Smaller Cities and Other Governmental Units* is the result of one such effort. The report cites five major variables that contribute to fiscal decline.

Signs of Fiscal Decline

The five variables noted in the MFOA report and the trends which local officials should monitor in guarding against fiscal decline are described in the following sections.

The Economic Base of the Municipality

A strong economic base produces the revenue to support services and creates the community environment which attracts residents and business. Moreover, when the economic base is strong, the need to expend public funds on such services as police protection, social services and housing rehabilitation is less severe. The following specific trends may indicate that the economic base of the community is declining:

- Appraised value of real estate per capita in the community is growing too slowly or declining;
- Number and value of building permits are declining or growing too slowly;
- Number and value of business licenses are declining;
- Retail business is declining or growing at a slower pace;
- Expenditures for police and social services are growing as a percentage of total expenditures;
- Total population is declining; and
- Income per capita is declining.

Financial Independence of the Local Government

Typically, a financially sound municipality has sufficient control over its finances to enable it to weather financial problems and emergencies without a crisis. In addition, such municipalities usually have the financial flexibility to respond to the need to support critical programs. This flexibility is a by-product of financial independence; it permits a jurisdiction to control its own destiny.

Financial independence can be lost in several ways:

- Becoming overly dependent on volatile outside funding sources, with their matching fund and administrative requirements;
- Incurring excessive debt, which creates heavy demands on future revenues; or
- Committing funds to programs whose costs cannot be readily controlled.

Specific trends to watch in this area include:

- A growing percentage of expenditures for basic services funded by categorical grant funds;
- A growing proportion of own-source revenues committed to matching funds;
- Tax rates in key tax sources approaching legal ceilings;
- A growing debt burden;
- A steady pattern of budget overruns in specific programs; and
- Rapid increases in fringe benefits for employees.

Municipal Productivity

Municipal productivity is not an easy factor to measure because many of the services and benefits which municipalities provide are intangible. The following trends are generally useful measures:

- The number of municipal employees per capita is increasing;
- Municipal expenditures after adjustments for inflation are increasing;
- Municipal enterprises are incurring operating losses;
- Customer rates for municipal enterprises are rising rapidly; and
- Unit output per dollar expended in selected local services is not increasing.

The Amount of Current Costs Deferred to the Future

Trends which should be closely watched to determine if an unreasonable level of cost is being deferred to the future include:

- Short-term debt and other obligations outstanding at year end growing as a percentage of total own-source revenues;
- Long-term debt being applied to operating programs;
- Declining funding of capital items such as street repaving, new equipment, etc.; and
- Increasing deferral of current pension costs.

The Effectiveness of Financial Management Practices

Sound financial management practices can provide information which local officials need to evaluate the fiscal posture of their jurisdictions. Financial management is a factor which is under direct management control. Thus, problems in financial management may be easier to solve than those in the other subject areas just discussed. There is no acceptable justification for having inadequate financial management practices.

Some trends which could indicate that a municipality's financial practices are inadequate include the following:

- Real estate assessments vary greatly from true market value;
- Earnings on short-term investments are declining;
- The interest cost of short-term loans is increasing;
- The incidence of budget-expenditure over-runs is increasing;
- The incidence of estimated/actual revenue short-falls is increasing;
- The amount of taxes and fees uncollected at year end is increasing; and
- The municipality consistently fails to obtain an unqualified opinion on financial statements from an outside auditor.

Procedures for Developing Indicators

The indicators just described can be developed and analyzed on a regular basis. The process would include the following steps:

1. Assemble the data needed to compute the indicators;
2. Calculate the indicators for each of several (at least five) prior years; and
3. Identify significant trends and assess the underlying causes for those trends.

If potentially unfavorable trends are identified, underlying causes should then be ascertained. A trend which appears unfavorable on the surface may be harmless. Its impact cannot be known until a background analysis has been completed. The development of the indicator is not the end, but rather the beginning of the analysis.

This portion of the process is the most subjective and, therefore, requires the greatest degree of analytical skill. It is also the most important task because the results will indicate whether the unit of government is heading for financial trouble. To assist in performing the analysis of underlying causes, a checklist of the most likely causes associated with each indicator should be developed as a guide.

Bibliography

Aronson, J. Richard. *Municipal Fiscal Indicators: An Information Bulletin of the Management, Finance and Personnel Task Force of the Urban Consortium.* Washington, D.C.: Urban Consortium, 1979. 40 pages.

Describes efforts to develop fiscal indicators and concludes with recommendations for topics requiring further study. Also describes the methodology and conclusions of recent research on fiscal indicators. Available from Urban Consortium, 1140 Connecticut Ave., N.W., Washington, D.C. 20036.

Bahl, Roy. *The Fiscal Outlook for Cities.* Syracuse, N.Y.: Syracuse University Press, 1978. 136 pages.

A series of papers which assess the fiscal outlook for cities against a background of current federal policy toward cities. The writings cover four topics regarding federal policy–the particular case of distressed Northeastern cities, capital obsolescence and financing, federal grants, and the impact of the federal budget. Available from the publisher, Syracuse, N.Y. 13210.

Clark, Terry N. *Urban Fiscal Strain Research Project Publications.* Chicago: University of Chicago Press, 1976 and 1977.

A series of papers that look at various indicators of fiscal strain. Sources of strain analyzed include intergovernmental relations, loss of jobs, the poor and municipal employees. For further information contact the author, University of Chicago, 1126 E. 59th St., Chicago, Ill. 60637.

Dearborn, Philip M. *Budget Performance. Measuring Liquidity. Payment of Debt Service.* Series of three reports. New York: First Boston Corporation, 1977.

Describes elements of municipal fiscal analyses. Two reports present methods of identifying a municipality nearing a financial emergency; the third examines debt-related factors to determine how an investor may be treated in a financial emergency. Available from First Boston Corporation, 20 Exchange Place, New York, N.Y. 10005.

Groves, Sanford M., and Godsey, W. Maureen. *Evaluation of Local Government Financial Condition. Financial Trend Monitoring System: A Practitioners Workbook for Charting Trends and Interpreting Results. Financial Jeopardy: Practices and Policies That Can Affect Financial Condition. Financial Performance Goals: A Guide for Setting Long-Range Policies. Tools for Making Financing Decisons.* Series of five handbooks. Washington, D.C.: International City Management Association, forthcoming 1980.

Five practical handbooks designed to help local government managers assess their fiscal condition. They focus on three broad variables: external influences such as local demands for resources and national and regional economy; organizational issues including management practices and policies; and internal financial characteristics such as revenue and expenditure patterns, debt, and unfunded liabilities. For information contact ICMA, 1140 Connecticut Ave., N.W., Washington, D.C. 20036.

Hubbell, L. Kenneth, ed. *Fiscal Crisis in American Cities: The Federal Response.* Cambridge, Mass.: Ballinger Publishing Company, 1979. 341 pages.

Examines the scope of the federal government's response to the fiscal crises of cities. Provides an extensive discourse on the emergency measures and programs enacted during the mid-seventies. Changes in the more established programs of the late sixties and early seventies are also scrutinized. Taken together, the assembled papers evaluate the bulk of the federally initiated programs aimed either directly or indirectly at assisting financially troubled cities over the past decade. Available from the publisher, Cambridge, Mass. 02138.

Peterson, John E., and Rafuse, Robert W. "Big City Finances in 1982: Will Closing Budgeting Gaps Cause Financial Strain?" Draft paper. September 1979.

Intended to help clarify the debate over what constitutes fiscal stress and how it might be measured. Seeks to determine whether any major cities may face a financial emergency by 1982, given a number of possible economic and policy scenarios.

Rosenberg, Philip, and Stallings, C. Wayne. *Is Your City Heading for Financial Difficulty?: A Guidebook for Smaller Cities and Other Governmental Units.* Chicago, Ill.: Municipal Finance Officers Association, 1978. 43 pages.

Provides local officials with step-by-step procedures for analyses of their government's fiscal condition. Focuses on five major variables that contribute to fiscal decline: economic vitality; financial independence being lost; declining municipal productivity; deferral of current municipal costs to the future; and, ineffective municipal financial management practices. A series of detailed indicators is presented to assess each variable and a methodology for collecting and analyzing data on the variable is outlined. Available from MFOA, 180 N. Michigan Ave., Chicago, Ill. 60601.

Touche Ross & Co. and First National Bank of Boston. *Urban Fiscal Stress: A Comparative Analysis of Sixty-Six U.S. Cities.* New York: Touche Ross & Co., 1979. 118 pages.

The results of a study that focused on the impact of economic-social-structural-financial linkages on local government fiscal stress. The study found that fiscal distress is not the necessary result of a weakening economy. Available from Touche Ross & Co., Client Services and Development, 1633 Broadway, New York, N.Y. 10019.

U.S. Department of Commerce, Bureau of the Census. *City Government Finances.* Washington, D.C.: U.S. Government Printing Office, annual publication.

Presents statistical information on various elements of municipal finances of individual cities, towns, and townships having 50,000 population or more. Updated regularly.

U.S. Department of Commerce, Bureau of the Census. *Governmental Finances.* Washington, D.C.: U.S. Government Printing Office, annual publication.

Provides estimated nationwide financial aggregates covering local government, together with state and federal government data.

Revenues

7 Revenue Sources

Arthur A. Mendonsa

Taxes

Taxes can be defined as "compulsory charges made against the public by a government to obtain the money it needs to finance its activities." Tax charges are levied against values. These values may be contained in property, in income, and in the gross receipts of a business.

The amount of taxes which will be charged to a member of the public is calculated by applying a tax rate to the values which he owns. This tax rate is usually equal to some percentage of the values being taxed. For example, if a tax is levied against property, the tax rate might be set in an amount equal to 2 percent of the value of the property. Or if a tax is levied against sales, the tax rate might be set at 3 percent of the value of the sales.

The values which are taxed by local governments can be divided into two groups: those contained in property and those produced by business activity. Let's look at each of these groups.

Tax on Property

Local governments levy taxes against three classes of property:

1. Real property. Real property consists of land and buildings or other permanent fixtures and improvements.
2. Personal property. Personal property is the property owned by a person or enterprise which can be moved with relative ease from one location to another. Included in this category are such things as vehicles, furniture, inventories, boats, and machinery.
3. Property of a privately owned utility. The property of a privately owned utility includes both real and personal property. However, utility property is in a special class since the values placed on it for tax purposes are set by the state.

The amount of the value which is placed on each of these three classes of property for tax purposes is dictated by state law and by court decisions. Usually, these values have some relationship to the "market" value. In some cases, it may actually be market value; in other cases, it may represent some percentage of market value. The techniques and principles by which this is done are too complicated and will not be discussed here. However, there are certain basic principles which should govern the assignment of these values. These may be summarized as follows:

1. Properties having approximately equal market values should be assigned approximately equal taxable values and should be charged about the same amount of tax. This can be accomplished only by using uniform procedures to establish taxable values. It cannot be accomplished if these values are assigned by whim.

Reprinted from Simplified Financial Management in Rural Government *(Athens, Ga.: University of Georgia Institute of Government, Institute of Community and Area Development, Center for Continuing Education, 1969).*

2. The taxable value placed on property should be adjusted periodically to reflect changes in market value. If market values rise, taxable values should be increased. On the other hand, taxable values should be decreased when market values drop.
3. All property subject to the property tax should be found and taxed. Real property is relatively easy to find since it cannot be moved. The techniques for finding such property include the use of aerial photographs, field surveys, and property record investigations.

   Personal property, because of its movable nature, is more difficult to find and tax. The techniques for finding personal property include making field surveys, comparing utility customer records with personal property tax rolls, and other search and find techniques.

The amount of taxes due from the owner of a taxable property is calculated by applying a rate to the taxable value which has been assigned to the property. We can illustrate this procedure with an example. We will assume that a taxing authority has established a tax rate equal to 2.3 percent of the taxable value of property. (The tax rate is usually stated in terms of mills. Ten mills equal 1 percent. Twenty-three mills would equal 2.3 percent.) We will further assume that a Mr. Smith owns property which has been assigned a taxable value of $2,000. To calculate the amount of taxes that Mr. Smith must pay, we multiply the value of his property, in this case $2,000, by the tax rate, in this case 2.3 percent or 23 mills. When this is done, we find that the amount of taxes due from Mr. Smith totals $46.

A number of bookkeeping transactions can be encountered in the administration of the property tax. Some of the more common transactions are listed and discussed below.

Accounting for Property Tax Revenues on an Accrual Basis

The revenues earned from a property tax levy can be accounted for on an accrual basis. When this practice is followed, the tax levy is recorded as revenue at the time it is imposed. The property tax lends itself to the accrual basis of accounting since the taxable values of the properties to be taxed are known in advance. Thus, the amount of taxes the properties will produce can be calculated by applying the tax rate to these values . . . .

Accounting for Property Tax Revenues on a Cash Basis

When tax revenues are accounted for on a cash basis, taxes are recorded as revenues when they are collected. The merit of the cash approach is that it helps a town to keep its spending within the amount of cash it receives. This is more difficult when tax revenues are recorded on an accrual basis, since there is a tendency on the part of the uninitiated to assume that accrued revenues represent actual cash on hand and to spend accordingly . . . .

Tax on Business Activity

A tax on business activity can take a variety of forms:

It can be applied against a business as a percentage of the gross receipts of the business.

It can be applied against the consumer as a percentage of the purchase price.

It can be applied as a fixed charge on each unit of a commodity. For example, a fixed charge can be made on specified quantities of beverages such as beer, wine, or alcohol.

The types of business taxes a town can levy are fixed by state law.

Accounting for Taxes on Business Activity

The tax on business activity is sometimes called a self-assessing tax because the primary responsibility for calculating and reporting the tax liability lies with the taxpayer rather than the tax collector. For example, the gross receipt tax on insurance premiums is applied against the premiums reported as collected by the insurance company. The beverage tax, on the other hand, is frequently administered through a beverage stamp system whereby the beverage retailer purchases the stamps from the tax collector and then affixes the stamps to the beverage containers.

There is usually no way to determine in advance the amount of taxes due from the levy of a business tax. The tax rate can be fixed, of course, but the value against which the rate will be applied cannot be fixed.

Administering the Tax on Business Activity

There are at least two problems which may arise in the administration of a self-assessing tax on business activity. First, it is sometimes difficult to identify all of the firms which are subject to the tax. Second, since the amount of the tax liability is usually calculated by the taxpayer, there is a degree of uncertainty about the accuracy of the liability reported.

Both of these problems can be minimized for a beverage tax program by making use of tax stamps. Under this plan, tax stamps are purchased by the beverage retailer and then affixed to the beverage containers. Visual inspections of beverage retail outlets are made, to insure that beverages are not being sold without stamps and that all liable companies are paying the tax.

Both of these problems are more difficult in the case of an insurance premium tax since a tax stamp plan cannot be used. In the absence of tax stamps, some means must be found to identify the companies which are subject to the premium tax and to check the accuracy of the tax liabilities reported by these companies. It is somewhat easier to identify the companies than it is to confirm the accuracy of the tax liabilities reported. The telephone book will include the names of most of the companies. In addition, the records of the State Insurance Commissioner can be of help in compiling a list of liable companies. However, there is no certain way to confirm the amount of taxes reported as due by these companies. In the final analysis, a town must depend on the integrity of the companies which supply this information.

Another problem in the administration of the self-assessing taxes is verifying that the taxes have been collected. Again, this problem is simplified in the case of the beverage tax when stamps are used, since it is a simple thing to audit the number of stamps issued and reconcile this with cash. Collections from the insurance premium tax are more difficult to verify. Pre-numbered receipts are of some help. In addition, a checklist of the companies subject to the tax can be prepared and periodic checks can be made to verify whether or not payments have been received from the companies on the list. This system can help to insure that collections will not be misplaced.

Non-Tax Revenues

A town may obtain revenue from a variety of non-tax sources. Some of these are listed and discussed below. Where appropriate, comments are made about problems which can be experienced in administering these revenues.

Licenses and Permits

Licenses and permits can be defined as "special rights or privileges granted to an individual or business by a governmental unit in return for the payment of designated fees." The fees collected for licenses or permits are classified as revenue. Licenses are issued to conduct a business, to engage in a profession, to park on the city streets, and to obtain a variety of other privileges. Permits are issued to construct a building, to dig a well, and to authorize other regulated activities.

The charges made for licenses and permits vary from community to community. There is no uniform standard for setting such charges. In some instances, the charges may be calculated to cover part or all of the cost of operating a regulatory program such as a building code. In other instances, the charge is levied primarily for revenue purposes and so is actually a tax.

A license and permit program is relatively easy to administer and control. This is because a document of some type is usually issued when a license or permit is purchased. Thus, pre-numbered documents can be used to provide a means of auditing the payments received from the purchase of licenses and permits. In addition, records which show the number of licenses or permits issued by month and year can be used to help measure the extent of annual compliance with licensing requirements. When the record shows a sharp drop in the number of licenses issued in relation to past trends, it can indicate a significant degree of non-compliance with licensing regulations.

One license fee which is difficult to administer is the parking meter fee. Meters can be robbed or meter fees can be misappropriated by the collector. One means of controlling these problems is to account for meter fee collections on a block-by-block basis. Significant fluctuations in the fees produced by meters in a particular block may indicate that meters are being pilfered or that collections are being misappropriated.

Fines, Forfeits, and Penalties

This class of revenue includes fines and penalties charged as a punishment for violating a law or for neglect of a public duty. It also includes forfeits of money posted as security to guarantee appearance before the court or to guarantee performance. Revenues obtained from this source are derived primarily from the activities of the police or the courts.

Control to prevent intentional or unintentional misplacement of payments received from fines, penalties, and forfeits is extremely difficult. Proper control over the collections received from court fines requires the use of pre-numbered receipts combined with a court docket which identifies each court case by number and which shows the disposition of each case. Control over fines for parking and traffic violation can be obtained through the use of pre-numbered traffic citation forms which are audited periodically to determine their disposition. Monthly and annual records of collections from fines, penalties, and forfeitures can provide some indication of possible misplacement of collections from these sources. However, these records can also indicate changes in the fining policies of the court.

Revenues from the Use of Money and Property

A town, like other enterprises, may obtain revenues by investing its money or by renting or leasing property. Revenues can also be obtained from the sale of concession rights to operate enterprises, such as refreshment stands, at favored locations.

Revenues from Other Agencies

Included in this category are revenues obtained from payments received from federal, state, and county governments; and from gifts, donations, and unclaimed money. For this category of revenues, the town is merely a recipient of the money. It does not impose a levy and it has no control over the formula for distributing the money.

Charges for Current Services

Among the current services for which charges are sometimes made are weed cutting, sidewalk repairs, recording fees, building inspections, waste collection and disposal charges, publicly operated concessions, and fire protection.

Revenues from Utility Charges

Most small towns operate one or more utilities from which they derive revenues. These include water, gas, and electrical utilities. Utility charges are calculated by applying a predetermined rate to a measured volume of service received by a utility consumer. Thus, the amount of revenues due from the utility charges is known before payments are actually received. For this reason, revenues from utility charges can be accounted for on an accrual basis.

Other Revenues

This classification is applied to revenues which do not fall into any of the other groups we have described. Included in this category are revenues from such sources as charges to departments, special assessments, sales of bonds, premiums on bonds sold, sale of fixed assets, contributions from other funds, and surplus from discontinued funds.

Included in the "other revenue" category is a revenue classification designated as "contributions from other funds." Interfund payments are usually made when one fund purchases services from another fund. For example, a Utility Fund may purchase bookkeeping service from the General Fund. Occasionally, however, a fund may be required to supply revenues to another fund which has been created for a special purpose. For example, the General Fund may be required to contribute money to a Pension Fund for city employees, or the General Fund may be required to contribute money to a Debt Retirement Fund. In all of these cases, a situation is created in which the expenditures of one fund become the revenues of another fund.

8 Federal Grants Management

Background

A considerable portion of all local government current revenues are received in the form of intergovernmental grants or transfers. The funds received may be for specifically defined purposes or may be designated for certain broadly defined purposes. Some funds must be formally applied for by a locality, whereas others are automatically distributed by formula or program criteria.

The receipt of grants funds by a municipality typically imposes new demands on its financial management systems and procedures. There are specific reporting, accounting and program requirements which must be met by a grantee. These compliance features may not be compatible with the city's fiscal period, chart of accounts, reporting formats, etc. Failure to comply with grant regulations and rules could result in the municipality having to repay grant funds. Consequently, grant financial administration and management systems are important elements of local government's overall financial management system.

This selection reviews the following issues in grants management: impact of grants on local financial management, categorical grants, block grants, general revenue sharing, advance funding of federal grants, integrating grants into local management and federal management circulars.

Reprinted from Elements of Financial Management 10 *(Washington, D.C.: Government Finance Research Center, Municipal Finance Officer's Association, May 1980).*

Impact of Grants on Financial Management

The management principles for federal programs frequently are at odds with accepted local practices. For example, the standards for accounting may be different for federal programs than for local programs. Consequently, a dual management system at the local level is sometimes created–one to deal with federal programs and another to provide management support for locally funded program activities. Management elements that might be affected by a dual system include:

- Timing;
- Location and format of financial records;
- Planning;
- Management capacity;
- Operating and maintenance costs;
- Local government priorities;
- Flow of revenues; and
- Compliance with federal requirements.

Timing Problems

The difference between a municipality's fiscal year and the associated budget preparation cycle, on the one hand, and the federal program year and grant application cycle, on the other, makes it difficult to determine the total resources required to provide necessary services. It can also complicate grants reporting, which typically must be done according to the federal program format.

Location and Format of Financial Records

Financial records for an individual federal program are often separately maintained by the local government department or agency responsible for carrying out the federal program. Whether these separate accounting systems are maintained by line departments or independent agencies, their existence means that local government administrative departments, which are legally responsible for this function, may lack the necessary fiscal information and control over federal program funds. Although federal financial management requirements do not mandate the accounting basis upon which a local government's records must be kept, the unit must be able to report on the accrual basis of accounting. In addition, the variety of federally prescribed budget formats may be inconsistent with local expenditure categories.

Uncertainty in Planning

Recognizing that there are no guarantees that the funds requested will be received, local officials may be either unwilling to include them in the annual budget or prohibited by statute from doing so. The variations in federal program requirements and funding cycles from year to year inhibit the development of an overall, standardized monitoring, reporting and evaluation framework. As a result, chief executives and local legislative bodies are not able to consider overall service levels or determine total resource commitments, and implementing agencies are unable to coordinate or effectively program expenditures over a uniform period.

Management Capacity

Federal grant programs frequently place additional management responsibilities upon local governments. These responsibilities are sometimes inconsistent with local practices and procedures. They often require system control and monitoring capabilities that do not currently exist within the city. Furthermore, certain federal programs require additional staff to adequately manage the programs. There is hesitation on the part of some local officials to hire the needed staff due to the uncertainty of future funding. The decision not to hire additional staff places additional duties upon existing staff.

Impact of Grants on Operating and Maintenance Costs

Federal construction programs may provide facilities that the local government could otherwise not afford. However, federal funds typically do not finance operating and maintenance costs. This could result in additional stress on the city's own source revenues and staff.

Local Planning Skewed

Local government program priorities often do not correspond with federal program priorities. This frequently results in local governments adjusting priorities in order to match those of the federal program.

Dependency on Federal Monies

As current economic and financial conditions reduce local governments' ability to support services and programs with own-source revenues, the governments become more dependent on federal monies. This increased dependence on federal funds decreases local governments' autonomy and also places them in an untenable position if federal programs are discontinued.

Compliance Features

Along with federal monies comes an array of compliance features, many of which must be satisfied prior to expenditure of the funds. Often, if the compliance features are not met prior to the expenditure of federal funds, the noncompliance will be the subject of audit findings. More importantly, however, this may result in the local governments being required to refund the federal funds.

Categorical Grants

According to the Advisory Commission on Intergovernmental Relations, the number of categorical grants . . . available to state and local governments has almost tripled since 1963, while funding has increased tenfold in that period . . . . These grants are directed at specific programs and limited to narrowly defined activities.

Categorical grants have many positive features.

- They stimulate state and local governments to meet specific national goals such as antidiscrimination, environmental protection, or the promotion of arts and culture;
- They act as a catalyst in numerous program areas that warrant exploration, such as national research and demonstration in health and natural resources;
- They attract the attention of appropriate aid recipients; and
- They ensure, as a result of the various strings and conditions attached to the funding, that the monies are used for the purposes intended by Congress.

However, the categorical grant system makes it difficult for local government to plan and manage a unified local program area. Each program has its own budgeting, financing, accounting and reporting forms and requirements. In addition, categoricals tend to be overly specific, fragmented or duplicative, and difficult to administer.

Block Grants

Block grants offer the potential for removing many barriers to improved budgetary and financial management of all the resources to be spent in a locality. Local officials are now able to play a far more substantive role in determining how federal funds may be allocated locally.

The basic characteristics of the block grant are:

- The eligible activities are fairly broad and stated in general terms within an overall program area;
- The amount to which a local government is entitled is determined by a formula;
- Local officials have the opportunity to determine their own priorities and allocate resources to meet identified local needs within broad national objectives;
- An annual application indicates the activities to be financed and how resources are to be distributed; and
- In lieu of lengthy application requirements and extensive application reviews, emphasis is placed on post-approval monitoring and audits.

The block grant approach affords local government certain advantages:

- Local government program consolidation [facilitates] better use of central administrative functions (such as budgeting and accounting);
- The program year may be made coterminous with a local unit's own fiscal year, thus facilitating monitoring and performance evaluation; and
- Block grants provide greater flexibility and fluidity in local decision making, thus permitting local priorities to be reconsidered and funds reallocated during a program year.

General Revenue Sharing

In response to pressures from local officials to provide predictability and flexibility to the flow of funds and the discretion on how to use and manage them, the federal government enacted the general revenue sharing (GRS) program in 1973. Transferring more power regarding grants to state and local governments, general revenue sharing funds are distributed by formula with very few restrictions concerning their use.

The revenue sharing program affords recipient governments the ability to:

- Plan, control and modify expenditures and tax policies, as well as assimilate citizen views into the budget process;
- Define, address and act on community problems;
- Promote and adopt new and innovative programs; and
- Improve planning due to the five-year certainty of the program, the simple availability of more money, and the opportunity to make needed expenditures.

The State and Local Fiscal Assistance Amendments of 1976 extended the general revenue sharing program for another three and three-quarter years. This act allows local governments virtually complete freedom in determining the use of the monies. On the other hand, the amendments extended the nondiscrimination provision to encompass religion, age and handicaps and to require that, with limited exceptions, each recipient obtain an audit of all its funds and groups of accounts in accordance with generally accepted auditing standards at least once every three years. Recently, the predictability in the program has been placed in jeopardy by calls for the removal of states from the general revenue sharing program and for the reduction in the amount of funds to local governments.

Advance Funding

While there may be an increase in the number of both categorical and block grants available to local governments, the delivery mechanism for these grants may be revised to reduce many of the uncertainties associated with the flow in federal funding. An important way to accomplish this would be through multiyear budgeting on the part of the federal government. For most expenditures, the approach seems feasible and has been recommended by the Congressional Budget Office. Such forward budgeting would make it easier for local governments to plan, budget and implement grants programs.

Integrating Grants Management at the Local Level

Officials should review their systems to determine the local unit's capacity to undertake integrated grants management, i.e., the incorporation of grant program management elements with local government management systems and procedures. This review should compare existing organization, policies, personnel skills and support systems with estimated resource requirements for the described integration process. To facilitate this review, officials should analyze current practices. For example, in the areas of budgeting and accounting, a government may review its existing structure and process to determine the following:

- How federal program and project cost estimates are aggregated into an overall budget within the grant limit;
- The relationship (both programmatically and in terms of timing) between the grant budgeting process and the city's normal budget process;
- The format for the prescribed grant activity budget, e.g., program versus line item, project versus objects of expenditure;
- The format employed for the city departments compared to that used for grant budget estimates and with any impediments to a common budget process and format;
- The approach and method used to account for grant programs and projects; and
- The relationship between grant program/project accounting and the municipality's own accounting and record-keeping practices, on the one hand, and impediments to an integrated program/project accounting system, on the other.

After such self-analysis, local government officials may wish to design and implement integrated grants management.

Federal Management Circulars

Regardless of how a local government chooses to manage the various elements of a federal program, it may comply with the ever-increasing requirements that various federal agencies impose in the audit, accounting and reporting areas.

The two major documents that govern the administration of federal grants at the state and local levels are Office of Management and Budget Circular A-102 and Federal Management Circular 74-4. Circular A-102 sets grant administration procedures in a number of areas, including financial management, and is designed to restrain federal agencies from imposing additional requirements on grantees, although it does not preclude them from doing so. While it does not impose or describe specific procedures, Attachment G of Circular A-102 presents the following standards for an adequate grant financial management system:

- Current, accurate and complete disclosure of financial results;
- Records that identify the source and application of funds;
- Effective controls and accountability for funds, property and other assets;
- Comparison of actual expenditures and budgeted amounts;
- Methods that minimize the time between receipt and expenditure of funds;
- Financial and compliance audits at least every two years; and
- Accounting records supported by source documentation.

Within this context, recent studies have shown the need for a single total audit, one in which an organization as a whole is audited, not just individual grants. Numerous federal audits, each attempting to examine a particular program, become wasteful of both federal and local resources and disruptive to operations.

In response to these demands for a "single audit," OMB recently published Attachment P to Circular A-102. Attachment P states that grantee audits are to be made on an organizationwide basis, rather than grant by grant. Furthermore, the authority of federal agencies to make audits of a recipient organization is limited. However, if independent audits arranged for by state and local governments meet the requirements prescribed, all federal agencies must rely on them, and any additional audit work should build upon the work already done.

Federal Management Circular 74-4 provides uniform rules for determining costs applicable to grants and contracts with state and local governments. It defines allowable costs and sets forth the procedures to recover them. The costs may be direct or indirect, but must be necessary, reasonable and directly related to the grant. The basic underlying intent of the circular is that federally assisted programs bear their fair share of costs. The circular also provides that one federal agency will negotiate a grantee's indirect cost (indirect or overhead costs which are common to two or more projects or operations) on behalf of all other federal agencies.

The federal executive branch has sought to coordinate, standardize and simplify categorical grant application and administrative procedures through governmentwide management and other circulars, organizational reforms and decentralization of management responsibilities to the federal field offices. Nevertheless, the record thus far would indicate there is much to be done.

Bibliography

Advisory Commission on Intergovernmental Relations. *Improving Federal Grants Management.* Report A-53. Washington, D.C.: U.S. Government Printing Office, February 1977. 287 pages.

Focuses chiefly on organizational and procedural efforts undertaken at the federal level to remedy some of the operational defects in the intergovernmental grant system. In addition, ACIR has published numerous books and articles related to grants management. For more information, contact ACIR, 1111 20th St., N.W., Washington, D.C. 20575.

Association of Government Accountants. *Review Guide for Grantees' Financial Management Systems.* Washington, D.C.: U.S. Office of Management and Budget, 1978. 32 pages.

Highlights most grantors' financial management requirements and discloses the adequacy of grantees' financial management systems. Covers grantees' accounting, budgeting, procurement and property systems. OMB is asking federal agencies to test the guide as a method of simplifying federal grant program administration. Available from U.S. Government Printing Office, Washington, D.C. 20402. Stock No. 041-001-0062-0.

Comptroller General of the United States. *Guidelines for Financial and Compliance Audits of Federally Assisted Programs.* Washington, D.C.: U.S. General Accounting Office, February 1980. 67 pages.

A guide for use in auditing federally assisted programs. Replaces almost a hundred individual program guides that were previously in use. Issued as part of an overall program of improving government accountability. Available from the General Accounting Office, Distribution Section, Room 1518, 441 G St., N.W., Washington, D.C. 20548.

Grants Management Advisory Service. *Federal Grants Management Handbook.* Washington, D.C.: Grants Management Advisory Service, 1978.

A detailed basic resource on federal grant administration. Identifies and analyzes the major requirements affecting federal grants. Organized in a looseleaf binder, fully indexed and cross-referenced. For information contact the publisher, 2120 L St., N.W., Washington, D.C. 20037.

National Council on Governmental Accounting. *Statement 2: Grant, Entitlement, and Shared Revenue Accounting and Reporting by State and Local Governments.* Chicago: Municipal Finance Officers Association, 1979. 5 pages.

Enunciates the applications of generally accepted accounting principles to grants, entitlements and shared revenues received by state and local governments. Available from MFOA, 180 N. Michigan Ave., Chicago, Ill. 60601.

National Association of Counties. *A Guide to Grants-in-Aid in County Government.* Washington, D.C.: National Association of Counties, 1978. 59 pages.

Designed to acquaint county officials and their executive officers with the need for a coordinated and properly managed federal/state grants-in-aid program. Documents the growth and changing nature of federal grants-in-aid. Sets forth the need for a grants management system, maintaining that effective use of grants by a county can help elected officials provide the most economical and efficient county government. Describes in detail the position and functions of the grants coordinator and presents organizational models from five counties from various parts of the country. An appendix lists federal grants programs and the requirements for notifying the appropriate planning and development clearinghouses of intent to apply in accordance with OMB Circular A-95 (Revised). Available from NACo, 1735 New York Ave., N.W., Washington, D.C. 20006.

Richtern, Albert. *Federal Grants Management: The City and County View.* Washington, D.C.: Urban Data Service, International City Management Association, 1976.

This publication reviews the management impact of federal grants on county and city government. Available from ICMA, 1140 Connecticut Ave., N.W., Washington, D.C. 20036.

Rosenberg, Philip, and Dalton, John. *Community Development Block Grant: Budgetary and Financial Management.* Chicago: Municipal Finance Officers Association, 1978. 135 pages.

A guide for local government officials. Intended to provide constructive guidance to improve management of the Community Development Block Grant. Although the manual deals specifically with one program in the panoply of federal grants to local governments, the principles and methodologies should also have applicability to many other federal grant programs. It should be of special interest to those interested in integrating the financial management of the grants with the city's financial management. Available from MFOA, 180 N. Michigan Ave., Chicago, Ill. 60601.

U.S. Congress, Congressional Budget Office. *Advance Budgeting: A Report to the Congress.* Washington, D.C.: U.S. Government Printing Office, March 1977. 205 pages.

A compendium of technical background papers. Focuses on the feasibility and advisability of advancing all or some budget decisions so that instead of making them just before the start of a fiscal year, they would be made at least 12 months earlier. Available from U.S. Government Printing Office, Washington, D.C. 20402.

U.S. Office of Management and Budget. *Circular A-102.* Washington, D.C.: OMB, 1977. 63 pages.

Sets forth uniform financial and other administrative requirements for grants to state and local governments. Only those specific requirements imposed by legislation establishing a grant program can take precedence over Circular A-102. Available from the Publications Office, OMB, Washington, D.C. 20503.

U.S. Office of Management and Budget. *Federal Management Circular 74-4.* Washington, D.C.: OMB, 1974. 17 pages.

Establishes principles and standards for determining costs applicable to grants and contracts with state and local governments. Available from the Publications Office, OMB, Washington, D.C. 20503.

U.S. Office of Management and Budget. *Financial Management of Federal Assistance Programs.* Washington, D.C.: OMB, 1980. 24 pages.

Summarizes a series of federal circulars, including A-102, that establish uniform simple rules for dealing with the federal government. Since many of the circulars use rather technical language, this booklet is intended to provide a brief overview in layman's terms of their various requirements. Available from the Publications Office, OMB, Washington, D.C. 20503.

U.S. Senate, Committee on Governmental Affairs. *Federal Grants Management Reform Hearings before the Subcommittee on Intergovernmental Relations, July 27, September 6, and October 3, 1979.* Washington, D.C.: U.S. Government Printing Office, 1979. 639 pages.

A report on a series of hearings exploring suggestions for improving the management of the federal grants system. The goal of the hearings was to seek ways to reduce the red tape and high overhead which prevent the grant dollars delivered to state and local governments from being used as effectively and efficiently as Congress intended. Available from Government Printing Office, Washington, D.C. 20402.

White, Virginia P. *Grants.* New York: Plenum Press, 1975. 354 pages.

Explains what the grant business is all about, from what a grant is to how to find out where the funds are, to how to go about getting a project supported properly. A good introduction to grants and the types of grants available. Available from the publisher, 227 West 17th St., New York, N.Y. 10011.

Wright, Deil S. *Understanding Intergovernmental Relations.* North Scituate, Mass.: Duxbury Press, 1978. 410 pages.

A description of intergovernmental fiscal relations. Provides much detail for a better understanding of fiscal federalism in its actual perspective. Available from the publisher, 6 Bound Brook Court, North Scituate, Mass. 02060.

9 User Charges and Service Fees

Paul B. Downing

Introduction

Inflation and the cost of energy have caused the cost of local government to increase rapidly over the last several years. Recession further increases local government expenditures for social services. At the same time, local government revenues have failed to keep pace with these cost increases. Sources of local revenue, especially the property tax, have been inflexible. Attempts to increase property tax revenues are constrained by legal limits and/or are subject to powerful political opposition. The resulting revenue "shortfall" has been felt in most urban governments. No longer is New York alone. Cleveland, Chicago, Washington, D.C. and Tampa, among others, are faced with substantial cuts in expenditures unless new sources of revenue are found. *User charges and fees are one source of new revenue urban governments are increasingly employing.*

The 1970s have seen a continual and accelerating shift in the methods of financing local governments. Property tax revenues increased 31.8 percent during the 1973-1977 period, but revenue from charges and fees increased 57.0 percent and revenue from sales and gross receipts taxes increased 62.7 percent. Adjusting for inflation, property tax revenues have been approximately constant, while user charges and fees have grown. While some of this growth—especially in the form of utility charges—can be attributed to increased energy costs, the overall growth in user charges and fees can be argued to be primarily an attempt by local governments to replace property tax revenues. This trend away from property taxes and toward user charges and fees is detailed in Table 1 and can be expected to continue through the 1980s.

In addition to their potential as a revenue source, *charges and fees can reduce the cost of government services.* Cost savings result from two phenomena. First, they cause people who consume a government service to consider the cost of its provision, which is reflected in the charge or fee. This added cost will lead to some reduction in use and, thus, in some cost savings. Second, the charge or fee gives better signals to government managers about the appropriate size of public facilities. If there are large numbers of users of a service when a charge equal to the cost of producing the service is levied, then the government manager can be reasonably sure that an expansion is warranted and will be self-financing. If not, then the city's limited resources can be better used elsewhere. This will lead to efficiently sized facilities and cost savings to the community.

User Charges v. Service Fees

The distinction between user charges and service fees is a fine one, and one that will be overlooked throughout this [article]. As a result of this decision, the terms "charges" and "fees" will be used interchangeably, and both will refer to "user charges

---

Reprinted from "User Charges and Service Fees," in Urban Consortium Information Bulletin, *Office of Policy Development and Research (Washington, D.C.: U.S. Department of Housing and Urban Development, January 1982).*

Table 1: *Selected City Government Revenues (1972-73 to 1976-77) (Dollar Amounts in Millions)*

	Fiscal Years					Percent Change From 1972-73 to 1976-77	
Source of Revenue	1976-77	1975-76	1974-75	1973-74	1972-73	Current Dollars (%)	Constant (1972) Dollars (%)
Charges (total)	17766	15869	13852	12167	11316	57.0	19.7
Current Charges*	6872	6161	5443	4927	4533	51.6	15.6
Utility Revenue	19682	9504	8217	7067	6619	61.4	23.0
Liquor Store Revenue	212	204	192	173	164	29.3	-1.4
Taxes (total from own sources)	26067	23336	21135	19434	18477	41.1	7.6
Property Taxes	15653	14165	13046	12244	11879	31.8	0.5
Sales and Gross Receipts Taxes	5805	5109	4555	3931	3567	62.7	24.1

*Current charges include "amounts received from the public for performance of specific services benefiting the persons charged and from sales of commodities and services. . . . Current charges include fees, toll charges, tuition, and other reimbursements for current services . . . ."[1]

Source: *City Government Finances in 1976-77* (Washington, D.C.: U.S. Bureau of the Census, 1979), Table 1.

and service fees." Nevertheless, there are some differences.

User charges are very much like prices charged for privately produced goods. That is, they *represent payment for services which would not be provided to the individual if the charge were not paid.* For example, an individual will be excluded from playing on a municipal golf course unless the required charge is paid. However, in some cases, the individual or firm is not given the right to refuse the service and thus cannot avoid having the services performed and paying the charge. Refuse collection is one example of this form of user charge. Utility type services, such as electricity and water supply, employ user charges which vary with the amount of the service used. In these cases, the user can avoid some (or all) of the charge by reducing his consumption.

Fees, on the other hand, *represent compensation paid to the government for expenses incurred in providing special services.* The expense of police services such as crowd control at private events are typically charged to the sponsor. Fees are also charged for administrative paperwork which primarily benefit specific individuals. Examples include development permits and tract map filing fees. License fees are often designed to cover the additional expenses to the local government of private activities such as carnivals. They are also used to provide revenue to oversee the operation of private enterprise. And in some cases, license fees are essentially a method of governmental sharing in the profit of a private enterprise such as taxi service. In this case, they are similar to sales or gross receipts taxes.

The various types of charges and fees are outlined in Table 2.

Setting Charges and Fees to Recover Costs

The degree to which charges and fees are intended to cover the costs of supplying the good or service will vary among services. Some services are considered to be an ordinary function of the local government for which charges are not appropriate. Schooling services are an example of this type. In other cases, charges are considered to be appropriate and are designed to cover all the costs of producing the service. Airports are an example of this form of operation. In still other cases, charges are used as a revenue source or a method of allocating the service among users, and there is little relationship between the fee and current outlays for the service. Parking fees on existing city streets are one example of charges as a revenue source. Finally, there are services for which charges do not cover full costs. As Table 3 indicates, sewerage, sanitation, parks, hospitals and highways fall in this intermediate group.

Potential Applications

Charges and fees are applicable to many more activities than are commonly assumed. Many activities of seemingly general public services such as police are really rendered to specific individuals, classes of users, or areas. These specific services can be financed with charges if the dis-

Table 2: *Types of Fees, Charges, and Licenses*

- Police Protection
  - special patrol service fees
  - parking fees and charges
  - fees for fingerprints, copies
  - payments for extra police service at stadiums, theaters, circuses
- Transportation
  - subway and bus fares
  - bridge tolls
  - landing and departure fees
  - hangar rentals
  - concession rentals
  - parking meter receipts
- Health and Hospitals
  - inoculation charges
  - x-ray charges
  - hospital charges, including per diem rates and service charge
  - ambulance charges
  - concession rentals
- Education
  - charges for books
  - charges for gymnasium uniforms or special equipment
  - concessions rentals
- Recreation
  - greens fees
  - parking charges
  - concession rentals
  - admissions fees or charges
  - permit charges for tennis courts, etc.
  - charges for specific recreation, services
  - picnic stove fees
  - stadium gate tickets
  - stadium club fees
  - park development charges
- Sanitation
  - domestic and commercial trash collection fees
  - industrial waste charges
- Sewerage
  - sewerage system fees
- Other Public Utility Operations
  - water meter permits
  - water services charges
  - electricity rates
  - telephone booth rentals
- Housing, Neighborhood and Commercial Development
  - street tree fees
  - tract map filing fees
  - street-lighting installations
  - convention center revenues
    - event charges
    - scoreboard fees
    - hall and meeting room leases
    - concessions
- Commodity Sales
  - salvage materials
  - sale of maps
  - sale of codes
- Licenses and Fees
  - advertising vehicle
  - amusements (ferris wheels, etc.)
  - billiards and pool
  - bowling alley
  - circus and carnival
  - coal dealers
  - commercial combustion
  - dances
  - dog tags
  - duplicate dog tags
  - electrician-first class
  - electrician-second class
  - film storage
  - foot peddler
  - hucksters and itinerant peddlers
  - heating equipment contractors
  - junk dealer
  - loading zone permit
  - lumber dealer
  - pawnbrokers
  - plumbers-first class
  - plumbers-second class
  - pest eradicator
  - poultry dealer
  - produce dealer-itinerant
  - pushcart
  - rooming house and hotel
  - secondhand dealer
  - secondhand auto dealer
  - sign inspection
  - solicitation
  - shooting gallery
  - taxi
  - taxi transfer license
  - taxi driver
  - theaters
  - trees-Christmas
  - vending-coin
  - vault cleaners
  - sound truck
  - refuse hauler
  - landfill
  - sightseeing bus
  - wrecking license

Source: Selma J. Mushkin and Charles L. Vehorn, "User Fees and Charges," *Governmental Finance* (November 1977), p. 48.

Table 3: *Charge Revenue as a Percentage of Expenditures (1976-1977)*

Parking	128.8%
Water Terminals	127.5
Airports	96.9
Sewerage	37.7
Hospitals	34.0
Highways	17.6
Parks and Recreation	15.6
Sanitation	10.3

City Government Finances in 1976-77 (U.S. Bureau of the Census, 1979), Table 8.

tributional consequences of doing so are not excessively adverse. In the case of services such as water supply and sewerage, the use of charges is more common but by no means universal. Charges for these services are now being combined in some areas with development charges and adequate public facilities regulations to more fully reflect the cost of serving new developments.

The expanded application of user charges and their extension to new areas can substantially improve the financial structure and efficiency of local government, and user charge/fee systems could be developed for various municipal services, including refuse collection, storm water sewerage, fire and police protection, emergency rescue, road and bridge tolls, public transit, street lighting, parks and recreation, libraries, water supply, and sanitary sewerage.

User charges can, however, have negative effects. The next section outlines the basic principles behind designing new user charge/fee systems and discusses several potential problem areas to avoid. Keep in mind that attention to detail is essential when designing new user charges and fees.

Principles of User Charge Design

In order to explain the principles which should be employed in the development of a user charge system for publicly provided services, it is convenient to discuss the form of pricing systems in the private economy.

The price you pay for a soda, for example, reflects the cost of producing that soda and the cost of transporting that soda from the site of production to the place where you purchase it. Thus, the price charged for a soda will be higher in areas where the cost of transportation is higher. The relevant costs are the increase in costs of production and transportation (distribution) as the output of sodas is increased by a small amount. Economists refer to this as the marginal cost of production and distribution. Under usual circumstances, firms will find it most profitable to charge a price equal to this marginal cost.

Your willingness to pay for a soda depends upon the satisfaction you expect to receive from consuming it. In general, you will purchase the soda if you expect to enjoy it more than you would enjoy something else you could purchase for the same amount of money. You will demand more sodas if the satisfaction you get increases as, for example, on hot days. You will also demand more sodas when the price goes down. The relationship between the cost of supplying sodas and the demand for sodas by all consumers determines the price. Producers set the price of soda to cover their costs. This price then determines the number of sodas supplied and consumed.

These pricing principles have relevance for certain kinds of publicly supplied goods. User charges should reflect the cost of providing additional units of the publicly provided good. This cost often varies by location. For example, it is more costly to collect refuse in low density areas far away from the landfill site than to collect in high density areas near the landfill. Efficiency requires that the user charge be higher for the first area.

User charges can perform another function of private prices. Charges can allocate demand to those users who value the good or service most highly. For example, by charging for the use of a bridge, those who value the services of the bridge highly would pay the charge and use the bridge, while those who do not value the bridge would neither use it nor pay for it.

Cost Factors

Since user charges should reflect the cost of providing a service, it is necessary to explore how costs are affected by changes in important parameters. There are three important variables: output, distribution, and demand variation over time.

Output

The cost of producing a public service increases as the output is increased. Depending upon the service, output may be measured in terms of some variable such as volume or time, or it may be measured in terms of people served. As facilities are expanded costs increase. The change in costs as output is expanded, called the long run marginal cost, may increase, decrease, or remain constant. Thus, expanding services may increase or decrease the cost of serving new residences depending upon the service being considered, the current population served, and other variables. Once a facility has been constructed or once an operation such as police protection has been organized to serve a population, the cost of changing output is different. Buildings cannot be easily expanded or reduced. Other equipment is likewise inflexible. Thus the ability to respond quickly to increase in demand is limited. This limitation is more severe for structures such as water treatment plants and bridges than it is for services like police. Once design capacity for such structures is exceeded, costs rise very sharply as output continues to increase.

Distribution

The relationship between volume and cost is well understood. Less commonly discussed is the relationship between the location of the customer, the density of development at his location, and the cost of serving him. There have been several studies over the past 20 years which have explored the effects of residential development patterns on the cost of service.[2] Primary emphasis has been on density of development. These studies show that the cost of service declines per household as density of development (number of households per acre) increases. For services like water supply, it is easy to see why this is so. Water pipe is laid down the center of a street and individual service lines extend from the water main to each building. Higher density of development means more dwelling units per mile of water main, and at high density, the number of connections can be reduced as well. Furthermore, the cost of laying water mains increases in proportion to their diameter but the volume of water a main can carry increases more than proportionally.

Estimates of the relationship between cost of service and density of development for some selected services are presented in Table 4. These estimates indicate that the variations in cost of service among densities and development types can be substantial. Low density single family housing is five times as expensive to serve as high-rise apartments, from $3,311 per household per year at one dwelling unit per acre to $655 per household per year at 60 dwelling units per acre. This difference was calculated employing a 5 percent interest rate. At today's higher interest rates, the difference in costs would be substantially increased. Capital intensive services such as water, sewerage, and drainage exhibit very large differences in capital costs, but the differences in operating costs are much smaller. For example, the capital cost of sanitary sewers is almost eleven times greater for low density single family than for high-rise apartments, yet the operating cost differential is less than two. Less capital intensive services such as police have operating expense differentials substantially higher than their capital differentials.

The above cost differentials are based solely on differences in the density of development. Consequently, they tell only part of the story. Many services are not produced at the site of consumption but must be transported between the production and consumption sites. For most services, this transportation cost will be substantially greater for outlying low density areas than for central high density developments. Estimates of this distance component of public service costs are presented in Table 5. It is clear that since the figures in Table 4 do not include distance costs, and since low density developments are typically also more distant, Table 4 understates the true differences in cost of service. However, the differentials will change depending upon local conditions. These numbers are presented only as a guide.

In order to economize on the transport or distance costs, many services are produced at more than one site within the metropolitan area. Police and fire stations are located in various neighborhoods. However, there is a limit to this potential for cost saving. Too many production sites can lead to higher output costs. For example, the increase in water production costs from the construction of several treatment plants instead of one will usually exceed the savings in costs of distribution. Nevertheless, each service will have a different combination of number of sites of production and transportation costs which will minimize the total costs of supplying all customers.

Demand Variation Over Time

Once decisions have been made about the location and the output capacity of the production facilities and about the capacity and the location of distribution facilities, and once these facilities are put in place, another aspect of cost becomes important. At some point at or beyond the designed capacity of the facility, the short run marginal cost of serving additional users increases sharply. If the demand for the service varies significantly over time, the facility may periodically face this capacity constraint. This periodic heavy demand is commonly called "peak load." If the facility is financed through

Table 4: *The Cost of Providing Public Services, by Property Type and Density (1973)*

	Single Family Homes (1,000 Units)				Multi-Family Homes (1,000 units)					1 Unit/acre as a Percentage of 10 units/acre	1 Unit/acre as a Percentage of 60 units/acre
					Townhouses	Walk-Up Apartments		High-Rise Apartments			
	1 unit/acre	2 units/acre	3 units/acre	5 units/acre	10 units/acre	15 units/acre	30 units/acre	30 units/acre	60 units/acre		
Capital Cost											
Police	$ 113,852	$ 111,752	$ 109,652	$ 105,452	$ 104,852	$ 104,252	$ 103,652	$ 103,652	$ 103,052	108%	110%
Fire	119,918	108,368	96,818	73,718	52,974	52,974	52,974	52,974	65,474	226	183
Sanitation	29,220	27,620	25,220	23,140	21,244	18,140	17,380	15,796	14,820	138	197
Schools	5,353,582	5,353,582	5,353,582	5,353,582	4,538,155	4,538,155	4,538,155	1,646,167	1,646,167	118	325
Water supply	7,529,720	3,833,744	2,563,857	1,739,362	1,163,154	855,900	485,304	566,792	334,777	647	2,249
Storm drainage	4,835,868	2,420,383	1,595,857	1,068,046	710,649	462,420	231,274	284,552	117,684	680	4,109
Sanitary sewerage	2,963,624	1,586,257	1,121,045	813,398	594,021	438,451	354,678	345,062	274,509	449	1,080
Total capital cost	$20,945,784	$13,441,706	$10,866,031	$9,176,698	$7,185,049	$6,470,292	$5,783,417	$3,014,995	$2,556,483		
Yearly capital cost	1,828,203	1,167,283	939,488	788,740	617,607	555,001	494,079	264,018	222,446	296	822
Operating Cost											
Police	$ 69,817	$ 66,267	$ 62,717	$ 55,617	$ 52,067	$ 49,700	$ 46,150	$ 46,150	$ 42,600	134%	164%
Fire	135,711	116,011	96,311	56,911	41,589	41,589	41,589	54,722	54,722	248	326
Sanitation	36,287	33,142	30,315	27,780	25,469	21,686	20,760	18,850	17,640	138	200
Schools	1,168,258	1,168,258	1,168,258	1,168,258	988,526	988,526	988,526	269,598	269,598	118	433
Water supply	31,821	31,821	31,821	31,821	30,103	30,103	30,103	25,538	25,538	105	125
Storm drainage	-	-	-	-	-	-	-	-	-	-	-
Sanitary sewerage	41,289	34,401	32,133	30,604	28,022	27,250	26,679	22,825	22,476	147	184
Yearly operating cost	$ 1,483,183	$ 1,449,900	$ 1,421,555	$1,370,991	$1,165,776	$1,158,854	$1,153,807	$ 437,683	$ 432,574	127	343
Total Annual Costs per Dwelling Unit	$ 3,311	$ 2,617	$ 2,361	$ 2,160	$ 1,783	$ 1,714	$ 1,647	$ 702	$ 655	186%	505%

Source: Paul B. Downing and Richard D. Gustely, "The Public Service Costs of Alternative Development Patterns: A Review of the Evidence," in Paul B. Downing (editor), *Local Service Pricing Policies and Their Effect on Urban Spacial Structure* (Vancouver, B.C.: University of British Columbia Press, 1977), Table 8.

Table 5: *The Annual Cost of Providing Public Services per Mile Distance from Public Facility Site (1973)*

	Capital or Operating Costs Per Mile
Police	$ 438*
Fire	216*
Sanitation	3,360***
Schools	19,845***
Water Supply	21,560**
Storm Drainage	6,187**
Sanitary Sewers	12,179**
Total Cost	$63,785

*Includes only operating costs

**Includes only capital costs

***Includes both capital and operating costs

Source: Paul B. Downing and Richard D. Gustely, "The Public Service Costs of Alternative Development Patterns: A Review of the Evidence," in Paul B. Downing (editor), *Local Service Pricing Policies and Their Effect on Urban Spacial Structure* (Vancouver, B.C.: University of British Columbia Press, 1977), Table 9.

general revenues or if a low "average cost" charge is employed during these peak demand times, the result may be an overuse of the facility. Overuse is generated because the cost of serving one more user or one more unit of use far exceeds the charge. Thus, users are comparing the value of use to them to a price which is below the true cost of their use. At this low price, demand will be high relative to capacity and the facility is overused. This overuse manifests itself in various ways. In water supply, pressure is lost. In electricity supply, brownouts occur. In highway or bridge travel, traffic jams and delays are generated. In such cases, social costs are increased and the private costs associated with the consumption rise as the quality of service declines. This potential overuse could be eliminated if an increased charge which reflects the true cost were levied during these peak load times.

What Costs Count? In general, user charges for public services should reflect the full costs of service. They should include both operation and maintenance costs and the cost of the capital employed in their production and distribution (see Table 4). The calculation of these costs may not be easily accomplished, however, because municipal accounting systems are not designed to serve this purpose. In particular, the current value or the cost of past capital investment may not be available. This is most often true of long lived assets such as water mains and sewers. The result of this is that costs of service estimates for user charge purposes often do not reflect all the capital costs. Hence, they understate the true costs. This can lead to undercharging and more expansion of services than is justified. That is, because the user charge is below the cost of service, residents will demand and consume more units of service. In the end, this will raise total social costs for everyone.

There are, however, cases where charging the full cost of producing the service is not desirable. One such case occurs when the consumption of a particular public good or service by certain individuals is thought to benefit the entire community. Such goods and services are called merit goods. A user charge equal to the full cost of production would reduce consumption of the merit good by some group of residents, usually the poor. Reduced consumption would lead to reduced generation of benefits to others in the community. Therefore, the user charge should be reduced or eliminated for these consumers so that their consumption remains high.

While there is substantial debate over whether any particular public service is a merit good, local governments do use this concept. Two applications which are fairly universal are education and recreation. The implication of a reduced charge for merit goods is that one group, usually the most affluent, is subsidizing the consumption of a second group, usually the poor. This is a form of income redistribution, but it differs from other more direct methods, i.e., transfer payments, in that it requires consumption of a specific good. The group which provides this form of subsidy recognizes that consumption of these goods by the poor benefits the subsidizing group. Recreation improves health and reduces social unrest. Education improves productivity and makes the community more pleasant to live in. The result in both cases is a reduction in costs to the subsidizing group.

The "Ideal" User Charge

User charges should be designed to reflect the costs of providing publicly supplied services just as prices for privately produced goods reflect their costs of production and transportation. Considering the costs outlined above, the ideal user charge for most services would have three components: (1) a quantity charge, (2) a capacity charge, and (3) a location charge.

The Quantity Charge

One part of the user charge would reflect the short run cost of current output. Generally, this can be done with a single charge which varies with the quantity of the service consumed. In cases where there are significant peak load problems, the quantity charge should be higher during these peaks. Thus, the quantity charge would reflect the short run costs of services at the time the service is produced and consumed.

Capacity Charge

The second part of the user charge would be a payment to cover the difference between the quantity charge and the full costs of production at the designed capacity level. This difference is the result of potentially high construction costs or fixed costs. This charge could be allocated on the basis of the potential for use of the designed capacity by each customer. In cases where fixed costs are not very high, this charge might not be levied since it would be very small or possibly zero.

The Location Charge

The third part of the user charge system would be a location charge which reflects the long run cost of serving residents at each location and development density.

The capacity and location charges could be paid monthly, or they could be paid as a connection charge when the area is initially served. A special assessment can be a close approximation to these charges.

The end product of this user charge system is a combination of charges which are higher for high demanders of the service and higher for residents who live in areas that are particularly expensive to serve. Because they reflect the costs of serving people, the charges provide residents and managers with information on the desirability of increasing the supply. Developers and prospective new residents will decide whether the value to them of developing a new area is greater than the cost of providing the public services. Managers of the public facility can observe the quantity demanded during peak times at the higher peak load price. If the revenues exceed the cost of expansion, it is worthwhile to expand the facility. If not, expansion probably would be wasteful. Such a system has substantial potential for improving the provision of public services because it provides more accurate information on the desirability of expanding service and because it allocates the available supply to those who value it most.

Practical Considerations

The ideal user charge would be designed as a three-part user charge (time variable/peak load quantity charge, capacity charge, and location charge) which reflects the costs of serving various residents. However, practical considerations may alter the form of the user charge.

Administrative Costs

One such consideration is the administrative cost of implementing the charge system. Administrative costs include primarily the cost of collecting data on the individual's consumption of the public service, calculating the costs of serving that resident at that volume of use, and billing for and collecting the user charge. For some services these administrative costs can be large. For example, it may be relatively easy and inexpensive to install a water meter, but it is much more difficult and expensive to monitor the volume and noxiousness of sewage put into the treatment system.

A calculation of the monitoring costs may lead the decision-maker to conclude that quantity charges are not justified. However, before such a conclusion is reached, it is desirable to look to other possibilities. One might consider indirect methods of measuring the quantity of use. A commonly used approach is to base sewer service quantity charges on the volume of water consumed. In cases such as this where there is a reasonably consistent relationship between what is measured and what one wishes to know, such indirect measurements can be less costly. When employed, they can retain the advantages of the quantity charge without excessive administrative costs. Nevertheless, it should be recognized that there is a quality problem here. Household sewerage may not be as difficult to treat as industrial waste. Consequently, use of water volume as an indicator of industrial waste may lead to errors and additional information on quality may be desirable.

The costs of billing may also be substantial. It is possible that they would be so high that it would not pay to implement a periodic billing system. However, in this age of inexpensive computers, it would be unusual for this to be the case. When a municipality is already preparing periodic bills for some services, the cost of adding another item to the process is usually very small.

One last point should be made about the administrative costs of user charges. There are many public services for which the use rate among residents is quite constant. In such cases, the difference in costs of service among residents may be small. The administrative cost of employing variable charges based on quantity may be higher than the cost savings. In such circumstances, variable charges would be undesirable and a flat charge per user would be appropriate. A similar circumstance may arise when variations in cost of serving residents at different locations and densities are small. Again, the extra administrative cost of instituting a variable charge may outweigh any gains in efficiency.

In some cases the cost of measuring the quantity of use of a service may be high, but it can be easily determined that different classes or groups of users have different average utilization rates. A user charge based upon these differences in class may be inexpensive to employ. Likewise, suppose some classes or groups are more expensive to serve because of their location, density, or for some other reason. Again a special class charge could be imposed relatively inexpensively.

Resident Acceptance

A second practical consideration is resident acceptance. This acceptance is based upon an understanding of what the user charge is for, and how it was calculated. When the benefits of the public service are easily identified by those using it, being charged for use is easily understood. Water consumption is one such case. Green fees for public golf courses, charges for tennis courts, and bridge tolls are others. It is hard for a resident to argue that he or she did not benefit from a service when it is obvious that they used it. However, charges which cannot be easily related to use may not be easily understood and may be resisted.

Tax Deductibility

A third practical consideration, and one related to resident acceptance, is the fact that while local taxes are deductible from a resident's federal income tax, user charges are not. This means that a dollar paid in user charges is more costly to a resident than a dollar paid in property taxes. The amount of this difference depends on the resident's marginal income tax rate. Thus, the extensive use of user charges can make local government services more expensive to residents.

This phenomenon will be most significant for high income residents and for high income communities. Kemper and Quigley have estimated that in New Haven, Connecticut, the average federal income tax savings per dollar of property tax was only $0.01, while in Woodbridge, Connecticut, the average savings was $0.21.[3] The reason for this is that New Haven has more low income people who do not itemize and, even if they do, they have lower marginal tax rates. For incomes over $25,000, the savings ranged from $0.21 to $0.46 in New Haven, and from $0.30 to $0.66 in Woodbridge. This finding suggests that high income people are more likely to be resistant to user charges.

Incidence/Equity

A fourth practical consideration has to do with the impact of user charges on people in various income classes. It is generally preferred that low income people pay less for public services because they have less ability to pay. While there are many ways to define what is meant by paying less, perhaps the most common comparison is to calculate the payment as a percent of the person's income. A financing system which requires a payment which is a higher percentage of income for higher income people is called a progressive system. A system which charges lower income groups a higher percentage of their income than it charges high income groups is called a regressive system.

There have been only a few studies of the distributional effects of user charges. The studies that have been done compare the distributional effects of user charges to the revenue source they would replace, the general property tax. In a study of refuse user charges based only on the volume of refuse collected (not the full multi-part user charge described above), Kemper and Quigley show that the user charge is mildly progressive as compared to the property tax.[4] Downing, on the other hand, found that a well-designed multi-part user charge which reflects all the differences in cost of service among users was somewhat regressive as compared to the property tax.[5] The differences in measures of costs between these two studies suggest that a well designed user charge for refuse is not likely to be much different in its distributional effects than the property tax it replaces.

In a comparison between a fixed user charge for refuse collection based on the average cost of servicing all users and the multi-part user charge, however, Downing has shown that fixed rate charges are much more regressive than multi-part charges. The reason for this is that high income people tend to live in larger homes at lower density and more distant locations. Since a multi-part user charge reflects these costs, it is likely to cause high income people to pay substantially more than lower income groups for the same services. For similar reasons, low income people may pay more than the cost of serving them and end up subsidizing high income residents when a fixed rate charge is used. The multi-part user charge eliminates this subsidy, but its high cost to high income people, coupled with the explicitness of the charge, is likely to increase political opposition to user charges from higher income groups.

While a well-designed user charge generally will be more progressive than the fixed rate user charges typically employed by local governments, it does not change one potential problem. That is, user charges in any form allow high income people to purchase more and better services than provided to the general populace. This could result in a politically difficult situation–low service levels for low income people, and high service levels for high income people.

Employee Acceptance

A fifth practical consideration is employee acceptance. Government employees have a widespread dislike for user charges.[6] Many apparently feel more comfortable with the politics of their existing budgetary process than with the uncertainty of relying upon income from user charges.

Legal Considerations

The legality of user charges for utility type services like water, sewerage and refuse has been clearly established. However, location charges have not been used very often so their legality remains somewhat in doubt. While user charges and fees for special police services have become accepted practice, the legality of other police charges, as well as those for fire protection, has yet to be tested. However, if a city can show a "reasonable" relationship between the cost of a service and the charge, these charges will probably pass the legal test. Road, bridge, transit fees and recreation fees are common and legal. Street lighting fees and library charges have been employed less frequently, but apparently are also legal.

Notes

This paper is based in part on "User Charges and Special Districts" by Paul B. Downing and Thomas DiLorenzo in Aranson and Schwarts (eds.) *The Management of Local Government Services* (International City Management Association, 1980) and is used with ICMA permission.

1. U.S. Department of Commerce, Bureau of the Census, *1967 Census of Governments: Historical Statistics on Government Finances and Employment,* p. 135.
2. See, for example, Walter Isard and Robert Coughlin, *Municipal Costs and Revenues* (Wellesley, Mass.: Chandler-Davis, 1957); Paul B. Downing, *The Economics of Urban Sewage Disposal* (New York: Praeger Publishers, 1969); and Real Estate Research Corporation, *The Costs of Sprawl,* Report prepared for the Council on Environmental Quality, Department of Housing and Urban Development, and the U.S. Environmental Protection Agency (Washington, D.C.: Government Printing Office, 1974).
3. P. Kemper and J. Quigley, "Refuse Collection Policy," in J. Meyer and J. Quigley (eds.), *Local Public Finance Squeeze: A Case Study* (Cambridge, Mass.: Ballinger, 1977), p. 108.
4. Kemper and Quigley, Note 3.
5. This has been shown in Paul B. Downing, "The Distributional Effect of User Charges," unpublished paper, October 1974.
6. Communications between Bruce G. Steinthal, Project Director, Public Technology, Inc. and Donald N. Johnson, Associate Director, Bureau of Governmental Research and Service, University of Oregon, May 13, 1980, and subsequent personal communications with Mr. Steinthal, May 15, 1980.

10 Projecting Local Government Revenue

Charles D. Liner

We cannot foresee changes in the many economic, political, and administrative factors that affect local government revenue. Nor can we expect statistical methods, techniques, or computers to do the impossible. Still, certain methods, techniques, and approaches can aid local governments in estimating future revenue. By analyzing current trends and the forces that underlie them, we can make a projection of future revenue.

Projection: An estimate of future possibilities based on current trends.

Webster's Dictionary

The key to good projections is good analysis. Good analysis requires understanding the revenue system and the forces or events that have affected past revenues, having adequate and timely information, and exercising good judgment. This article presents an introduction to one approach–time-series analysis. Although this approach incorporates certain statistical methods that may be helpful, the value of the approach lies in its emphasis on analyzing current trends by dividing the past record of collections (the time series) into its component parts and using this analysis as the basis for making projections.

For a revenue projection method to be useful to local governments, it must meet certain criteria:

– It must be straightforward and uncomplicated so that local officials untrained in mathematics, statistics, or economics can use it during the budgeting process.
– It must require only information or data that are easily obtainable on a timely basis from local government administrative records or from the state government.
– Finally, it must be possible for the required calculations to be performed manually rather than by computer, since many local governments do not have computers.

Some methods proposed for local government revenue projections–for example, multivariate-regression analysis–do not meet these criteria. Time-series analysis, on the other hand, is a method that can be understood easily and requires only simple computations that can be performed on a hand-held calculator. It does not require projections or current data on population, per capita income, retail sales, gross national product, or other variables. Instead, it involves analysis of data readily available from internal records or recent state government reports. Even when a computer is available, manual computations and graphing techniques are preferable to use because they give the analyst a better "feel" for factors that affect revenues. Finally, the projections can be understood by members of governing boards, who are responsible for the budget and for making long-range plans.

The first step in making a time-series analysis is to separate total revenue into its major components–funds, local revenues, state-shared and state-

Reprinted from Popular Government 43 *(Spring 1978): 32-45.*

collected revenues, and individual revenue sources. This break-down is necessary because different sources are affected by different variables and because budgeting requires some separation of revenue sources. Once total revenue is separated into its components, the analyst must decide whether to analyze *actual* revenues or the *base* of the revenue source. For example, property tax revenue is the result of several factors—the total assessed value of taxable property (the base), the tax rate, and the collection rate; therefore, the base should be projected separately from the tax rate and the collection rate. It may be necessary to divide the property tax base into its components—real versus personal property or residential versus commercial property. For other revenue sources it may be infeasible or unnecessary to analyze the base. For example, it is usually sufficient to analyze retail sales tax collections rather than retail sales, which is the base, because the tax rate is not expected to change and because the composition of the base is not likely to change in a way that will affect revenues significantly.

Once the analyst has broken down the revenues into components, he must decide how to allocate his time. Usually it does not pay to spend much time on minor revenue sources. These sources can be projected by using the previous year's collections or by using the department heads' judgment. The analyst should devote most of his attention to important revenue sources.

The next step is to collect the historical record of actual collections or the tax base for each year. This chronological series of data is a "time series." A time-series component is a factor that causes the time series to change over time. The object of time-series analysis is to break the time series down into its components in order to analyze the components separately. Four types of components will concern us—trend, cyclical, seasonal, and irregular. These are discussed below.

Time-Series Components

Trend

A trend is a continuing direction of movement in the time series. The trend is the most important type of time-series component for use in projecting local government revenue because many revenue sources are affected by long-term trends in underlying economic and demographic variables. Communities with growing population and increased economic activity are likely to have an upward trend in their property tax base and in retail sales tax collections. A dramatic example of a downward trend appears in Figure 1, which shows the time series of parking fee revenue in Durham. The downward trend in revenue is due to the long-term downward trend in shopping and commercial activity in Durham's central business district.

Underlying trends in population and economic activity that are stable over time can be used to project revenue if we can assume that the same trends will continue or if we can forecast future changes that may occur in the trends. Population trends are not entirely stable over time because they depend on changes in birth, death, and migration rates. But these rates do not change dramatically or unexpectedly over short periods of time, and we are generally aware of changes that are occurring. In fact, past changes in birth rates, such as the "baby boom" after World War II and recent declines in birth rates, provide good clues to future changes in family formations, school enrollments, age distribution, and other factors that will affect local governments.

Similarly, although economic activity is very susceptible to business cycle influences, economic growth or decline in local areas is usually based on fundamental trends that can be expected to continue for several years. For example, in the 1960s and early 1970s the southern states have had economic growth rates higher than those in other regions of the country, and the basic economic and social factors that contributed to these growth rates should continue in the near future. One of the most pervasive causes of population and economic change in recent decades has been the long-term downward trend in the rural farm population and the large increase in urban and nonfarm rural population. Another basic trend that has had important implications for local governments is the decentralization of economic activity within communities. Growth has tended to occur outside or at the edge of municipal boundaries, and as a result many central business districts have declined and changed in character.

Thus a key to analyzing local government revenue is to analyze basic trends that affect the local revenue base. Current trends are the best indication of future trends, providing the basis for making assumptions about the future and alerting us to those factors that may change in the future and thus affect future revenue.

Cyclical Factors

Revenues may be affected by cyclical, or wave-

Figure 1: *Parking Meter Receipts, City of Durham*

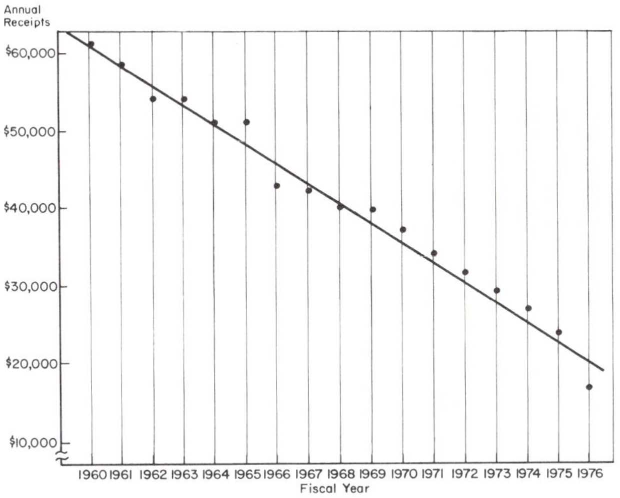

like, movements that occur irregularly over a period of several years. Three types of cycles may affect revenues: business cycles, interest-rate cycles, and stock-market cycles. Although related, they must be analyzed separately.

The most important cyclical influence on local revenues is the business cycle, wavelike fluctuations in the general level of economic activity. Business cycles tend to affect almost all economic activities and are characteristic of modern industrial economies in which economic decisions are largely decentralized. Production, employment, income, retail sales, property values, and prices affect local revenues either directly or indirectly and are affected by the phases of the business cycle—expansion, downturn, contraction, and recovery. Business cycles do not occur regularly, and it is difficult to foresee their occurrence or their size.

In projecting revenues, it is important to have some appreciation of the current state of the economy and the current phase of the business cycle. Although the analyst cannot be expected to make sophisticated economic forecasts, he should be aware of current analyses and forecasts of economic conditions, which are reported frequently in newspapers, news magazines, financial publications, and government publications.

If revenue projections are to be based on past trends in revenue collections, it is essential to analyze the effects of previous business cycles. The historical pattern of business cycles can be seen in time series of gross national product, industrial production indexes, employment, or unemployment rates. Figure 2 shows the Federal Reserve Board index of industrial production from 1950 to mid-1977. The major downturns, or recessions, are readily apparent. The 1973 recession began as a "business slowdown" that in the fall of 1974 turned unexpectedly into one of the most severe recessions of the postwar period. In the few months between November 1974 and April 1975, when the index bottomed out, the index fell from 121.7 to 109.9, a drop of over 9 percent. The North Carolina economy suffered immediate effects and fared worse than most states. Massive layoffs occurred throughout the state, and 11.6 percent of those eligible were drawing unemployment compensation by March 1975. After spring 1975, however, the economy recovered steadily, and by mid-1977 the industrial production index was above 138.

The effect of business cycles on tax revenues is usually not as dramatic as the effects on such economic variables as production, income, and employment. Tax revenues may not fall precipitously during recessions, and they may not increase proportionately during expansions. People who become unemployed during recessions must still buy food, utilities, and housing. Unemployment compensation and personal savings permit many families to maintain their standard of living. Since property is usually assessed only every eight years in North Carolina, normally the tax base would not fall, even if property values fall, but growth in the property tax base may lessen and some collections may be delayed. Sales tax collections, franchise tax revenues, and privilege license tax collections should not reflect the full extent of economic recessions.

Figure 2: *Federal Reserve Board Index of Total Industrial Production, 1950 to mid-1977*

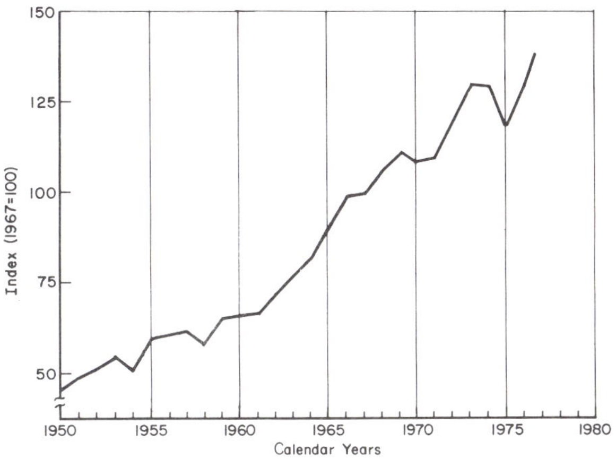

Cyclical fluctuations in interest rates have two effects on local government revenue: they affect the cost—and therefore the desirability or feasibility—of government borrowing, and they affect the property tax by influencing the amount of new construction, which is sensitive to changes in mortgage rates.

A final but less important cyclical effect in North Carolina comes from stock-market cycles. Since the value of stocks owned by residents is part of the base of the intangible property tax, revenue from this tax may respond somewhat to fluctuations in stock prices.

Seasonal Components

Revenue collections during the course of a year may vary according to seasonal influences. For example, parking fee revenues and retail sales tax collections will vary with seasonal patterns of shopping. Utility franchise tax collections, which depend on consumption of electricity and gas, will also vary with the season. Recreational fee revenues will usually be much higher in summer than in winter. In these cases revenue collections vary seasonally because the base varies seasonally. Legal and administrative provisions of revenue sources are another important cause of seasonal variations. For example: most property tax collections occur in the late fall, local governments receive their share of state-shared and state-collected taxes quarterly.

In analyzing and projecting revenues it is usually necessary to examine both annual and monthly time series. Normally, one analyzes annual data to study long-term trends and cyclical influences, but in making projections for the coming fiscal year it is often necessary to examine monthly data for the most recent years. Annual data will not reflect seasonal variations—the only components will be the trend, cyclical, and irregular components; but in a monthly time series, the seasonal component may have the strongest influence on variations.

Figure 3 demonstrates seasonal variation in retail sales tax collections. Sales tax collections increase dramatically in December because of Christmas shopping. Since we are interested in the long-term trend underlying the monthly data, we must smooth out the seasonal variation to establish the trend. This can be done by calculating a twelve-month moving average and plotting the average in the seventh month. (The box on page 88 shows how to calculate a moving average.) The twelve-month moving average eliminates the seasonal variation and also smooths variations due to irregular and cyclical influences; the plotted average indicates the underlying trend, although cyclical influence may also be revealed. For example, in Figure 3 retail sales tax collections exhibit a strong upward trend, but the dip in the moving average during 1974 and 1975 reflects the cyclical effect of the recession that occurred in those years.

Figure 3: *Monthly Collections, N.C. 3% Retail Sales and Use Tax, 1970-1976*

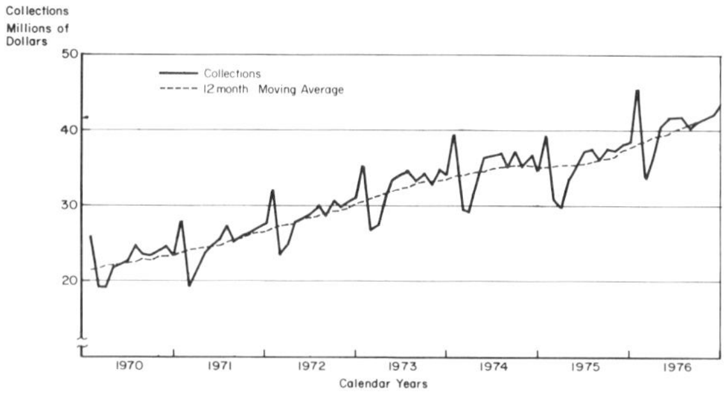

During the course of a year it may be useful to analyze monthly collections from some local or state sources to see whether collections are in line with previous estimates and to detect cyclical or other changes that may be affecting collections. But it is often very difficult to analyze weekly or monthly collection data because of seasonal or irregular influences. For example, unusually large collections may occur in one period or differences in the number of business days in each month may affect collections. A good example is provided by the record of monthly gasoline tax collections shown in Figure 4. It shows a seemingly erratic pattern of collections. Calculating and plotting a seven-month moving average, as shown in Figure 4, reveals a regularly occurring seasonal pattern. Monthly collections of gasoline taxes fall in the winter months and then increase during the spring and summer as the number of miles driven increases. The seven-month moving average also smooths out unusual variations in collections. For example, collections were unusually low in April 1973 and unusually high in the following month, presumably because some collections that normally would have occurred in April were collected in May. The seven-month moving average smooths these large variations and shows them to be in line with the normal pattern of collections.

A moving average of less than twelve months also gives an indication of trend and cyclical effects without completely eliminating the seasonal component. The seven-month moving average plotted in Figure 4 permits the trend of collections from

Figure 4: *North Carolina Gasoline Tax Monthly Collections*

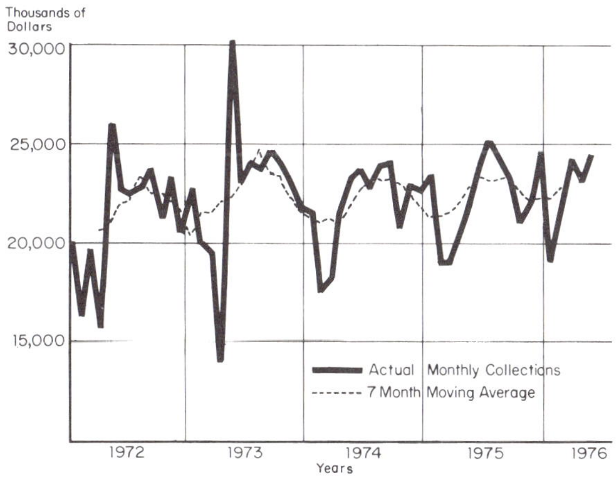

year to year to be evaluated. For years before 1973, the seven-month moving average would reveal a continuing increase in the level of seasonal collections. The moving average for 1973 is similar to that of 1972 but at a higher level. However, the sharp increase in gasoline prices late in 1973 and early 1974 had an important effect on gasoline consumption and therefore on revenue collections, which are based on the number of gallons sold. This effect is not immediately apparent from actual collections but is readily apparent from the moving averages. The moving average for 1974 shows the same seasonal pattern but at a lower level, while the moving average for 1975 appears to be roughly at the same level. This pattern is confirmed by total collections for calendar years—collections increased 6 percent in 1973, declined 2.6 percent in 1974, and increased only 1.4 percent in 1975.

Irregular Components

Irregular components of time series include a multitude of possible events, legal and administrative changes, or other factors unrelated to trend, cyclical, or seasonal components. Irregular components show up as deviations from the trend or from cyclical patterns. We should devote our time and efforts to analyzing the trend and cyclical components and those irregular components that can be explained easily or have had significant effects on revenues. Since so many factors or variables can affect revenues, and since these factors or variables change constantly, almost every number in a time series will be affected by irregular or erratic components. We have neither enough information nor enough time to investigate each variation from the trend or cyclical pattern.

For some revenue sources the irregular components may have such an important effect on revenues that no trend or cyclical components are apparent. This may be true, for example, of a time series of water tap charges. These charges are assessed when a home or building is connected to a public water system, not necessarily when the structure is built. The amount of water tap charges may depend on such irregular events as the extension of sewer line to an existing neighborhood, annexation, the construction of a new industrial plant, additions to water system capacity, or construction of new homes near existing water lines. Revenue from parking fines may vary with administrative policies regarding enforcement. Other revenue sources that are likely to have strong irregular components are the municipal property tax (due to annexations or revaluations), sewer assessments, sewer charges, street cut revenues, and interest on investments of idle cash.

For some of these sources, analysis of trend and cyclical components may not be very helpful in projecting revenues; for others, such as the property tax, the analysis must account explicitly for irregular components such as annexations and revaluations as well as trend and cyclical components. It may be possible to discover some pattern or causative factor associated with variations and to use this information in estimating future revenue. Sometimes it may be appropriate merely to use some rough average or an informed guess to estimate future revenues, especially if the amount is not large relative to total revenue. In any event, the time-series analysis methods discussed below will be of little value when the irregular component overwhelms trend, cyclical, or other components.

For revenue sources that are not overwhelmingly affected by irregular components and have important trend or cyclical components, two types of irregular components are very important in analyzing local revenues: tax-rate and tax-law changes (including enactment of new taxes), and specific occasional factors that significantly affect revenue.

Revenue projections must, of course, take into account expected changes in tax rates and in the tax laws, but past changes must also be taken into account in order to analyze past trends in revenues. For example, a time series for municipal franchise tax revenues from fiscal years 1968-69 through 1971-72 would seem to indicate a very strong upward trend. However, much of this increase was due to the legislated increase in the municipal share

Calculating a Moving Average

For a three-month moving average, add the amounts for the first, second, and third time periods and divide by three to obtain the moving average, which should be centered in the second time period. Then add the amounts for the second, third, and fourth time periods and divide by three. And so on. Thus:

Month	Collections	Moving Average (rounded)
1	$21	
2	16	(21+16+20) ÷ 3 = 19
3	20	(16+20+15) ÷ 3 = 17
4	15	(20+15+16) ÷ 3 = 17
5	16	(15+16+22) ÷ 3 = 18
6	22	(16+22+22) ÷ 3 = 20
7	22	(22+22+23) ÷ 3 = 22
8	23	(22+23+21) ÷ 3 = 22
9	21	(23+21+23) ÷ 3 = 22
10	23	(21+23+20) ÷ 3 = 21
11	20	(23+20+22) ÷ 3 = 22
12	22	

For a seven-month moving average, add the amounts for the first seven time periods, divide by seven, and center in the fourth time period. Then add the amounts for the second seven time periods, divide by seven, and so on. A moving average for an even number of time periods must be placed off-center (e.g. the seventh month for a twelve-month moving average). Reference: F.E. Croxton and D.J. Cowden, *Applied General Statistics,* 2nd ed. (New York: Prentice-Hall, Inc. 1955).

from three-fourths of 1 percent to 2 percent of gross receipts in fiscal year 1969-70 and to 3 percent of gross receipts in fiscal year 1971-72. Analysis of property tax revenue requires distinguishing between tax-rate changes and tax-base changes.

Revenue projections and analysis of past trends must also take into account specific events and developments that have had or are expected to have an effect on revenues. One example, previously mentioned, is the sharp rise in gasoline prices in 1974, which caused a decrease in gallons of gasoline purchased and, therefore, of funds available for municipal street improvements. Revaluations of property is another important example. The opening of a new shopping center may affect sales tax revenue if it draws customers from outside the county. A new industrial firm or the closing of an existing firm may have a significant effect on revenue.

Analysis of Trend

For many local revenue sources the trend component will have a strong influence; therefore analysis of the trend component will be the basis for making projections. Once the trend is estimated, the influence of cyclical and irregular components can be analyzed, since they will show up as deviations from the trend. The trend in time series can be estimated by "fitting" a straight line to the time series so that the line approximates the trend.

Graphing the Time Series and the Trend Line

Although it is preferable to calculate trend lines from the actual data in the time series rather than to fit a trend line visually, it is important to plot the time series on graph paper. In fact, graphing each time series may be the single most important part of the analysis. A graph gives a picture of the basic pattern of each revenue source. It immediately calls to attention major variations in the time series, and it forces the analyst to explain the revealed patterns. The graph can also be used to plot the calculated trend line so that variations from the trend line can be analyzed and so that the trend line can be projected to future periods. Figure 1 is an interesting example of such a graph, which shows the pattern of parking meter collections in Durham. As stated previously, the graph reveals a consistent downward trend in parking meter receipts in a city that has experienced a decentralization of shopping and other economic activity from the central business district. Variations from the calculated trend line are relatively small, suggesting that the underlying trend is very important in determining collections and that cyclical and irregular components have had relatively little influence on collections. The calculated trend line can therefore be expected to serve well as the basis for projecting future collections. (Rate changes, of course, will have to be taken into account.)

Calculating the Trend Line

The trend line can be calculated quickly and simply from the time series by using a short-cut "least-squares" method. The least-squares method produces a straight line that minimizes the sum of deviations from the line and the actual data. It provides an estimate of the slope and level of the trend and allows us to calculate and plot future trend values. But this method must be used with judgment and discretion since the calculated line does not necessarily produce a good fit with the data and does not necessarily reflect a true trend. The actual trend in the time series may be a curve rather than a straight line, or irregular influences may produce such large variations from the calculated trend that the calculated trend is meaningless.

A trend line is defined by its level and slope. The level is represented by the calculated value of

Calculating and Plotting a Least-Squares Trend Line

The object is to calculate a trend line for the time series for fiscal years 1972-73 to 1976-77 (in actual practice a longer period would normally be used), plot the trend line along with the actual data, and project the trend line for fiscal years 1977-78 and 1978-79. The first step is to calculate the slope and level in the central year.

Column (a) Fiscal Year	Column (b) Collections (thousands)	Column (c) Years from Central Year	Column (d) Cross-products (b) x (c)	Column (e) Years-squared (c) x (c)
1972-73	$142.8	-2	-285.6	4
1973-74	105.8	-1	-105.8	1
1974-75	166.5	0	0	0
1975-76	173.0	+1	+173.0	1
1976-77	213.9	+2	+427.8	4
Total	802.0		+209.4	10

Calculate the slope:

$$\text{Slope} = \frac{\text{cross-products total}}{\text{years-squared total}} = \frac{209.4}{10}$$

Calculate the level in the central year:

$$\text{Level in central year} = \frac{\text{total collections}}{\text{number of years}} = \frac{802.0}{5} = 160.4$$

Calculate the trend line and project the trend line to fiscal years 1977-78 and 1978-79:

Fiscal Year	Level in Central Year		Number of Years from Central Year		Slope		Trend Line Value
1972-73	160.4	+	(-2	x	20.9)	=	118.6
1973-74	160.4	+	(-1	x	20.9)	=	139.5
1974-75	160.4	+	(0	x	20.9)	=	160.4
1975-76	160.4	+	(+1	x	20.9)	=	181.3
1976-77	160.4	+	(+2	x	20.9)	=	202.2
1977-78	160.4	+	(+3	x	20.9)	=	223.1
1978-79	160.4	+	(+4	x	20.9)	=	244.0

Graph the time series and the trend line:

1. Plot actual revenues.
2. Plot the trend-line values for 1972-73 and 1978-79 and connect with a straight line.

Calculating a trend line for an even number of years is similar except that the "central year" is between the two central years. For these two central years, the trend-line values are calculated by adding or subtracting half the value of the calculated slope to or from the calculated "level in the central year."

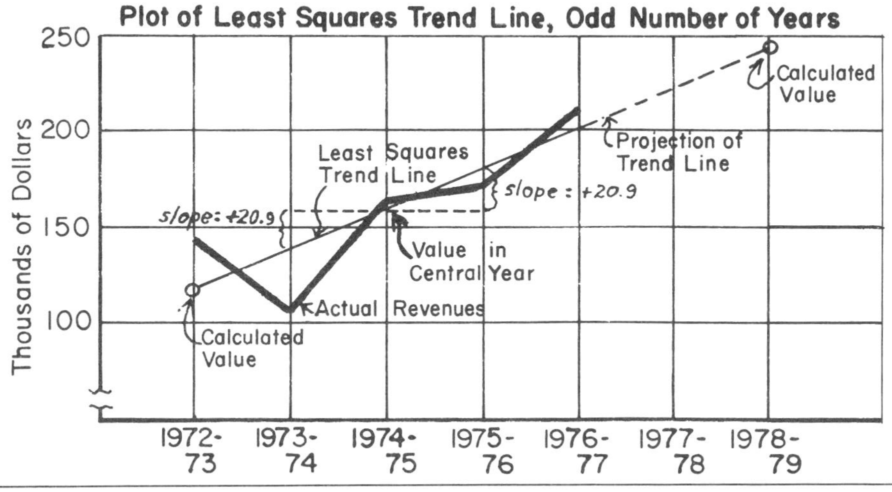

the trend line in a given year. The slope represents the change in the time series for each period of time. The slope may be negative or positive, depending on whether the trend is down or up. The slope is the change in the calculated value of the trend line for each period. The change will be the same for each period. In the short-cut least-squares method the trend values for each year of the time series are calculated according to the following formula:

> Calculated trend value = level in central year + (slope x number of years from central year)

To calculate the trend line, we must (1) calculate the "level in central year," and (2) calculate the slope of the trend line (as explained in the box in the next column). Calculation of the trend values is simplest when the time series has an odd number of years. The middle year then is the "central" year. For an even number of years, the "central" year is between the two central years, and the calculations must be adjusted accordingly. The slope will be a positive (+) number for upward trends and a negative (-) number for downward trends. After the level in the central year and the slope are calculated, one can calculate the values of the trend line for each year in the time series and project the trend line to future years.

Adjusting for Trend

The least-squares trend line can be used to project revenues into the near future as long as there is no reason to believe that the trend will change. Before using the trend line for this purpose, however, we will need to know how much confidence we can place in the trend as a predictor of future revenues. We also will need to analyze the contribution of cyclical and irregular components to the behavior of the time series in order to adjust the projections according to our assumptions about future cyclical and irregular influences. One method that can be used for both purposes is to "adjust the data for trend."

To adjust the data for trend, the actual data for each year are divided by the calculated trend value for that year and multiplied by 100 to produce the "percentage of trend." The formula is as follows:

$$\frac{\text{Actual collections}}{\text{Calculated trend value}} \times 100 = \text{Percentage of trend}$$

The calculation is illustrated in the box on this page.

Calculation of Percentage of Trend

Fiscal Year	Actual Collections (thousands)		Calculated Trend Value		Percentage of Trend
1971-72	($142.8	÷	$118.6)	x 100 =	120.4%
1972-73	(105.8	÷	139.6)	x 100 =	75.8
1973-74	(166.5	÷	160.4)	x 100 =	103.8
1974-75	(173.0	÷	181.3)	x 100 =	95.4
1975-76	(213.9	÷	202.2)	x 100 =	105.8

The percentage of trend is a useful measure of the relative variation of the actual data from the trend line. If the percentage-of-trend values are all close to 100 percent, this suggests that most of the variation in actual collections is due to the underlying trend, and we can have more confidence in projections based on the trend. On the other hand, if the percentage-of-trend values vary significantly above or below 100 percent, the actual data are clearly being influenced importantly by cyclical or irregular components in addition to, or instead of, a trend, and the trend line will not give us a means for making trend-line projections with confidence.

Adjusting for trend may be helpful in analyzing cyclical and irregular components. Besides analyzing the percentage-of-trend values for each year, it may be helpful to graph them. Cyclical components will show up as high or low percentage-of-trend values during years of expansion and contraction, respectively. Major irregular components may show up as one-time deviations.

Projecting Revenues

Time-series analysis provides an approach to understanding the trend, cyclical, seasonal, and irregular influences on local government revenues. The knowledge that we gain from time-series analysis can serve as the basis for projecting revenues into the future. But a word of caution is in order. Time-series analysis is a method for analyzing revenues, and the analysis can serve *as the basis* for making revenue projections. But simply calculating a trend line and projecting the trend line into the future does not necessarily produce reliable estimates of future revenue. Time-series analysis must be used with good judgment and discretion.

Analysis of trend is the starting point for projecting revenues when trend is found to be an important influence. If it is apparent that the trend is an important component of the time series, a study should be made of the factors that account for the trend. For example, the property tax base should be analyzed by looking at the record of changes in components of the base in past years. Trends in commercial, residential, and apartment construction should be understood. Local population and economic trends should be analyzed. After the basic trend is analyzed, deviations from the trend should be analyzed. Are the deviations due to cyclical influences, to changes in tax law, or to special events? How sensitive are local revenue sources to the business cycle? Do current collections suggest any changes from the trend?

After the time-series components have been analyzed, assumptions must be made about the future. Projecting a trend line into the future involves the implicit assumption that the underlying trend will not change and that cyclical or irregular factors will not cause future revenue to depart significantly from the trend. The assumptions should be explicit. For example, explicit assumptions should be made about population growth, the level of economic activity, the business cycle (e.g., "the national economy will continue to recover from the recession," or "there will be no recession during the next two years"), interest rates, new major industrial firms, annexations, and so forth. It may be advisable to have alternative assumptions—pessimistic and optimistic, high and low, for example—and to make different projections according to the alternative assumptions. Analysis of each major revenue source enables us to know what assumptions are necessary or important. The projections then follow according to the assumptions.

Summary

The reader may be disappointed to find that no mathematical, statistical, or mechanical methods have been presented that would enable him to produce precise projections for each revenue source. Unfortunately, such techniques do not exist. We cannot produce adequate projections by feeding data into a computer. Rather, good projections must rest on thorough analysis, good judgment, realistic assumptions, and a sound approach.

The reader who wishes to know more about time-series analysis and other methods of forecasting and projecting should see Frederick E. Croxton and Dudley J. Cowden, *Applied General Statistics,* 2d ed. (New York: Prentice-Hall Inc., 1955), and Steven C. Wheelwright and Spyros Makridakis, *Forecasting Methods for Management,* 2d ed. (New York: John Wiley and Sons, 1977).

11 Evaluating Public Expenditures
A Guide for Local Officials

Therese A. Freeman, Ernest G. Niemi, and Peter M. Wilson

Fundamental Concepts: Community Resources, Costs, and Benefits

Public expenditures almost always have impacts that extend beyond the budget. When local officials consider only the budgetary effects of a public program, they may be ignoring some other important effects that influence the program's desirability to the community. The full range of public and private impacts should be evaluated to determine if, on balance, a program is worthwhile.

Consider a hypothetical public program. Before the program begins, the community (individuals, businesses and the government) possesses a set of "resources." These resources include all the community's goods and services: money, real property, labor, governmental services, clean air, civic pride, etc.—everything of value. Carrying out the program uses some of these resources—public as well as private, monetary as well as nonmonetary. In return, the program creates a new set of resources which would not have been available without it. The resources that a program uses are the program's *costs.* The new resources that exist as a result of the program are its *benefits.* In addition to the program's effect on the total amount of resources available to the community, it may redistribute resources among individuals. Both aspects are important in evaluating the program.

The Beginning Steps: Clearly Defining the Situation

Because public programs can affect a community and its resources in complex ways, completely evaluating a program's costs and benefits may be difficult. The magnitude and value of a program's costs and benefits often cannot be predicted with certainty. The resources devoted to evaluation will depend on the nature of the program. Some programs, due to their size and expense, will warrant a full-scale look at costs and benefits. For many other programs, much simpler evaluations will suffice.

Evaluating a program in terms of its effects on community resources will indicate the extent to which the program contributes to the community, even in cases where the costs and benefits cannot be assigned monetary values. The critical tasks are to decide which costs and benefits are relevant to the expenditure decision and identify the resources the community would possess with and without the program. Therefore, an evaluation should begin with the following two steps:

> *Step 1:* Define the community whose resources are relevant to the program evaluation.
> *Step 2:* Identify all the changes in the community's resources (public and private) that will occur if the program is undertaken.

Many government programs will affect people who live outside the boundaries of the governmental entity. Step 1 involves deciding whether or not to include these effects in the analysis. Usually this decision is based on the community's political situation and each program's individual characteristics.

> *EXAMPLE 1-1: Building an Athletic Field*
> The city of Newport is considering a proposal to build a multiple-use athletic field. Opponents of the program argue that many of the

Reprinted from a document prepared by the Department of City and Regional Planning, Harvard University, under contract to the Massachusetts Executive Office of Communities and Development, Division of Community Services, June 1978.

field's potential users will not be residents of Newport, and that the city should not build facilities for nonresidents. Proponents argue that for recreational facilities, the concept of community should include not only the city's residents but also their close neighbors.

Which view of the community is correct? There is no "correct" answer to this question. The city's political process will have to provide the answer.

Step 2 sets the stage for determining the program's costs and benefits. As the following sections explain in detail, the new resources available to the community as a result of the program are the program's benefits and the decreases in available community resources are program costs. Figure 1 summarizes the logical sequence of steps for thoroughly evaluating a program's impacts on a community.

Costs

This section (1) defines in more detail the concept of a program's costs to the community; (2) discusses why it is valuable for local officials to consider this concept of costs when making spending decisions; (3) explains how to distinguish between real costs to the community and "transfers" between individuals; (4) describes how to measure costs; and (5) illustrates how to use the cost concept in making decisions.

Defining Costs

The costs of a local government program are the resources used in carrying it out. From an overall community perspective, costs are relevant whether they are incurred by government or directly by households and businesses. They also are relevant whether they entail dollar outlays or the use or consumption of nonmonetary resources. The following four categories cover the complete range of resources that should be considered as costs if used by public programs.

Group 1: Resources purchased by the government for the program.
Outlays of public funds for construction, equipment, or salaries are examples of this type of cost. Standard financial budgetary analysis usually deals with only this type of cost.

Group 2: Resources already owned by the government.
When a program uses a previously acquired government asset such as land or office space, a real cost is incurred even though there may be no dollar outlay related directly to the program.

Group 3: Resources owned or purchased by local residents.
Some government programs use or consume privately owned resources, thereby imposing costs on the community. For example, if a program requires households to use larger septic tanks, the extra costs to the households should be counted as part of the program's costs.

Group 4: Intangible resources.
Programs often require some sacrifice of community resources such as clean air or uncongested streets. While such losses can be important

Figure 1: *Steps for Analyzing Public Programs*

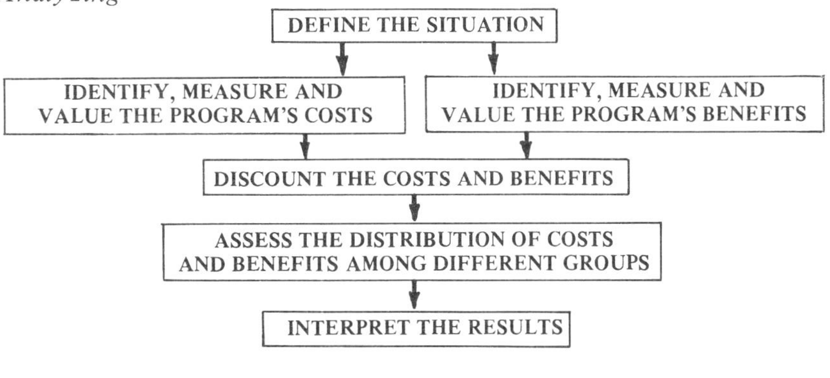

costs, their monetary value usually cannot be estimated. However, these sacrifices can sometimes be quantified in physical terms; for example, congestion could be measured by a change in traffic flow.

When important choices between programs must be made, a full accounting of each of these four types of costs is worthwhile even if some estimates must be very rough.

Distinguishing between Real Costs and Transfers

When resources are neither used up nor created but just shifted from one set of individuals to another, the shift is called a *transfer.* A transfer differs from a cost in that it does not decrease a community's total amount of resources. Instead, it changes the shares of those resources enjoyed by different individuals.

EXAMPLE 2-1: Abating Local Property Taxes
Riverside is considering a program that would abate the property tax payments of elderly persons. If the program is implemented, the taxes of other taxpayers would increase to compensate for the abatements. Some opponents of the program claim that these tax increases would be an excessive cost for the community.

The abatement program does *not* have a cost from the perspective of the community as a whole. The program would make elderly persons better off and nonelderly persons worse off than they would be without it, but it would not decrease the community's total amount of resources. The program would, in effect, only transfer resources (tax money) from nonelderly taxpayers to elderly persons.

Of course transfers are important attributes of government programs and have considerable bearing on local officials' decisions. However, when evaluating programs it is important to distinguish between transfers and real program costs. Later sections further discuss transfers.

Measuring Costs

Determining Monetary Values

Whenever possible, costs should be valued in monetary terms so that different types of costs are measured in the same units. In principle, a program's costs should be valued according to individuals' general willingness to pay for the resources the program will use. For goods and services in Group 1, willingness to pay is indicated by the price the government must pay to buy them. When a program uses publicly owned assets in Group 2 it is necessary to estimate what the value of those assets would be on the open market. For example, if a program uses office space in a government building, the program's costs should include the estimated rental value of that space. Costs in Group 3 should be valued in the same manner as those in Groups 1 and 2.

It is much more difficult, however, to assign a monetary value to a program's effects on intangible resources such as clean air or quiet streets. A community's willingness to pay for intangible resources must be determined through the judgment of local officials.

EXAMPLE 2-2: Removing Snow
Youngsville must decide between continuing municipal snow removal and contracting with a private company. To determine the annual cost of the current snow removal program the finance committee examines the budget. They find that only direct salaries are reported separately for snow removal. Outlays for pension benefits, administrative expenses and vehicle maintenance are reported in the municipal accounts as single "line items" encompassing many programs. How can the actual costs of the current snow removal program be determined?

The problem of determining a program's true total costs comes up repeatedly when decisions must be made about continuing existing programs. Budget costs are an example of the costs in Group 1, resources purchased by the government for a particular program. Although they are reflected in the budget, they are not always apparent. To make a choice, the finance committee needs to know the total cost of the service. The committee should therefore estimate the portion of the line-item costs attributable to the snow removal service, and add these to the salaries.

The committee also should look beyond the budget and estimate the value of the trucks, equipment, storage area and other previously acquired resources that are part of the current program. These resources are important elements of the program's costs, and if the committee excludes them from its calculations, it will underestimate the program's full costs.

EXAMPLE 2-3: Constructing a Parking Garage
Louisburg is considering two ways of developing a downtown block which is owned by the city. One option is for the city to build and operate a parking garage. The other is to sell the site to a private firm which would construct a parking garage.

Proponents of a municipally built garage argue that it would be less expensive for the city to build the facility than for a private operator. They claim that, since the city already owns the land, the only costs under this option would be for construction and operations. Since a private firm would have to buy the land, it would need to charge higher fees in order to recover its costs.

From a community-wide perspective, the proponents' argument is *not* correct. There is no saving in land costs if the city builds the garage. The costs of using scarce publicly owned land, buildings, and equipment are sometimes overlooked because they do not entail a dollar outlay. Yet these resources have many alternative uses, so committing them to one program has a cost, namely the lost opportunity to use them for other purposes. Therefore, using the site has the same real costs whether the site is privately or publicly owned. The same scarce resource is used in either case. The cost calculations for each option should contain the land's estimated market value.

Determining Values in "Constant Dollars"

When programs involve costs occurring at different times, the values of the costs should be expressed in terms of "constant dollars," that is, in terms of the present purchasing power of dollars without building in inflation. For example, if a program presently uses an office that rents for $4,000 per year and will continue to use the same office in future years, the program's cost calculations should show this amount as the value of the office for each future year. Using constant dollars insures that all costs are measured in dollars with the same purchasing power.

Benefits

Benefits are the resources which the community will gain as a result of a public program. This section (1) defines benefits in detail; (2) explains the differences between real benefits to the community and transfers of resources among individuals; (3) demonstrates how to measure benefits; and (4) shows how to use the benefit concept to make spending decisions.

Defining Benefits

Benefits are the resources the community will possess if a program is undertaken but will not possess if it is rejected. Thus, a program can produce benefits by making resources available to the community. Resources created, freed from other uses, or conserved by a program are all considered benefits.

EXAMPLE 3-1: Renovating an Office (Part 1)
The city of Rimpton wants to renovate a usable but deteriorated office. The benefits of this project will not be the value of the entire renovated office. Instead, the benefits will be just the value of the improvements made to the office. Since some aspects of the office (walls, windows, etc.) are not new resources made available by the project, they should not be viewed as benefits.

Distinguishing between Real Benefits and Transfers

When a program redistributes resources between groups of individuals, these actions often are mistakenly counted as a benefit instead of a transfer. From the recipient group's perspective the program appears to produce benefits; however, the gain to the recipient group is a loss to some other group in the community. From a community-wide perspective, the program has not made any new resources available.

EXAMPLE 3-2: Constructing New Bleachers
A citizens' group in Scranton has urged the School Committee to construct bleachers at the high school's football field and to charge admission to the school's games. The group claims that within 10 years, the admissions fees will have covered the construction costs. The group also claims that, "This project will benefit the entire community not only by giving us a set of bleachers, but also by creating added revenues for the school from the eleventh year onward."

In this example, the bleachers clearly would be a benefit. However, it is incorrect to consider the admissions fees as benefits—even during the first ten years. No new resources will be created when spectators pay money to sit in the bleachers. Because the admission fees can be used to support school expenditures, they represent a transfer from spectators to taxpayers. Counting the fees as benefits would be double-counting, i.e., counting the benefits from the bleachers twice.

The following impacts are frequently cited as benefits, but they usually are transfers among individuals: increased revenues, increased taxes, increased sales, and increased property values. These impacts are benefits only if they make new resources available to the community.

EXAMPLE 3-3: Developing a New Playground
Riverton is considering developing a new playground. In a feasibility study, a consultant stated that the project would "benefit Riverton in two ways: (1) provide 10,000 user-days of recreational opportunities annually and (2) increase the value of surrounding residences by a total of $95,000."

It is not correct to count as benefits both the additional recreational opportunities *and* the increased property values. The additional recreational opportunities are the only new resources and thus the only benefits. The property value increases do not represent new resources, they only indicate that the surrounding property owners will have access to the playground, and, in a rough sense, will be the recipients of the project's benefits.

(Note that if the value of the additional recreational opportunities cannot be measured directly, the property value increases can be used as an *indirect* measure. Either the direct or the indirect measure–not both–must be chosen to represent the project's benefits.)

Measuring Benefits

Whenever possible, a program's benefits should be measured by estimating how much the community values them. Placing a value on benefits is important because a program's desirability primarily depends on whether the value of its benefits exceeds the value of its costs.

As earlier noted, the fundamental measure of a resource's value is the community's willingness to pay for it. However, public programs often produce benefits for which it is difficult to determine this measure. Consequently, for measurement purposes, benefits can be divided into three groups:

Group 1: Resources measurable in monetary terms.
Group 2: Resources measurable in physical units, but not in monetary terms.
Group 3: Resources valued by the community, but not measurable by any means.

Benefits in Group 1 typically are (or are similar to) goods and services that are sold in the marketplace. In such cases, the value of the benefits is the market price of the good or service. As earlier explained, these resources should be valued in constant dollar terms if they occur at different times in the life of the program.

EXAMPLE 3-4: Renovating an Office (Part 2)
This example in the previous section demonstrated that the benefits from a renovation would be the improvements to the office. To find the value of these benefits, it is necessary to first estimate what the price would be for a comparable, renovated office in the private real estate market. From this value should be subtracted the price that people would have paid in the private market for an office comparable to the deteriorated office before it was renovated. The difference between the two prices represents the value of the renovation's benefits.

Although the monetary value of the benefits in Groups 2 and 3 cannot be determined, these benefits are no less important than those in Group 1. Personal judgment must be relied upon for estimating the value of these benefits to the community.

The important difference between the benefits in Group 2 and Group 3 is the amount of information available to help local officials make their judgments about value. By definition, officials have a nebulous idea of the value of the benefits in Group 3. The benefits in Group 2, on the other hand, can be estimated in discreet physical units. Clearly, in most instances, this additional information can be useful.

The playground in Example 3-3 illustrates the difference between the last two groups of benefits. Assume that, besides the 10,000 user-days of recreational opportunities, the program will produce another important benefit, increased neighborhood pride. Neither of these benefits can be measured in monetary terms. However, the increased recreational opportunities can be measured in physical terms (10,000 user-days); this benefit belongs in Group 2. The increase in neighborhood pride, which cannot be measured at all, belongs in Group 3.

Discounting

The costs and benefits of public programs can occur in complex patterns over time. To compare and evaluate programs, each program's stream of future costs and benefits–in constant dollars–must be converted to a single value by discounting. This section introduces the discounting concept. It discusses (1) what the discount rate means; (2) the mechanics of discounting; and (3) the ways discounting can aid individuals making public spending decisions.

Defining Discounting

A familiar notion is that a dollar tomorrow is worth less than a dollar today. This notion is partly based on inflation, but it is also true with the constant dollar concept used for evaluating a program's costs and benefits. One way to look at the impact of time on the value of money is to consider that, through investments, money can "grow." For example, suppose someone asks to borrow $100 from you today and gives you a guaranteed promise to repay $100 (in constant dollars) in one year. You probably would not accept the offer because having $100 now is more valuable to you than having $100 next year. One reason for this is that if you keep the money you can invest it and by next year have more than $100. If your best investment opportunity pays 10 percent annual interest you would have:

$$\underset{\text{This Year}}{(\$100)} \times (1 + \text{interest rate}) = (\$100) \times (1.1) = \underset{\text{Next Year}}{\$110}$$

As a result, you would consider $100 today to be equal in value to $110 next year. Unless the person promised to repay this amount, you would not make the loan.

What if the person wanted to borrow the money for two years? In this case, if you make the loan you will forgo a second year of interest. You would consider $100 to be equal in value to:

$$\underset{\text{This Year}}{(\$100)} \times (1.1) \times (1.1) = \underset{\text{In Two Years}}{\$121.00}$$

When evaluating public programs the role of time is the same but the perspective is reversed. One knows the program's stream of estimated future costs and benefits for which monetary values can be determined. The objective is to find out how much a specific dollar amount that will be realized in a future year is worth today. For example, how much money today would be equivalent to having $100 a year from now? To find the *present value* of $100 a year from now you *discount* using a *discount rate,* which is another term for the interest rate. With a 10 percent discount rate, the present value is:

$$\underset{\text{Next Year}}{(\$100)} \times \left(\frac{1}{1 + \text{discount rate}}\right) = \$100 \times \left(\frac{1}{1.1}\right) = \underset{\text{This Year}}{\$90.91}$$

This reasoning also applies to longer periods. A $100 payment two years from now has a present value of:

$$\underset{\text{In Two Years}}{(\$100)} \times \left(\frac{1}{1.1}\right) \times \left(\frac{1}{1.1}\right) = \underset{\text{This Year}}{\$82.60}$$

In practice, a table of *discount factors* is used rather than the preceding calculations. Discount factors show how much $1 in a future year is worth today. A table of discount factors appears on page 101. The following equation uses the discount factor to recalculate the present value of a $100 payment two years from now:

$$(\$100) \times (\text{Discount factor: } 10\% \text{ per year for two years}) = (\$100) \times (0.826) = \$82.60$$

Discounting can be used to convert any flow of dollar values in future time periods to an equivalent single present value. The dollar amounts in each year are multiplied by the appropriate discount factor, then added together to produce a single present value. The examples and cases that follow illustrate the uses of discount factors.

How Discounting Can Aid Local Spending Decisions

Discounting is useful whenever dollar *flows* are compared over time. If dollar values can be estimated both for a program's costs and its benefits, discounting can be used to calculate the program's *net present value.* For each year of the program, costs and benefits are added together to give a net cost or benefit. Then the net cost or benefit for each year is multiplied by the appropriate discount factor. These yearly values are summed to give a net present value. If the net present value is positive, the program's benefits exceed its costs; if the net present value is negative the costs are greater than the benefits.

Discounting also can be used to compare alternative programs that differ in the timing of their costs and/or benefits. If a net present value can be determined for each alternative, the program with the greatest net present value has the greatest surplus of benefits over costs. If it is necessary to compare just the costs or just the benefits of the alternatives, discounting can indicate which alternative is least costly or most beneficial.

EXAMPLE 4-1: Upgrading a Rural Road
Pine County wants to upgrade a dirt road to accommodate more traffic. Either graveling or paving would be adequate to carry the road's traffic. The county wants to choose the option with the lowest costs over an 11 year period. Paving would have a high initial cost of $35,000 but low maintenance costs of $1,000 per year. Graveling would have a lower initial cost of $28,000 but higher maintenance costs of $2,000 per year. Which alternative is less costly for the county?

Discounting can yield the answer by converting the stream of costs for each alternative to a single equivalent present value. Pine County has a 10 percent discount rate. The costs are shown on the following page in thousands of dollars.

If annual costs were simply added together with the initial expense, graveling would have a total cost of $48,000 and paving would have a total cost of $45,000, but this would neglect the time value of money. Future costs are less of a sacrifice than current costs, since until they are used for this project, resources can yield a return in other uses. By applying discounting to each flow of costs, each alternative can be expressed as a single present value. Using a discount rate of 10 percent (see "Choosing a Discount Rate," p. 100), the cost of the gravel alternative has a present value of $40,260; the paving alternative cost has a present value of $41,140. Discounting indicates that graveling is the least expensive alternative.

Choosing a Time Period for the Analysis

To calculate a program's present value, it is necessary to choose a time period for the analysis. In other words, it is necessary to decide how far into the future to count the program's costs and benefits. Sometimes the time period can be determined by the lifetime of a program or the local government's official planning period. In other cases, a program may have a very long or indefinite lifetime, and it is necessary to choose a somewhat arbitrary period of analysis. As a general rule, a time period of less than 15 years is adequate for most present value calculations. Using a period longer than 15 years rarely yields results much different than using a 15-year period, because discounting greatly reduces the present value of costs and benefits that will occur in the distant future.

Incorporating Capital Costs in Present Value Calculations

Recognizing Capital Costs

Because capital investments last for many years, they require special consideration in present value calculations. The first consideration is that if land, buildings, and equipment are purchased for use in a program, their full value should be recorded as costs in the year in which they are purchased. This is the case regardless of the pattern of cash outlays such as bond payments for the assets. When resources are committed to a program, they are unavailable for other uses for the rest of the time period of analysis. Their full cost should be recognized in the year they are committed to a program.

A second consideration is that land, buildings, and equipment that are already part of the community's total resources when a program is being evaluated must be included in present value calculations. In the present value analysis the use of capital stock that is already owned should be treated just like an initial purchase. When it is committed to the program its full estimated current market value should be recorded as a cost.

A third consideration is that neither depreciation nor finance charges are counted as part of a program's costs. This follows directly from the concept of costs as resources used by the program. Depreciation is an accounting technique that is not applicable in present value calculations. Since costs should be recognized when the resources to be used by the program are committed to it, the full values of capital investments are counted at the time of their purchase. Subsequently including depreciation as costs would therefore be double-counting. Similarly, including financing charges—interest and principal repayments—as costs would also be double-counting. The discounting procedure automatically accounts for interest. Principal repayments have already been charged to the program by counting capital investments at the time of purchase.

Table 4-1: *Summary of Costs for Example 4-1*

Year:	This Year	+1	+2	+3	+4	+5	+6	+7	+8	+9	+10
Annual Costs in Constant Dollars (In Thousands):											
1. Graveling	28	2	2	2	2	2	2	2	2	2	2
2. Paving	35	1	1	1	1	1	1	1	1	1	1
3. Discount Factor at 10 Percent	1	.91	.83	.75	.68	.62	.56	.51	.47	.42	.39
Present Values at 10 Percent (Costs x Discount Factor):											
4. Graveling (line 1 x line 3)	28	1.8	1.7	1.5	1.4	1.2	1.1	1.0	.94	.84	.78
5. Paving (line 2 x line 3)	35	.91	.83	.75	.68	.62	.56	.51	.47	.42	.39
Total Present Values at 10 Percent (Sum of Costs x Discount Factor):											
Graveling (sum of line 4):	$40,260										
Paving (sum of line 5):	$41,140										

Accounting for Salvage Value

If capital investments are not completely consumed during the time period of analysis, their remaining value should not be counted as a program cost. For example, a new vehicle that is purchased and used for two years has a resale value at the end of the two-year period. In this instance, the resale value of the vehicle should be deducted from program costs in the year of its sale. Similarly, capital investments used in ongoing programs may have some value at the end of the time period used for analysis. This remaining value should be discounted and deducted from the program costs in the final year of analysis.

Salvage value is the term used for the resale value of capital items and the remaining value of capital investments at the end of the period. Salvage value is deducted from program costs to show that the program has not consumed the capital asset entirely; some of the resource still remains available for additional uses. An equivalent procedure is to add the salvage value to program benefits. The important point is to account for the resource's remaining value.

EXAMPLE 4-2: Estimating the Capital Costs of an Existing Building
Glenville is assessing the costs of its recreation program over the next ten years for comparison with other programs. The recreation program uses a building which has an estimated market value of $100,000. Because of aging, wear and tear, the building will be worth less (in constant dollars) 10 years from now than it is worth now. The assessors' office judges that 10 years' aging will reduce the building's value to $80,000. In calculating the present value, the planning department accounts for the capital cost of the building in the following way:

1. The building's existing market value is recognized as a cost in the initial year of the time period.
2. Its salvage value at the end of 10 years (in constant dollars) is discounted and deducted from costs in the final year.

The following entries are made in the present value worksheet:

	Capital Costs for Building (This Year)	Salvage Value (+9)
	-$100,000	+80,000
10% Discount Factor	1.000	0.424
Present Value	-$100,000	+$33,920
Net Present Value	-$66,080	

The discounting calculations show that using the building for ten years costs the community $66,080.

EXAMPLE 4-3: Leasing Versus Buying a Typewriter
The Holfield Senior Citizen's Council needs another typewriter. The typewriter can be leased for $280/year or purchased for $815. The typewriter company requires a 15 percent

downpayment with the balance repayable over two years at 12½ percent interest. The council routinely replaces the typewriters it owns every two years. Past experience has shown the resale value of a two year-old machine to be about 50 percent of its original price. Should the Council lease or buy the additional typewriter?

Year:	This Year	+1
LEASE OPTION		
1. Costs	-$280	-$280
2. Resale Value	0	0
3. Net Value	-$280	-$280
4. 10% Discount Factor	1.000	0.909
5. Present Value (line 3 x line 4)	-$280	-$255
6. Net Present Value (sum of line 5)	-$535	
PURCHASE OPTION		
7. Costs	-$815	0
8. Resale Value	0	+$408
9. Net Value	-$815	+$408
10. 10% Discount Factor	1.000	0.826
11. Present Value (line 9 x line 10)	-$815	+$337
12. Net Present Value (sum of line 11)	-$478	

The above table illustrates the net present value (NPV) calculations for each option. A two-year time horizon is used in the analysis because of the council's typewriter replacement policy. The leasing costs for a two-year period when discounted at 10 percent yield a NPV of -$535. The NPV of the buy option is -$478. Note that interest and principal repayments are not counted as costs in this calculation. Interest is accounted for by the discounting procedure; the price of the typewriter is counted as an initial investment so that including the payments would be double-counting. The typewriter can be resold after its two years of use, hence the positive entry in year +1. A two-year discount factor is used here because the typewriter is held for two years and sold at the beginning of year +2. The NPV calculations show that the council would save $57 in present value terms by purchasing rather than leasing the typewriter.

Choosing a Discount Rate

The example at the beginning of this chapter explained that a person generally does not lend money to someone else unless the borrower agrees to repay at least as much as the lender would have by investing the money and earning interest. The same principle applies for the resources used in public programs. A public program should not be undertaken unless its benefits are worth at least as much as the resources the community would have without it (except where equity impacts override this conclusion as explained in the next section). The discount rate represents the average rate of interest that public funds would earn if, instead of being used on a public program, they were returned to private households and firms. Thus, the discount rate is the cost of drawing resources from the private sector for use in the public sector.

Local governments using discounting need to choose a single discount rate and apply it to each program that is evaluated. Discount rates of between 5 and 15 percent are commonly used. The local government's bond rate is sometimes used as the discount rate, on the principle that it measures the cost of public funds. This is not correct, because the bond rate represents only one source of public funds. The discount rate should reflect the average cost of all public funds, whether acquired through borrowing or taxes.

The Federal Office of Management and Budget has estimated the cost of public funds to be 10 percent. This rate is widely used by federal agencies for program evaluation. Because it is quite difficult to determine a community's exact discount rate, it is recommended that local governments also use the 10 percent rate.

The choice of a discount rate can sometimes affect the ranking of alternative programs. High discount rates give a relatively heavy weight to dollar flows in the first year of a program, while low discount rates give relatively more weight to dollar flows further in the future. In Example 4-1: Upgrading a Rural Road, discounting at 10 percent indicated that the costs of the gravel alternative had the lower present value of the two options. If Pine County considered 10 percent too high a time value of money, and instead used 5 percent, then the ranking of the alternatives would be reversed. Paving would have the lower cost in present value terms ($42,720 for paving versus $43,440 for graveling). Because graveling has a lower initial cost but higher future costs, it becomes relatively less attractive with a lower discount rate.

For some programs it is useful to see if the present values change considerably when different discount rates are used. A reasonable range of alternative rates is 8 to 12 percent. However, for most cases, the 10 percent rate will be appropriate.

Discount Factors

The following table presents discount factors that show how much \$1 in a future year is worth today. The table includes discount factors for discount rates of 8, 10, and 12 percent. The discount factor for a given discount rate and a time in years into the future is determined using this formula:

$$\text{Discount factor} = \left(\frac{1}{1 + \text{Discount rate}} \right)^n$$

The discount factor for the present year (n=0) is 1.000.

Discount factors are used to discount (convert) dollar amounts occurring in future years to their equivalent present value. The formula for discounting is:

$$\text{Present value} = \underset{\text{at year n}}{(\text{Dollar amount})} \times \underset{\text{for year n}}{(\text{Discount factor})}$$

Discount Factors: How Much \$1 in a Future Year is Worth Today

	Discount Rate		
Year	8%	10%	12%
This Year	1.000	1.000	1.000
+1	0.926	0.909	0.893
+2	0.857	0.826	0.797
+3	0.794	0.751	0.712
+4	0.735	0.683	0.636
+5	0.681	0.621	0.567
+6	0.630	0.564	0.507
+7	0.583	0.513	0.452
+8	0.540	0.467	0.404
+9	0.500	0.424	0.361
+10	0.463	0.386	0.322
+11	0.429	0.350	0.287
+12	0.397	0.319	0.257
+13	0.368	0.290	0.229
+14	0.340	0.263	0.205
+15	0.315	0.239	0.183
+16	0.292	0.218	0.163
+17	0.270	0.198	0.146
+18	0.250	0.180	0.130
+19	0.232	0.164	0.116
+20	0.215	0.149	0.104

Equity Impacts

Very few programs will affect every member of the community equally. If a program involves transfers, one group within the community acquires resources from another group. For some programs one group may receive most of the benefits without incurring many of the costs.

Since the distribution of costs and benefits can have important consequences for the community's overall well-being, identifying and considering this distribution is as important as looking at a program's total levels of costs and benefits. For example, because of its distributional consequences, a program may be judged to be undesirable even though its benefits outweigh its costs. This section (1) introduces the concept of a public program's equity impacts; and (2) presents a method for evaluating these impacts.

Defining Equity Impacts

A program's equity impacts are its effects on the distribution of resources among different groups within a community. Note that EVERY PUBLIC PROGRAM HAS SOME IMPLICATIONS FOR EQUITY, either because it changes the present distribution or because it keeps this distribution the same.

Assessing Equity Impacts

Although methods exist for extensively evaluating programs' equity impacts, the focus here is limited in the most fundamental and important steps—identifying and roughly measuring the impacts. These objectives can be accomplished by following three steps:

Step 1: Identify which group receives each benefit and which group incurs each cost.

Step 2: Quantify, as far as possible, the program's impact on each group.

Step 3: Determine whether the pattern of distribution of costs and benefits affects the program's desirability.

Successfully completing Step 3 is the crux of our concern with equity impacts. Note, however, that a local official can complete Step 3, deciding on the importance of the equity impacts, only by using his/her judgment. A concern for equity involves feelings about justice—feelings that are personal and subjective.

Steps 1 and 2 can systematically explain what a program's equity impacts will be and provide useful information for making decisions. Merely identifying each group's costs and benefits (Step 1) may sometimes be sufficient. The equity impacts may be so obviously overwhelming or inconsequential that further consideration is unnecessary. If more information is needed, then the costs and benefits each group will experience should be quantified (Step 2).

Following these steps requires classifying members of the community into groups. The following list presents several commonly used distinguishing characteristics.

–Income and Wealth	–Homeownership
–Geographic Location	–Age
–Race or Ethnic Group	–Family Size

EXAMPLE 5-1: Locating a Day-Care Center
The director of the city of Banfield's subsidized day-care program is considering expanding the program. Residents in the Fairmount neighborhood have asked that a new day-care center be located in their neighborhood. Fairmount is a low-income area and residents have complained that it is very costly for them to take their children to the existing, downtown center. However, the director's staff recommends that the existing center be expanded since, although both alternatives would yield the same benefits, the expansion alternative would have lower costs. Although most costs would be the same for both alternatives, a new center in Fairmount would require additional new equipment and an extra supervisor. The total annual additional costs for the new center would be $20,000. However, the director's staff estimates that if the new center were located in Fairmount, residents in the area would save a total of $4,470 each year in transportation costs. Thus, the net additional costs for the new center would be $15,530 a year (the additional costs to the city minus the savings to the Fairmount residents).

Which alternative should the director choose? There is no obvious answer. The community, as a whole, would be better-off with the expansion, but the residents of Fairmount would be better-off with the new center. Although the director still must base the decision on judgment, the analysis of equity impacts and costs and benefits gives him/her a clear understanding of the implications of each alternative.

Interpreting the Results of a Program Analysis

This section (1) suggests how to summarize the findings of a program analysis to highlight the critical choices which must be made; (2) discusses how to assess the effect on the analytical results of alternative assumptions about future conditions; and (3) provides a checklist of questions which should be asked when reviewing an analysis to ensure that it has been conducted appropriately.

Summarizing the Findings of a Program Analysis

An analysis of spending alternatives provides officials with predictions about the outcomes of different proposals. These predictions provide a good basis for choosing an alternative. However, in almost any decision, officials must add their own judgment of community needs and priorities to the findings of a program analysis in order to make a choice. Cost and benefit estimates need to be closely scrutinized. Costs and benefits expressed in monetary terms should be compared with those that are measured in units other than dollars. Concerns for equity should be weighed against other objectives.

Consideration of all the impacts of alternative programs is made easier if impacts are placed in a summary format. A program analysis should include a table summarizing the costs, benefits and equity impacts of each spending alternative. Costs and benefits in a summary table can be divided into those which have been estimated in monetary terms and those which are measured in non-monetary units. Costs with monetary values should be given as a total, with a listing of the cost elements included in the total. Benefits with monetary values should be summarized in the same way. When alternatives differ in the time-flow of costs or benefits, discounted present values should be given in the table. Costs or benefits which are not measured in dollar terms should be represented by other measures such as "number of persons served," or "increase in daily traffic," or "change in water quality."

Often, statements of program impacts can include a measure of "cost effectiveness," which is the cost per unit of output or capacity. Cost effectiveness measures are most useful for programs which have benefits that cannot be valued in monetary terms. For example, the cost per sewer connection for alternative sewer plans or cost per student for special education programs are measures which can aid decisions in the absence of quantified benefits.

EXAMPLE 6-1: Choosing a Landfill Site
Bayport is seeking a site for a new sanitary landfill. Alternative sites are being evaluated

on several criteria, including acquisition cost, capacity, potential pollution hazards, and recreational value. Officials wish to minimize any hardships on nearby residences from odors or traffic, and they would prefer to purchase a site from an owner willing to sell rather than using eminent domain. The following costs and benefits have been discussed and measured in either quantitative or qualitative terms:

Monetary Costs:
- -Site acquisition costs (present value)
- -Site development costs (present value)
- -Operating costs (present value)

Other Costs:
- -Potential for groundwater pollution (none; slight; moderate; serious)
- -Suitability of site for recreational use (no potential; some potential; great potential)
- -Proximity to residential areas (number of homes within ¼ mile of site)

Benefits:
- -Site capacity (tons of solid waste)
- -Market value of site after it is filled and landscaped (present value)
- -Potential for public reuse as recreational land (no potential; some potential, great potential)

The costs, benefits and equity impacts for each alternative site are summarized in a table similar to the table in the next column.

Using Site #1 will concentrate collection truck traffic on Fuller Street, and create congestion at the intersections with Oregon Avenue and California Avenue.

With the analytical findings summarized in this form, Bayport officials have some useful information to make complex tradeoffs between good and bad features of each site. Officials must decide which site would yield the greatest net benefits, and they must assess whether use of that site would be equitable for the site owner and for nearby residents.

Summary of Estimated Impacts for Site #1

Costs	
Monetary Costs* (Present Value)	$600,000
Other Costs	
Potential for Groundwater Pollution	Slight
Lost Recreational Value	None
Number of Affected Residences	22
Benefits	
Market Value After Rehabilitation (Present Value)	$100,000
Capacity	40,000
Recreational Reuse Potential	None
Cost Effectiveness: Dollar Cost per Ton of Capacity	$15.00
Equity Impacts	
Site #1 is occupied and farmed by an elderly man who has lived there all his life. He has stated that he would not be willing to sell the farm and move to another residence.	

*Includes costs for site acquisition, development operations, and rehabilitation. Discounted at 10 percent over the expected life of the landfill.

Changing the Assumptions of the Analysis

In estimating a program's costs and benefits, many assumptions must be made about future conditions in order to estimate the most likely values of the program's expected impacts. However, there may be a great deal of uncertainty about the true magnitude of some cost or benefit elements. It is important to know how a program's desirability would change if the assumptions prove to be incorrect. Sometimes large uncertainty about a particular cost or benefit estimate will be inconsequential because the item is only a small part of total costs or benefits. In other cases, changing one assumption may greatly affect a program's attractiveness. In the latter instance, further research may reduce the uncertainty of the original assumption, but frequently local officials will have to rely on their judgment about the likelihood of future events.

The importance of an uncertain assumption to a program's desirability can be tested in the following manner:

Step 1: Determine a range of plausible values for the uncertain cost or benefit.
Step 2: Re-estimate the program's impacts using the lowest and highest values of the range.
Step 3: Summarize the results and compare them with the original results using the most likely assumption.
Step 4: Where possible, indicate the likelihood that the cost or benefit will be higher or lower than the most likely value.

EXAMPLE 6-2: Increasing the Frequency of Bus Service

Parking congestion is a problem in Pelman's business district. One proposal to reduce congestion is to increase the frequency of downtown bus service. It is projected that 500 drivers per weekday could be attracted to the transit system with a particular expansion in bus service. The service expansion would be costly, however, because new buses and additional drivers would be required. It is estimated that the cost of expanding service would be about 5 times as great as the additional revenues which could be expected. Officials rejected the proposal because the city has a policy of implementing service expansions only if additional revenues will cover at least one-half of additional costs.

There could be objections to the decision not to extend service based on the possibility that the projected ridership increases are too low. However, ridership must increase by more than 1,000 riders per weekday for revenues to cover one-half of the additional costs. An increase in ridership of this magnitude is considered extremely unlikely. Therefore officials have a strong basis for rejecting the proposal, even though ridership estimates are somewhat uncertain.

A Checklist for Reviewing an Analysis

The following questions are presented for local officials to use as a checklist for determining if a program has been analyzed thoroughly and correctly.

1. Have the program's objectives been clearly and completely stated?
2. Has the population affected by the program and relevant to the analysis been identified?
3. Have the program's costs been estimated correctly?
   a. Are the estimates of future budget outlays complete, or have some important expenditures been overlooked?
   b. Have the costs of land, building space, or equipment already owned by the government and used by a program been included as a program cost?
   c. Have other non-budget costs been overlooked?
   d. Have any costs been counted more than once?
4. Have the program's benefits been estimated correctly?
   a. Have all of the benefits been identified?
   b. Have any benefits been overstated or counted twice?
5. Has the time value of money been accounted for by discounting those future costs and benefits for which dollar values can be determined?
   a. Have present values been computed?
   b. Was an appropriate discount rate used in the present value calculations?
6. Have the program's distributional impacts been considered?
7. Have the findings of the analysis been tested for their sensitivity to changes in assumptions about the magnitude of important costs or benefits?

Implementing the Use of Program Analysis

This section (1) suggests criteria for choosing the issues which should be analyzed; (2) discusses the resources needed to undertake program analysis; and (3) suggests how program analysis can be incorporated into local government operations.

Selecting Programs to Analyze

The issues and methods discussed in this guide can be applied to virtually all local government expenditure decisions. However, for many programs a simple "back of the envelope" analysis of costs, benefits, and equity impacts can provide local officials with sufficient information. In addition, because thorough investigations of program costs and benefits do take time and money, officials will have to set priorities on which decisions will be aided by extensive analysis, and which will be subject only to cursory analysis.

Several criteria can be used to choose whether a spending decision should be analyzed in detail:

1. *The magnitude of the program.* The greater the cost of proposed programs or projects, the greater the potential savings from a systematic comparison of alternatives.
2. *The length of the program.* Which decisions will have impacts over a long time period? If a project will have a long life, then a projection of future conditions, costs and effects is worthwhile.
3. *The political nature of the program.* Which decisions are likely to be controversial? If

a consensus exists that a particular spending proposal should be approved, then an elaborate comparison with "straw man" alternatives will be of little use. However, if a lively debate about a program is expected, then the factual base provided by a systematic evaluation can help focus the arguments on the important issues.

Resources Needed to Analyze Programs

The major resource required for analytical studies is the time of skilled personnel. Program analysts need not have a great deal of specialized training, but they should be familiar with basic analytical techniques and the use of quantitative data. They also need an ability to clearly define the problems being analyzed and to identify the alternative ways of solving those problems. Persons with backgrounds in engineering, economics, public administration, planning or business usually have the skills necessary for program analysis. A single individual with administrative experience, analytical skills and familiarity with the needs of local officials can effectively direct analytical efforts of other personnel who may lack extensive experience or training in program analysis.

The cost of a program analysis will depend on the complexity of the issues, the availability of data, the experience of the analysts, and the thoroughness of the study.

Incorporating Program Analysis into Local Government Operations

Having the in-house capability to do program analysis has strong advantages over the use of consultants. Local government personnel have an on-going familiarity with the policy issues faced by officials. Consultants hired for a single study must first familiarize themselves with the unique circumstances of the locality. At the conclusion of a consultant's study, the expertise gained by the consultant is usually not available to local officials in the future. Studies which are performed in-house can be considered investments in the knowledge and skills of government personnel as well as aids for specific decisions. In addition, in-house analyses are likely to be less costly than analyses performed by consultants. For major studies requiring highly specialized knowledge, use of consultants is advantageous. However, for regular reports of modest scale, government staff members are usually preferable to consultants.

States and large cities which are using program analysis often place responsibility for program analyses within a special department which may also undertake evaluations of the performance of existing programs. These departments usually are closely associated with the budget office. Small cities or towns may find that analysis can be introduced most effectively by individuals within an operating department, with the encouragement of the executive officer.

12 Monitoring Performance

An Overview

A popular interpretation of "productivity" among many government officials is that the best way to increase productivity is to work harder. This implies that low productivity is directly related to people. However, there are many other factors affecting productivity that are often overlooked by management. Some of these include equipment, working conditions, availability of supplies and materials, planning and scheduling problems, work force composition, physical layout of a community, and so forth. Working harder is rarely the best way to improve productivity. Often, more can be accomplished through improved planning and scheduling.

Officials and managers of smaller local governments who are trying to improve productivity should be aware that often no single factor determines any given level of productivity. Usually a mixture of variables should be looked at before action is taken. For a director or manager to begin to get a handle on productivity, a system is necessary to highlight both regular accomplishments and problems that arise.

In approaching productivity measurement and improvement, several steps can be taken. The following discussion provides a framework or approach—not a formal process—for the analysis of alternatives to improve productivity. Included in this framework is the use of productivity measures.

Reprinted from Performance Measurement and Cost Accounting for Smaller Local Governments *(Providence: Rhode Island Department of Community Affairs, n.d.).*

Any manager or department director is constantly engaged in the process of looking at needs, delivering services to answer those needs, and evaluating those services. While this process is almost self-evident, there are some opportunities for a manager to incorporate productivity and accountability more strongly into department operations. Breaking down this constant daily management process can illustrate the point. Managers in the public sector

- Review the public service needs of the community and existing policies aimed at meeting those needs.
- Set objectives of service and determine how best to meet those objectives, i.e., what type and level of service.
- Evaluate whether any improvements in procedures or organization of resources is possible.
- Monitor the performance.
- Analyze the results and take management action to make needed improvements.

One of the key stages where productivity measurement becomes important is monitoring. That is the feedback link, giving managers the data with which to determine whether the particular service delivery system is on target.

Accountability

Managers have always been accountable on a daily basis to the chief administrative officer and on an annual basis for their budget. However, the factual, quantified record of performance on which to base good accountability has been less than adequate. Smaller communities simply do not have enough detailed records to really analyze their performance. The reason lies in daily pressures and lack of a system which could remove the daily burden from the department director. As a result, many department directors have relied on informal review of performance through supervisors or been reactive to whatever is the most pressing issue at the time, reviewing performance in that area in detail, and ignoring other activities temporarily. When issues arise or at annual budget hearings, expenditures are justified in terms of dollars, not output; and facts on what cutbacks would mean in terms of less service are lacking.

This handbook is based on the premise that department directors in smaller communities can set up a manual system to be accountable for productivity in two ways:

1. To see that local services are truly meeting needs of the community (i.e., they are effective); and
2. To see that local services are improved within available resources wherever possible (i.e., if they can be made more efficient, they will).

Accountability operates to insure the best use of the tax dollar. The purpose of this [selection] is to outline a system of performance measurement that, with a little initial effort, a manager in a small community can use to effectively quantify performance, monitor and report on all functions he or she is accountable for.

Right now the kind of performance measures which can really help highlight efficiency and effectiveness are not there, but they can be developed. They will be useful both internally and at budget hearings as factual data supporting each functional expenditure at the requested levels. Such detailed backup information is more and more being required by taxpayers.

What to Measure

A manager must be concerned with both efficiency and effectiveness which together constitute productivity. Both these aspects of service delivery should be measured. The types of measures that will indicate effectiveness are quite different from those which will help a manager to evaluate efficiency.

A. Effectiveness

The broadest level of decision about effectiveness involves the decision whether or not to provide a particular service at all, i.e., is there a true identified need or can a service that does not seem necessary be eliminated partially or in total. This type of decision will take place at a higher level of management. With services that are being provided, a department director needs to know if they are effective, if they do provide good quality service. Meeting the established public view of what constitutes an effective level of service is important.

The issue of effectiveness and effectiveness measures can be thought of as an evaluation of the service from the consumer's perspective to some extent. The quality of service is not always easy to quantify, but by using the "consumer" perspective certain general types of effectiveness measures can be identified:

Percentage or volume of community use of a service;
Percentage of community reached (i.e., by area, economic groups, by age group, "reached on schedule," etc.);
Percentage of citizen satisfaction (survey of types of recreation programs wanted, for example);
Response time (in public safety areas especially);
Visual inspection using some type of rating system and trained observers to see that quality work is being done;
Citizen complaints.

Other examples of the major types of effectiveness measures can be found in the publication of the Urban Institute and ICMA entitled *How Effective Are Your Community Services?*

For a smaller community, the key to selecting measures of effectiveness is the cost of data collection. Several of the types of measures just suggested are feasible because data can be collected through regular department record keeping. For example, citizen complaints, volume of use of facilities or percent of community reached are data easily collectible in standard message forms, schedules of use or by simply adding one or two pieces of data to collect on existing forms. Response time, likewise, can be monitored by most police and fire departments using radio equipment.

One of the most reliable measures of the quality of physical work performed which includes most public work and maintenance type activities is visual observation. While smaller communities will probably not use the highly developed system of ratings and trained observers suggested in the referenced publication, their size is, in fact, an advantage in being able to have someone out in the field periodically observing the quality of work. This particular individual may be required to be on site of the work anyway. Some regular follow-up discussion of observations may be all that is necessary.

While the type of rigorous measurement of effectiveness suggested in the literature is very often too costly to smaller communities and not worth the effort, a department director should definitely consider some of the effectiveness measures suggested as part of a system of measurement. The general objective is to use every possible method available to check on the overall quality and effectiveness of major services. If some quantifiable measure is not possible, the alternative is frequent firsthand observations of work quality.

B. Efficiency

After looking more broadly at measures of the general effectiveness of services, a director will want to look more closely at the details of how services are delivered. How have resources been allocated to each function, and what kinds of operating procedures, planning, etc., go into the actual accomplishment or performance of the activity? Is it being done efficiently?

At this point, the question of what level of work to monitor arises—a task, group of tasks, unit or an entire department? Selection of the appropriate level at which to measure efficient performance should be governed by the following rule:

> Ideally, performance measurement should begin at the lowest productive level—the level at which the work is actually done.

This means that where possible and practical, measures for each unique task should be identified.

Why measure each task? From the standpoint of the role of the accountable manager, the reason is that each task represents a specific cost to government involving a unique combination of men, equipment, materials and time; and also produces a specific result for which the manager is responsible. If it can be quantified, then it is a measurable activity and output obtained for dollars expended can be reported.

From the standpoint of the manager's own need to have information with which to manage, information resulting from the measures can be used to plan, execute and control future operations. As a practical matter, however, smaller local governments may not be able to afford the time required to gather information at the lowest productive level in every instance. Therefore, in some instances, productivity measures can and should be accumulated at some higher level, possibly at the lowest formal organizational level such as unit or section.

Before going into more detail on the process of selecting measures, it may be helpful to outline some circumstances which can help a department director determine the right balance between too much and too little measurement information.

A director should consider *detailed performance reporting* when—

> The activity is the subject of special attention by the Council or the public;
> The activity has not been looked at in detail in a long time, i.e., no updating of operating procedures, etc.;
> The activity is a labor intensive one which represents a large cost in the budget;
> A problem is known to exist which will require some sort of public policy decision in the near future involving expenditures;
> Existing data indicates a potential problem (e.g. once a community has set some targets, they are being missed by substantial amounts);
> A specific project is underway which involves a new method for delivering a service, especially designed to improve performance; there is a need to evaluate its effectiveness and efficiency compared to the previous method.

Less detailed performance reporting is satisfactory when—

> Good records are already kept at the work-level and they are always available to look at for analysis if the more general measures being reported indicate a problem;
> The activity is regularly observed firsthand by a supervisor who regularly reports to management, and has a good feel for whether problems exist without detailed reporting by employees;
> The activity was recently reviewed in detail and is not of great concern because it is performed adequately or improvements were made and verified.

Each department director must carefully weigh the advantages and disadvantages involved in monitoring at a detailed task level. This decision can be made for each function and in no way has

Exhibit 1

Department PUBLIC WORKS

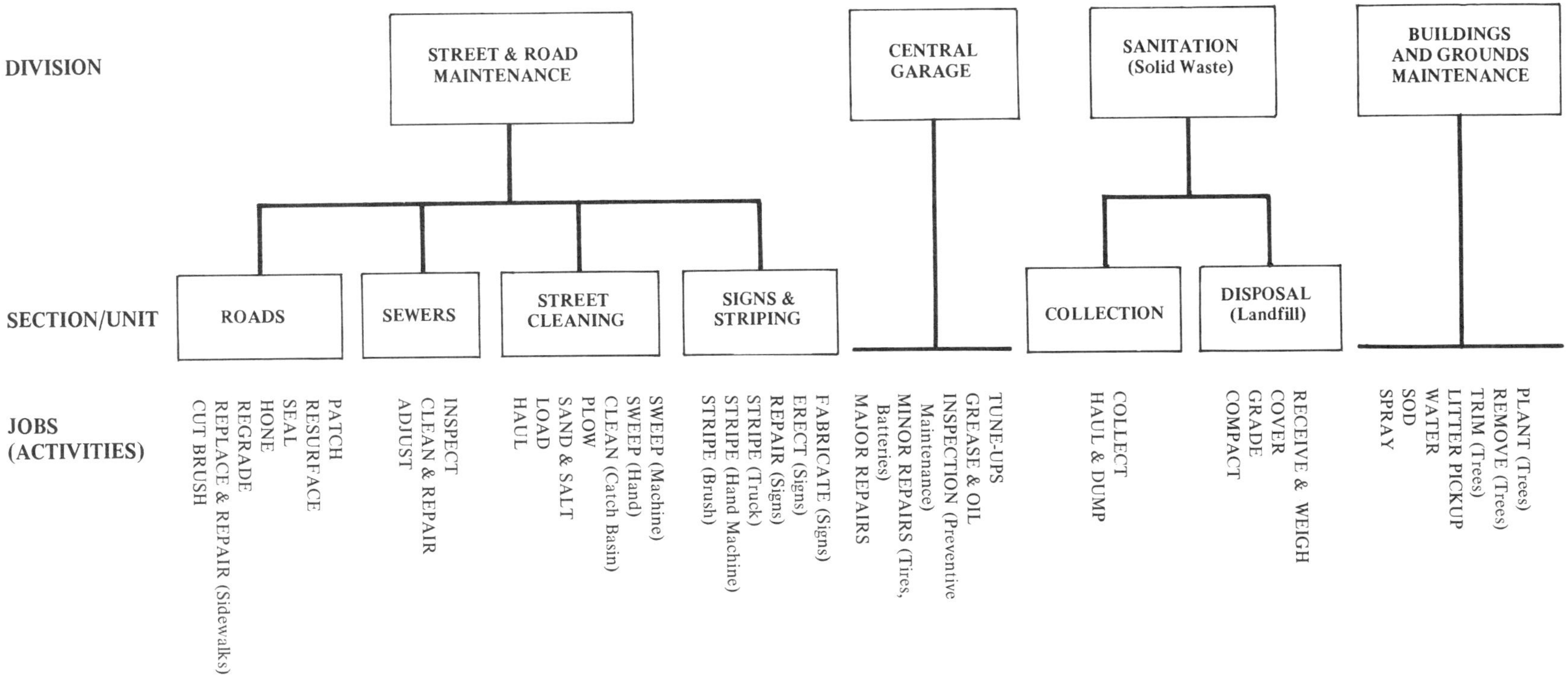

Exhibit 2: *Program Structure, Community Protection*

MAJOR PROGRAM AREA	SUBPROGRAM	ACTIVITY	ELEMENT
COMMUNITY PROTECTION	Law Enforcement	CITIZEN PROTECTION	Foot Patrol Vehicle Patrol Court Appearances Detention
		CRIME PREVENTION	Community Relations Records Communications Juvenile
		CRIME INVESTIGATION	Investigation Support Research Court Liaison
	Accident Prevention	TRAFFIC CONTROL	Selective Enforcement Maintenance
		STREET LIGHTING	Installation Repair
	Fire Safety	FIRE PREVENTION	Inspections Community Relations
		FIRE CONTROL	Fire Fighting Equipment Maintenance
	Construction	BUILDING INSPECTION PLUMBING INSPECTION ELECTRICAL INSPECTION	Permits Inspecting Reinspecting

to be uniform among all work responsibilities in the department. Detail can vary.

What exactly is the best way to identify the lowest productive level? Street maintenance, for example, includes a wide variety of productive activities ranging from patching, resurfacing, and sweeping to snow removal and catch basin cleaning. As another example, a smaller community may have a buildings and grounds division or crew. Such a unit does many things including mowing, trimming, painting, etc.

There is a process which department directors can follow before deciding which "level" of activity to measure. Whether or not a department has a formal organization chart, for purposes of setting up a performance monitoring system, a department director can develop a work responsibility chart which simply lists all the various functions associated with the department, down to the level of detail of each task involved. Such a chart will help identify all tasks that could possibly be measured for results. In deciding the "level" to measure, a director can first consider each task. If this is impractical, then the chart helps group tasks together so that measuring productivity can be feasible at a "higher" level.

Exhibits 1 and 2 show two examples of detailed charts which list all tasks performed. Now, on the basis of reviewing the chart, a public works director may decide to measure a task, such as mowing, or a group of tasks, such as landscaping, which includes mowing, trimming, weeding, planting, etc. The same director may also choose simply to measure at an even "higher" or divisional (grounds and buildings) level which may include even more activities than mowing, weeding and trimming, such as tree removal, pest control and so forth. On the other hand, for central garage operations, a very detailed accounting of time and resources used in each task may be required for decision making on vehicle replacement.

Creating a detailed work responsibility chart which lists every task permits the director to start by considering measures at this level, where the work is performed. To restate the point, there are advantages to measuring at the task level, not only for an accountability system but for internal use in planning, executing, and controlling operations. Not only can *street miles swept* indicate the level of service and measure performance, the records which provide this data also show whether scheduled work is too great, too little, whether machines are breaking down and unavailable, etc. In general, *more detailed* measures at the task level lead to:

Equal accountability for all, i.e., it is easier to pinpoint responsibility for performance on specific individuals or work units;
Data immediately available to more sharply define problems and help determine potential solutions;
Less likelihood of any activity being overlooked, i.e., no reporting required, therefore supervisors pay less attention.

In certain instances, a director may reject measuring a task because of unavoidable problems, such as—

Time consuming;
Staff inadequate or retraining too difficult, placing accuracy of data in doubt;
Data too difficult to read and interpret, i.e. the sheer volume overwhelms a manager and/or the most useful data is hard to pick out.

The general rule for managers is accountability for efficient, effective management. A department director should have all the records and measurement data on performance which is needed for good accountability for all functions in the department. If there is no other apparent use for the information either immediately or in the future, excessive detail should not be required. Each decision should of course be reviewed at least annually, and preferably more frequently: each time the community's reporting system requires a performance report.

Selecting Measures

Once those activities which will be measured are identified, several steps are involved in selecting the measures to be used to implement performance monitoring.

A. Identifying the Work Unit

How can the activity be quantified? "Unit" in this sense means the physical unit of work accomplished which describes the activity for purposes of evaluation, such as miles, tons, number (made), calls answered. The unit plus the appropriate verb constitutes a workload measure. Workload measures are not too difficult to identify; miles traveled, tons collected, inspections conducted and calls received are a few examples. Exhibit 3 lists other examples of work units and the related workload measure.

Exhibit 3

Measuring workload can be a first step in establishing a PERFORMANCE MONITORING SYSTEM which will provide a department director with valuable information for planning, scheduling, and budgeting. Below is an example of some types of measures for monitoring performance at the function (activity) level where the work is performed.

FUNCTION	WORK UNIT	WORKLOAD (OUTPUT)
PUBLIC WORKS		
Streets and Highways		
Sweeping	Tons	# Tons Collected
	Miles	# Miles Swept
	Areas	# Areas Cleared
	Tons	# Tons/Area
PUBLIC WORKS		
Central Garage		
Maintenance	Tune-ups	# Tune-ups
	Changes	# Grease & Oil Changes
	Repairs	# Repairs
	Inspection	# Inspections
POLICE		
Uniform Service		
Patrol	Miles	# Miles Driven
	Beat Miles	# Beat Miles Covered
	Arrests	# Arrests
	Responses	# Responses
	Calls	# Calls for Service

Review the measures to make sure they actually define or reflect the activity. In areas such as public works, the measures are fairly straightforward. In crime prevention, there is obviously no way to measure "crimes prevented." In this instance, number of crimes reported and arrests made is the closest approximation, and the limitations of this data as a measure of crime prevention should be recognized.

Can the data be fairly easily identified and collected to provide the kind of information desired, i.e., useful for accountability, planning, scheduling, controlling? The "state of the art" in public sector productivity is not sufficiently defined that all measures suggested by the literature are applicable for the needs of smaller local governments. For example, some effectiveness measures require elaborate systems to collect data which may not be that necessary in a small community.

B. Identify All Appropriate Measures

Is a single measure adequate or are several necessary? In setting up a performance monitoring system, a director should consider a gradual implementation process. However, it should be pointed out that workload measures just discussed highlight output but do not really measure efficiency or effectiveness. Eventually, a manager must measure input, (i.e., costs) including manpower, materials used, etc., to evaluate efficiency. Other measures tell a manager whether the quality of work was satisfactory (effectiveness). A smaller community may "measure" workload at first but managers should look ahead to eventually reaching the stage of measuring efficiency and effectiveness. Workload measures are a beginning. Measures of costs and quality are the ultimate goal.

C. Identify Forms on Which Data Can Be Collected

Can the data be collected accurately and reliably? This is critical. Accuracy demands a consensus on the data being collected, and the source of the data being collected. Is everyone defining terms the same way? Are there existing forms and procedures to gather and report the data, such as work order forms, logs, summary reports, etc.? If not, can they be easily designed? If individual employees have to report data, forms used should be preprinted, simple check-off or fill-in style that minimizes work and leaves less room for interpretation.

D. Identify Personnel Responsible for Data Collection

Are adequately trained personnel available to gather and report data? Will individual employees need to provide data or can supervisors maintain records? The more people involved in reporting source data, the more opportunity there is for inaccuracy. If a supervisor can handle the forms, there are likely to be fewer problems.

E. Identify All Data Needs

For what purposes are the productivity measures being collected? For immediate performance improvement? For the Council? For Departmental planning? This purpose relates to "level" of detail. Are major system changes required? The ability of existing budgeting and accounting systems to support the accumulation and analysis of output data with cost data must be considered.

In sum, selection of measures involves: Determining the work unit for the basis of measurement; reviewing forms and records to ensure that they support collection of good data. Ensuring that there is consensus on the data and source of data. (Is everyone defining terms the same way?) Assigning responsibility for collecting the data. One point to remember is that the more people involved in reporting source data, the more opportunity there is for inaccuracy.

Using Measures to Evaluate Efficiency

After a local government has selected and implemented measures of workload for each task, it has the capacity to monitor the existing output of any given unit. The next step is to determine what inputs were necessary to produce the performance. Measuring inputs is a necessary step to measuring efficiency.

Manhours is the largest single input or cost. It is important for a city or town to monitor manhours *at the same work level at which measures of output are being used.* This is critical. The weekly time sheet indicates total hours worked by the individuals assigned to the street crew, but does not tell how much time was spent patching vs. cutting brush. That data has to be recorded daily on *actual* performance, not assigned time. The amount of labor time which it actually takes to accomplish the outputs being measured for each function is the major factor a department director needs to

PUBLIC WORKS
Streets and Highways

ACTIVITY (FUNCTION): SWEEPING

INPUT (COSTS): MANHOURS, SUPPLIES, (GAS), EQUIPMENT, REPAIR.

WORK UNIT	WORKLOAD (OUTPUT)	÷ INPUT = EFFICIENCY MEASURES
Tons	No. of Tons Collected	Cost per Ton
Miles	No. of Miles Swept	Cost per Mile
Areas	No. of Areas Cleared	Cost per Area
Tons	No. of Tons Per Area	Cost per Ton per Acre

PUBLIC WORKS
Central Garage

ACTIVITY (FUNCTION): MAINTENANCE

INPUT (COSTS): MANHOURS, PARTS, SUPPLIES, ETC.

WORK UNIT	WORKLOAD (OUTPUT)	÷ INPUT = EFFICIENCY MEASURES
Tune-Ups	No. of Tune-Ups	Cost per Tune-Up
Changes	No. of Grease and Oil Changes	Cost per Grease and Oil Changes
Repairs	No. of Repairs	Cost per Repairs
Inspection	No. of Inspections	Cost per Inspection

POLICE
Uniform Services

ACTIVITY (FUNCTION): PATROL

INPUT (COSTS): MANHOURS, EQUIPMENT, SUPPLIES.

WORK UNIT	WORKLOAD (OUTPUT)	÷ INPUT = EFFICIENCY MEASURES
Miles	No. of Miles Driven	Cost per Mile
Beat Miles	No. of Beat Miles Covered	Cost per Beat Mile
Clearance	No. of Clearances	Cost per Clearance

know, not only to report efficiency but also to plan and schedule future operations in order to control costs. Knowing the *manhours* involved in an activity is essential.

Monitoring manhours can be accomplished in a number of ways. The supervisor who assigns crews or the dispatcher who assigns patrol cars, etc., is probably the best source. A simple code can indicate the type of work assigned, number of men in the crew, and even equipment or materials being used.

When measuring output at the task level, it is essential to record the number of hours each individual spends on each task. Three men working three hours on painting equals nine (9) manhours of painting.

It is possible to identify other inputs directly connected to particular activities by keeping some simple, but specific, records. These would relate to materials and supplies used, fuel consumed, equipment repair required, and other objects directly associated with performing each function.

By associating these inputs of labor, materials, supplies, and equipment which represent the *direct* cost involved with workload measures, a performance monitoring system can be developed for measuring efficiency. With data provided by line departments on all inputs, the finance department can calculate costs.*

Using Targets to Evaluate Efficiency and Effectiveness

Once a community has begun to use performance measures to get a clearer picture of existing levels of service delivery, several things may occur. A department director may spot areas where procedures have tended to get inefficient, and he may change some procedures to improve work. At the next level once improvements are made, a community may wish to have an ongoing way to compare performance from one year to the next. A very simple way to provide this point of comparison for analysis and decision-making is the use of targets. Targets are simply the planned level of service for a given time period. They may be informal, implied or specifically stated as part of an objective. For example, "to improve response time to breaking and entering incidents to three minutes." Three minutes is the target. Or, "to increase summertime streetsweeping operations and completely sweep the city once every month and the downtown area once a week." The target would be total miles of sweeping X number of sweepings for the time period involved, possibly 1,800 miles of sweeping that quarter.

Targets can be developed several ways:

1. Based on historical records—match or better last year's performance or meet the average of the last five (5) years.
2. Productivity improvement goal—based on careful analysis of existing performance and resulting work improvement efforts, a specific new level of performance is expected, e.g., a 10% increase in inspections.
3. Engineered standards—more and more communities have used industrial engineering techniques to carefully analyze the steps involved in a task. Based on the number of men and equipment involved, a standard of output is set. Several states are using standards for public works activities. This type of target works best with very repetitive, standardized operations where the same steps are used each and every time.

Whatever the source of the target, it is a highly effective means of analyzing productivity. It forms the basis of planned vs. actual reporting and is the type of accountability which can lead to productivity improvement when carefully analyzed and used for decision-making.

This [selection] recommends that smaller local governments measure activities over a period of time and then develop their own targets from this historical data. In some areas targets are not so easily defined. To further complicate the problem, performance targets derived in one community are not usually directly transferable or comparable in another community. Targets should be constantly evaluated, not used as a black and white measure of success or failure.

Summary

A community should aim to achieve a balance between efficiency and effectiveness. Measures of both should be used. Targets should be careful not to sacrifice quality for quantity. If concern for efficiency indicates that a more intense schedule would save dollars in terms of the inflationary cost of materials, concern for quality must be weighed and the results of any decision translated in terms of its effects on service.

---

*See "Cost Accounting," p. 210.

This [selection] has discussed the process of setting up a productivity measurement system to aid in making these decisions based on:

Efficiency Measures—quantified indicators of *both* the direct outputs of each unique task (wherever possible) and the direct inputs required to produce that particular output (manhours, materials, etc.).

Effectiveness Measures—quantified indicators of the quality or level of accomplishment of major services.

Targets—based on analysis of historical performance, efforts to improve existing performance where possible, and finally establishing ***measurable*** targets which are carefully and periodically reviewed by management.

The process of improving services relies heavily on effective evaluation of existing services—on being able to spot the difficulties and understand them, in order that they might be overcome. This vital step in the management process is monitoring performances . . . .

Effective performance monitoring involves knowing what to measure and how to measure it. It is understanding how the relationship of cost to results can point to ways in which services might be made more efficient. And it is being able to determine whether the service effectively meets the needs of the community.

13 Calculating Compensation Costs

Marvin Friedman

"Compensation" consists of both salaries and/or wages and fringe benefits. It encompasses all forms of wage payments (including, for example, bonuses, commissions, and incentive payments) as well as the cost to the employer of all types of fringes.[1] Obviously, the higher-paid, senior employees in the bargaining unit tend to enjoy higher compensation, while the compensation of those at the opposite end of the salary and seniority spectrums tends to be lower.

For bargaining purposes, the most relevant statistic is the unit's average compensation or, more specifically, its *weighted* average compensation. The weighted average compensation (hereafter "average compensation" or, simply, "compensation") is merely an expression of how much it costs the employer, on the average, for each person on the payroll. It is this figure which presumably will be increased through negotiations.[2]

Although precision in computing these compensation costs depends very much on detailed data usually available only in the employer's payroll records, it is possible to develop some reasonably accurate approximations even without such detailed information.

Indeed, the ability to do so may be quite important in making judgments as to whether a settlement proposal is or is not satisfactory. Moreover, an awareness of the concepts and techniques that are involved in these computations can prove invaluable in carrying out the bargaining dialogue or in dealing with a third-party neutral.

These computations, it must be remembered, are not performed simply to engage in a mathematical exercise. The reason for seeking out this type of information is its usefulness at the bargaining table.

The value of salaries and fringe benefits must be known so that the value of any bargaining offer or settlement can be judged. Logically, therefore, the base compensation costs as of the point in time of negotiations—or, more accurately, immediately prior to the receipt of any increase—must be known.

The information that is needed in most cases in order to compute compensation costs is (a) the salary scales and benefit programs, (b) the distribution of the employees in the unit according to pay steps, shifts, and length of service, and (c) for purposes of some medical care programs, the employees' coverage status. If this information is in hand, just about all but one item of compensation can be readily computed.

The sole exception is the cost of the overtime premium. Overtime is apt to vary widely from week-to-week or month-to-month. Consequently, the data for any one pay period are an inadequate gauge where overtime is concerned. Simply by chance, it may cost the employer more one week than the next. It is common practice, therefore, to cost-out the overtime premium by averaging the cost of that benefit over the prior 12 months.

So far as the other elements of compensation are concerned, however, it is not necessary to study a full year's experience. With salaries, vacations,

Reprinted from The Use of Economic Data in Collective Bargaining *(Washington, D.C.: U.S. Department of Labor, 1978.)*

holidays, etc., the costs can be based on a snapshot taken at a fixed point in time on the basis of the provisions in the current collective bargaining agreement and the current distribution of the employees in the bargaining unit. That snapshot of compensation costs should be made as of the time the parties are at the bargaining table.

The purpose of this essay is to provide guidance on how to perform those computations, as well as the computations to determine the cost—the value—of an *increase* in compensation. The development of such compensation information gives the parties a basis for weighing the value of any particular wage and fringe benefit package.

Before the value of cost impact of any increase in compensation—whether in salaries, fringes, or both—can be gauged, the first step is to develop the base, or existing, compensation figure. A pay increase of $500 per employee, for example, means something different for a bargaining unit whose existing salary and fringe benefit cost per employee amount to $20,000 per year than for a unit whose compensation is $10,000. In the latter case, it represents an increase of 5 percent, but on a base of $20,000 it amounts to only 2½ percent. Thus, the base compensation figure is essential in determining the percentage value of any increase in compensation.

In order to demonstrate the computation methods for arriving at the base compensation figure, a Sample Bargaining Unit has been constructed and certain levels of employment, salaries, fringe benefits and hours of work have been assumed:

Exhibit 1

Sample Bargaining Unit

(a) Employment and Salaries

Classification	Number of Firefighters	Salary
Probationary		
Step 1	5	$10,100
Step 2	10	11,100
Private	65	12,100
Lieutenant	15	13,500
Captain	5	14,500
	100	

(b) Longevity Payments

Longevity Step	Number of Firefighters	Longevity Pay
Step 1	20 Privates	$ 500
Step 2	10 Privates	1,000
Step 2	15 Lieutenants	1,000
Step 2	5 Captains	1,000

(c) Hours of Work

The scheduled hours consist of one 24-hour shift every three days (one on; two off), or an average of 56 hours per week and a total of 2,912 hours per year.

(d) Overtime Premium

All overtime hours are paid at the rate of time-and-one-half. The Sample Bargaining Unit is assumed to have worked a total of 5,000 overtime hours during the preceding year.

(e) Shift Differential

The shift differential is 10 percent for all hours between 4 p.m. and 8 a.m. However, 10 members of the unit work exclusively on the day shift, from 8 a.m. to 4 p.m.

(f) Vacations

15 employees—(probationers) 5 shifts
35 employees—(privates) 10 shifts
50 employees—(all others) 15 shifts

(g) Holidays

Each firefighter is entitled to 10 paid holidays and receives 8 hours pay for each holiday.

(h) Clothing Allowance

$150 per employee per year.

(i) Hospitalization

Type of Coverage	Number of Firefighters	Employer's Monthly Payment
Single Coverage	15	$20.00
Family Coverage	85	47.00
	100	

(j) Pensions

The employer contributes an amount equal to 6 percent of the payroll (including basic salaries, longevity, overtime and shift differentials).

Computing Base Compensation

On the basis of the foregoing information on employment, salaries and benefits, we are now in a position to compute, for the Sample Bargaining Unit, its average base compensation–in essence, the cost of compensation for the average employee.

Exhibit 2

The Cost of Compensation for an Average Bargaining Unit Employee

(a) Average Straight-time Salary

(1) Classification	(2) Number of Fire-fighters	(3) Salary	(4) Weighted Salaries (2) x (3)
Probationary			
Step 1	5	$10,100	$ 50,500
Step 2	10	11,100	111,000
Private	65	12,100	786,500
Lieutenant	15	13,500	202,500
Captain	5	14,500	72,500
	100		$1,223,000

Average Annual Basic Salary =

$1,223,000 ÷ 100; or $12,230 per year

(b) Longevity Pay

(1) Longevity Step	(2) Number of Fire-fighters	(3) Longevity Pay	(4) Total Longevity Pay (2) x (3)
Step 1	20	$ 500	$10,000
Step 2	30	1,000	30,000
			$40,000

Average Annual Longevity Pay =

$40,000 ÷ 100;* or $400 per year

*Since the unit is trying to determine its average base compensation–that is, all the salary and fringe benefit items its members receive collectively–the total cost of longevity pay must be averaged over the entire unit of 100.

The combined average salary cost and average longevity cost amount to $12,630 per year. On an hourly basis, this comes to $4,337 ($12,630 ÷ 2,912.

Exhibit 3

(c) Average Cost of Overtime

Overtime work for the Sample Bargaining Unit is assumed to be paid for at the rate of time-and-one-half. This means that part of the total overtime costs is an amount paid for at straight-time rates and part is a premium payment.

	(1) Annual Cost	(2) Number of Firefighters	(3) Average Annual Cost (1) ÷ (2)
Straight-time cost ($4.337 x 5,000 overtime hours)	$21,685.00	100	$216.85
Half-time premium cost (½ x $21,685.00)	10,842.50	100	108.43
Total Overtime Cost	$32,527.50		$325.28

It can be seen from the overtime-cost calculations that the half-time premium is worth $108.43 per year on the average, while the straight-time portion is worth $216.85. This means, of course, that total pay at straight-time rates amounts to $12,846.85 ($12,630 plus $216.85) per firefighter.

Exhibit 4

(d) Average Cost of Shift Differential

The Sample Bargaining Unit receives a shift differential of 10 percent for all hours worked between 4 p.m. and 8 a.m. But 10 members of the unit who work in headquarters are assumed to work hours that are not subject to the differential. This leaves 90 employees who receive the differential.

Since the differential is paid for hours worked between 4 p.m. and 8 a.m., it is applicable to only two-thirds of the normal 24-hour shift. It, therefore, only costs the employer two-thirds of 10 percent for each 24 hours. That is the reason for column (5) in the following calculation. Each employee receives the differential for only two-thirds of his 24-hour tour.

(1) Classification	(2) No. on Shift Pay	(3) Salary	(4) 10% of Col. (3)	(5) .667 of Col. (4)	(6) Total Cost (2) x (5)
Probationary					
Step 1	5	$10,100	$1,010	$ 674	$ 3,370
Step 2	10	11,100	1,110	740	7,400
Private					
Longevity-0	35	12,100	1,210	807	28,245
Longevity-1	17	12,600*	1,260	840	14,280
Longevity-2	7	13,100*	1,320	880	6,160
Lieutenant	12	14,500*	1,450	967	11,604
Captain	4	15,500*	1,550	1,034	4,136
	90				$75,195

Average Annual Cost of Shift Differential = $75,196 ÷ 100,** or $751.95 per year

*Basic salary plus longevity pay.
**Since the unit is trying to determine its average base compensation—that is, all the salary and fringe benefit items its members receive collectively—the total cost of the shift differential must be averaged over the entire unit of 100.

Exhibit 5

(e) Average Cost of Vacation

Vacation costs for the unit are influenced by (a) the amount of vacations received by the employees with differing lengths of service, and (b) the pay scales of those employees.

(1) Classification	(2) Number of Firefighters	(3) Hourly Rate*	(4) Hours of Vacation**	(5) Total Vacation Hours (2) x (4)	(6) Total Vacation Costs (3) x (5)
Probationary					
Step 1	5	$3.468	120	600	$ 2,080.80
Step 2	10	3.812	120	1,200	4,574.40
Private					
Longevity-0	35	4.155	240	8,400	34,902.00
Longevity-1	20	4.327	360	7,200	31,154.40
Longevity-2	10	4.499	360	3,600	16,196.40
Lieutenant	15	4.979	360	5,400	26,886.60
Captain	5	5.323	360	1,800	9,581.40
	100				$125,376.00

Average Annual Vacation Cost = $125,376 ÷ 100; or $1,253.76 per year

*Derived from annual salaries (including longevity pay), divided by 2,912 hours (56 hours x 52 weeks). The 10 firefighters who do not receive shift differential would be on a regular 40-hour week and would, therefore, have a different hourly rate and vacation entitlement. The impact on cost, however, would be minimal. It has, therefore, been disregarded in this computation.

**Since each firefighter works a 24-hour shift, the hours of vacation are arrived at by multiplying the number of work shifts of vacation entitlement by 24 hours. For example, the figure of 120 hours is obtained by multiplying 5 shifts of vacation x 24 hours (one work shift).

Exhibit 6

(f) Average Cost of Paid Holidays

Unlike vacations, the number of holidays received by an employee is not typically tied to length of service. Where the level of benefits is uniform, as it is with paid holidays, the calculation to determine its average cost is less complex.

In the Sample Bargaining Unit, it is assumed that each firefighter receives 8 hours of pay for each of his 10 paid holidays, or a total of 80 hours of holiday pay:

(1) Average Annual Cost of Paid Holidays = $346.96 (80 hours x $4.337 average straight-time hourly rate), or

(2) Total Annual Cost of Paid Holiday hours per year = 8,000 (80 hours x 100 employees)

Total annual cost of paid holidays = $34,696.00 (the unit's average straight-time hourly rate of $4.337 x 8,000 hours)

Average annual cost of paid holidays = $346.96 (34,696.00 ÷ 100 employees)

Exhibit 7

(g) Average Cost of Hospitalization

(1) Type of Coverage	(2) Number of Fire-fighters	(3) Yearly Premium Cost to Employer	(4) Total Cost to Employer (2) x (3)
Single	15	$240	$ 3,600
Family	85	564	47,940
	100		$51,540

Average Annual Cost of Hospitalization = $51,540 ÷ 100; or $515.40 per year

(h) Other Fringe Benefits

(1) Pensions cost the employer 6 percent of payroll. The payroll amounts to $1,370,723 (salary cost–$1,223,000; longevity cost–$40,000; overtime cost–$32,528; and shift differential cost–$75,195). Six percent of this total is $82,243 which, when divided by 100, yields $822.43 as the average cost of pensions per firefighter, per year.

(2) The yearly cost of the clothing allowance is $150 per firefighter.

As the recapitulation in Exhibit 8 indicates, total compensation–salary plus fringes–for each firefighter averages $16,795.78 per year.

Once having determined the base compensation costs, it is now possible to compute the value–or cost–of any increase in the items of compensation. The methods used to make these computations are essentially the same as those used to compute the base compensation data.

Before proceeding to that exercise, however, a general observation about the computation of base compensation should be made. Since the purpose is to produce an average *total* cost per employee–whether by the hour or by the year–it follows that the objective must be to capture and include in the computation, for each item of compensation, the full amount of the employer's expense. This is why accurately maintained payroll records are desirable. Among other things, such records can help to resolve what might otherwise be protracted debates over approaches to the costing-out process on certain complicated benefit programs.

Exhibit 8

Average Annual Base Compensation for the Sample Bargaining Unit

(a) Straight-time earnings		$12,846.85
Basic salary	$12,230.00	
Longevity pay	400.00	
Overtime	216.85*	
(b) Fringe benefits		$ 3,948.93
Overtime premium	$ 108.43	
Shift differential	751.95	
Vacations	1,253.76	
Holidays	346.96	
Hospitalization	515.40	
Clothing allowance	150.00	
Pension	822.43	
(c) Total		$16,795.78

*This is only the straight-time portion of overtime pay. The premium portion appears with the fringe benefits.

One such item that comes to mind is paid sick leave. Many paid sick leave programs permit the employee to accumulate unused sick leave. Suppose, for example, the employees are allowed five paid sick leave days each year, with the opportunity to "bank" the unused days and, upon separation or retirement, to receive pay for one-half of the days in the "bank."

With such a program, it is likely that not all of the employees in the unit would use all five days each year. It would be incorrect, however, to cost out sick leave on the basis of the days actually taken each year since, at some subsequent point, there would be partial reimbursement for the unused days. Further complicating matters is the fact that the employee's rate of pay at the time the reimbursement takes place will very likely be higher than it is when the unused days are put in the "bank." Obviously, there is no way of knowing what that future rate of pay will be, so there is no way to determine now how much those "banked" days will be worth at the time of reimbursement.

One way to cost out the unit's paid sick leave in any year may be simply to charge everyone with five days. Needless to say, this may misstate the true cost and may generate controversy and debate.

Such disputes may be avoided if the actual total dollar cost of the sick leave program for the year can be derived. To do this, however, it would be necessary to have the dollar costs for each piece—that is, in our example, the cost of the days used in the year plus the cost of the reimbursements made in the year—in order to produce a total annual cost. That total, divided by the number of employees in the unit or by the number of hours worked by the unit during the year, would then yield the cost per employee or per hour for this particular benefit.

In a case such as the sick leave program cited, the availability of dollar amounts reflecting total annual costs would, as mentioned earlier, help to forestall controversy over the procedure to be used for costing out the benefit. And this approach would be consistent with the basic concept that is involved in costing out the other elements of employee compensation. That approach, as was also mentioned earlier, seeks to capture and include in the computation the full amount of the employer's expense for each item of compensation.

Computing the Cost of Increases in Items of Compensation

In order to demonstrate how to cost-out any increases in compensation, it will be assumed that the Sample Bargaining Unit negotiates a settlement consisting of the following package:

- An increase of 5 percent in basic salaries;
- Two additional shifts of vacation for all at the second step of longevity;
- An improvement in the benefits provided by the hospitalization program, which will cost the employer an additional $4.00 per month for family coverage and $2.50 for single coverage.

The cost of this settlement—that is, the amount of the increase in compensation that it represents—would be computed in the manner presented below, starting first with the cost-impact of the salary increase. As will be noted, the objective of the computation is to find the *average* cost of the increase—that is, the cost per firefighter, per year.

(a) *Increase in Cost of Salaries.* The increase in average annual basic salary (0.05 x $12,230) is $611.50. The cost of longevity pay does not increase. This is because longevity increments for the unit are fixed dollar amounts. If these payments were based on a percentage of salary—that is, if they were linked to the pay scales—then the cost of the longevity payments would also have risen by 5 percent. However, as a fixed dollar amount, these payments remain unaffected by the increase in basic salaries.

As a result, the increase in the unit's total average salary ($12,230 in basic salary plus $400 in longevity) is, in reality, not 5 percent, but only 4.8 percent ($611.50 ÷ $12,630).

This difference is important because of the way in which pay increases impact on the cost of fringe benefits. This is commonly referred to as the "roll up." As salaries increase, so does the cost to the employer of such fringes as vacations, holidays, overtime premiums, etc. This increase in cost comes about even though the benefits are not improved.

Some fringes, however, are not subject to the roll up. This is the case with respect to those fringe benefits that are not linked to pay rates. Examples of this type of fringe benefit include shift differentials that are stated in cents-per-hour (in contrast to a percentage of salary), a flat dollar amount for clothing allowance, and most group insurance programs.

(b) *Cost Impact of the "Roll up."* The increase in average straight-time pay (basic salary plus longevity pay) of the Sample Bargaining Unit was shown to be 4.8 percent. This means that the average cost of every benefit linked to salary will likewise increase by 4.8 percent. In our example, therefore, the average cost of compensation will go up by $611.50 per year in salaries, plus however much this adds to the costs of the fringe benefits as a result of the roll up.

But there is more. For our example, it is also to be assumed that the Sample Bargaining Unit will gain a vacation improvement—two additional shifts at the second step of longevity—and an improved hospitalization program.

The employer's contribution for the hospitalization program of the Sample Bargaining Unit is a fixed dollar amount and is, therefore, not subject to any roll up. Thus, we need in this instance be concerned only with the costing-out of the improvement in that benefit.

This is not the case with the vacations. Here the cost-increase is double-barreled—the cost of the improvement *and* the cost of the roll up.

None of the other fringe benefits of the Sample Bargaining Unit will be improved. Consequently, so far as they are concerned, we need only compute the increases in cost due to the roll up. The fringes which fit this category are overtime premiums, holidays, sick leave, shift differentials, and pensions.

As is indicated in Exhibit 9, column (3)—the added cost due to the roll up—is obtained by multiplying the base (pre-settlement) cost by 0.048. Obviously, if shift differentials and/or pensions were based on a set dollar (or cents) amount (instead of a percentage of salary), there would be no roll up cost associated with them. The only increase in cost that would result in such a situation would be associated with an improvement in the benefit item.

Exhibit 9

(1) Fringe Benefit	(2) Base Average Annual Cost*	(3) Roll up Factor	(4) Increased Cost (2) x (3)
Overtime			
Straight-time	$216.85	0.048	$ 10.41
Premium	108.43	0.048	5.20
Shift differential	751.95	0.048	36.09
Holidays	346.96	0.048	16.65
Pensions	822.43	0.048	39.48
			$107.83

*See Exhibits 2-8 for derivation of these costs.

Having performed this computation, we can now begin to see the impact of the roll up factor. As a result of the increase in pay, the four fringe benefit items will together cost the employer an additional $107.83 per firefighter, per year.

(c) *Increase in Cost of Vacations.* As noted earlier, the vacation improvement of two shifts—48 hours (2 shifts x 24 hours)—is to be limited to those whose length of service is equal to the time required to achieve the second step of longevity in the salary structure. Thus, it will be received by 30 members of the unit—10 privates, 15 lieutenants, and 5 captains.[3]

The first step in the computation is to determine the cost of the *new* benefit under the *existing* (old) salaries—that is, before the 4.8 percent pay increase (Exhibit 10):

Exhibit 10

(1) Number of Firefighters	(2) Hours of Increased Vacation	(3) Total Hours (1) x (2)	(4) Existing Hourly Rates*	(5) Cost of Improvement (3) x (4)
10 Privates	48	480	$4.499	$2,159.52
15 Lieutenants	48	720	4.979	3,584.88
5 Captains	48	240	5.323	1,277.52
				$7,021.92

*See Exhibit 5 for derivation of hourly rates.

The calculation thus far reflects only the additional cost of the vacation improvement based on the salaries existing *prior* to the 4.8 percent pay raise. In other words, if there had been no pay increase, the vacation improvement would result in an added cost of $7,021.92. But there was a pay increase. As a result, the base year vacation costs—including now the added cost of the improvement—must be rolled up by the 4.8 percent factor. Every hour of vacation—the old and the new—will cost 4.8 percent more as a result of the pay increase:

Exhibit 11

(1) Classification	(2) Existing Vacation Costs*	(3) Increase in Cost**	(4) Adjusted Base Costs (2) + (3)	(5) Roll up Factor	(6) Increased Cost from Roll up (4) x (5)
Probationary					
Step 1	$ 2,080.80	—	$ 2,080.80	0.048	$ 99.88
Step 2	4,574.40	—	4,574.40	0.048	219.57
Private					
Longevity-0	34,902.00	—	34,902.00	0.048	1,675.30
Longevity-1	31,154.40	—	31,154.40	0.048	1,495.41
Longevity-2	16,196.40	$2,159.52	18,355.92	0.048	881.08
Lieutenant	26,886.60	3,584.88	30,471.48	0.048	1,462.63
Captain	9,581.40	1,277.52	10,858.92	0.048	521.23
	$125,376.00	$7,021.92	$132,397.92	0.048	$6,355.10

*The base (or existing) vacation costs are from Exhibit 5.
**From data in preceding table.

By adding the two "new" pieces of cost—$7,021.92, which is the cost of the improvement, and $6,355.10, which is the cost due to the impact of the wage increase—we obtain the total increase in the cost of vacations. It amounts to $13,377.02. In order to figure the *average* cost, this total must be divided by the number of firefighters in the Sample Bargaining Unit. The increase in the average cost of vacations, therefore, is—

$13,377 ÷ 100, or $133.77

Had the vacation improvement been granted across-the-board, to everyone in the unit, the calculation would have been different—and considerably easier. If the entire unit were to receive an additional 48 hours of vacation, the total additional hours would then be 4,800 (48 hours x 100 employees). These hours would then be multiplied by the unit's old average straight-time rate ($4.337), in order to arrive at the cost of the additional vacation improvement which, in this case, would have come to $20,817.60 (4,800 hours x $4.337). And, in that case, the total cost of vacations—that is, the across-the-board improvement, plus the impact of the 4.8 percent salary increase—would have been computed as follows:

(a) Roll up of old vacation costs = 6,018.05
($125,376 x 0.048)
(b) Cost of vacation improvement =$20,817.60
(c) Roll up cost of improvement =$ 999.24
($20,817.60 x 0.048)

These pieces total to $27,834.89. When spread over the entire Sample Bargaining Unit, the increase in the average cost of vacations would have been $278.35 per year ($27,834.89 ÷ 100 employees).

This latter method of calculation does not apply only to vacations. It applies to any situation where a salary-related fringe benefit is to be improved equally for every member of the unit. An additional paid holiday would be another good example.

(d) *Increase in Cost of Hospitalization.* In this example, it has been assumed that the Sample Bargaining Unit has negotiated as part of its new package an improvement in its hospitalization programs. As with most hospitalization programs, the one covering this unit is not linked to salaries.

This improvement, it is assumed, will cost the employer an additional $4.00 per month ($48 per year) for family coverage and $2.50 per month ($30 per year) for single coverage. Thus, based on this and previous information about the breakdown of employees receiving each type of coverage, the calculation of the increase in hospitalization costs is as follows:

Exhibit 12

(1) Type of Coverage	(2) Number Covered	(3) Annual Cost of Improvement	(4) Total New Cost (2) x (3)
Single	15	$30	$ 450
Family	85	48	4,080
			$4,530

The unit's average hospitalization cost will be increased by $45.30 per year ($4,530 ÷ 100 employees).

The Total Increase in the Average Cost of Compensation

At this point, the increase in the costs of all the items of compensation which will change because of the Sample Bargaining Unit's newly negotiated package has been calculated. All that is left is to combine these individual pieces in order to arrive at the total increase in the unit's average cost of compensation. This is done in the tabulation which appears below (Exhibit 13).

Exhibit 13

Increase in Average Annual Cost of Compensation for Sample Bargaining Unit

(a) Straight-time earnings		$621.91
Basic salary	$611.50	
Longevity pay		
Overtime (straight-time portion)	10.41	
(b) Fringe benefits		$276.49
Overtime premium	$ 5.20	
Shift differential	36.09	
Vacations	133.77	
Holidays	16.65	
Hospitalization	45.30	
Clothing allowance		
Pensions	39.48	
(c) Total increase in average annual cost of annual compensation		$898.40

As the recapitulation shows, the average increase in salary costs amounts to $621.91 per year, while the average increase in the cost of the fringe benefits (including *new* benefit costs, as well as *roll up* costs) comes to $276.49, for a total increase in average annual compensation of $898.40 per firefighter, per year. That is the total annual cost of the settlement per firefighter.

There remains one final computation that is really the most significant—the *percent* increase that all of these figures represent. The unit's average base compensation per year was $16,796. The total dollar increase amounts to $898. The percent increase, therefore, is 5.3 percent ($898 ÷ 16,796) and that is the amount by which the unit's package increased the employer's average yearly cost per firefighter.

Computing the Hourly Cost of Compensation

The increase in the cost of compensation per *hour* will be the same. The approach to the computation, however, is different than that which was used in connection with the cost per year. In the case of the hourly computation, the goal is to obtain the cost per hour of *work.* This requires that a distinction be drawn between hours worked and hours paid for. The difference between the two is leave time.

In the Sample Bargaining Unit, for example, the employee receives an annual salary which covers 2,912 regularly scheduled hours (56 hours per week, times 52). In addition, he works an average of 50 hours of overtime per year. The sum of these two—regularly scheduled hours and overtime hours, or 2,962—are the total hours paid for.

But they do not represent hours worked, because some of those hours are paid leave time. The Sample Bargaining Unit, for example, receives paid leave time in the form of vacations and holidays. The number of hours actually worked by each employee is 2,600 (2,962 hours paid for, minus 362 hours of paid leave).[4]

The paid leave hours are, in a sense, bonuses—hours paid for, above and beyond hours worked. Thus, in order to obtain the hourly cost represented by these "bonuses"—that is, the hours of paid leave—the annual dollar cost of these benefits is divided by the annual hours *worked.*

It is the same as if we were trying to compute the per-hour cost of a year-end bonus. The dollar amount of that bonus would simply be divided by the total number of hours worked during the year.

So it is with *all* fringe benefits, not only paid

leave. In exchange for those benefits the employer receives hours of work (the straight-time hours and the overtime hours). Consequently, the hourly cost of any fringe benefit will be obtained by dividing the annual cost of the benefit by the annual number of hours *worked.* In some instances that cost is converted into money that ends up in the employee's pocket, as it does in the case of fringe benefits like shift differentials, overtime premiums and clothing allowances. In other instances—such as hospitalization and pensions—the employee is provided with benefits in the form of insurance programs. And in the case of paid leave time—holidays,[5] vacations, sick leave, etc.—the return to the employee is in terms of fewer hours of work.

The average annual costs of the fringe benefits of the Sample Bargaining Unit were developed earlier in this [selection] in connection with the computations of the unit's average annual base compensation. They appear in column (2) below.

In order to convert the costs of those fringe benefits into an average hourly amount, they are divided by 2,600—the average hours worked during the year by each employee in the unit. As can be seen, the hourly cost of all fringe benefits amounts to $1.518.

Exhibit 14

(1) Fringe Benefit	(2) Average Annual Cost	(3) Average Hours Worked	(4) Average Hourly Cost (2) ÷ (3)
Overtime Premium*	$ 108.43	2,600	$0.042
Shift Differential	751.95	2,600	0.289
Vacations	1,253.76	2,600	0.482
Holidays	346.96	2,600	0.133
Hospitalization	515.40	2,600	0.198
Clothing Allowance	150.00	2,600	0.058
Pensions	822.43	2,600	0.316
	$3,948.93		$1.518

*Includes only the premium portion of the pay for overtime work.

In addition to the fringe benefit costs, compensation includes the basic pay. For our Sample Bargaining Unit this is $12,630 per year (average salary plus average cost of longevity payments). On a straight-time hourly basis, this comes to $4.337 ($12,630 ÷ 2,912 hours). Even with the straight-time portion for the year's overtime included ($216.85), the average straight-time hourly rate of pay will, of course, still remain at $4.337 ($12,846.45 ÷ 2,962 hours).

A recapitulation of these salary and fringe benefit cost data produces both the average *annual* base compensation figure for the Sample Bargaining Unit and the average *hourly* figure:

	Yearly	Hourly
Earnings at Straight-time	$12,846.85 ÷ 2,962	= $4.337
Fringe Benefits	3,948.93 ÷ 2,600	= $1.519
Total Compensation	$16,795.78	$5.856

As indicated, on an annual basis, the average compensation cost comes to $16,795.78, a figure that was also presented earlier in this [selection]. And on an hourly basis, the average compensation of the unit amounts to $5.856.

Essentially the same process is followed if the *increase* in compensation is to be measured on an hourly (instead of an annual) basis.

The 5 percent pay increase received by the Sample Bargaining Unit would be worth 21 cents ($12,230 x 0.05 = $611.50; $611.50 ÷ 2,912 = $0.21). The annual increase in the unit's fringe benefit costs per firefighter—$276.49 for all items combined—works out to 10.6 cents per hour ($276.49 ÷ 2600 hours).

Together, these represent a gain in average compensation of 31.6 cents per hour, or 5.4 percent ($0.316 ÷ $5.956). This is one-tenth of a percentage point off from the amount of increase (5.3 percent) reflected by the annual data—a difference due simply to the rounding of decimals during the computation process.

Notes

1. Technically, employee compensation may also include the cost of legally required employer payments for programs such as social security, unemployment compensation, and workers' compensation. These items are disregarded in this analysis.
2. It is also referred to as the "base" compensation—that is, the compensation figure against which the cost of any settlement will be measured in order to determine the value of the settlement.
3. In costing out an improvement in vacations, the computation should cover the cost impact in the first year *only*. There is no need to be concerned with the impact in subsequent years when, supposedly, more and more employees become eligible for the improved benefit. For computational purposes, it must be assumed that the average length of service in the unit remains constant. This constancy is caused by normal personnel flows. As the more senior staff leave because of retirement or death, the staff is replenished by new hires without any accumulated seniority. Thus, for this type of computation, it must be presumed that the proportion of the workforce which benefits from the improved vacation will be constant year after year.

   It should be noted that an improvement in vacations (or any other form of paid leave) that is offset by corresponding reductions in on-duty manning does not represent any increase in cost to the employer.
4. Each firefighter receives 80 hours in paid holidays per year. The average number of hours of vacation per year was derived as follows:

15 firefighters x 120 hours (five 24-hour shifts)	=	1,800 hours
35 firefighters x 240 hours (ten 24-hour shifts)	=	8,400 hours
50 firefighters x 360 hours (fifteen 24-hour shifts)	=	18,000 hours
		28,200 hours

   This averages out to 282 hours of vacation per firefighter (28,200 ÷ 100) which, together with 80 holiday hours, totals 362 paid leave hours.
5. Typically, of course, firefighters do not receive time off, but are paid an extra day's pay for working a holiday.

14 Budgeting Capital Outlays and Improvements

A. John Vogt

Several years ago a medium-sized city spent $265,000 to replace pumps for its sewerage treatment plant and another $195,000 to pave streets in low- and moderate-income neighborhoods. A metropolitan county will spend about $700,000 next year to acquire 30 acres for a sanitary landfill site, and a nearby city spent $575 last year for a movie film projector to be used in the city's fire prevention program. These expenditures, different in nature and amount, are alike in one way—they are all capital expenditures.

This article will examine the elements involved in planning and budgeting capital outlays and improvements and develop a model of capital budgeting for state and local governments. Whereas we have a well-defined model for operating budgeting in the public sector, this is not the case with capital budgeting—a truth made evident in that while many states require their local governments to have annual operating budgets and prescribe specific steps for preparing that budget, few states require a special process for local government budgeting of capital expenditures. Similarly, while we have numerous books and manuals on operating budgeting which portray a fairly uniform process, we have few books and manuals on capital budgeting, and their treatment of the process and techniques varies greatly. Moreover, most of these latter books and manuals typically cover only one phase or aspect of capital budgeting, such as capital improvement programming, borrowing to finance capital improvements, or quantitative methods for evaluating capital project proposals.

The model of capital budgeting developed in this article consists of three stages: planning, budgeting, and implementation, and it shows how different techniques and approaches like capital programming fit into each stage and the entire capital budget process.

First, however, we will define capital outlay, discuss what capital outlays and projects should be reviewed and approved in a separate capital budget process, and consider why a special process or set of procedures have evolved in many jurisdictions for capital budgeting.

What Is a Capital Outlay?

Capital outlays are different from other expenditures. Capital outlays are durable—that is, they yield benefits for many years, or they result in the acquisition of property that has a long life. Capital outlays do not usually recur each year, and irregular intervals of time elapse between periodic replacements. Capital outlays are also typically expensive, requiring large expenditures compared with most on-going current expenditures.

Two formal definitions of capital outlay are available in the literature. One is from economics, and it gives a broad meaning to the concept. The other is from accounting, and it provides a more restricted definition.

Economics states that a capital outlay is any

This article was written especially for this volume. A. John Vogt is associate professor of public law and government, The University of North Carolina, Chapel Hill.

expenditure that will produce benefits in future years or for at least more than one year, whereas a current expenditure yields benefits for only the current year.[1] Under this definition, whether the capital outlay results in the acquisition of specific property is irrelevant. Thus, even advertising expenditures made to attract new industry to a state or community, which accounting practices would charge to a current account, would be considered to be capital expenditures because they are made to obtain benefits or revenues in future years. This is clearly a broad conception of capital outlay.

Accounting, on the other hand, says that a capital outlay is an expenditure of significant value that results in the acquisition of an addition to a fixed asset.[2] "Significant value" can be $50, $100, or several hundred dollars, depending on the size of the jurisdiction. If an item costs less than the significant dollar amount, the expenditure for it is an operating outlay even though it would otherwise qualify as a capital outlay. The term *fixed asset* refers to tangible property that is held or used for a long period of time or at least more than one year. "Fixed" as used here does not mean immobile; thus an automobile is commonly classified as a fixed asset. The major difference between these two definitions from accounting and from economics is whether a fixed asset is acquired. Economics says that any outlay that produces future benefits, whether or not a fixed asset is acquired, is a capital outlay. To qualify as a capital outlay under the definition from accounting, however, an expenditure must produce future benefits and result in the acquisition of a fixed asset or add to an existing one. Indeed, it is through the use of the fixed asset that the future benefits are realized.

The definition from accounting is the one generally used in government financial practices, and that is the meaning intended for capital outlay in this article. The major categories of capital outlay under this definition are as follows:

1. Land. This blanket term includes land; legal, brokerage, and other expenses incidental to the purchase of land; and land-preparation costs.
2. Buildings. This designation refers to permanent structures for housing persons or property, and equipment or furnishings that are fixed or attached to such structures. The costs for legal, architectural, and engineering services related to building construction also belong here.
3. Improvements other than buildings. Examples in this category are streets, bridges, tunnels, and water or sewer lines.
4. Unattached equipment or furnishings. Included here are trucks, automobiles, desks, and other equipment that is used for more than one year or fiscal period.

What Capital Outlays Belong in the Capital Budget?

Not all capital outlays should be included and reviewed in the capital budget process. The annual or biennial operating budget is the best place for capital outlays that will not involve a great deal of money. These expenditures typically are for unattached equipment and furnishings, small parcels of land, and minor construction projects. A dollar cutoff that ranges from $500 to as much as $25,000 or so (depending on the size of the jurisdiction) serves as the instrument for deciding which capital outlays are large enough to place in the capital budget. Thus while the accountant for a state government or large city will record an expenditure of $800 for an electric typewriter as a capital outlay, the budget officer of that jurisdiction would include and review such an expenditure in the operating budget; the item would be classified under "capital outlay" or "permanent property" in the operating budget.

The capital budget should also not include capital outlays that recur each year, even though the total outlay or outlay per item is above the dollar cutoff for determining which capital outlays belong in the capital budget. For instance, a large city may have a capital budget with a dollar cutoff of $25,000; a capital item that will cost over $25,000 is included in the capital budget, and a capital item that costs less than $25,000 is placed in the operating budget. The city may be replacing one fire department pumper truck each year, at a current cost of $80,000 per year. This expenditure is for a long-lived capital asset and it is more than $25,000, and on this basis, the expenditure for the fire trucks should be placed in the capital budget. However, since the expenditure occurs each year, it should be placed in the operating budget. The operating budget is able to finance an annual capital outlay as readily as annual operating expenditures for salaries, fringe benefits, supplies, etc. The capital budget therefore should be reserved for capital outlays that are costly, i.e., above a specified dollar cutoff, and that do not recur each year.

Some planners and managers say that the capital budget should include *all* extraordinary, unusual, or large nonrecurring expenditures, and not just those that result in the acquisition of a fixed asset. They argue that all of these expenditures, whether current or capital, draw on the jurisdiction's capital resources and therefore should be evaluated together in the capital budget process. Examples of expenditures like this are a one-time extra Medicaid payment of $500,000 by a medium-sized county or $30,000 spent by a small city for a management improvement study. The former is clearly not a capital outlay. The latter could qualify as a capital outlay under the economist's but not the accountant's definition of capital outlay. The danger of putting large operating expenditures that do not recur each year into the capital budget is that if the capital budget is financed with bonds, this practice opens the door to financing current expense items—those that benefit only the current year—with bond proceeds. Bond proceeds, which are paid back in the future, should be used to finance only outlays that produce benefits in the future—or better still, the accountant would say, to finance only capital or fixed assets that will last or be used for many years into the future.

Why Capital Planning and Budgeting?

Why would a local government establish a special process or set of procedures for making and implementing capital outlay decisions? The first reason is the sheer magnitude of many capital outlays, especially for the construction of buildings or improvements. A lot of money is at stake in these decisions, and a government should try to make sure that these decisions are the right ones and that the money is not wasted. Moreover, because capital outlays are often so large, the decisions of government to undertake them can shape the most basic features of a community. For example, a school board's decision to locate a new high school on the north side of a city can speed major new development there and indirectly slow growth in other parts of the city. Moreover, the consequences of a capital outlay decision usually extend well into the future. In other words, the impact of the decision is probably irreversible for as long as the useful life of the facility or equipment acquired with the outlay. Thus, when the city council decides to build a new city hall in a particular style and at a specific site, the community will have to live with that decision, whatever its merits, for perhaps 30 or 40 years—there is not much of a market for a secondhand city hall. Similarly, if a small town buys a new fire truck, it has committed itself to the technology represented by the new truck's capabilities for perhaps 10 years.

Another reason for capital budgeting arises because the same capital outlay decisions do not recur each year. In the operating budget, expenditures recur each year and officials have the current year's experience to guide them in making decisions for the coming year, which reduces the risks of error in these decisions. On the other hand, major capital outlay decisions do not recur every year, and officials do not have the previous years' experience to guide them in making these decisions. The consequent risk of error is much higher for these decisions, which is a good reason to set up a separate process for capital budgeting to assure that major capital decisions are fully considered before they are approved and funded.

Since capital outlay decisions are frequently financed in whole or in part with bonds, the risk of default in bond financing is another reason for having special procedures for making these decisions. Moreover, when it commits its government unit to bond financing, the governing board this year binds future governing boards to pay annual principal and interest installments on the bonds. In other words, the present governing board exercises authority over those that follow it—a fact that obliges the board to take great care in making capital outlay and financing decisions.

Capital planning and budgeting helps a community provide for the orderly replacement and development of public facilities. To maintain the quality and efficiency of public services like water and sewer systems, public transportation, schools, or recreation, the facilities involved must be replaced or upgraded periodically. Moreover, new buildings or equipment are usually needed to meet the growth in service demand. Both the replacement and new capital needs must be taken care of within the limited capital resources of the community. A capital budget process helps achieve this purpose—not by lessening the need for new or replacement facilities or by increasing the resources to meet capital needs but by setting priorities to meet the most pressing needs first, by submitting projects to several analytic stages to eliminate poor or very low-priority projects, by carefully scheduling approved projects, and by providing revenue projections to help a community avoid overextending itself financially in meeting capital needs.

Capital Planning and Budget Process

What is a capital budget process? How does it work? The model of capital budgeting presented here divides the process into three stages:

1. Planning stage.
   - Classification and initial analysis of capital requests.
   - Ranking capital requests into priority. Although this ranking is tentative and will be reviewed and most probably revised later on in the process, decision-makers should begin to think about the community's most pressing capital needs at this initial stage of the capital budget process.
   - Preparation of a capital improvement program (CIP) that schedules capital requests for approval, funding, and implementation over a five- to seven-year future planning period.
   - Forecast of financial resources that will be available to fund capital requests over the same planning period spanned by the CIP.
2. Budget stage.
   - Project evaluation. This is a feasibility study that precedes the decision whether to undertake a capital project or buy a capital item. If the project or item is of major size, the study is likely to be contracted out to an engineering consulting firm. Project evaluation, whether done by in-house staff or contracted, may involve the use of quantitative analysis.
   - Selection of financing for capital requests. Such financing can come from operating revenues, bond proceeds, capital reserves, and other sources.
   - Approval of capital requests and appropriating money to fund them.
3. Implementation stage.
   - Acquiring, managing, and investing the revenue available to fund capital requests.
   - Buying equipment, land, and other capital assets.
   - Designing, contracting for, and supervising construction projects.

All three stages with their steps constitute a full capital budget process. We should note here that the appearance of a capital or fixed-asset statement in a local unit's budget does not mean necessarily that the unit has a separate process or special procedures for making capital expenditure decisions. A statement in the budget documents can be used to show what expenditures are capital and how much of the budget they take. Many jurisdictions, including the federal government, use such a statement in their budget books without having either a full-fledged or even a partial capital budget process. Such a process implies that decisions on proposed capital outlays are treated differently in the review and approval process from decisions on current operating expenditures.

Capital Planning: Identification and Initial Analysis of Requests

Identification and initial analysis occurs when the need for a capital outlay is recognized and the request to meet the need is first made. If a government has no CIP or other type of long-range capital plan, most capital requests probably will be formulated and made just before the final decision must be made on whether to approve the request. However, we place "identification and initial analysis of requests" as a step in the planning stage to suggest that capital needs should be identified several years ahead of the time when decisions to meet those needs have to be approved and funded. This permits a governmental unit to have a planning stage in its capital budget process and to carefully plan individual capital requests.

The initial analysis of capital requests includes several steps: (1) deciding whether particular requests are in fact capital and whether they belong in the capital budget or in the operating budget; (2) determining that each request is a practical and low-cost way of meeting the need in question; (3) determining that all costs that should be charged to a capital request are counted, and making sure that cost items that are not capital in nature are excluded from the request; (4) analyzing the capital costs for each request and estimating the impact that each will have on the operating budget; and (5) beginning to consider what source or sources of financing should be used to fund each request.

Capital Planning: Establishing Priorities

Few organizations have sufficient resources to meet all of their capital needs. Only some requests can be funded at any one time. Because capital needs or requests compete with one another for limited resources, a critical question to ask about any one request is how great the need for it is compared with the need for other requests. To answer this question, the requests must be ranked into priority. Such ranking occurs throughout the capital budget process as capital needs are assessed and reassessed. However, a preliminary ranking should be made in the planning stage before the capital improvement program (CIP) is proposed. The CIP allocates the costs for capital requests among the years of the CIP planning period, and costs allocated to the first few years of the planning period are presumed to have a high priority and costs allocated to the latter years a low priority. Thus some sort of priority-setting has to occur before the CIP is prepared.

There are different approaches to priority-setting. Decision-makers can simply rank capital requests from high to low on the basis of their judgment about the relative need for each request. Or they can first establish categories of capital need and then examine the requests and allocate them among the categories. An established priority ranking system for capital construction projects might have the following categories, ranging from high to low priority:

1. Repairs or construction to ensure the safety of persons or property.
2. Construction to complete projects previously authorized.
3. Major renovations or additions to provide fuller use of existing facilities.
4. New facilities to reduce overcrowded conditions or relieve obsolescence.
5. New facilities to meet increases in demand.
6. New facilities to provide for improvements in programs.
7. New facilities for new programs or services.

The ranking categories of this system favor renovation and repair projects over new facilities to accommodate program expansion or new programs. However, officials could just as easily devise another system with different categories or different priorities among the categories.

Some governments have used a two-dimension rating system for ranking capital requests. With a two-dimension system, two types of priorities are established, the categories for each are ranked and assigned a numeric score, and the scores for the categories from one dimension are multiplied by the scores for the categories from the other dimension to produce a matrix of ratings like that shown in Figure 1. The two dimensions used for the matrix are degree of urgency and priority of function, and the categories for each from high to low are as follows:

Degree of Urgency

1. Legislation: Required by legislation or regulation of federal or state government.
2. Hazard: Removes an obvious or potential hazard to public health or safety.
3. Efficiency: Replaces equipment or a facility that is obsolete, or would be too costly to repair, or maintains and better utilizes existing equipment and facilities.
4. Standard of service: Maintains or provides existing standard of service in developed areas, or provides comparable standard of service in newly developed areas.
5. Economic advantage: Directly benefits the city's economic base by increasing property values or other revenue potential.
6. Increased service: Expands or increases a service or improves a standard of service.
7. New service or convenience: Makes possible a new service or increases convenience or comfort.

Priority of Function

1. Protection of persons and property: police, fire, rescue, inspections, etc.
2. Environmental health: water, sewer, sanitation, public health, etc.
3. Housing: public housing, rehabilitation of housing, etc.
4. Pedestrian and vehicular transportation: street construction and maintenance, mass transit, parking, etc.
5. General maintenance of city-owned property.
6. Recreation: parks, athletic programs, etc.
7. General government: office facilities, central services, etc.
8. Heritage and cultural: education, libraries, etc.

Using a matrix like the one in Figure 1, decision-makers can rank capital requests by assigning each a rating from the matrix. A low rating from the matrix indicates a high priority and vice versa.

A priority ranking or rating system is a useful device in capital budgeting because it provides a common framework for decision-makers to rank requests. It is particularly helpful to decision-makers in ranking medium-priority requests. The high and low-priority requests are likely to be

Figure 1: *Two-Dimension Rating Matrix for Capital Proposals*

Urgency		**Function**							
		Protection 1	**Environ-mental Health 2**	**Housing 3**	**Transpor-tation 4**	**General Mainten-ance 5**	**Recrea-tion 6**	**General Govern-ment 7**	**Heritage and Cultural 8**
Legislation	1	1	2	3	4	5	6	7	8
Hazard	2	2	4	6	8	10	12	14	16
Efficiency	3	3	6	9	12	15	18	21	24
Standard of service	4	4	8	12	16	20	24	28	32
Economic advantage	5	5	10	15	20	25	30	35	40
Increased or improved service	6	6	12	18	24	30	36	42	48
New service or convenience	7	7	14	21	28	35	42	49	56

Source: This model is adapted from the matrix used by the City of Durham, North Carolina.

readily apparent, but the "correct" ranking among requests that fall in the middle are not so clear-cut. The major problem in using a priority ranking or rating system lies in selecting the categories, setting them into priority in a way that satisfies different decision-makers, and then staying with these categories during the ranking process. A ranking or rating system is not likely to work if the decision-makers disagree significantly about the priorities, or if the categories are changed to accommodate individual requests.

Capital Planning: The Capital Improvement Program

The capital improvement program (CIP) is at the heart of the planning stage of the capital budgeting process. As already mentioned, a CIP lists capital projects and outlays that a government expects to undertake. Most CIPs extend five to seven years into the future. A forecast period much shorter than this does not allow enough time for planning major projects. While some CIPs extend as much as 10 years, requests made for years that far into the future are likely to be based on "wish-listing" rather than serious planning.

The essential feature of a CIP is the apportionment of capital costs among the years covered by the CIP. On the CIP summary form in Figure 2, the column designated "Prior Year's Costs" is used for capital projects that are now under way. The column "Coming Budget Year" lists capital costs that will be incurred in the upcoming year. These costs can be for projects in process or for projects or outlays that are in the final stage of review in the current year's CIP. The latter projects and outlays will be funded either in the capital budget or the coming year's annual budget, or else postponed to a later year in the CIP or dropped altogether. The columns on the CIP form for the planning years show forecasted costs for projects in process, projects getting under way in the budget year, or projects or outlays scheduled to start in one of the planning years. The column for years beyond the CIP is for the costs of projects that get under way in the CIP planning period but carry beyond that period before the projects are finished.

The CIP is conceived of as an annual process, and most jurisdictions that use the CIP repeat it each year. Annual repetition provides for a recurring assessment of capital needs and updates the CIP every year to account for new needs. Use of a CIP presumes that capital needs are foreseen and requests will be placed in the CIP in one of the distant planning years. Then the requests are reviewed each year when the CIP is repeated. When the requests that survive reach the budget year, they are approved and funded, rejected, or perhaps postponed another year. Of course, not all capital needs can be recognized five or six years ahead of the time when the final decision to approve or reject them must be made. Some will have to be

Figure 2: *Capital Improvement Program*

Project and Project Elements	Total Project Costs	Prior Year's Costs	Coming Budget Year	Planning Year One	Planning Year Two	Planning Year Three	Planning Year Four	Planning Year Five	Years beyond CIP Period

approved and funded almost immediately upon first request. However, if this happens for many requests, the CIP loses most of its value as a planning tool.

In simple form, a CIP may be no more than a list prepared by the administration that shows future capital outlays by year. However, in both content and process, a CIP usually evolves into something more elaborate, especially for state governments and medium-sized or large local governments. In a more elaborate CIP process, requests are subjected to review by different public bodies or officials. A planning agency or citizen's group typically makes one review. This review evaluates each request in terms of need, conformity to the comprehensive development plan (if there is one), and whether alternatives are available to the request. The planning agency may hold public hearings on the capital requests. The chief executive officer also reviews capital requests for the CIP. This review considers the feasibility of requests, ranks the requests into priority if this has not already been done, and compares the total dollar cost of all the requests with the financial resources available for capital purposes over the period covered by the CIP. The governing or legislative body or a committee thereof makes a final review of CIP requests. More public hearings may be held at this stage, with popular feelings on projects weighed against need, financial feasibility, and other factors. When its review is finished, the governing board can stop here, or it can adopt a formal resolution approving the CIP. This latter course is recommended by most authorities, since it formalizes the CIP process. However, such a resolution typically neither commits funds to a project nor gives the go-ahead to start construction or to make a purchase. The resolution is basically a statement of governing board intent.

As this description of the CIP process suggests, the total time required for CIP preparation, review, and approval may span three or more months for states and large local governments and perhaps a month for small local governments. An important question with regard to timing is whether the CIP process should occur before, simultaneously with, or after the annual budget process. In one city with a July 1-June 30 fiscal year, the CIP process starts in early fall and is completed in February when the annual budget process begins. Thus the CIP is one factor that sets the stage for the annual operating budget in that city. The other factor is a five-year projection of annual operating needs. Without such a projection, preparing the CIP before the annual operating budget runs the risk that capital plans will be formulated without regard for program or annual operating needs. Probably the best timing is to proceed with the CIP and annual budget process simultaneously. The inherent difficulty in such a schedule is that each process requires much work, in both preparation and review, and doing both together is very difficult in practice.

Capital Planning: Revenue Projections

Revenue projections are undertaken to provide an estimate of the financial resources available for capital outlay purposes for the same period that the CIP covers. Such projections are important because having a CIP without knowing about revenues in effect proposes capital decisions without regard for a jurisdiction's financial ability to fund the decisions. Moreover, projecting the revenue available for capital outlays means that future operating needs are also projected. Because capital outlays are frequently financed with current revenue, the revenue available for capital outlays cannot be predicted realistically without also forecasting how much revenue operating needs are likely to absorb in the future.

Four projections are involved in predicting revenue available for capital outlay purposes: annual operating revenue and expenditures, intergovernmental aid, outstanding debt, and annual debt-service payments.

Projections of annually recurring revenue are usually based on past trends in existing revenue sources.[3] In looking at the trends, natural growth must be distinguished from growth resulting from changes in a revenue or tax base or rate enacted by the legislative body or governing body. Since the revenues from individual sources usually grow at different rates, projections are better based on the individual trend for each revenue source followed by summation than on the total revenue trend. If changes in revenue classifications have been made during the trend period, past classifications must be adjusted to make them consistent with existing ones. Finally, in making the projections, existing revenue sources and tax rates are assumed to continue through the planning period, but then the trends, as carried into the future, must be adjusted for changes in fiscal conditions or decisions that will affect revenues during that period.

Two major local operating revenue sources are the property tax and income from water-sewer systems. Projection of future revenue from the property tax must consider existing assessed valuation, future building activity, any revaluation or annexation that will occur during the planning period, the assessment ratio if property is not assessed at market value, and the expected collection rate. When water-sewer operations are self-supporting, cost is the best base for projecting revenue from them. This involves predicting the number of water-sewer customers (by category if applicable), the average consumption per customer, and cost per unit of consumption, e.g., 1,000 gallons, at the expected level of consumption. Information on these variables can then be combined in a formula to calculate the amount of revenue that must be secured to cover costs.

As with operating revenues, the projection of operating expenditures should be based on historic trends and adjusted for conditions expected to prevail in the planning period. The expenditures should be grouped by fund, department or function within each fund, and major line-item classes within each department or function. Only a few general line-item classes need to be used: salaries, fringe benefits, contractual services, supplies, permanent property, and contributions to individuals, organizations, or other governments. Adjustments to historic expenditure trends in anticipation of future decisions and developments should consider salary and wage increases likely to be awarded in the future; changes or improvements in fringe benefits; inflation on contractual services, operating supplies, and permanent property; the probable addition or deletion of positions to meet changes in workload requirements and new positions for improvements in services or new services slated for the planning period. Adjustment to the historical trends to account for changes in policies, developments beyond the trends, etc., are likely to be greater for expenditures than for revenues.

If operating revenues exceed operating expenditures in a particular year, the sum can be transferred to the capital budget to finance capital improvements and outlays. Or it could be left in the operating fund balance and carried forward to the next year without being appropriated to the budget for that year. Such a balance serves as an operating reserve to meet unforeseen operating expenses and to pay expenditures during cash-lean periods of the year when disbursements exceed receipts. But operating fund balances are sometimes built up to amounts greater than needed for this purpose and then drawn down to finance capital projects and outlays. The revenue projection for capital planning should therefore also forecast operating fund balances during the planning period.

Federal aid and grants are a major source of financing to state and local government for capital projects and outlays, and state grants generated from operating revenue or state bond proceeds provide another source of capital financing for local governments in many states. Projecting the amount of federal or state aid available to a governmental unit in the future is problematic. The degree of difficulty depends greatly on the legal and administrative provisions governing the distribution of that aid.

General federal revenue-sharing is one major source of federal aid. Some state and large local governments and many medium-sized and smaller local units have spent their federal revenue-sharing mainly for capital purposes.[4] Money from federal revenue-sharing has been distributed in entitlements according to formulas that have remained the same since the revenue-sharing program began in 1972. Moreover, the U.S. Treasury distributes revenue-sharing directly to individual state and local governments. Federal administrators and state legislative bodies or administrators have no say about how much revenue-sharing is or should be allocated to a particular state or local government. Consequently, the amount of revenue that individual state or local units have received over the years has not fluctuated greatly and projecting revenue from this source has been relatively easy to this point.

Federal grant money is an important revenue source for a wide range of state and local government capital projects: water-sewer, mass transit, recreation, education, law enforcement, etc. Projecting such grant money is hazardous because the grants are awarded on the basis of a federal administrator's judgment on whether a local or state applicant meets qualifications for the grant. Moreover, many governments compete for the grant money, and usually only some can be funded even though all may qualify. Despite these difficulties, federal grant money likely to be available for capital projects in the future should be projected, with a very conservative margin for error or with the option left open to drop the project if the grant does not materialize.

Projecting outstanding debt and annual debt service is important for capital planning purposes because state and local governments issue bonds to finance major capital improvements. If the improvements in question are for general government functions, the bonds are likely to be general obligation (G.O.) bonds. Such bonds are backed or secured by a government's unlimited taxing power. For local governments, the term "unlimited taxing power" refers to the local unit's legal authority to levy property taxes without limit as to rate or amount to make debt service payments on the bonds.

Most states have constitutional or statutory debt provisions that restrict the amount of G.O. debt that local government can issue to some percentage of that unit's assessed or appraised valuation for property tax purposes. For example, North Carolina limits a city or county's outstanding and authorized but unissued G.O. debt to 8 percent of the appraised value of the unit's property that is subject to taxation.[5] The 8 percent limit does not include either revenue bonds (bonds backed solely by the net earnings of a public enterprise or a limited pledge of a unit's tax or revenue raising power) or G.O. bonds for self-supporting municipal or county utilities. The 8 percent limit is one benchmark for determining how much G.O. debt a local government in North Carolina can safely borrow. However, it is an *outside* limit; most localities in the state try to keep their outstanding G.O. debt within 3 to 6 percent of appraised valuation[6] so that they can sell their bonds at low interest rates. The ratio of outstanding debt to appraised valuation is a less than adequate measure or boundary of safety in borrowing because real property is appraised for tax purposes only at widely spaced intervals in most states (in North Carolina once every eight years). Also when property is appraised, it is often valued at varying percentages of market value depending on local appraisal practices. As a result, appraised (and assessed) values diverge from true market value depending on state property tax laws and local appraisal practices.

Other fiscal indicators help determine the boundary of safety in borrowing. One is the ratio of annual debt service payments to annual operating revenue (excluding federal revenue and grants and enterprise revenue pledged to secure revenue bonds, but including state shared revenues in the case of local governments). Nearly all state and local government G.O. bonds have serial maturities—that is, a portion of the bonds are retired or paid back each year, usually over 20 to 25 years. Annual debt service payments include the amount of bonds or debt retired that year plus interest owed at a specified rate on the amount of debt outstanding for the year. A rough rule of thumb is that annual debt service payments on G.O. bonds should not exceed 20 percent of annual operating revenues.[7] Conservative jurisdictions try to hold debt service to 15 percent or less of such revenue. Future annual debt service on bonds to finance a proposed capital facility can be added to the schedule of debt service on existing outstanding debt and the sum divided by projected operating revenues to determine whether future operating budgets will be able to make the future debt service payments without strain.

Another measure for determining the boundary of safety in borrowing is the ratio of outstanding G.O. debt to annual operating revenue. The rule of thumb is that outstanding G.O. debt should not exceed some percentage, e.g., 200 percent, of annual operating revenue.[8] The exact percentage of the limit applicable to a specific state or local government should depend partly on growth prospects of that state or locality.

Debt limitations for revenue bonds are usually stated in terms of a coverage ratio. Coverage is the ratio of net earnings to annual debt service for the enterprise or facility to be financed with the revenue bonds. Net earnings equal operating revenues less operating expenses, depreciation excluded. Since net earnings are the major (and probably sole) security for the bonds, investors will require a coverage ratio well over 1.0 for projects to be financed with revenue bonds. The ratio required by investors varies by the type of enterprise financed with the bonds.[9]

Capital Budgeting: Project Evaluation

Project evaluation refers to a detailed and often technical study of a capital outlay proposal, and it is usually done late in the planning stage or early in the budget stage. It is the study that a locality does (or has done) just before it decides finally whether to commit funding to a capital outlay or project. As such, it relates more to capital budgeting than to capital planning.

Project evaluation can be conducted by in-house staff or contracted out to a consulting firm. If the project is large and involves technical considerations, part or all of the evaluation will be contracted out to an engineering consulting firm. The purpose of evaluation, no matter who does it, is to help determine the need for and/or economic viability of the project. For capital construction, the study is also likely to involve the preparation of general plans and specifications.

The methods or techniques for project evaluation range from approaches that rely on observation and judgment to very sophisticated quantitative analysis. Informed judgment based on field study or inspection is the simplest and probably the most often used of all evaluation methods. It is most applicable when the outlay being considered is a relatively small construction project or the purchase of equipment or when the priorities among competing or alternative outlay proposals are fairly clear. It generally involves consulting with manufacturers and those who will use the facility or equipment and visiting other jurisdictions that have a similar facility or piece of equipment. Such an approach makes no claim of technical certainty, for the result it produces rests ultimately on the personal judgment of whoever is the decision-maker.

Quantitative techniques can be used for project evaluation when a project will generate a stream of revenue over the period of its useful life. Government activities or projects that produce revenue are those financed in significant part with user fees—for example, water-sewer operations, mass transit, some recreation programs, and sometimes solid-waste pickup and disposal. Quantitative analysis can also be used to evaluate a capital project or piece of equipment that generates a stream of savings over the period of its useful life. For example, a municipality may be renting privately owned office facilities, and the question arises whether the cost of a new city office building will be compensated for in whole or part by the savings in private office rentals (less annual maintenance cost on the city hall) by having the city-owned facility.

Various economic techniques can be used to evaluate capital projects.[10] One technique widely used in the private sector is to calculate the payback factor—that is, the number of years required before the annual net cash income from a project recoups the original capital cost or investment. The payback method is simple and also when capital funds are lean it favors projects that return income or capital to the locality quickly. Its disadvantages are that (1) it fails to consider earnings after the investment has been recouped; and (2) it values earnings in different years equally. Because of the uncertainty or risk associated with the future, this year's earnings should be valued higher dollar for dollar than earnings next year and earnings next year more than earnings two or more years from now.

A second economic technique that can be used for project evaluation in the public sector is the present-value method, which considers the time value of money. This method (1) lists all net cash revenues or savings for each year over the useful life of a project; (2) discounts the annual net revenues or savings to the present, using a chosen interest rate; and (3) compares the total present worth of net revenues or savings with the original capital investment. If the present worth of the future annual net revenues or savings exceeds the investment, the project is presumably economically viable. The present-worth method is superior to payback because it considers annual revenues or savings over the full useful life of a project and takes into account the time value of money. But present worth is more difficult to compute than payback, and it assumes the ability to forecast receipts and costs far into the future. It also presents the problem of having to select an appropriate discount rate. Possible rates for discounting are the rate at which a government can borrow money, the rate it can earn by investing idle cash, or the rate that private citizens could earn if the money were kept and invested by them.

Another problem with the present value method (shared by all economic analysis techniques) is that it gives undue emphasis to benefits that can be quantified. The capital outlays or projects of local government usually have important nonmonetary benefits, and economic techniques do not take them into account. Indeed, when economic analysis is used for project evaluation, nonmonetary benefits and costs are too often neglected by decision-makers.

Capital Budgeting: Project Financing

In the capital planning process, financial projections are made to set long-term capital needs within the expected level of available funding. The principal financial issue at the budgetary stage is what source(s) of financing should be selected to fund individual capital requests and how heavily should a government rely on each alternative funding source for the whole of its capital budget. A capital request can be financed by one or a combination of several sources, including operating revenue, bond proceeds, capital reserves or fund balances built up from prior years' revenue, lease-purchase agreements, equipment-purchase revolving funds, special assessments, and, of course, federal and state grants.

The use of operating revenue to finance capital outlays or projects is commonly called pay-as-go financing. The capital budget of a state or local government may be financed entirely or partially on a pay-as-go basis. Full pay-as-go funding is practical only when a government spends more or less the same amount for capital purposes each year. The most common types of capital outlays financed on a pay-as-go basis are equipment purchases, land acquisition, and minor construction and remodeling projects.

The advantages of pay-as-go financing for capital outlays are that (1) it encourages responsible spending by requiring the same officials who approve projects or outlays also to levy the taxes to pay for them; (2) it avoids paying the interest charges that are involved with bonding; and (3) it avoids the accumulation of large, fixed principal and interest payments in the operating budget.

A second method for financing capital projects is borrowing, which is designated pay-as-use because the financing comes ultimately from annual debt service payments made while the capital facility or equipment is being used. Pay-as-use financing is commonly employed when the project is very large relative to the community's resources and when the project need not be replaced for many years, e.g., a city hall or sewerage treatment plant. Pay-as-use financing is also necessary in communities that are growing rapidly. Such communities typically face substantial and rather immediate needs for public facilities that can be provided only through borrowing. Pay-as-use financing is often involved in annexation, in which extending municipal services to a new area requires new public facilities. Equipment acquisitions and remodeling or minor construction projects are usually not financed by borrowing.

Borrowing or pay-as-use financing for capital projects has several advantages. First, through annual debt service payments spread over the useful life of a project, the users of a project are charged for its costs plus interest. Second, in a period of inflation, pay-as-use financing enables a locality to borrow dear or expensive dollars and pay back with cheap ones. Third, when operating revenue or reserves are used to finance capital projects, the projects may have to be delayed until the funds are accumulated. Pay-as-use financing enables a capital need to be met almost immediately. Finally, although borrowing carries an interest cost, the use of operating revenue for capital projects has a corresponding opportunity cost, which is equal to the rate of return that the locality or its citizens could have earned by investing the current revenue rather than allocating it to finance the capital project.

Capital outlays or projects can also be financed with money accumulated in one or more capital reserve funds.[11] Once a reserve is established, monies can be accumulated in it by annual appropriation from the operating budget, interest earnings on money accumulated in the fund and invested, and other sources. When the reserve is big enough to pay for a project or outlay, it is spent on the project. Thus the timetable for reserve financing of capital outlays is opposite that for bond financing. In reserve financing, annual installment payments are made before the capital item is acquired, while in borrowing or pay-as-use financing, the annual debt service payments are made after acquisition.

Capital reserve financing is feasible for purchases of land and major equipment items. It can also be used for building projects of modest scope or to accumulate funds to match federal grants for large construction projects. Capital reserve financing is not practical to accumulate 100 percent of the funds required for a major construction project. The need for such a project cannot be seen far enough ahead to accumulate sufficient money to finance the project.

As already mentioned, some governments build up operating fund balances to amounts greater than needed as operating reserves and the balances are then drawn down to finance capital projects or outlays. The use of operating fund balances in this way is similar to capital reserve financing of capital requests. The difference is that state or local law often requires that money placed in a capital reserve be used only for capital purposes. On the other hand, money that is accumulated and held in fund balance can be used either for operating expenditures or for capital projects and outlays. This is a problem in building up and counting on "excess" operating fund balances to finance future capital outlays. The money being accumulated from year to year in this way can be drawn off very easily to finance operating expenditures rather than the capital project or outlay for which it was originally intended. Moreover, taxpayers sometimes object to the accumulation of large balances in operating funds. They may not understand that the money is being held for future capital purposes.

Lease-purchase agreements are an increasingly popular method of financing the acquisition of equipment, such as computers, fire trucks, sanitation vehicles, etc. Under a lease-purchase agreement, a government unit acquires possession and use of (if not title to) the equipment and agrees to make annual payments over a period ranging from two to ten years to pay for the equipment. The annual payments cover the original cash price of the equipment plus interest on whatever portion of the cash price is outstanding. If the unit fails to make one or more of the payments, the vendor can repossess the equipment. Once the annual lease payments are complete, the government owns the equipment free of lien. Long-term lease-purchase agreements are also used by some state and local governments to acquire major facilities like office buildings.

The disadvantage of lease purchase financing is that it is more expensive than pay-as-go or bond financing. Pay-as-go financing involves neither interest charges nor profit paid to the vendor for financing. Bond financing involves interest charges but no vendor's or finance company's profit, and the interest charged is at low tax-exempt rates rather than the higher taxable or private-sector rates. Some finance companies are, however, starting to offer tax-exempt interest rates on lease-purchase agreements to their governmental clients.

A revolving or intragovernmental service fund can also be used to finance equipment purchases. Such a fund is first established by transferring seed money from the general fund, but thereafter it is financed by annual rental charges to the line departments that use the equipment purchased and owned by the fund.

Special assessments are levied on property to finance specific improvements or services that benefit the property. Street-paving, curb and gutter, sidewalks, and water-sewer and other utility-line extensions are improvements for which special assessments are often charged.[12] Special assessments are supposed to be levied in proportion to the benefit that accrues to each property from a project, but as a practical matter, each benefiting property shares in a project's cost in the proportion that its area or front footage bears to the area or front footage of all property that benefits from the project. Still, property owners seldom pay the full cost of a project financed with special assessments. The governmental unit usually pays part of the cost because the community as a whole presumably benefits from most any project for which special assessments are levied. The special assessments owed by property owners can be paid in a lump sum or in installments plus interest over a multiyear period. If paid in a lump, the assessment revenue can be a significant source of financing for the project in question. If the project extends over many years and is divided in phases, installment payments resulting from assessments levied for work done in the earlier years of a project can be used to help finance the project in later years.

Federal grants and revenue sharing are another major source of financing for state and local government capital projects. We have already discussed the problems of projecting federal and state aid or grants in capital planning. A question to resolve at the budget stage of the capital budgeting process concerning federal grants or revenue available for capital purposes is whether the availability of such outside money should raise the priority of a request or move up the funding timetable for it. If the grant finances 100 percent of a project's cost, if the project will not lead to significant increases in operating expenditures, and if it benefits some group in the community, there is little reason not to go ahead and fund the project immediately. Or if a project is scheduled for implementation sometime in the near future and a grant becomes available for the current year to finance part of the project's cost, this is reason enough in most cases to proceed with the project ahead of schedule. On the other hand, the availability of a federal grant should not lead a government to undertake a project that it would not otherwise approve if the project entails significant capital or future operating costs for the government.

Capital Budgeting: Authorization of Capital Outlays

The third step in the budgetary phase of the capital budget process is the authorization of capital requests and the appropriation of money for the requests. This is usually done by the legislative or governing body, but occasionally legislative bodies provide a lump sum of money for capital requests for the year and delegate the authority to approve and fund individual requests to executive officials or a joint legislative-executive board. The usual vehicle for capital project authorization and appropriations are:

1. The annual or biennial budget ordinance or bill.
2. A capital projects ordinance that provides funding for all capital requests approved that year—these requests can come forward from the capital improvement program or from separate capital projects ordinances that are enacted throughout the year for for individual capital requests.
3. A bond order(s) approved by the governing board and perhaps by the voters.

Each method of authorizing capital outlays has advantages and disadvantages. Authorization in the annual or biennial budget helps assure that capital expenditure decisions are coordinated with operating budget decisions. Moreover, because annual or biennial budget authorization is only for a year or two at a time, it provides for periodic review of projects in process or under construction.

The disadvantages of authorizing capital outlays in the annual or biennial budget apply mainly to large multiyear projects. One is the incongruity of authorizing a project only a year or two at a time when in fact contracting and spending for the project and construction will take several years. A more difficult problem is that authorizing capital outlays in the annual operating or biennial budget can cause that budget to fluctuate erratically, so that confusion arises as to the amount of the on-going budget. Also, it can camouflage substantial growth in the operating budget. For example, a major increase in the operating budget can be obscured by the completion of a capital project and its removal from the annual or biennial budget in the same year.

The disadvantages of capital outlay authorization in the annual or biennial budget are addressed or overcome by using a capital projects ordinance.[13] This type of ordinance, whether comprehensive and embracing all major projects to be authorized in a year or broken into separate ordinances for individual projects, continues in force until the item is acquired or the project built. In other words, the authorization and the money appropriated by it do not lapse at the end of a fiscal year if not contracted or spent. Second, by authorizing capital projects separately from operating ones, current expenditures and the benefits flowing from them are matched more readily with annual revenues. Large capital outlays with benefits that occur in future fiscal years are segregated, and this helps decision-makers and the general public to determine precisely what the operating budget is and to identify and deal with changes and increases in that budget from year to year.

The disadvantages of relying on a capital projects ordinance to authorize capital outlays lie, first, in deciding whether all capital outlays or only those that are above a certain dollar level or of a specific nature—for example, those involving construction—will be authorized through such an ordinance. Presumably, small recurring capital outlays would be authorized in the operating budget, while major capital outlays would be approved by a projects ordinance. Second, if a capital projects ordinance is passed at a different time from the annual or biennial operating budget, capital decisions may be reached without giving adequate regard to their effect on annual operating needs. Finally, enacting capital project ordinances for individual projects or outlays may foster a fragmented approach to capital decision-making, each capital outlay being evaluated on its own merits but without regard to any priorities among different capital needs.

An approved bond order authorizes a jurisdiction to issue bonds to finance a capital request or project.[14] Passage of the bond order is also tantamount to authorizing a project, although officials can still choose not to issue the bonds and thereby block or postpone the project. In some states and jurisdictions, no further authorizing action or capital appropriations are necessary after the bond order has been passed. In other states and jurisdictions, the legislature or local governing body has to appropriate bond proceeds previously authorized by a bond order in the annual or biennial budget or in a capital projects ordinance before the bond proceeds can be spent. In these instances, the authorization process has two steps.

Implementing the Capital Budget

The last step in the capital planning and budget process is implementation. Failure here can put all the plans and financial arrangements made in the earlier stages of the process down the drain. Key facets of capital budget implementation are management and investment of the revenue available to finance a project, equipment purchases, and design and construction of buildings or improvements.

Management of revenue proceeds available for capital outlay purposes usually requires an investment plan. A locality may have revenue accumulated to finance a project well before the revenue must be spent. For example, on a construction project, bond proceeds are typically issued at the start of the project—preferably just after the bids for construction are received, and the proceeds are spent throughout the construction process. This means that idle funds are available that can be invested during construction. A plan should be formulated for investing these funds so that they do not lie idle in the locality's checking account but rather earn interest during construction and become available in cash in the appropriate amounts to meet payments to vendors and contractors when the payments are due.

Two important factors in implementing equipment purchases are timing and bid procedures. Equipment purchases are often financed from current revenue. This being so, such purchase should be timed to coincide with the period of greatest revenue in-flow from operating sources. Unlike expenditures for salaries and supplies that must be made regularly throughout the year, equipment purchases can be made when a government chooses. And since such purchases usually require substantial money, making them when revenue inflow is large eases a jurisdiction's cash-flow problem.

Equipment purchases must also be made according to the applicable purchasing laws. For example, in North Carolina any piece of equipment that costs $2,500 or more must be purchased according to formal bid procedures that involve public advertisement and submittal of sealed bids.[15] Moreover, any equipment that costs between $1,000 and $2,500 must be purchased using informal bid procedures, i.e., bids secured by telephone or in a similar manner.[16]

Implementing capital outlay decisions that involve construction is more complex. First, if the project is of any magnitude, an architect or engineer is usually employed to draw up plans and specifications. State law often requires that this be done when the cost of the project exceeds a certain amount[17] and, legal requirements aside, securing an architect usually pays off in avoiding costly construction mistakes. Architects are seldom selected by bidding. They are chosen through private negotiation focused primarily on design considerations, though if special skill or experience is not required, some jurisdictions select the architect by simple rotation. Architects are paid on a sliding scale, which starts with a flat fee plus a percentage of the project's cost, ranging from 3 or 4 to 10 percent, depending on the size of the project. Some governments employ one architect to draw the preliminary design for a project, and a second to do the final blueprints and specifications and to supervise construction. In reviewing architectural proposals and plans, local officials must balance high construction costs and low maintenance costs later versus low construction costs and high maintenance costs later.

Implementing a construction contract and supervising construction under a contract for a capital project carry special concerns. First, state law typically requires that any contract involving an estimated expenditure above a certain amount (e.g., $30,000 in North Carolina[18]) be let through formal bid procedures. Second, separate contracts may be required for different types of construction—general construction, heating, air conditioning, plumbing, electrical installation, and refrigeration.[19] Third, a performance bond or the equivalent is often required on any construction project. This bond protects the government financially from the contractor's failure to complete his work. A retainage provision written into the contract has a similar effect. Such a provision allows a locality to hold back a portion, usually 5 to 10 percent, of each month's payment to the contractor for work done during the month and construction materials delivered to the site. This money is not paid to the contractor until construction is complete and is satisfactory to the locality. Finally, during construction, the work done should be inspected frequently, daily if possible, by either the architect or the government's own engineer or building inspector.

Conclusion

We might ask here whether a particular town, city, county, or state should establish special procedures or a separate process for capital planning and budgeting. But the actual experience of state and local governments in making capital outlay decisions indicates that this would be an inappropriate question. Most governments of any size already use some of the steps that are described here as elements of capital budgeting. State legal provisions require the performance of some steps, especially those having to do with project authorization and implementation, and some of the other steps simply represent common-sense approaches to planning and carrying out capital outlay decisions.

Therefore, perhaps the better questions to ask are whether the individual procedures that a government has for making capital expenditures should be pulled together into a coordinated capital budget, and whether other missing elements or procedures—for example, the capital improvement program or long-range revenue forecast—should be added to form a more complete process for capital budgeting. Some of the criteria that will help a government answer these questions go back to the reasons cited for capital budgeting at the beginning of the article. Thus the more the following conditions hold, the more likely a government is to benefit from having a separate capital budget process: (1) the unit faces large capital needs requiring the expenditure of substantial amounts of money; (2) meeting these needs is likely to shape or alter the basic features of the community; (3) bonding will be required to meet at least some of the needs; and (4) other procedures will probably not guarantee that the needs are met in an orderly and fiscally sound manner.

A final factor that bears on whether a government should have a special process for capital budgeting and how complete the procedures in that process should be concerns the availability of investment funds to state and local governments in the future. Because of taxpayer revolts, G.O. bond issues will be much more difficult to pass in the future. Moreover, spending limits and high interest rates will make any borrowing that is done more expensive. The combination of these factors suggests that investment funds for state and local government capital projects and outlays will be in short supply in the future, adding another important reason for state and local governments to have full-fledged capital budgeting so that capital outlay allocations make the best use of limited resources.

Notes

1. G. David Quirin, *The Capital Expenditure Decision* (Homewood, Ill.: Richard D. Irwin, Inc. 1967), pp. 1-2.
2. National Committee on Government Accounting, *Government Accounting, Auditing and Financial Reporting* (Chicago: Municipal Finance Officers Association of the United States and Canada, 1968), p. 155.
3. See Charles D. Liner, "Projecting Local Government Revenues," *Popular Government* 43, no. 3 (Spring 1978), pp. 32-38, for a summary of revenue forecasting that is based on historical trends.
4. See "Urban Data Service," David A. Caputo and Richard L. Cole, *General Revenue Sharing: Initial Decisions* (Washington, D.C. International City Managers Association, Vol. 5, No. 12, December 1973). In North Carolina, some of the larger cities and counties have used most of their federal revenue sharing money to fund operating expenditures while the medium-sized and smaller cities have restricted revenue sharing for the most part to capital outlays.
5. N.C. Gen. Stat. §159-55.
6. The ratio of outstanding debt to appraised valuation of taxable property for all North Carolina cities and counties is maintained on file by the North Carolina Local Government, State Treasurer's Office, State of North Carolina.
7. J. Richard Aronson and Eli Schwartz, *Management Policies in Local Government Finance* (Washington: International City Managers Association, 1975), p. 325.
8. This method or measure of limiting local government debt is discussed in Lennox L. Moak and Albert M. Hillhouse, *Concepts and Practices in Local Government Finance* (Chicago: Municipal Finance Officers Association of the United States and Canada, 1975), pp. 278-79.
9. See Lennox L. Moak, *Administration of Local Government Debt* (Chicago: Municipal Finance Officers Association of the United States and Canada, 1970), Chapter 12 on "Revenue Bonds," particularly pp. 317-18.
10. For a discussion of payback, present worth, and other quantitative methods for evaluating capital projects, see National Association of Accountants, *Financial Analysis Techniques for Equipment Replacement Decisions* (New York: National Association of Accountants, 1965).
11. The use of capital reserve financing is discussed by Alan Walter Steiss, *Local Government Finance: Capital Facilities Planning and Debt Administration* (Lexington, Mass.: Lexington Books, 1975), pp. 105-107.
12. The use of special assessments by local governments is explained in Glen W. Fisher, *Financing Local Improvements by Special Assessments* (Chicago: Municipal Finance Officers Association of the United States and Canada, no date), pp. 59.
13. North Carolina municipalities and counties can appropriate money for capital outlays either in the annual budget ordinance or in a separate capital projects ordinance. See N.C. *Gen. Stat.* §159-13, -13.2.
14. See, for example, N.C. *Gen. Stat.* §159-54.
15. N.C. *Gen. Stat.* §143-129.
16. N.C. *Gen. Stat.* §143-131.
17. See, for example, N.C. *Gen. Stat.* §133-1.1 as amended.
18. N.C. *Gen. Stat.* §143-129 as amended.
19. See, for example, N.C. *Gen. Stat.* §143-128 as amended.

Unit II

Budget Execution

15 Introduction

This unit examines activities involved in performing the budget. Several operations receive attention, mainly management of *cash flow, debt* (including how third parties analyze a city's credit risk), *risks* broadly defined, *pension liabilities,* and *purchases.* Attention then turns to financial and administrative controls, with special attention directed at how the accounting system can provide data for management decision making. A section on reporting practices provides background on how reporting of financial and other data serves various needs. The last section on accountability pinpoints the purposes and usages of auditing.

Operations

This first section examines various operations involved in carrying out the financial plan of the governmental unit. Business managers historically have viewed liquidity (the flow of available cash) as fundamental. Governmental financial managers have started paying more attention to the flow of cash in an effort to identify periods when excess cash (more than needed to meet immediate needs) is on hand and periods when cash might be insufficient to meet demands. This topic is reviewed in Harold I. Steinberg and Donald Tashner's "Cash Management for Local Government." Astute management allows investment of excess cash, which results in added revenues without tax increases. As with most areas of public budgeting and finance, state laws often govern investment of idle cash. For instance, investments earned from monies retained in some earmarked account might be restricted for use only in that account. Thus, pooling of all excess cash might be hindered. Further, certain investment instruments—such as common stock—almost always are off limits for governments.

For Steinberg and Tashner, annual cash flow projections are the "basic tools" for monitoring a city's financial condition. However, quarterly cash flow projections are vital for daily control.

Forms and statements can provide basic information on where a government stands. However, effective managerial control is still the vital link between data collection and the conversion of the data into useful information. Nevertheless, there are some individuals in management positions—usually in staff or finance positions—whose contribution to the organization is often not clear. Techniques involved in cash management, such as setting the return on investment, can help "finance people" demonstrate their usefulness to the organization.

A deficit cash position during parts of the year might lead to the use of short-term borrowing. How can relying upon debt offer managers additional fiscal options? Debt management policies are especially important when financing large, costly capital improvement items that are to be paid for over a long period of time; debt management policies can also offer methods for dealing with short-term liquidity problems. Of course, short-term debt can be, and has been, misused in such cities as New York City and Cleveland.

A selection from the Governmental Finance Research Center ("State and Local Debt Policy and Management") offers instruction for developing sound debt policy for a local government. Debt management involves relations between the government and creditors located in New York City and other financial centers.

The Governmental Finance Research Center report brings forth clearly the implication a "debt policy" has for a local government:

> First, debt sold today must be repaid in the future and with interest. This will create an added fixed obligation in subsequent budgets. Furthermore, according to both practice and law, most long-term borrowing is done for purposes of financing long-lived, major capital projects. These projects become part of the public physical establishment and thereby influence patterns of growth and generate future operating expenditure requirements.

Investors in governmental debt instruments look to third-party assessments (ratings) of the government's credit risk. Two firms, basically similar in credit analysis methods utilized, dominate in this service to investors: Moody's Investors Service and Standard and Poor's (S&P) Corporation. A report by Standard and Poor's, "Municipal Bond Ratings," offers key insights into the bond rating process, especially for general obligation and revenue bonds. Credit analysis involves an attempt to determine the affected government's financial condition; adverse findings by credit rating firms, however, result in high interest rates for the debt issue. According to Standard and Poor's, rating the credit standing of private and public organizations has become essential today because of the large amount of money available for investment in the United States.

Weak and ineffective management may affect a government's credit rating. Moreover, governments often neglect the financial risks associated with inadequate insurance coverage, poor control of worker's compensation claims, and overly generous employee benefit plans. By paying closer attention to risk management principles, these and other exposures to financial loss can be identified and adequately handled.

"Advantages of a Risk Management Program," by Gerald Miller and Bartley Hildreth, offers an introduction to this long-neglected area of financial liability. Risk management and its liability protection program are based on four principles: ". . . identification, measurement, control, and finance." With its concern for loss prevention and control, risk management serves to unite the activities of safety, insurance, and some elements of employee benefits under one responsibility function. Once risks are better managed, cost savings can and have resulted.

On a related issue, pension plan administration deserves close scrutiny by budget makers. While costing out such a benefit is important, managing the pension program is even more critical. Poor management of pension program resources has led many governments to face financial difficulty. Why are pension plans so difficult to administer and what options are available for managers? Hildreth and Miller address these points and others in "Pension Policy and Management." Even governments operating under a state-controlled local pension system should become familiar with the pressures and issues facing pension administrators. The impact on the budget remains, regardless of whether local governments have direct control over the pension plan. No matter who controls the plan, the employer pays for employee pension benefits, and benefit levels are influenced by other compensation and work practices.

In closing this section, one last operational issue deserves attention—the government's purchasing policy. Though it is often neglected, purchasing can have important implications. Poor financial management practices, including delays of payments to vendors, can lead to an insufficient number of bidders for a government's needed purchases (such as garbage trucks, asphalt for the roads, and office supplies). The cost of items might increase because of this lack of competition among bidders. Furthermore, effective purchasing procedures offer opportunities for cost efficiencies. David Neuman and Paul Carren discuss two approaches in "Public Purchasing—Principles and Recommended Practices" that offer great cost-saving potential: centralized and cooperative purchasing. Like other areas of financial operation, purchasing practices depend upon a sound method for monitoring the condition of the city— the use of internal controls.

Controls

Internal control rests upon an accounting system. However, as Price Waterhouse and Company (one of the "big-eight" accounting firms) demonstrates in "Accounting and Administrative Controls," a comprehensive internal control system has both financial and administrative elements. Elements of financial control include methods to protect the integrity of transactions and assets, while administrative control mainly focuses upon the assignment of responsibility.

While accounting data is the "currency" of any control system, the overall accounting system serves as a data collection, storage, and format system for managers. That is, various records dealing with the receipt of money (e.g., property bills, court fines, license fee receipts) and its disbursement (e.g. payroll sheets, vouchers) must be organized and recorded in a way that gives decision makers an understanding of the organization's financial condition. Thus, the manner in which the accounting system is constructed and operated says much about the manager's ability to answer financial questions. Robert Reny offers a basic introduction to practical governmental accounting in "Municipal Accounting" and provides information on both double-entry bookkeeping and the critical elements of governmental accounting. He concludes by stressing the basic objective of municipal accounting and indicates how this type of accounting differs from, but is similar to, accounting in the private sector.

Readers must understand that "experts" disagree on proper governmental accounting principles. The National Council on Governmental Accounting, a spin-off of the Municipal Finance Officer's Association, offers its pronouncements, and the American Institute of Certified Public Accountants provides its *Industry Guide.* There is much agreement, but debate still rages over some elements. For example, accountants with strong private sector ties call for governments to use standard business practices, including the use of full accrual accounting, not modified accrual practiced by the more managerially advanced governments. Many suggest that governmental accounting is different from business accounting, in great part because of legal controls that result in the use of many specialized "funds" to segregate city monies according to use or sources.

A specialized form of accounting, cost accounting, provides essential data for managers planning to use advanced forms of budgeting (e.g., zero-base budgeting) that require efficiency and effectiveness measures. The total costs for a program, activity, or function depend upon figures for direct labor, services, and supplies and all indirect, or overhead, costs. "Cost Accounting," part of a manual prepared for local officials by the state of Rhode Island, introduces cost accounting and shows how it can be used.

Reporting

Communicating the government's financial profile to interested persons is important. The most common device is the annual audit, which conveys an end-of-year financial picture of the government's operation. Much controversy has arisen about the type of information that this report should present. One debated topic is the inability of most governmental financial statements to consolidate all operations into one statement of financial position. Governments traditionally resort to separate financial tables for each "fund." The result, as one study found, is a confusing mass of data, unlike reports compiled by business firms. For instance, General Motors used 24 pages (14 of which contained financial information) to convey in one of its recent annual reports that it had $31 billion in gross revenues with 734,000 employees. In contrast, a city with $1 billion in gross revenues and 50,000 employees required nearly 225 pages to show the results of its yearly operation. Most of the tables were, of course, of use only to management, not to citizens or other external readers.

Is there any hope in trying to read and interpret a government's financial statement? Yes, but first one must gain a basic understanding of governmental accounting concepts, such as those provided in the earlier selection by Reny. Building upon that knowledge, Vincent Pivnicny dissects a financial statement in "A Primer on Reading Local Government Financial Statements." Pivnicny converts a cash-based statement to a modified accrual one. Along the way, he clarifies many accounting concepts. Furthermore, he explores additional accounting and budgeting concepts, such as the "balancing" of a municipal budget.

Besides the government's annual report, other types of financial communications are important, including interim, official, and special purpose reports. "Financial Communications," a report by Coopers and Lybrand (another big-eight firm), provides an outline to the different types of financial reports. In it, the big-eight accounting firm underscores the fact that most financial reports can and should contain not only financial data but also social, economic, and basic administrative material. This is especially true when official statements are prepared to secure favorable bond ratings for debt obligations, given the earlier finding from the Standard and Poor's report that bond analysts examine a wide variety of data, such as changing demographic data.

Who uses governmental financial communications? A variety of people have some interest in the operation of a particular governmental unit. While elected officials, managers, and employees have perhaps the most direct personal interest, citizens (the owners, so to speak) also have a vested interest, however unarticulated it may be. Even some outsiders have an interest, namely investors in the government's debt. Thus, financial communications must respond to various users' needs. Are the needs of all users the same? No. While state auditors might want detailed data to check on local compliance, citizens might express little interest in anything other than a brief summary. Investors, however, might have the most vocal demand for specialized information.

Sidney Davidson and his colleagues, in "The Needs of Users of Governmental Financial Statements," explore the uses to which financial statements can be put by state and local governments. Users of financial information center on four groups:

1. the general public, made up largely of the taxpayers of the governmental unit preparing the report;
2. investors and creditors (and their advisors), both present and potential, of the governmental unit;
3. employees and potential employees of the governmental unit; and
4. officials, both elective and appointive, of the governmental unit.

Accountability

The budgetary system can be viewed as a way to hold public officials and managers accountable for the manner in which the public's tax dollars are allocated and spent. Auditing has evolved as a formalized approach for dealing with the accountability question. While auditing has linkages with accounting controls used, more is involved. Harold Steinberg ("Understanding Municipal Financial Audits") shows what guides the auditors' work (auditing principles) and what goes into expressing an audit opinion.

The U.S. General Accounting Office (GAO) has adopted a body of audit standards applicable to governmental programs that calls for more nontraditional ways of using the auditor. These standards are not obligatory in all situations, but local government managers can learn from the GAO's clear enunciation of the features of an audit. Even more, the GAO calls for movement away from sole reliance upon auditing for mere *financial compliance* and into auditing of *economy/efficiency* and *program results.*

Building upon the GAO standards, Alfred Cancellieri and Darryl Enstrom ("The Expanded Scope of Government Auditing") give examples of what is involved in each of the three elements of auditing—financial and compliance; economy and efficiency; and program results—and seek a better sense of the "expanded scope" of public sector auditing as proposed by GAO. This expanded scope should benefit government, especially in today's climate of scarcity and cutback.

What is involved in the actual audit process? A guide for local officials in the State of Massachusetts ("The Municipal Audit: Choice and Opportunity") provides a summary of the audit sequence. Fundamentally, the selection demonstrates why elected officials should involve themselves in choosing an auditor and in monitoring the audit itself, and how officials might pursue this responsibility to achieve some of the benefits of having an independent audit.

Summary

As this collection of essays shows, development and execution of the local government budget is based on assumptions, knowledge, and skills. An effort has been made to highlight critical concepts and practices that might enable budget participants to understand and use the budget-making authority of local governments better. Moreover, the approach taken here has attempted to reveal how budgeting can, and is, integrated with features of accounting, auditing, and financial reporting, evaluation, and operations.

16 Cash Management for Local Government

Harold I. Steinberg and Donald Tashner

[Editor's Note: While this article reports on trends that are somewhat dated, it does represent a comprehensive guide of significant use.]

The objective of cash management for local government is to produce as much revenue from the investment of available cash as is practicable. Since most villages, towns or cities obtain most of their cash from tax receipts during two short periods of the year, but spend it evenly throughout the entire year, they frequently have substantial sums available for short-term investment. Income from such investment can help to offset at least partially the need for additional taxes. There are other advantages to cash management that this article will touch on as the subject is developed in the form of a series of recommendations designed to achieve a sound cash management program for a local government entity (later referred to, for convenience, as the "city"). These recommendations are discussed under the following four categories:

Bank relations. This involves determining the appropriate number and type of bank accounts for fulfilling the city's needs, and then selecting banks and establishing bank relationships on a mutually beneficial basis.

Collections. The emphasis here is on obtaining and depositing funds due as quickly as possible.

Cash flow planning and management. Eventually, all monies collected must be used to discharge obligations. The payment of these obligations, however, can be so managed as to increase their availability for investment purposes.

Investment policy and practices. The manner in which available funds are invested in various investments for given periods has a major impact on cash management results.

Bank Relations

Proper banking relationships are an important element in cash management. Banks can help the city and particularly its cash managers with such valuable services as lock box operations and transfer services to accelerate the collection and investment of cash, account reconciliation services to assist in the timely reconciliation of cash balances, and repurchase agreements for short-term investing purposes. Equally important, the city has a chance to support those financial institutions which in turn support the local economy.

Overriding this whole aspect of cash management is a need to conduct bank relations on an ethical and business-like basis. A city must choose its depositories on the basis of services rendered to and prices paid by the city. To do otherwise would impose a less than optimal condition on the city government. Likewise, the city must allow the banks to recover demonstrated costs and earn a reasonable profit. Any other policy is at best unfair and likely to undermine the banks' viability.

Reprinted from Management Controls 23 *(January-February 1976): 22-28. By permission of Peat, Marwick, Mitchell, & Co.*

Minimize Number of Bank Accounts

Cities frequently have an excessive number of bank accounts, with many accounts having small or zero balances and a limited amount of activity. With so many accounts, much time is required to prepare deposits and checks, transfer excess sums, and reconcile balances each month. From a cash management point of view, the city loses the opportunity to operate with balances that are substantial enough either to elicit attractive proposals for maintaining its accounts or to invest meaningfully. Under these circumstances, consolidating existing bank accounts into a fewer number is often desirable. It should be noted that the emphasis should be placed on the reduction in the number of bank accounts, not the number of banks. The selection of the appropriate banks is another topic for discussion.

The criteria for making the consolidation should include the following:

- Size of the average balance.
- Nature of receipts and disbursements.
- Need to facilitate interaccount transfers.
- Existence of restrictions against commingling.

There are several other considerations that also apply. Certain banks with which a city might want to do business may be relatively small and might not, under state banking regulations, be permitted to maintain large balances of government funds. Hence, certain accounts might have to be reduced to a size that permits these smaller banks to be accommodated. Also, in some instances, several small accounts can be combined into a single account without disturbing the ability to maintain individually reconcilable sub-disbursement accounts.

Establish Bank Relationships That Permit Reduction of Bank Balances

Once accounts are consolidated, a city should distribute its funds to various banks and maintain balances at appropriate levels, that is to say, at a level sufficient to pay the bank for services rendered plus a profit, but not in excess of that amount. By so doing, larger amounts of funds will be available for investment. One way of accomplishing this objective is for the city to define the types and magnitude of the services required and then ask banks to submit competitive bids. Larger banks will usually identify their costs and the balance necessary to offset the costs. In the absence of formal cost systems, smaller banks may specify only the required compensating balance.

There are other benefits accruing to a city using this approach. Specifically, it:

- Frees the city administration from any possible suggestion of favoritism.
- Provides for fair competition based upon service requirements established by the city.
- Encourages banks to add services to the basic requirements.
- Minimizes the cost of services.

It should be noted that it is sometimes desirable or necessary to give preference to locally-based banks, particularly if their loan and investment activities are oriented toward the city.

Review Bank Charges

At this point, a discussion of bank costing practices would be helpful to describe how charges and compensating balances are determined.

Banks typically are compensated for the services they provide by means of compensating balances. Compensating balances are collected deposits net of checks paid that are left on deposit by the bank's customers. The bank uses these sums (net of their reserve requirement) for making loans and investments to generate bank income. Since the amount of compensating balances required is dependent upon the types of services provided and the volume of transactions, it is first necessary to determine what banking services are needed or desired. Some examples of services are:

- Checking services. (The number and type of transactions–i.e., deposits, checks, wire transfers–should be estimated.)
- Lock box and window collection services.
- Daily armored car pickup.
- Night depository bags.
- Bank reconciliation of accounts.

The banks handling the city's accounts should be asked periodically to report their charges for these services and the offsetting compensating balance required. Quotations to service particular accounts should be obtained from banks other than the current depository, simply to ensure that the city is obtaining a reasonable price, and that a change to a more favorable situation is not warranted. As indicated, smaller banks may not have data available regarding their costs of services, and consequently they might specify only a required compensating balance and refrain from identifying specific charges for services rendered.

Exhibit 1 illustrates how a determination may

Exhibit 1: *Determination of Minimum Balances and Investable Funds*

Month of July:

Average gross balance	$ 2,073,332
Less average uncollected funds (bank float)	140,924
Average balances available to support bank services	1,932,408
Less average balances required to support bank services	314,081
Excess (deficient) collected bank balances	$ 1,618,327

Account charges:

Monthly activity	Quantity	Unit price	Total cost
Account reconciliation	3,329	.023	$ 76.57
Checks paid	6,910	.108	746.28
Deposits	13,411	.040	536.44
Other debits	–	–	–
Other credits	131	.30	39.30
Wire transfer	3	4.000	12.00
Lock box	2,721	0.149	405.43
Other services	–	–	–
Total activity charges			$ 1,816.02

Average balance required to support services:

Total activity charges	$ 1,816.02
Divided by earnings allowance–8.260%	21,985.71
Multiplied by 12 months	263,828.52
Divided by 1 – .16 (16% reserve requirement) to obtain average balances required to support services	$314,081.57

Note: If more than one account is maintained at the same bank, the calculation should be made on a combined basis.

Explanation of terms

- *Average gross balance*–the total account balance according to the demand deposit records of the bank. It represents total deposits less checks paid and any bank charges made directly to the account.
- *Average uncollected funds*–that portion of the gross balance which has not cleared through the banking system and is therefore not available for investment purposes. There are three classes of funds: immediate availability; one-day float; and two-day float. Float days are based upon the location of the bank on which the deposited checks were drawn according to a standard established by the Federal Reserve Bank. The computation is usually made based upon a weighted average float computed on a daily basis.
- *Average balances available to support bank services*–the difference between the average gross balance and the average uncollected funds. It represents the average collected balance for the period.
- *Average balances required to support bank services*–the collected balance that must remain on deposit with the bank as compensation for the services provided.
- *Excess (deficient) collected bank balances*–average amount of collected funds available for investment by the city during the period. When this is a negative number (deficient), the bank is not able to recover the costs of servicing the account and earn a reasonable profit.
- *Account charges*–the bank's prices for the services provided during the period.
- *Total activity charges*–the sum of the individual service charges for the month.

be made of the compensating balance required to service an account. The same approach may be used to verify bank charges for services provided and to adjust balances left with a bank to support these services. It should be remembered, however, that total activity charges will vary from month to month so that the required compensating balance will also vary.

Have Banks Telephone Collected Balances Daily

In order to maximize its investment opportunities, a city should know at all times the precise amount of collected funds in its major accounts. Hence, banks should be directed to telephone a designated city employee each morning to provide up-to-date information as to collected balances. Such information is also useful in verifying the bank's calculations of required compensating balances. It can be used to refine the city's estimates of average float, which in turn are used in the projections of future cash balances. ("Float" is the term used to describe the amount of funds available in a bank account as a result of checks written but not yet presented for payment. It must be reduced by the amount of checks deposited but not yet collected by the bank. As the latter is usually the smaller amount, organizations often have a positive float.)

Utilize Restricted Funds for Compensating Balances

In the case of some federal and state grants, investment of these special funds prior to the time they are disbursed for the purposes of the grant is not permitted. With others, the funds can be invested, but the interest must be transmitted to the funding agency or included with the original grant and expended according to the grant's provisions. The investment income cannot be credited to the city's general fund. State Aid to Disadvantaged Children, Elementary and Secondary Education Act, Title I and Adult Basic Education grants are examples of the latter.

When such funds exist, they can be used to satisfy, at least in part, compensating balance requirements. By so doing, city funds otherwise required for compensating balances will be freed for investment purposes.

Collections

The efficient collection of cash receipts is the second element in an effective cash management program. A lock box system for collecting current tax receipts is one example of how monies can be deposited into a bank quickly and thus be available for subsequent investment. Discussed below are recommendations for improving other aspects of the cash collection process.

Provide Return Envelopes Addressed to Lock Box

While a bank lock box is often made available to collect semi-annual real estate tax payments and annual personal property and motor vehicle taxes, many taxpayers may nevertheless remit payments directly to the tax collector's office or other city departments. If all payments are mailed to the lock box, clerical effort can be reduced and receipt of cash by the bank accelerated. Therefore, return addressed envelopes, imprinted with the lock box number, should be provided with all tax bills. Consideration should also be given to the advisability of imprinting a return postage permit number as a further inducement for earlier tax payments to the bank lock box. Needless to say, even without a lock box system, return addressed envelopes expedite the tax collection process.

Minimize Number of Lock Box Exceptions

A number of exceptional conditions can exist in a lock box system which preclude the bank from processing the tax payment check immediately. In those circumstances, the check, along with the tax bill and other identifying material, are transmitted to the city tax collector. Many of these conditions, however, do not warrant delay in depositing the checks. Examples are checks which do not match the amount of the tax bill or are received without a tax bill or with the wrong bill.

In such instances (and if the check is not marked paid in full), the check should be deposited immediately and a photocopy of the check along with other supporting documents forwarded to the tax collector. The follow-up effort required to reconcile the discrepancies should still be made but the time involved in sending checks to the tax collector and getting them back for deposit would be eliminated. Hence, greater sums would be available sooner for investment purposes.

Monitor and Expedite Receipt of Grants and Subsidies

A substantial amount of local government revenues is received each year from various federal and state agencies in the form of grants and subsidies. Examples include educational grants, payments in lieu of taxes, and tax abatement payments. Maximum monies can be made available if the local government knows in advance when grant monies are to be received, and the schedule of grant payments is adhered to. Unfortunately, this is not always the case. One of the main reasons for such delays is that the liaison function for grant applications and follow-up is typically dispersed among various local government offices. Since the various programs are usually not adversely affected by a delay in grant receipts, there is little motivation for liaison personnel to vigorously pursue the earliest possible collection.

To overcome this situation, a grant-monitoring system should be established that enables the city's director of finance or other responsible official systematically and continually to be aware, for cash forecasting purposes, of the size and timing of grant receipts. Further, if applications are required for the monies to be paid, the monitoring function can ensure that the applications are filed on a timely basis. And finally, if the payments are not received as scheduled, this procedure would facilitate follow-up.

It should be emphasized that this system is not a grant-locating or program-monitoring system. Those functions remain with personnel in the operating departments. This procedure is simply a means of ensuring that the major sums represented by grants and subsidies are received on time. There is nothing improper, however, in several municipalities joining together with their state association and attempting to persuade the state or other grantee to adopt grant payment dates that are more favorable to the individual cities.

Accelerate Collection of Large Tax Receipts

Some tax receipts are so large that their collection by the bank and their availability for investment even a few days earlier than normal can have considerable monetary value. Some of these checks may be drawn on out-of-state banks. Consideration should be given to making arrangements for the local deposit of such checks and immediate wire transfer of the funds to the city's tax collection bank.

There are other procedures that may be instituted to accelerate collections. For instance, cities provide many services for which monies are collected. Parking meter collections are periodically brought to central collection points; traffic fines are collected at the police station or courts; monies are received in the building and other departments for licenses and permits; golfers remit green fees at the golf course; etc. A well-run city reviews these collection procedures periodically to make sure that they are operating efficiently, that the money is deposited intact daily, and that the central treasury is immediately advised of the amount of the deposit.

In line with this concern, a city can benefit greatly by improving the sensitivity of its many cash-handling employees to efficient cash management. Some cities conduct a cash management seminar at which are explained reasons and methods for improved cash management. Local banks are usually quite willing to help conduct such seminars.

Cash Flow Planning and Management

Cash flow planning and management has two aspects. One is determining and recording projected cash receipts and disbursements so that information is available upon which optimal investment decisions can be made. The other is scheduling outflows of cash in order to maximize the availability of funds. Following are some recommendations pertaining to these essential activities.

Prepare Annual Cash Flow Projections

While short-term cash forecasts are very useful to help in day-to-day investment decisions, they do not portray adequately the flow of funds over an entire year. An annual cash plan is a necessity since it:

- Provides a reasonable approximation of the availability of and need for cash during the entire year, and this in turn permits an overall investment strategy to be developed.
- Constitutes a framework from which the quarterly cash forecasts can be developed.
- Indicates potential difficulties caused by cash receipt and disbursement timing differences so that early corrective actions can be taken.
- Encourages "cash consciousness" on the part of all who are involved in providing information and developing the projections.

The annual cash plan should be developed in terms of months rather than the exact dates receipts and disbursements will occur. Also, it need not be precise as to amounts since it is impossible to forecast exactly in advance such items as payroll requirements, rate of tax collections, and receipts from other sources. The quarterly cash flow projections are the vehicle to determine more precise timings and dollar amounts.

Specifically, a cash plan should be developed prior to the beginning of each fiscal year to set forth the pattern of cash flows during the year. It should include projections of cash receipts and disbursements for each month of the coming fiscal year. The plan should be constructed from the information contained in the operating budget, tax schedules, the capital budget, and such other pertinent data as notifications of state revenues to be received on a reimbursement basis. An analysis of the preceding year's monthly receipts and disbursements will provide helpful input. Interviews with key administrators might indicate new factors to consider. The annual cash flow projection, moreover, need not be done in exhaustive detail but can be limited to the major categories of receipts and disbursements, such as taxes, grants, payrolls, accounts payable, capital projects, and pension payments.

Prepare Quarterly Cash Flow Projections

An annual cash flow projection is the basic tool for determining the overall flow of funds and monitoring a city's liquidity. It does not, however, provide the detail necessary for guiding specific actions. Thus, for day-to-day control, detailed quarterly cash flow projections should be maintained. Exhibit 2 is an illustration of a quarterly cash flow projection format. The following are some pertinent procedures:

- Project weekly cash receipts from all sources, including tax collections, grants and subsidies, bond proceeds, and maturing investments.
- Project weekly cash needs for the subsequent three-month period by:
  (a) Determining payroll.
  (b) Estimating disbursements required for accounts payable. The disbursements should be made, if possible, on Thursday or Friday so that the checks will not reach the city's bank until after the weekend, thus making additional float available for investment purposes. Also, purchase invoices should not be paid until just prior to the time cash discounts expire or payment is due.
  (c) Obtaining estimates of the required rates for construction payments from capital projects coordinator.
  (d) Listing debt service payments requirements.
  (e) Listing pension payment requirements.
- Calculate weekly cash flow excess or deficiency.
- Calculate closing cash balances for the banks based upon opening balances plus (or minus) the excess (deficiency) cash flow for the week. Subtract the amounts that are to be left as compensating balances to obtain the book balance available for investment.
- Estimate the amount in float.

The resulting figure is the amount available that week to be invested until again needed for normal disbursements.

Exhibit 2: *Quarterly Cash Flow Projection, Three-Month Period*

	Week-ending		
	7-x	7-x	Etc.
Cash receipts:			
City tax collections			
Federal and state grants and subsidies			
Proceeds from bond sales			
Maturing investments			
Interest on investments			
Other			
Total projected cash receipts	____	____	____
Cash disbursements:			
Payroll			
Accounts payable			
Construction payments			
Debt service			
Pension payments			
Other			
Total projected cash disbursements	____	____	____
Excess (deficiency) of weekly cash flows	====	====	====
Cash balances:			
Opening balance			
Excess (deficient) cash flow			
Closing balance	____	____	____
Minimum balances to be left on deposit	____	____	____
Bank balance available for (required from) investments			
Estimated float	____	____	____
Balance available for investments	====	====	====

Note: This cash flow projection is a work sheet for managing cash resources. As such, changes in cash flow expectations should be recorded as they occur. In addition, at the beginning of each month the forecast should be updated to include the forthcoming three-month period.

Monitor Actual Cash Flows against Projections

It is one thing to project cash flows and make decisions based upon those projections, but it is quite another to fulfill the projections so that the decisions are always the best. The quality of projections can be continuously upgraded if the actual flows are constantly monitored against the projections.

Monitoring requires a comparison of the actual book and bank balances with the original projections on a fairly regular basis. When there are major variations between the projected book and actual book balances, it is usually because of some identifiable condition such as a different-than-anticipated spending rate or slow tax collections. The appropriate corrective actions should be taken and future projections modified.

If the projections and actual book balances are fairly close but the bank balances vary materially, it is likely that the float is different than anticipated. Again, the reason must be identified and the remaining projections modified, if appropriate.

Pay Particular Attention to the Scheduling of Large Payments

As indicated, small recurring payments should be scheduled to provide the city with maximum float. For example, accounts payable checks should be mailed Thursday to arrive Friday and reach the city's depositories no earlier than after the weekend. Attention should also be given to construction, pension and other large payments in order to (1) know precisely when they must be made, and (2) adjust these payment dates, if possible, to take better advantage of float. The idea is to avoid unexpected large payments to contractors that become due suddenly. Perhaps the easiest way to avoid this problem is to maintain close internal communications. For instance, if a capital projects coordinator monitors construction projects, he should be responsible for advising the finance department regularly as to the status of projects and the impact of payment requirements.

Investment Policy and Practices

Investment policy and practices is the last element in an effective cash management function, and the one that enables the city to gain monetarily from the previous efforts. There are some basic rules and approaches to follow, but, in the final analysis, success in short-term investing is the result of alertness, experience with the process, and finesse.

The first rule is that the highest interest rate is not always the best rate; safety and liquidity are vital considerations. Another consideration is that monies should only be invested in securities that will mature prior to the time the funds are required for operating purposes. Furthermore, even if the monies will not be needed for operating purposes, the rates projected to be available when the investments mature must be considered.

The first step in the investment process is to aggregate as large a sum as possible. Decreasing the number of banks and bank accounts, as described in the first section of this article, will contribute to this. When there are funds available for investment in more than one bank account, consideration should be given to pooling the funds.

Next, an investment strategy should be developed. Most strategies involve the purchase of treasury bills and/or certificates of deposit maturing each week in an amount sufficient to cover the disbursements projected for that week. When the investments come due, part of the proceeds is placed in demand deposit accounts and part is invested in repurchase agreements to mature on subsequent days as checks are presented for payment. Indeed, some banks offer automatic repurchase agreement plans under which the bank automatically invests excess balances.

Funds available for investment should be offered to several banks in order to obtain the most desirable interest rate. This is particularly important when securities are "rolled over." Banks should not be permitted to reinvest automatically since the interest rate a particular bank will apply to an extended investment may not be the best rate available that day. Furthermore, including the funds from maturing investments in the total funds available for investment that day increases the amount available for investment.

Incidentally, while laws vary from state to state, in most instances a city need not limit itself to the interest rates offered by local banks. If the local rates are not sufficiently attractive, a city is obligated to its taxpayers to consider rates from out-of-town banks, including those located in the state capital.

Conclusion

Interest rates in 1974 were extraordinarily high, and municipal officials were using cash management as a painless way to raise funds to offset ever-increasing levels of expenditures. In some communities, as much as 4 percent of total revenues was raised through investment income. Interest rates in 1975, however, were lower and it probably will be more difficult to raise equivalent monies through investment income. For that reason alone, finance directors, controllers, and others concerned with municipal management should make sure that their city's cash management function is as effective as possible.

Directors of finance occupy a difficult and rather unique position. The heads of the many departments that provide citizens with services are responsible for substantial expenditures. However, many program objectives are imbedded within those departments' programs, by reference to which they can demonstrate and even report improvements in efficiency and effectiveness. By contrast, it is the hapless role of the director of finance to control the expenditure of funds but there is less opportunity to judge his contribution to their effective management. Setting investment return as one of the objectives for the director of finance and then evaluating performance in relation to that objective is one way by which he can demonstrate his contribution to the ongoing efforts to which all conscientious government officials are dedicated—the achievement of more effective and economical government.

17 State and Local Debt Policy and Management

Even for the smallest governments, the raising of capital through the selling of securities to private investors can involve unfamiliar processes, technical experts and relatively large amounts of money. Therefore, public officials and administrators are well advised to be aware of the fundamental procedures and practices used in designing and marketing municipal securities. This paper reviews the following elements: formulating a debt policy, uses of debt, types of instruments, design and sale of issues, debt limitations, debt capacity and credit ratings.

Formulating a Debt Policy

Because of its visibility and long-term consequences, debt management can be a particularly important element in local government decision making. In order to borrow, governmental borrowers must appeal to the investing public for their funds. Emergencies have arisen from time to time that have caused defaults or near-defaults on the part of state and local units. Along with high rates of interest, such periods—as occurred in 1975 and again in 1980—usually bring intense examination of the public's debt.

Debt management policies and issuing procedures should meet four requirements:

- Guidelines as to the appropriate and prudent uses of borrowing;
- Statutory and constitutional requirements placed upon the use of debt;
- Acceptable disclosure practices as enforced in the private financial markets; and
- Consideration of questions of timing and design to maximize the efficiency of borrowing under various market conditions.

For most governments, debt management involves a complex of factors born out of both practical necessity and legal tradition. A "debt policy" as such is seldom found in a particular document or set of principles, and the financial planner must take into consideration several factors in policy formulation. First, debt sold today must be repaid in the future and with interest. This will create an added fixed obligation in subsequent budgets. Furthermore, according to both practice and law, most long-term borrowing is done for purposes of financing long-lived, major capital projects. These projects become part of the public physical establishment and thereby influence patterns of growth and generate future operating expenditure requirements.

Uses of Debt

Most borrowing is done to finance capital facilities. This is true not only because of restrictions on the use of public debt, but also because capital facility financing possesses certain attributes that make the use of credit efficient and equitable. Capital investments are those whose useful lives exceed more than one period and, therefore, whose benefits accrue over time. Such expenditures in some cases may be financed by current taxes or grants, but they are usually financed by borrowing.

Reprinted from Elements of Financial Management *(Washington, D.C.: Government Finance Research Center, Municipal Finance Officers Association, May 1980).*

The need for borrowing to finance public facilities may be particularly great in growing areas. Growth in population and income almost always requires capital outlays that anticipate the ultimate growth in tax revenues. Exclusive reliance on the pay-as-you-go approach to finance capital investments out of current savings can inhibit the growth of a jurisdiction and deter the efficiency of capital investment.

Overall debt policy must be meshed clearly with growth planning and a prudent concept of what the fiscal and economic capacity of the debtor will be in the future. It should be integrated with the process of capital programming and budgeting. Making commitments to carry out specific projects necessarily involves planning for their financing. If the capital improvements program is to be an effective guide for financial planning and a means of achieving a government's long-range physical, social and economic goals, then the capital planning and budgeting process should connect all projects systematically.

Types of Borrowing

There are two basic choices that must be made at the outset of a borrowing decision: the type of security and its maturity.

General Obligation vs. Revenue Bonds

As a general rule, the securities market is sensitive to the differences among the security types. Given a level of indebtedness, the broader the security base in terms of potential revenues to repay the obligation, the better the market will treat the security.

With general obligation debt, the general taxing power of the jurisdiction is pledged to pay both principal and interest. To sell such debt, voter approval may be required, and various debt and tax limitations usually restrict its use.

Various types of limited obligations, known as revenue bonds, frequently are sold for purposes, such as water and sewer systems, that produce revenues. Such bonds usually are not included in debt limits, as are general obligation bonds, nor do they usually require voter approval because they are not backed by the full faith and credit of the local jurisdiction, but rather are repaid from various service charges or fees.

Generally speaking, tax-supported general obligation debt is considered a superior form of debt by the market because of its standing as a full-faith obligation of the unit. It typically carries a lower interest rate than revenue-secured debt. There are many circumstances, however, where revenue-secured debt has advantages, particularly when it comes to allocating the costs of facilities to the actual users. But, the most frequent reason for using the revenue bond (and associated special-purpose funds or districts) has been to circumvent debt and referendum requirements or to finance purposes that are beyond the legal authority of a general unit of government.

The rapidly growing use of revenue bonds to finance a variety of quasi-public purposes (such as industrial development, housing and pollution control) has added greatly to the size and complexity of the tax-exempt bond market.

Long-Term vs. Short-Term Borrowing

Another important choice in security type is between long-term borrowing (that which extends beyond a year) and short-term borrowing (that with a maturity of a year or less).

There are three types of short-term debt: (1) the bond anticipation note, which anticipates the ultimate sale of a long-term bond; (2) the tax anticipation note, which is sold to bridge gaps between expenditures and expected tax proceeds; and (3) revenue anticipation notes, short-term securities that are sold in anticipation of general revenues or grant receipts. The bond anticipation is the form of short-term security most suited to the overall problem of debt management, whereas short-term instruments in anticipation of taxes and revenues typically are cash management concerns.

Debt Issue Design and Sale

Bond issues may have several characteristics which can either detract or enhance their marketability and can either simplify or complicate the problems of debt management. It is possible to design bond instruments and sales to attract the most favorable bids and to time sales to coincide with accommodative market conditions. Among the technical features of bonds are the choice of maturity structure and the total maturity, the type of sale (competitive or negotiated), and whether or not the bonds will be subject to call prior to the stated maturity date. Sometimes, these characteristics are set by state law and are not subject to tailoring at the local level.

Most experts favor giving officials charged with bond issuance as much flexibility as possible in order to tailor bonds for the market. Unusually complex situations or the issuer's status as a "difficult deal" may require a negotiated sale. But normally, award after competitive bidding is preferable.

Another matter of growing importance is disclosure, that is, the design and dissemination of information provided to investors in conjunction with the bond sale. Recent bond market difficulties and concerns about legal exposure under antifraud provisions has greatly increased the amount of detail supplied in a bond sale. Underwriters and investors are now demanding and receiving much more extensive documentation, often including a statement by officials that the information contained in a document represents the situation truthfully.

Another aspect of selling bonds that has attracted some attention is the use of the true interest cost method (TIC) instead of the conventional net interest cost method (NIC) in making awards. The arguments involved in favor of the TIC have to do with the subtleties of present-value mechanics. Nonetheless, it has been amply demonstrated that the use of the NIC procedure can be inefficient and can result in higher than necessary interest costs for state borrowers.

Debt Limitations

Most states have enacted constitutional or statutory restraints on the debt powers of local government units. The two primary types of restrictions that have been applied to local jurisdictions are:

- A limit on the level of debt outstanding (frequently expressed as a percentage of the taxable real property in the jurisdiction); and
- A requirement for a local referendum to authorize the issuance of bonds.

Over the years, several problems have arisen with the use of legalistic controls on local debt activity. Debt limitations and restrictions on the use and design of financing instruments frequently proved to be too restrictive and inflexible in the flow of changing conditions. The referendum requirement likewise proved to be an obstacle to financing projects that many voters—if not a majority—thought unnecessary. Major consequences of the traditional requirements were the development of the "special fund" doctrine and the "limited obligation," and the birth of special districts and authorities that have been empowered to issue debt outside of the traditional constraints.

Debt Capacity

Legal limitations on the amount of outstanding debt provide a ceiling that is seldom hit by borrowers. Of greater practical importance is how much debt and what composition of debt is acceptable to the municipal bond market. The market is particularly concerned about the unit's capacity to support debt-service payments along with its other expenditures, and its overall economic and fiscal climate. Furthermore, the market's perceptions of what is desirable or at least acceptable will change, depending on conditions in the securities market.

Not surprisingly, the bond market does not use one individual indicator of debt capacity. Standard measures of debt capacity usually relate to the revenue base and the general level of economic activity. They can also be heavily influenced by the unit's fiscal behavior, whether or not it has operating deficits, and also the market's perception of the desirability and financial integrity of the programs being financed.

Credit Ratings

The great number of state and local issues that come to market has led to an institutionalization of much credit opinion in the form of bond ratings. Issued by rating agencies, the best known and most widely accepted opinions are those of Moody's Investor Service and Standard and Poor's. For a fee, the agencies express an opinion as to the credit quality of individual bond issues or, in the case of general obligation issues, of the borrower itself. There is no formula for weighting factors that determine the agency's opinion, but they include fiscal standing of the borrower, general economic conditions, and certain legal and administrative qualities.

The most important thing about the rating is its impact on interest costs. Although the differences among the various security grades will fluctuate depending upon market conditions, the very highest grade bonds (Aaa) often sell at interest rates a full percentage point or more below those of the lowest grade securities (Baa).

For all practical purposes, a bond issue of even small size must have a rating in order to be sold in the national markets. Ratings typically cost between $1,000 and $5,000, depending on the size and complexity of the bond issue.

Bibliography

Calvert, Gordon, ed. *Fundamentals of Municipal Bonds.* Washington, D.C.: Securities Industry Association, 1972. 168 pages.

Provides a brief technical description of municipal bonds, how to issue them, and the parties involved in the various transactions. Available from the publisher, 20 Broad St., New York, N.Y. 10005.

Coe, Charles K., and Stallings, C. Wayne. *A Debt Management Handbook for Small Cities and Other Governmental Units.* Chicago: Municipal Finance Officers Association, 1978. 65 pages.

Provides basic information for those with little exposure to the area of municipal finance. Besides helping with the terminology, it gives a "how to" lesson, including making the decision to issue long-term debt, a step-by-step description of the process of issuing bonds and the administration of outstanding debt. Available from MFOA, 180 N. Michigan Ave., Chicago, Ill. 60601.

Doty, Robert W., and Petersen, John E. "The Federal Securities Laws and Transactions in Municipal Securities." In *Northwestern University Law Review,* vol. 71, no. 3 (July-August 1976).

A comprehensive treatment of the new role of financial reporting and disclosure in the municipal bond market. For information, contact Northwestern University School of Law, Chicago, Ill. 60611.

Forbes, Ronald W., and Petersen, John E. *Building a Broader Market.* Report of the Twentieth Century Fund Task Force on the Municipal Bond Market. New York: McGraw-Hill Book Company, 1976.

Discusses what should be done to improve the overall structure of the municipal bond market so that it can function effectively and equitably in serving local governmental borrowers, investors and the taxpayer. Available from the publisher, 1221 Avenue of the Americas, New York, N.Y. 10020.

Kaufman, George, and Hopewell, Michael. *Improving Bidding Rules to Reduce Interest Costs in the Competitive Sale of Municipal Bonds: A Handbook for Municipal Finance Officers.* Eugene, Ore.: Center for Capital Market Research, University of Oregon, in cooperation with the Municipal Finance Officers Association, 1977.

A detailed but easy-to-follow examination of bond sale procedures with emphasis on optimal bidding rules for competitive sales. Available from MFOA, 180 N. Michigan Ave., Chicago, Ill. 60601.

Moak, Lennox L. *Administration of Local Government Debt.* Chicago: Municipal Finance Officers Association, 1970.

A comprehensive textbook on all phases of debt administration and policy with numerous and detailed examples. Available from MFOA, 180 N. Michigan Ave., Chicago, Ill. 60601.

Moody's Investor Service. *Pitfalls in Issuing Municipal Bonds.* 3rd ed. New York: Moody's Investor Service, Inc., 1978.

A guide for local governments in "avoiding needless errors, omissions and faulty planning which can weaken or doom to failure an otherwise feasible financing." Available from the publisher, 99 Church St., New York, N.Y. 10007.

Mussa, Michael L., and Kormendi, Roger C. *The Taxation of Municipal Bonds: An Economic Appraisal.* Washington, D.C.: American Enterprise Institute for Public Policy Research, 1979. 228 pages.

A study of the issues surrounding the tax status of municipal bonds. Compares the current tax status of bonds (interest on them is exempt from federal income taxes) with the taxable bond option (an alternative proposed in 1978 under which municipalities could choose to issue taxable bonds with some of the interest paid by the federal government). Available from AEI, 1150 17th St., N.W., Washington, D.C. 20036.

Municipal Finance Officers Association. *Disclosure Guidelines for State and Local Governments.* Chicago: Municipal Finance Officers Association, 1979 edition.

The authoritative statement of information to be provided and disclosure practices to be followed in state and local security offerings. Available from MFOA, 180 N. Michigan Ave., Chicago, Ill. 60601.

Petersen, George E., with Cooper, Brian. *Tax-Exempt Financing of Housing Investment.* Washington, D.C.: The Urban Institute, 1979. 196 pages.

Studies the impact of the growth of these bonds on tax-exempt interest rates, tax revenues of the U.S. Treasury, local mortgage markets, the home buyer and urban development patterns. Available from the publisher, 2100 M St., N.W., Washington, D.C. 20036.

Petersen, John E. *The Rating Game.* Report of the Twentieth Century Fund Task Force on Municipal Bond Credit Ratings. New York: The Twentieth Century Fund, 1974.

Evaluates the municipal bond rating system in view of the changed nature of the market and demands with which it has had to cope. Available from the publisher, 41 East 70th St., New York, N.Y. 10021.

Petersen, John E. *Changing Conditions in the Market for State and Local Government Debt.* Prepared for the Joint Economic Committee of the U.S. Congress and published as a Joint Committee Print, Washington, D.C.: U.S. Government Printing Office, 1976.

Describes changing conditions in the municipal bond market and their effect on the availability and cost of state and local debt. Also describes recent changes in supply of and demand for tax-exempt securities. Available from GPO, Washington, D.C. 20402.

Petersen, John E. "Small Borrowers in the Municipal Bond Market: Does Size Matter?" In *Conference on Non-Metropolitan Community Services Research,* proceedings of a conference sponsored by the U.S. Senate Committee on Agriculture, Nutrition and Forestry. Washington, D.C.: U.S. Government Printing Office, 1977.

An analysis of the small local government borrower and how it fares in the municipal bond market. Available from GPO, Washington, D.C. 20402.

Smith, Wade S. *The Appraisal of Municipal Credit Risk.* New York: Moody's Investor Service, Inc., 1979. 442 pages.

A guide to the credit aspects of municipal bonds and notes. Divides the components of municipal credit evaluation into five areas: (1) population, wealth and income; (2) governmental organization and powers; (3) financial operations; (4) general debt obligations; and (5) special and limited debt obligations. An excellent reference. Available from the publisher, 99 Church St., New York, N.Y. 10007.

Standard and Poor's. *Municipal and International Bond Ratings: An Overview.* New York: Standard and Poor's Corporation, 1979. 84 pages.

Focuses on the factors included in the rating process. Includes specific discussions of general obligation bonds and of specialized types of revenue bonds. Available from the publisher, 25 Broadway, New York, N.Y. 10004.

18 Standard and Poor's Municipal Bond Ratings
An Overview

Introduction

The concept of a rating is simple—What is the probability of timely payment of interest and repayment of principal? It's in the implementation of the concept that things get complicated, primarily because of the number, diversity, and complexity of the variables involved. Our purpose in preparing this [selection] is to provide an overview of Standard and Poor's municipal and international bond rating process, including the fundamental factors of the evaluation. Our objective is to cast as much light as possible on the rating process; but it is obviously impossible to list and discuss all factors that might enter into an evaluation of all issues we may rate. Such a list would be different for major cities versus school districts, or water and sewer bonds versus municipal electric systems, etc. What we have attempted to do is to illustrate the key general areas of analysis that are intrinsic to most ratings, [and] to highlight certain new areas. . . .

Role of Ratings and Rating Agencies

Until fairly recent times, reasons to extend credit were based upon close personal relationships between the borrower and the lender whether credit was being extended to an individual, a corporation or a municipality. However, the sheer size of today's public market for corporate and municipal debt has made necessary some sort of impersonal credit judgment. No nation in history has been able to build the huge reservoirs of money available for investment that the United States has through its insurance companies, savings banks, trusts, mutual funds, profit sharing plans, pension plans and so on. AT&T alone is accumulating money in its pension plans at a rate of approximately $2 billion a year. These funds are invested in a multiplicity of debt and equity instruments, and one of the tools that has assisted in the investment of these monies has been the nationally recognized credit ratings of S&P and others.

These credit ratings help investors by providing an easily recognizable, simple tool that couples a possibly unknown issuer with an informative and meaningful symbol of credit quality. Issuers range in nature from public corporate utilities, such as Commonwealth Edison, to conglomerates, such as Gulf + Western. Municipal issuers range from California and Virginia to the New Jersey Sports and Exposition Authority (the Meadowlands) and the Yazoo Mississippi Delta Housing Corporation. To that are added foreign governments, such as Japan and Finland, and foreign corporations, such as Volvo of Sweden and ICI of England. Moreover, many issuers sell bonds with varying security pledges, such as first mortgage bonds and sinking fund debentures, and also issue bonds that are callable, convertible and complex.

Ratings are of value only as long as they are credible. Credibility arises primarily from the objectivity which results from the rater being independent of, and disinterested with respect to, the issuer's business. The investor is willing to accept

Reprinted from Standard & Poor's Municipal and International Bond Ratings: An Overview *(New York: Standard & Poor's Corp., n.d.), pp. 5-15, 29-32.*

the rater's judgment only where such credibility exists. Where enough investors are willing to accept the judgment of a particular rater, that rater is referred to as a rating agency.

Credibility is very fragile. S&P operates with no governmental mandate, subpoena powers or any other official authority. We simply have a right as part of the media to express our opinions in editorials written in the form of letter symbols.

In order to properly use the credit rating, one should understand what a rating is and is not. . . .

The bond rating is not a recommendation to purchase, sell or hold a security inasmuch as it does not comment as to market price or suitability for a particular investor. While we ask many questions in any number of areas as we proceed through the rating process, the rating does not represent that S&P has performed an audit or that S&P attests as to the authenticity of information provided by the issuer upon which the rating is based. Ratings can be changed, suspended, or withdrawn as a result of changes in, or unavailability of, information. A rating is also not a general purpose evaluation of an issuer. For example, a city that has an "AA" obligation outstanding is not necessarily "better than" a city with a "BBB" obligation outstanding inasmuch as the "AA" rating may be based primarily on the specific security underlying the bonds.

The ratings do not create a fiduciary relationship between S&P and any users of the ratings inasmuch as there is no basis for the existence of such a relationship. Ratings by themselves do not justify the purchase, sale, or holding of a particular security. The rating performs the isolated function of credit risk evaluation, which is only one element of the entire investment decision-making process and cannot in and of itself constitute a recommendation inasmuch as it does not take into consideration other factors such as market price and the personal risk preference of the investors.

The Rating Process

Types of Long-Term Obligations Rated

Standard and Poor's rates tax-exempt bonds upon the request of the issuer or its financial or legal representative. Virtually all types of general obligation and revenue bond issues are rated encompassing bonds of states, counties, cities, school districts, and special purpose taxing districts. Both limited and unlimited tax general obligation bonds of these issuers are rated. In addition, the following revenue bonds are rated: enterprise systems, such as electric, water, sewer, gas, airports, parking, ports, toll facilities, solid waste, transit, hospital, housing, race tracks (under certain conditions), stadiums (if additionally secured), telephone, marinas, and auditoriums; special tax revenue bonds, such as sales, franchise, hotel, utility, cigarette, business license, and fuel; special revenue bonds, such as higher education (tuition, fees, etc.), student loan, tax increment, state revenue sharing, and special assessments (if additionally secured); lease-rental obligations; guaranteed bonds; collateralized debt; moral obligations; debt service make-ups; and insured bonds. However, as a matter of policy, S&P does not rate bonds issued for:

1. Recreational, or sports arena, facilities which are secured solely by enterprise earnings therefrom
2. Special assessment projects which are not additionally secured by another revenue source
3. A start-up of a new hospital facility
4. Nursing home (extended care) or life-care facilities
5. Section 8 housing projects in which the sponsoring housing authority has no previous operating experience

. . . .

Fees for Domestic Long-Term Obligation Ratings

S&P charges a fee for its rating services, and it is normally paid by either the issuer, underwriter, or financial consultant. This fee is generally based upon the time and expense involved in determining and monitoring the rating. The size of the issue or the issuer is not a factor in determining the fee. Generally, the fees for domestic long-term bond issues range from $1,000 to $6,000. . . .

Types of Short-Term Obligations Rated

S&P as a matter of policy does not accept rating requests for most types of municipal short-term notes because, in our opinion, they have a variety of inherent weaknesses which could leave the investor exposed to financial loss. For example, we will not rate Bond Anticipation Notes, the repayment of which by definition depends upon the issuer's ability to borrow at some future date. By far the largest defaults on municipal securities in recent history were the short-term notes of New York City and the Urban Development Corporation (N.Y.), neither of which was ever rated by S&P.

However, S&P will rate short-term working capital notes of states and municipalities which have a maturity of one year or less, are general obligations of the issuer, and meet a variety of other criteria. . . .

How the Rating Process Works

Once a decision has been made that an issue will be sold either competitively or by negotiation, a rating request to Standard and Poor's Municipal Bond Department is initiated by either the issuer or its authorized representative, as shown in Figure 1: S&P's Municipal Bond Rating Process Generalized Flow Diagram. Because the analyses involved in determining a bond rating are now so complex, and in view of the greatly expanded amount of documentation involved, it is in the best interest of all parties concerned to allow at least three weeks before the sale date to complete the analysis and the release of the rating. In cases where a field trip is involved, an additional one or two weeks may be needed.

. . . . Once a rating request has been received at S&P, either by phone, letter or personal visit, the "Application for Rating" will be mailed or presented to the issuer or its authorized representative. Although S&P will initiate the rating process once all the documentation has been received, no conclusion to the rating process will result if the "Application for Rating" has not been received.

The events that follow the initiation of the rating process and which ultimately result in the assignment of a rating are depicted in the flow diagram.

As is illustrated in Figure 2, there are a number of parties involved in the sale and purchase of a debt issue. S&P as a rating agency is not involved with the actual structuring of a given issue—that is the function and responsibility of the parties in the "Inner Circle." S&P stands in the "Outer Circle" and is the recipient and user of materials prepared by those in a position to attest to their accuracy and completeness. While, particularly in new areas, we may react to a proposed financing and perhaps publish a paper outlining our criteria for that type of issue, S&P is unwilling to function as an investment banker or financial advisor. Performance of such a role would ultimately serve to impair our credibility by leaving us open to a charge of rating the issues we structured. . . . Credibility is vital to our continued performance as an independent rating agency.

Prior to the assignment of many ratings, it is necessary for us to meet with representatives of the issuing entity. In some areas, such as hospitals and housing, an issuer meeting is essential due to the complexities involved. These meetings generally occur at our offices or on site; and, in either case, they give the issuer an opportunity to make a presentation, give us an opportunity to resolve questions and uncertainties, and facilitate the highly important management assessment. S&P is represented by a minimum of two staff members, at least one of whom is a member of the Rating Board. The issuing entity is represented by personnel in the areas of finance, administration and governing body, plus technical assistance such as legal counsel and feasibility and engineering consultants. The underwriter and financial consultants are also frequently represented. The issuer's presentation can be either formal or informal in nature, although to assure that the meeting is as productive as possible we request that all documentation be furnished to us at least one week prior to the meeting.

(In order to provide a frame of reference for the discussion that follows, it is necessary to define two terms used therein—"investment grade" and "speculative grade." The term "investment grade" was originally used by various regulatory bodies to connote obligations which are eligible for investment by various institutions such as banks, insurance companies, and savings and loan associations. Over time, this term has gained widespread usage throughout the investment community. Issues rated in the four highest categories ("AAA," "AA," "A," "BBB") are generally recognized as being "investment grade." Securities rated below "BBB" are generally referred to as "speculative grade" securities. Neither term indicates which securities S&P deems worthy of investment inasmuch as an investor with a particular risk preference may appropriately invest in securities which are not "investment grade.")

Our analysis first centers on determining whether the issue is "investment grade" or "speculative grade" (see Figure 3). The differentiation is made by determining if there are any negative factors or uncertainties, for which there are not offsetting positive factors, which could lead to a significant possibility that less than 100 percent of the principal and interest will be paid on time. If such a determination is reached, the issue will not be rated "investment grade."

Bonds rated "AAA," "AA," "A," or "BBB" are those we have analyzed and for which we have found no known factors which would prevent timely payment of debt service. We then employ a "bottom up" analysis which determines

Figure 1: *S&P Municipal Bond Rating Process*

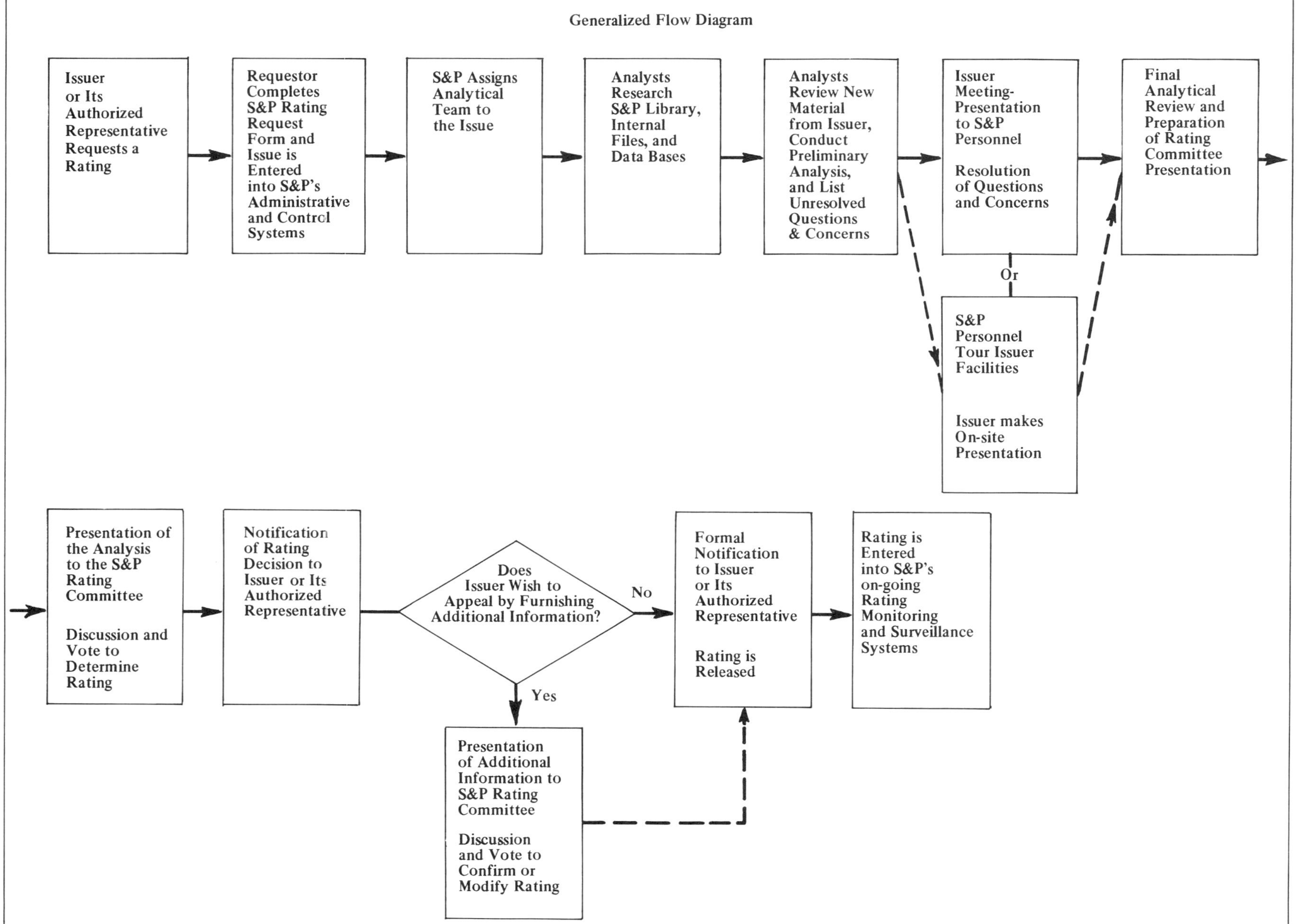

Figure 2

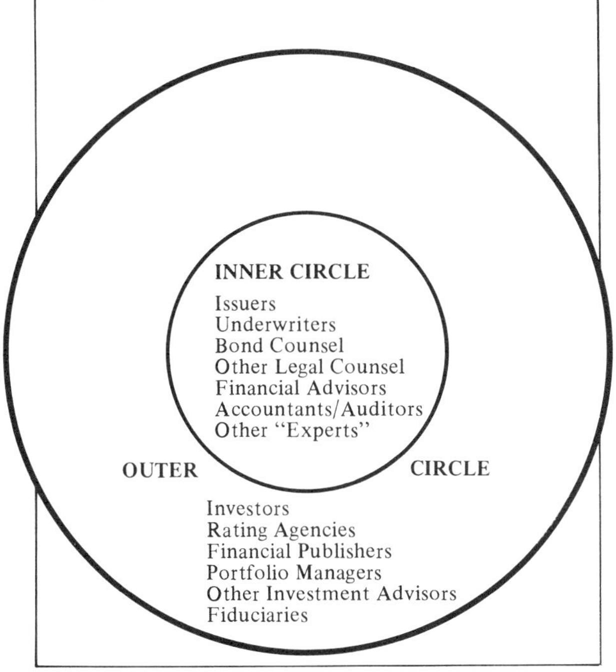

how much additional protection there is and, therefore, how far up the "investment-grade" scale the issue is rated.

Figure 3

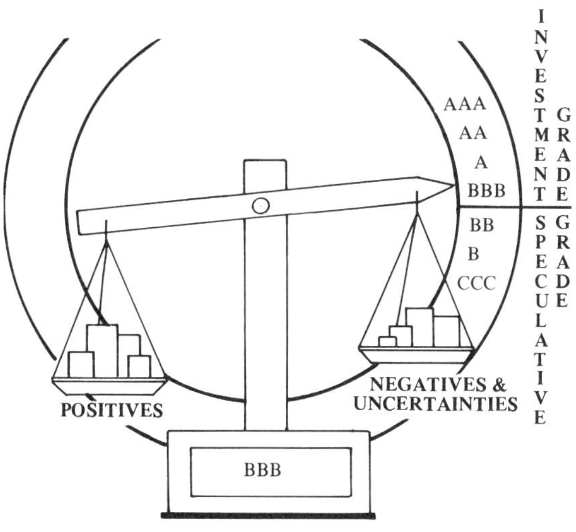

Bonds rated "BB," "B," "CCC" or "CC" are, on balance, regarded as possessing a speculative capacity to pay debt service because of the existence of negative factors or uncertainties for which there are not compensating positive factors. In these cases, we employ a "top down" analysis to determine just how speculative we think the likelihood of repayment is, and, accordingly, how far down the "speculative-grade" scale the issue is rated.

In addition, our analyses take into account security provisions and relative creditor standing in bankruptcy and any mechanisms for the prompt cure of a default. While the rating process generally does not attempt to determine the value of fixed assets in a forced liquidation, there are types of collateral whose value can be easily and reliably determined because of the continuing existence of highly liquid markets. For example, a portfolio of government securities or a pool of single-family residential mortgages can be disposed of quickly and at values that can be known at any time.

There are two ways in which the existence of such liquid collateral may enter into the rating process. The first is when the cash flow produced by such collateral or the proceeds resulting from the sale of such collateral are dedicated to the timely payment of debt service. The second is through the creation of bankruptcy rights to the collateral in the event of a default on the bond issue. The former is a somewhat stronger form of protection since it effectively precludes any economic loss to the bondholder; in the latter situation, some economic loss could stem from time delays encountered while the rights are being enforced.

For issues rated "AAA" and "AA" (the top half of the "investment-grade" category) security and seniority positions in the event of default are less important in the analytical process because default is deemed to be so unlikely. For issues rated "A" and "BBB," security and seniority positions are a somewhat more important factor, increasing as the bottom of the category is approached. For issues rated in the "speculative-grade" category, the presence or absence of a secured or senior position can be very important because of the greater possibility of default and a resultant need to address relative standing of issues in bankruptcy proceedings.

Once the rating has been determined in accordance with prevailing policies and criteria, the issuer, or the party acting on behalf of the issuer, is notified. At that time, the issuer has a right to submit information not previously supplied or to further clarify information already presented. Ultimately, however, a decision must be made, at which time the rating is published. The meetings in our offices and on-site visits are not limited to the new issue calendar. S&P encourages update meetings with issuers on an annual basis or more frequently if the situation warrants.

Once established, municipal bond ratings remain in effect for as long as current information is furnished regularly or until the next bond sale. For most issues we need annual audit and budget documents on an on-going basis. For revenue bond ratings involving construction financing, we also need at least quarterly progress reports covering the project involved. In lease-rental situations, where the lease rental payment is dependent upon completion and/or acceptance of the project by the lessee, we also request a copy of the "Certificate of Completion." Failure to supply the above information on a timely basis necessitates a suspension or withdrawal of the rating inasmuch as S&P's first rule of rating is that a rating must be based upon adequate facts.

An Overview of General Obligation Bond Ratings

Although General Obligation (G.O.) bonds now represent a smaller share of the total municipal bond market than they represented historically, G.O. bonds are expected to continue as an important financing vehicle for such municipal capital improvements as schools, streets, municipal buildings, etc. Of the total of $45 billion of long-term tax-exempt bonds sold in 1977, about $17.9 billion (or 40 percent) were G.O. bonds, and this same percentage pretty much held through the first nine months of 1978. While we expect G.O. bonds to remain a major force in the marketplace, there has been some erosion in confidence in this type of security which can be largely attributed to a lack of faith in the accounting, financial reporting and management systems used by some G.O. issuers. Moreover, it has become increasingly important to understand what is meant by a "full faith and credit" pledge, and how this identically worded pledge can differ greatly in meaning from issuer to issuer.

When an issuer sells a G.O. bond secured by its full faith and credit, it is attaching to that issue its broadest pledge, encompassing such things as its ability to levy an unlimited ad valorem property tax or other revenue streams, such as sales or income taxes. However, the issuer's ability to actually generate any such revenue depends upon numerous factors; for analytical purposes, we classify these factors under four broad categories: Socioeconomic (commonly referred to as "Economic Base"), Financial, Debt and Administrative.

Economic Base

We consider an issuer's economic base the most critical element in our determination of municipal bond ratings. It is axiomatic that a community's fiscal health derives from its economic health. Virtually all revenue sources, from sales and income taxes to permits and property taxes, are affected by economic forces. In addition, major expenditure categories, such as welfare, are directly influenced by economic conditions.

Among the factors considered in evaluating the economic base are income levels and the rate of income growth. When looking at income, we evaluate both per capita and per household income levels, since per capita numbers could be distorted by such things as large student or prison populations in a community. In either case, the income levels as well as the rate of growth thereof are measured against those for the region in which the community is located, the standard metropolitan statistical area (SMSA), the state and the nation.

Another important analytical factor is the employment mix analysis which can, for example, isolate areas of potential vulnerability in the employment base. These figures are also compared with regional, state and national figures, and long-term trend analysis is crucial when analyzing the employment base. While unemployment figures can be useful in some cases, the stress at S&P is on trends of employment and trends of labor force growth; these two figures together give a real indication of the expansion or contraction of the local economy. (Unemployment figures by themselves are of limited value because of the lack of standardization in their derivation and because a low unemployment figure may not portray what is really happening in the economy. For example, in the early 1970s when the aerospace industry stagnated and layoffs were on a large scale, several aerospace-dependent communities showed relatively stable unemployment rates. What had occurred, in fact, was that thousands of formerly employed residents had left these communities in search of employment elsewhere. Therefore, although the unemployment rate remained stable, it took an analysis of the size of the labor force and employment levels to show the dramatic shifts taking place.)

When analyzing population growth, we look at a four-decade trend as well as recent estimates, keeping in mind that the further we get from the last completed census, the more optimistic population estimates tend to become. Therefore, we go to several sources when conducting this analysis. It is also important to take into account the effects of annexations, or in some cases, de-annexations, on the population trend. Other aspects of population analysis include the age of the population (under 18 and over 65 are considered "dependent" population requiring more costly services) and educational attainment levels as they relate to wage-earning capacity.

The leading employers and taxpayers are weighed carefully in relation to the types of industry involved, their commitment to the area, expansion plans, etc. Any significant shifts in taxpayers or employers are analyzed for their impact on the economic base. Building activity is another good indicator of economic vitality and, of course, translates into higher property assessments and revenues. We look carefully at the mix of building activity (residential versus commercial and industrial) and the effects of various economic conditions on building activity. For example, many "growth" communities, particularly in the South and Southwest, experienced high levels of building activity in the early 1970s. Much of this activity has since stopped, and because of overbuilding, many builders (and taxpayers) went bankrupt. Caution is necessary when looking at building permit values as many communities include "exempt values" in the figures. While these may add to the short-term economic activity, they do not translate into increased assessments.

Other economic indicators include the age and composition of the housing stock, retail sales activity (which indicates whether a community is a local, regional or nationally important center) and bank deposits.

In summary, communities with higher income levels and diverse economic bases which provide protection against economic fluctuations clearly demonstrate a stronger capacity to pay the long-term bondholder. As previously stated, assessments of the economic viability of a community must take a long-term perspective because the issuer's ability to meet debt service is a long-term consideration. Economic change is generally slow but persistent, and a high capacity to pay at present may not translate into a long-term trend.

The source of data for our economic base analysis, must, in part, come from the issuer itself. We do, however, draw extensively from outside sources including publications of the Bureau of the Census (which is providing increasingly helpful income data between censuses), the U.S. Department of Labor, various state labor and commerce departments, *Sales Management Magazine* for retail sales data, and bank economic departments.

Financial Factors

Financial analysis first involves an understanding of the accounting practices employed and their impact on the operating statements of the issuer. Historical budget and audit report analysis is conducted with an emphasis on the issuer's revenue structure and how well it responds to various economic conditions. It is our opinion that a balanced composition of revenues, not unduly reliant upon one or two revenue sources or outside fiscal aids, gives an issuer the maximum flexibility to meet all its obligations, not just those due the long-term bondholder. The recent history of New York City shows that regardless of where the general obligation bondholder stands in the "flow of funds," an issuer must be able to function on a day-to-day basis, providing services and paying municipal salaries, to remain a viable entity.

S&P does not perform an audit function and we expect issuers to supply us with adequate and timely financial reports, preferably prepared by an independent certified public accountant in accordance with generally accepted municipal accounting standards. In instances where a community's finances are audited by the state auditor, or by the chief financial officer, we request that the accuracy and completeness of such statements be attested to by the appropriate party. In either case, the method of accounting for each of the funds and fund groups is noted, as well as any change in the method of accounting from previous periods, and most importantly the impact of such change of accounting on the operating statements is assessed. Complete footnotes to the financial statements are essential. We also request a copy of the management letter which accompanies the independent audit.

Current account analysis includes examination of the absolute size of the current budget, the trend in budget growth related to growth in other factors such as population and tax base, and the revenue/expenditure balance or imbalance over a period of years. Next, we analyze all the major revenue sources, their changing importance as part of the entire revenue picture, and the suitability of these revenue sources considering the economic base. Expenditure trends and categories are analyzed in the same manner. The balance sheet is examined to determine the "cumulative" effect of each year's revenue and expenditure position. A comparison of this year's budget document with actual operations is a significant indicator of both financial and managerial strengths. For purposes of the general obligation current account analysis, we concentrate on the main operating funds—that is, those funds which are basically tax supported, such as the general fund, debt service fund and perhaps a highway, welfare or road fund. The special revenue fund would be included if it was the recipient of federal revenue sharing monies which were used primarily for operating, rather than capital, purposes.

The need for and use of short-term financing and the implications thereof are closely examined. With the increased reliance on outside fiscal (state and federal) aids, plus a taxing calendar not geared to expenditure streams, cash flow problems have become more prominent in recent years. Improved cash management can help to minimize the problem, freeing an issuer from relying upon the goodwill of others for its fiscal survival.

While all areas of expenditure growth are significant indicators, those relating to pension fund requirements are particularly notable. Due to inflation, the aging of the workforce, and very generous public employee retirement benefits, annual benefit payouts are often rising at a rate significantly higher than asset accumulation in public pension funds. It is generally agreed that postponing or deferring the funding of pension benefits as they accrue encourages fiscal irresponsibility by minimizing the impact of wage settlements and other benefit enrichments on the current operating budget and lays the groundwork for future revenue imbalance. We expect issuers to provide recent and ongoing actuarial valuation reports, and in addition, those financial managers who are in charge of supervising pension plans need to have a sound working knowledge of the plans and their future cost implications. Our stress here is away from "unfunded accrued liabilities" as a significant indicator, and more toward the rate of asset accumulation versus accruing benefits. By a thorough analysis of the text accompanying the actuarial valuation report, we attempt to determine the suitability of the cost method being used to fund the pension system, and the adequacy of the assumptions employed. We then apply some "funding" ratios to each system. However, keeping in mind the limitations and lack of standardization in valuation studies, no system-by-system comparison analysis is undertaken. What we are doing involves trend data on individual systems, with the direction of such trends closely monitored.

Debt Factors

Debt factors include the nature of the security being pledged: Are the bonds secured by a limited or unlimited ad valorem property tax, and do the bonds constitute general obligations of the issuer? Next, such trends as debt issuance, debt history, debt burden, and debt payout schedules are addressed. The debt burden is measured against the issuer's total budget resources and income, which constitute its current ability to pay. The debt limitations and the unused margins thereof are important; an issuer should be able to operate within realistic debt limitations which allow on-going capital needs to be met. In addition, the debt payout schedule should generally correspond to the useful life of the facilities being financed. Projected debt requirements are also considered, and evidence of regular planning for capital improvements should be demonstrated. To help evaluate the willingness of an issuer to pay, the history of past voter approved bond authorizations is evaluated.

Administrative Factors

As municipal operations expand and become more complex, the form of the governing body is an increasingly important analytical factor. A professional manager is generally better able to implement budgetary cost controls and management systems and to deal with such sensitive issues as zoning and land use planning. An understanding of how a government is structured is essential to us since it bears on the "home rule" powers of the entity. Charter, statutory or constitutional limitations on tax rates or levies and bases of assessment obviously affect the ability to raise revenues and could severely impact an issuer's fiscal integrity. Also, the range and level of services provided by the issuer should be examined in relation to the capacity to provide such services. The relationship to and the areas of shared responsibility with overlapping governmental units should be defined.

Under administrative factors, we analyze the issuer's property valuations and assessment trends, changes in assessment ratios, and assessment procedures. We look at the valuations by categories (industrial, commercial, utility and residential) and how the assessment ratio is applied to these different classes of properties. Tax rates, levies, collections (on both a current basis and a total basis including delinquencies) and procedures are examined over a ten-year period. Tax due dates and delinquency rates are noted for their possible impact on cash flow. Possible litigation against local municipalities has become a reality, and this area should be analyzed for any fiscal impact. Our impressions of management fall under administrative factors and include, among other things, budgeting techniques, labor relations, management controls, and long range planning.

An Overview of Revenue Bond Ratings

Revenue bond financing is used for several reasons, the most common being the desire to have users of facilities pay for the financing thereof. Revenue bonds are also sometimes used when voter approval for general obligation bonds cannot be obtained; or because they are usually not subject to statutory or constitutional debt limitations; or because they may be the most convenient method for financing a capital program that benefits several governmental jurisdictions. Originally used to finance canals and turnpikes, their issuance was quickly expanded to include the financing of water and electric systems. Currently the various types of revenue bonds include those just mentioned as well as sewer, gas, telephone, airport, port, rapid transit, stadium and other recreational facilities, solid waste disposal, college, student loan, special tax and tax increment bonds. They are issued by both municipalities and special districts or authorities created to provide specific services. Issuers may include one community, several communities, combinations of incorporated and unincorporated areas, and in some instances even cross state lines.

Although there are many types of revenue bonds, there are certain basic documents that are common to them all. Those that are needed for analysis include the official statement, bond resolution, the most recent audits, current budget and the issuer's capital improvement program. In addition, many analyses require copies of engineering and/or feasibility studies, enabling legislation, lease agreements and customer contracts. Some official statements carry all these items in their entirety. Others carry some, and still others include only excerpts. The official statement includes background information on the issuer and service area and the purpose for the bond issuance. The bond resolution covers the security features of the issue, and the audits and budget provide the needed information concerning historical and current financial operations. The capital improvement program outlines the issuer's overall capital needs for the next several years. The enabling legislation documents the creation of an authority or district and outlines its purpose and powers. The engineering or feasibility report covers the technical aspects of a capital program and, based on financial projections, whether it can be successful. Lease agreements and customer contracts describe both the issuer's obligation to others and vice versa.

There are five broad areas of concern in every revenue bond analysis: legal, economic, debt, administrative and financial factors. But before looking at these areas, we first look at how bond proceeds are to be expended. The purpose could be to effect interest cost savings, change the security features of the bonds through refunding, or to extend the maturity schedule to avoid a default. If the issue is not a refunding, we need to determine such things as whether the bonds are being issued to purchase a private enterprise such as a private water company and, further, whether such enterprise is a profitable one or a bail-out situation. If the issue is being sold to finance construction, we determine if bond proceeds are being used to make minor improvements to an existing operation or to finance a start-up facility. If the project costs are being met partially from federal or state grants or loans, we need to know how certain the issuer is of receiving these grants or loans and the alternatives available should the monies not be received. Next, we examine the type of project being undertaken, its public purpose and its importance to the community. Is it a project operating as a monopoly, such as a water system, or does it have competitive aspects, such as a port, parking facility or college? Remedies available in the event that construction is not completed on time are investigated, and appropriate approval of all regulatory agencies for the proposed construction program should be in place.

Legal Analysis

The next item reviewed is the bond resolution which covers the issue's security provisions. Most revenue bonds are secured by the net revenues of the operation (net of the costs to operate and maintain the facility). Normally, no value is given to gross (before those expenses) revenue pledges since as a practical matter, revenues must be sufficient to meet operating charges as well as debt service requirements to keep the facility viable. The gross revenue pledge can be meaningful if there are other funds to meet the cost of operation and maintenance, such as the general funds of a college or a tax levy in the event of an earnings deficiency. Another exception would be a special tax revenue bond, such as a sales tax bond, which is structured in such a way that tax revenues are not affected by the closing of a facility.

The next step is to determine where this particular bond issue stands in terms of claim on revenues, i.e., whether the bonds hold a first claim on revenues or are junior and subordinated to others. If there are senior lien bonds outstanding, those liens should be closed so that additional senior bonds cannot be issued. This is an extremely important consideration since earnings protection can differ greatly depending on the lien status of the bonds and, obviously, the larger the senior lien debt, the less the protection for junior bonds. When examining revenue bonds with successive lien positions, the funding requirements of any reserves established under each bond resolution should be considered in addition to debt service payments, since they generally have to be satisfied first before principal and interest on the next succeeding lien bond can be paid. This can be ascertained by checking the flow of funds.

The flow of funds establishes the priority of all claims on revenues, from their collection to their final disbursement. A typical flow of funds starts with the revenue fund, where all revenues are collected. From there they are usually distributed on a monthly basis, usually in the following order: operation and maintenance fund, debt service fund, debt service reserve fund, renewal and replacement fund and surplus fund. There are many variations on this theme, such as the addition of an operating or emergency reserve prior to the surplus fund.

Reserve funds can be either funded "up front" from bond proceeds or funds on hand or are built up over a period of time, usually within five years. The purpose of a debt service reserve is to provide monies if earnings are insufficient to pay debt service on schedule. This buys time for the issuer, allowing it to correct its problems. The renewal and replacement fund is created to provide monies for extraordinary maintenance and repairs or scheduled replacements that are not large enough to warrant a bond issue. These funds are also available for debt service and provide another cushion for the bondholder. Surplus funds collect all remaining revenues. They can be either closed off to assure that any surplus remains in the system to be used for improvements, extensions or bond retirement or left open to be siphoned off by the municipality to support its general fund. In fact, many municipalities support a major portion of their general funds through surplus revenues generated by revenue bond financed operations. Where there is a substantial amount of tax-exempt property in a community this is an effective method of getting revenue from these facilities.

After the flow of funds, we analyze the rate covenant. This is the assurance given by the issuer that it will charge sufficient rates to pay all the costs of operation and debt service and maintain all funds at their required levels. Rate covenants may provide for more than sufficient coverage; this means that after the costs of operation and payments to reserves, net revenues must cover debt service by a particular coverage, such as 125 percent or 150 percent—the greater the coverage, the greater the margin for both error and the unforeseen. From a rating viewpoint, the issuer is better off when it has ultimate responsibility for rate setting without review by another body.

Revenue bond issuers generally want to retain the option to issue additional bonds to finance needed expansions if the existing facilities can no longer adequately serve the needs of the community. The additional bonds clause is designed to allow for such a probability. In some instances the lien is closed and only junior lien debt can be issued. In most cases, however, the lien is not closed and the clause includes a set of conditions governing the issuance of additional parity bonds to protect original bondholders against dilution of debt service coverage. Foremost among these conditions is the "earnings test" which establishes a minimum level of debt service coverage on all outstanding and proposed indebtedness as a precondition for the issuance of the new bonds. There is also usually a provision to increase the level of funding of the debt service reserve fund, to reflect the larger debt charges. The most conservative earnings test is based on current financial performance, such as the net revenues of the last completed fiscal year, or the average income of the preceding twenty-four months, against estimated future maximum annual debt service. Often the earnings test will be based on a combination of current revenues adjusted for rate increases and projected future earnings. This is usually typical of financings which involve major expansions to an existing project. If such is the case, there should be a requirement to perform a new or updated feasibility study prior to the issuance of the additional bonds. Extreme care should be exercised in situations where the earnings test is based fully on projected future revenues; this is the least conservative test.

Other protective covenants generally found in bond resolutions include: the maintenance of the system in an efficient manner; the maintenance of adequate insurance; no free services; the diligent prosecution of delinquent billings; not to sell or dispose of the physical plant unless bond retirement is provided for; and to keep all funds and accounts relating to the system separate from those of the municipality.

The bond resolution protects the bondholder in many ways but it cannot guarantee timely and full payment of principal and interest. Beyond the resolution one must look at the service area, administrative factors, and financial operations to complete the determination of creditworthiness and the rating.

Economic Analysis

Having completed the legal analysis and therefore having established in detail the type of entity we are dealing with, we can begin the highly important economic analysis of the service area. The primary motive for our concern with economic factors is that the financial health of the facility(ies) under examination obviously depends upon the economic health of the area it serves. In particular, we investigate vulnerabilities that might cause the issuer financial duress should there be a reduction in the economic revenue base. In addition to the economic base analysis outlined previously for general obligation bonds, economic diversity is of prime importance so as to minimize the impact of severe economic downturns related to key industries in the service area. A trend in customers, broken down by classification (i.e., industrial, commercial or residential) shows whether there is growth and a good balance among the sectors. Also important is a list of the system's major customers and the percentage of revenues each represents. If any one customer accounts for over 10 percent, we examine that customer's stability and commitment to the area.

Another important factor in the analysis of the service area is whether it is incorporated or unincorporated. The concern with unincorporated territory is that it may be annexed by another entity or form its own municipality. If this happens, customers may be lost, although the issuer should receive compensation to use for bond retirement. Another concern with unincorporated territory is that rates may be subject to review in that area. Rates may also be charged at a higher level in that area which may someday be cause for litigation. Furthermore, if there is a rate differential and the area is annexed, the issuer will lose the revenues generated by the higher rates.

Still other factors must be taken into account when analyzing a competitive situation. Whether it's an airport, toll road or parking garage, the service area must be analyzed with emphasis on demand for the services and the issuer's competitive standing.

Administrative, Debt, and Financial Analyses

Administrative, debt and financial factors are interrelated and are therefore analyzed together. The first item reviewed is management, including the board of directors, operating management, and the structure thereof, and whether the management structure is adequate for the size and complexity of the enterprise. While analyzing management is highly subjective, it is usually easiest to identify a weak management. In addition to management's operating capabilities, management's policy toward debt and its ability to formulate a comprehensive capital improvement program is important. Perhaps management's commitment and ability to maintain both a sound financial and operating system can best be determined by looking at the track record through an analysis of the audited financial statements for the most recent five years. Through a comparison of actual operating results and past budgets, one is in a better position to evaluate the accuracy of past projections. If a substantial variance is noted, then further investigation is in order.

In reading an audit, the first items to review are the auditor's opinion and footnotes. The footnotes will indicate the basis of accounting employed and usually tell many other things about management and the system itself. For example, they discuss pending litigation that may affect financial performance. Looking at the balance sheet, we examine the various "financial health" ratios, such as the ratio of cash and investments to current liabilities and total current assets to current liabilities.

The key to an issuer's ability to pay debt service on time is its operating statement. In analyzing this statement, operating and maintenance expenses, excluding depreciation, are subtracted from gross revenues to determine net revenues. If local taxes come before debt service they are included as an operating expense. If not, they are deducted. Net revenues are divided by debt service to derive debt service coverage. This is a key figure in revenue bond analysis. It indicates the cushion provided for bondholders—the greater the coverage, the greater the cushion. In analyzing a bond issue, we look at the issuer's debt service coverage on an annual basis and as it relates to the new bond issue. Historical coverage is an indication of the coverage levels management likes to maintain, but we, of course, check with management to see if policies have changed with the new bond issue. Historical coverage of at least 100 percent on future debt service including the new bond issue provides assurance that rates are already at levels sufficient to pay off these bonds. Since trend analysis is so important in rating bonds, coverage is analyzed over a period of years; in any one year extraordinary maintenance costs or unusually high revenues (such as connection fees, grant monies or interest income) may distort it.

One of the crucial components of the financial performance analysis, as well as being an indication of management's goals and operating philosophy, is the rate policy. Rates are viewed from both absolute and relative perspectives. The absolute component is the magnitude of rates and the ability to raise them quickly and effectively to meet unforeseen financial shortfalls. Obviously if rates are deemed to be high already, there will be a reluctance to raise them even higher and an even greater reluctance on the part of the ratepayers to pay them. Conversely, if rates are low, management should have the flexibility to raise them without too much controversy. The autonomy enjoyed by a municipal government over its own rate setting is an extremely important analytical factor, and we look closely in situations where municipal entities are subject to commission jurisdiction. The political climate should also be considered in this regard, for obvious reasons. Finally, the relative perspective on rates includes comparisons with neighboring entities, particularly so in competitive situations.

Another factor often used in assessing management efficiency and financial performance is the operating ratio, defined as operating and maintenance expenses divided by total operating revenues. However, it can be a misleading indicator whether it is used to compare one entity to another or to compare performance of the same entity from one year to the next. This is because the components of the ratio can be impacted by a variety of unusual factors, many of which do not relate directly to operations. For example, a community may have to raise revenues because of (a) increased debt, (b) increased capital improvements paid from current revenues, or (c) increased contributions to the general fund. The net effect in all cases would be a reduced operating ratio. Thus, use of the operating ratio as an analytical tool requires that it be gone into in considerable detail.

In summary, weak management usually shows through and ultimately affects financial performance in a negative way. Strong management is usually evidenced in forward planning and sound financial operations. But while good management and the resultant sound financial operations are comforting to the bondholder in the short term, such results may be difficult to maintain in the face of economic decline. Therefore, all these factors must be studied together always looking at trends and asking "why" whenever there is an aberration from a trend. Quantity of revenues and coverage is important, but quality is even more important. A reliable revenue stream at 120 percent coverage may be a better credit than one with 170 percent coverage currently but which is subject to fluctuation due to a variety of external factors.

The feasibility report is an absolute essential in the case of a major or new undertaking and should be prepared by a reputable and recognized independent consultant. It should provide projected balance sheets, income and expense statements, cash flow statements and changes in fund balances for a minimum of five years. The study should also include a full set of assumptions and rationale which support the financial projections. These relate primarily to levels of demand and usage of the services to be provided, all sources of revenue including schedules of fees and charges, operating and maintenance costs, competing facilities, the estimated interest rate on the bonds, and estimates of additional financing requirements. Since a feasibility study is based on suppositions of events that may or may not happen, a feasibility report should also include a sensitivity analysis to indicate what could happen to the projections when certain selected assumptions are changed. By having these additional results to compare against the basic projections, we have the capability to evaluate the project's earning capability under the worst possible set of events.

19 Advantages of a Risk Management Program

Gerald J. Miller and W. Bartley Hildreth

Introduction

Governments today face severe risks. The risks include property damage and loss; liability claims for damage to others' property, for government agents' implementation of unconstitutional policies, and for antitrust law violations; death or sickness of employees; and losses in productivity due to nonexistent or poorly planned pension programs. Facing uncertainty, government managers must confront, even manage, these potential losses.

Risk management provides a means or a strategy to protect governmental resources against accidental or anticipated losses. As a "planned" approach, risk management uses systematic analysis, often based on statistical or probability rules, to identify areas of potential loss, evaluate their potential severity and frequency, control or eliminate potential risk exposures, and provide the means to finance those losses which do occur (Valente, 1980).

The body of knowledge dealing with the management of risks developed as insurance programs to protect property against theft, fire, and flood. These early programs have evolved into broader management principles with programs specifically tailored to government activities.

Organizations began using the term risk management to describe a systematic approach to dealing with potential losses only recently. However, the risk management profession is older than the term "risk manager" or "risk management," having evolved from the insurance office.

Although the terms "risk management" and "insurance management" are often used interchangeably, there is a fundamental difference. Risk management is broader than insurance management in that it deals with both insurable and uninsurable risks and the choice of the most appropriate techniques for dealing with these risks.

Risk management also differs from insurance management in philosophy. Instead of the traditional focus in which an insurance buyer simply tried to get the most insurance for the least money, risk management emphasizes the reduction of risks and their costs by the most appropriate techniques. Insurance management involves techniques other than insurance, such as loss prevention and noninsurance, but these other techniques are generally considered primarily as alternatives to insurance. Under the risk management concept, insurance is viewed as simply one of several approaches for dealing with the risks the organization faces (Vaughan, n.d.).

Our purpose in this essay is to describe the principles of risk management which underlie a loss prevention program and which command systematic examination and disposal of potential losses. In a first section, we describe four principles which guide the vast majority of programs. Then, in the second section, we show why the government should assign responsibility to deal directly with potential losses—usually to a risk manager, who coordinates organization effort.

This article was written especially for this volume.

Loss Prevention Program Principles

The four principles which constitute a liability prevention program are identification, measurement, control, and finance. The process of risk management begins with the identification of possible threats to the public treasury, or simply, unanticipated or anticipated losses. These possible losses can then be measured in terms of how often they occur and how severely at each frequency. Among these possible losses, some the organization can avoid and others can be reduced, either in frequency or severity. Of the remainder, the organization may choose to retain some losses, finding them frequent enough and/or not severe enough to choose to transfer. Some, however, evade prediction and may have catastrophic impact, in which case the organization may choose to buy insurance in one form or another.

The process, of course, gets implemented both through the organization and through its management. The organization depends upon the size and complexity of the risks faced, often requiring a risk manager dealing with the problem full-time. Whether a delegate of the chief executive officer supervises the implementation of the risk management program or not, the management of the organization effort follows three basic steps: constructing rules and procedures to guide the program, training organization members, and monitoring organization performance.

We will expand the discussion of each of the elements in the risk management process in subsequent sections.

Identification of Risks

Risk identification is the process of isolating and analyzing potential sources of accidental loss. To the public organization, loss could be classified as that occurring to property or capital, such as damage to buildings or losses due to liability suits, or that occurring to people, such as death or accident, or the risk of economic insecurity after retirement. In all cases, assets of the jurisdiction are jeopardized. In response to these potential losses, managers now design property loss and liability prevention, life insurance, safety, and pension programs.

Risk identification is the first step in the design process. Initially, the manager's effort includes investigation, analysis of data, and classification of risks. Investigators attempt to find out what the potential losses are and where they lie. Surveys and questionnaires, examination of financial records, and study of operations flow charts usually constitute the means of investigation (Greene and Serbein, 1978).

Analysis of risks requires one to determine what potential losses loom largest or most frequent. Data generated during investigation suggest the frequency but give no reliable estimate of severity. Gaining knowledge of just how large a loss can be requires the perspective of other organizations. Therefore, analysis of risks necessitates an in-depth study based on a broad perspective.

Measurement of Risks

Based on identification and analysis, a manager can classify risks by measuring and evaluating them. A public official must determine the probability and financial impact of potential losses. In other words, how likely is a loss and how severely could the loss affect the budget? Not only should the information about one type of loss be identified, but public officials should also weigh the probability and severity of each type against others. Both the probability and financial impact of losses may be determined by maintaining complete and accurate records on the number and kinds of losses sustained in the past, both in the organization and in other governmental units.

What should one know? Liability suits affecting other jurisdictions provide one example. In this case, useful information might include the official sued, the management practice in question, the amount of the court judgment paid, attorneys' fees and other costs such as court costs, and the length of time spent by the official's professional and support staffs defending the suit. Why collect such detailed information on other governments? The low number of suits encountered by all but the largest governments results in sparse data. Other governments' experience can provide a fuller perspective. The same data requirements apply to the risks associated with an employee's death, disability, and loss of income at retirement.

Control of Risks

Not only must a public official identify and measure risks, he or she must also attempt to manage and control organizational practices which could lead to losses and to select methods of handling anticipated or accidental losses. In fact, control is the most important step in risk management. This effort encompasses all government activities and requires establishing, implementing, monitoring, and updating policies and procedures related to those practices identified as risks. Four suggested approaches are (1) avoiding risks, (2) reducing them, (3) retaining some, and (4) transferring others.

Avoid the Risk

Public officials can forego activities involving risk. Earlier identification of risky programs or activities can aid decision making. The nature of government programs, however, forestalls adequate use of avoidance. Few activities required of a public official can actually be avoided; therefore, careful scrutiny of legal requirements should precede efforts to avoid a particular activity. Moreover, all public officials want to provide a variety of facilities and services to citizens, even though some of these facilities and services can result in loss.

A city-owned swimming pool is one example. Adequate recreation facilities hallmark the policies of most public officials. Yet, the provision of swimming pools carries with it a number of potential losses. Inadequate security for the facility in winter months may result in destruction. Little regard for safety and supervision in summer months may lead to accidents and then liability suits. Providing the pool at all represents a desire to serve the community; however, no legal requirement necessitates a city's undertaking the responsibilities and the risks. Therefore, decision makers must balance the desire to provide services that improve the quality of life of citizens against the chance of financial loss.

Consider also safety of employees. Clearly, a safety program can isolate hazardous jobs or tasks, and, through conscientious implementation, the program can minimize the number of activities in which accidents occur. Yet, many risks will remain. For example, employees involved in police, fire, and military matters involuntarily face quite risky situations. In these areas, risk reduction may help.

Reduce the Risk

Officials' own efforts can reduce the probability of loss. Consider three available methods. First, carefully crafted policies and procedures can guide officials' actions as well as those of public employees, especially in high risk activities. Development and implementation of sound policies and procedures in these exposure areas can provide employees and officials with uniform guidelines.

Personnel administration, licensing decisions, and equipment operation provide examples. Policies can state explicitly how new employees get selected without bias, even to specification of procedures such as forms and action steps taken in handling job applications. Similar steps can state qualifications for a particular license, and procedures can prescribe hearing requirements in reviewing and deciding whether a particular applicant is qualified. Finally, safety guidelines can provide employees the wherewithal to reduce accidents while operating automobiles or construction machinery, and preventive medical checkups of employees might allow supervisors to remove the worker from potential disability-provoking work requirements.

Second, officials can follow sound management principles, such as adequate training and supervision of employees, to reduce risks. Thus policies in force are made part of the required training materials, and supervisors can inspect employees' work from time to time to ensure their compliance.

Third, clarifying responsibilities within the organization can often reduce risk. For example, having several different people responsible, in part, for one task increases risk. By consolidating functions or delimiting roles, managers can fill specialized jobs with highly skilled individuals. Such clear definition of work might prevent neglect or accident.

Retain the Risk

When public officials have avoided some risks and reduced the probability of others, they may retain many other risks through government assumption of financial losses. Research in risk management suggests guides for retaining risks (Greene and Serbein, 1978). The guides rest on the notion of frequency and severity of losses, a classification yielded by the original investigation and measurement of risks. There are four possible outcomes:

a. Low frequency, low severity
b. Low frequency, high severity
c. High frequency, low severity
d. High frequency, high severity

Risks that fall within categories a., c., and d. could be retained and budgeted for, avoided, or reduced. Greene and Serbein (1978) argue that only risk category b—low frequency, high severity—be transferred. Decisions about the amount to set aside for retained risks would, of course, also depend on the data generated by an identification and measurement of potential losses. A public entity can assume the financial consequences of a potential risk, absorbing the loss in the operating budget when the loss occurs. "Going bare," as absorbing a loss is called, would pertain, if ever, only to a low frequency, low severity risk.

A second method requires use of both organizational and outside resources. The public entity can assume either a small or large part of the loss, leaving the remainder to insurance coverage. The small loss retention results when the government assumes some in-kind services or the deductible on an insurance policy. For instance, the small loss situation may allow the government to reimburse officials for attorneys' fees and court costs should they be sued for actions taken in the performance of their jobs. Policies can also hold that the government's attorney defend officials if they are confronted with a personal liability suit. In these cases, the government entity will pay for what can be small losses, leaving court judgments to insurance. Workers' compensation claims can be covered by funds equal to probable losses and set aside systematically. Also, governments can retain larger deductibles with insurance contracts, resulting in possibly lower insurance premiums.

The large loss retention is arranged through government funds used with catastrophic insurance coverage. Government indemnity illustrates the use of government funds and perhaps insurance coverage. Indemnity may emanate from state provision of local government liability, or simply from allowing injured citizens to sue the government. State laws follow two basic approaches to indemnification—open-ended and closed-ended (U.S. Advisory Commission on Intergovernmental Relations, 1978).

Open-ended approach to indemnification. "Open-ended" indemnification suggests broad government responsibility for losses to citizens. This approach provides that the government is liable for all activities, unless an act is specifically excluded. Oklahoma law, for example, provides for open-ended liability except in specified instances generally relating to essential government functions such as legislative, judicial, and executive actions; taxing; inspections; and licensing. Liability of employees and the government is "merged" in the act; the governmental unit must defend the employees and pay any judgment if the employee was acting within the scope of his or her powers.

Most important, the Oklahoma law limits the amount of liability, establishes procedures for bringing claims against a government, and authorizes broad powers for governmental units to insure themselves against liability cases. In this case, the "open-endedness" creates a potential high frequency, high severity condition. To reduce the effects associated with the "high-high" condition, the government can share or partially transfer the risk. The government could pay part of the amount of any judgment, leaving all above to an insurance company.

Closed-ended approach to indemnification. "Closed-ended" liability narrowly defines indemnity. This approach provides for the exclusion of suits against governments except in certain instances. Missouri law, for example, provides that governments are immune except for damages caused by a public vehicle or a dangerous condition in public property—two areas dealt with in a 1977 state supreme court decision. Missouri law also places limits on the amount of liability.

Such an approach may yield a low frequency, high severity risk. The result would depend, as always, on the judicial interpretations of the law. If a large loss were probable, the deductible for almost total insurance coverage could represent some attempt to retain losses.

Retention of losses can require a self-insurance program. A self-insurance program systematically handles all of the functions of an insurance agency, but normally at a lower cost than the premiums paid to insurers. Thus the government accounts for amounts set aside to cover losses; measures the probability of losses; and administers adjusting, legal work, and payment for losses. The benefits gained from self-insurance are also measured against the costs in determining which losses to retain through self-insurance. Those losses that the local government can handle by itself at lower cost than insurance can be self-insured. Others can be transferred (Technical Standards Committee of the California Society of Municipal Finance Officers, 1980).

Prohibitive expense is not the sole reason for self-insuring. Insufficient insurance policy limits, insurance policy exclusions and deductibles, and unavailability of insurance expertise may necessitate a conscious and well-planned effort to create organization capacity to absorb losses.

Transfer the Risk

In deciding how to control risks, public officials may buy insurance after they have eliminated all other methods—avoiding, reducing, or retaining risks—as either impractical or impossible. Insurance for public employees and officials increasingly interests managers concerned with the uncertainty of the world in which they operate.

Two methods of insurance have gained wide acceptance: commercial insurance and interlocal insurance pools.

Commercial insurance. Using private companies to insure risks has traditionally served cities well in areas such as property damage and employee life and health. The area of liability, however, poses problems. Consider the assessment by the U.S. Advisory Commission on Intergovernmental Relations (1978: 22):

> The growing debate over the liability issue resulting from court and legislative actions has led to a tightening of the commercial liability insurance market and an increase in the importance of risk management as a component of financial management. In many instances, commercial coverage has become unavailable or premium costs have skyrocketed. Instances of insurance premiums doubling in one year even though no claims were filed in the previous year are not uncommon.

In response to the "tightening of the commercial insurance market," the International City Management Association, the National Association of Counties, and the National League of Cities, for example, have jointly established an insurance program.

What should one consider in purchasing insurance? Analysis of coverage, service, and cost yield particularly pertinent information to guide choice. First, the analysis of coverage expressed by an insurance contract yields answers to whether one is getting the coverage desired—has the coverage desired, in fact, been obtained?—and whether the obligations of buyer and insurer are clear. Various kinds of insurance policies cover various risks, and many authorities can assist in selecting the appropriate form (Greene, 1978). However, all insurance policies have four common features (Betterly, 1967: 9-85):

1. *Declarations* include names, location, amount, term, and premium. These should be checked for accuracy. Failure properly to name the insured or to designate the correct address has been the basis for more than one lawsuit by an unsatisfied insured.
2. *Insuring agreements* state what is covered. Although usually expressed positively, they do include limitations sometimes more significant than the exclusions. Be sure to clarify any ambiguity.
3. *Exclusions* are a necessary part of any insurance contract, but the type of exclusions and the number of them constitute significant points of comparison between two or more proposals.
4. *Conditions* include standard clauses required by statute, plus basic provisions common to a species of policy. Usually they can be broadened in favor of the insured, and such amendments may be necessary so that the insurance will do what the buyer intended.

Inter-local insurance pools. Governments can form funds to which several entities contribute and from which claims are paid (New York State Legislature, 1979). Each jurisdiction contributes regularly and assumes a set deductible amount in case of a claim. In 1979, an estimated 20 insurance pools were operating in nine states.

The decision concerning commercial insurance or interlocal funds depends upon the cost of each, of course. However, as ACIR suggests, the interlocal fund may sometimes be the only choice for risk transfer, given general economic conditions and the market conditions of the insurance industry.

Risk Finance

Budgeting and shrewd purchasing policies for insurance coverage clearly underlie a risk management program. Even more, self-insurance and interlocal insurance pools illustrate the government's need to connect financial planning and risk management. Risk funding requires setting aside funds to meet losses arising out of those uncontrolled risks that cannot be eliminated or transferred. If local or state law requires the government to assume certain losses in which insurance may incur prohibitive expense, prudent management dictates that public officials budget for the contingency.

The accounting methods have real importance in any risk financing plan (Technical Standards Committee of the California Society of Municipal Finance Officers, 1980). In other words, how should risks that the organization retains be controlled? An internal service fund provides one accounting method. This fund—a self-insurance fund—charges operating funds an amount equivalent to premiums based upon the identified and measured risks. Such a fund would not receive retroactive payments from operating funds when losses occur but would charge higher amounts in subsequent periods. The internal service fund aids managers in capturing the total cost of the risk management program and facilitates allocations of cost back to the various operating funds.

The self-insurance set-aside may also be accounted for through the General Fund and enterprise funds. This arrangement generally allows greater managerial flexibility, although the commingling of funds prevents segregation of the true costs of the risk management program. However, the philosophy of the program, more than the relationship of losses to total funds, may dictate spreading the cost over all departments.

As enticing as self-insurance sounds, the local government must be able to handle the financial necessities of such a fund without curtailing normal service activities or placing its assets in jeopardy. Similar comments, of course, apply in funding insurance schemes, especially in times of rapidly escalating fees. The watchword is prudent management of financial resources.

Administering the Risk Reduction Program

What does risk management require? Common sense supported by careful planning and supervision can result in sound management. Aided by systematic effort on all officials' parts, a risk management program can successfully reduce the threat of liability.

There are four major steps in setting up a risk management program:

1. Establish a management policy with local government goals in preventing and controlling risks, and organize risk management units, assigning responsibility to a risk manager on the local government staff.
2. Review and amend policies, procedures, and practices which create potential risks and isolate chronic risks in the organization.
3. Increase awareness among officials and employees of liability risks through memoranda and training.
4. Monitor officials' and employees' compliance with management policies and procedures and the risk management program through observations of on-the-job behavior and through citizen feedback.

Policy and Organization

Public officials guide the management of risks with dictates, adopting and announcing management policy that sets out the broad designs of the loss prevention and reduction program. Despite this logic, policymaking more often gets honored in its breach. For example, a 1973 public sector survey of cities in the United States (Roos and Gerber, 1973) reports only 10 percent of the sample had policy statements.

Formal policy may not guide a program in many cities, but a government concerned about liability risks must provide a coordinating unit responsible for risk management. Cities, again, have yet to emphasize organization. While data available (Roos and Gerber, 1973) are sparse, they do suggest that few cities have such a unit. In fact, the survey data indicate only 3 percent of cities in one sample have a full-time risk manager. Data derived from private sector surveys (Greene and Serbein, 1973) portray greater concern for risk management among U.S. companies. Thus 60-70 percent of companies responding (depending on the particular survey) had either a full-time risk/insurance department or a full-time risk/insurance manager.

Implementation of a risk management program is normally assigned to a professional risk manager, a practice especially noticeable in private sector organizations. The risk manager's office may report to or form part of a finance or personnel office or stand free of other staff departments, reporting only to the chief executive officer. The office, in any case, usually has staff status, associated with the chief executive.

Centralization or decentralization of structure varies. Basically, a risk manager must not only support individual departments in their risk management programs but also provide specialized expertise for elected or appointed officials on risk management aspects of new or existing policies.

The scope of duties given the risk manager may differ. A major part of the risk manager's responsibility is insurance management, but employee benefits often get added, at least in the private sector (Ivry, 1966). Most important, the risk manager coordinates the managerial aspects of risk prevention.

Implementation

After organizing the unit, risk managers must seize the early initiative by following at least three major steps: constructing sound practices for dealing with areas that create potential risks or ones chronically creating loss; training employees in these new rules and procedures; and monitoring compliance with the procedures so that early indicators of system failure or recidivism surface quickly and lead to corrective action.

The first ingredient is the construction of rules and procedures to define what may be done and how losses can be prevented. Initially, this may involve a survey to find out how the problem areas are currently being handled. It might be useful to evaluate current policy in light of other organizations' perspectives, legal trends, and other indicators such as citizen complaints. In such managerially important areas as personnel administration, for example, this would involve validated selection instruments and appropriate affirmative action procedures. Similarly, the due process rights of employees deserve special attention. When considering discipline or dismissal actions, local government officials should practice caution. Rash action in cases of employee misconduct should be tempered with thorough investigation and application of penalties consistent with past cases.

In each case, the risk manager and other public officials scrutinize the problems that create losses and attempt to deal with them reasonably and systematically. Whether the effort to be made by the official goes toward solving a problem, meeting a demand, or trying to comply with court orders, he or she must clearly determine what the object of the regulation will be and address it with applicable and reasonable rules. This step is crucial because all procedures, training, and monitoring will by definition be based on the efforts to grapple with this problem.

Comprehensive, on-going training, the second step, provides a special opportunity. Through training, risk managers can address safety, life/health, and liability questions constructively. Training programs can be instituted to familiarize employees with established policies and procedures conforming to safety standards and those complying with the law. Using case studies or actual court cases to outline potential risks, employees get special warning of the specific areas that can result in accidents or damage suits.

Two types of programs can be designed: one for skill updating and another for new employees. In each program the basic rules and procedures gain visibility and employees learn to use these rules and procedures with more facility.

A variety of training methods may be employed in the two programs, of course. For example, role-playing exercises efficiently illustrate the dynamics of safety and liability situations and provide experience in decision making under these constraints. One such approach has been designed by these writers in conjunction with colleagues and practitioners (Nigro, Rabin, Hildreth, and Miller, 1978). The approach has met with success in providing experiential training to a wide cross-section of public administrators. A by-product of training sessions such as these could well be the identification of previously undetected risks, adding an unexpected feedback element to the first step of constructing and reviewing rules and procedures.

Complementing this effective, but incidental, feedback will be the process of monitoring. Monitoring systems will help officials to check employees' performance, gain internal organization feedback, and govern the implementation of policies. Monitoring employees' compliance will strengthen the training process, demonstrate unclear training methods, reveal gaps in understanding, and isolate individuals who cannot comprehend the risks being taken. Internal organization feedback can help change managerial practices before their inadequacy leads to disruption, loss, or even litigation. Finally, monitoring the effect of policies and procedures will permit policymakers to adapt rules to the needs of clientele and point out unfair ways of dealing with problems.

Conclusions

The most positive implications of the legal challenges to management are the creation or encouragement of fair and effective management practices where none existed before and the recognition of risks and plans to deal with them. Thus, objective rule-making and fair procedures in applying them, rigorous and continual training, and constant monitoring of the effects of both rules and training can help. Moreover, following risk management principles can do more. As a result, no exotic remedies are called for in response to court judgments, legislative actions, and other risk threats. Rather, just and sound managerial approaches can control the challenge to public officials today.

Bibliography

Betterly, G. "Risk Management." *Handbook of Business Administration.* H.B. Maynard (Ed.). Chicago, Illinois: McGraw-Hill, 1967.

Greene, M.R., and Serbein, O.N. *Risk Management.* Reston, Virginia: Reston Publishing Company, 1978.

Ivry, D.A. "The Corporate Insurance Manager and Employee Benefit Plans." *Journal of Risk and Insurance* 33 (1966): 1-17.

New York State Assembly, Ways and Means Committee. *Municipal Insurance Pools–An Appropriate Alternative for Local Governments.* Albany, New York: New York State Legislature, 1979.

Nigro, F.A.; Rabin, J.; Hildreth, W.B.; and Miller, G.J. *Personal Liability in Government.* Southern Regional Conference, American Society for Public Administration, Montgomery, Alabama, 1978.

Roos, N.R., and Gerber, J.S. "Governmental Risk Management." *Urban Data Service Report* 5 (February 1973): 1-17.

Technical Standards Committee of the California Society of Municipal Finance Officers. "Self-insurance Concepts for Public Entities." *Western City* (February 1980): 6-8.

U.S. Advisory Commission on Intergovernmental Relations. *Intergovernmental Relations* (Winter 1978).

Valente, P. *Directory of Risk Management Practices.* Washington, D.C.: International City Management Association, 1980.

Vaughan, E. *Risk Management and Insurance Buying Guide for Kansas Municipalities.* Institute for Insurance Education and Research. Iowa City, Iowa: University of Iowa (n.d.).

20 Pension Policy and Management

W. Bartley Hildreth and Gerald J. Miller

The employee benefit package of nearly all full-time public employees includes a form of postretirement income protection, better known as a pension program. Whether the pension program is administered locally or by the state, or by the U.S. social security system, public employers face significant yearly appropriations to cover the employers' contributions to these employee retirement programs. Inattention to the purposes and management of pension programs can lead to poorly planned benefit packages, insufficient funding precipitating plan insolvency, and/or wasted appropriations of increasingly scarce public funds.

To provide a fuller understanding of public pension management, this essay explores distinguishing characteristics and major controversies. First, the purposes of pension programs are outlined. Then, public pension systems' development and administration will be sketched. Attention then turns to general but key features of pension benefits. Different ways of financing pension plans (such as pay-as-you-go and actuarial funding) are reviewed along with ways in which pension systems have an impact on public budgeting. We note changes in investment strategy, including socially beneficial investment. Finally, we focus on such issues as control, regulation, and reform of public pension plans.

Purposes

Pension systems benefit both the employee and the employer. The employee receives attention to economic and social needs; the political jurisdiction's personnel management objectives are also supported. Viewed from an *economic security* perspective, pensions systems can allow an accumulation of income to provide for retirement, disability, and/or income to survivors in case of death. While pension programs are often regarded as postretirement income, members generally receive disability and survivor's benefits too. Disability programs for public employees date from the Revolutionary War and are frequently found benefits under a pension plan (Bleakney and Maule, 1978).

Personnel management objectives have long been served by pension systems. An early reason for such public sector programs was the need to supplement the bureaucrat's low salary. Thus Tilove (1976) refers to "charity" as an important reason for public pension systems' development. Further, retirement systems have been viewed as fostering a career system with retirement benefits serving as compensation for a long public service career (Public Service Laboratory, 1975). Plans therefore have been constructed that grant increased benefits to organizational members of long-standing seniority (Munnell and Connolly, 1979).

Differing personnel management purposes have been served by military, police, and fire fighter pensions systems. Since uniformed work requires great personal risks, the desire for safe but quick response capabilities displaces the tenure requirements usually associated with adequate accumulation of pension contribution. The uniformed services, as a result, typically offer incentives for uniformed ser-

This article was written especially for this volume.

vice members to retire early, opening up opportunities to make the transition into a second career at a relatively early age (Tilove, 1976). Often this results in a person having sufficient time in a second occupation to qualify for another pension. An opportunity, such as in the uniformed services example, to earn two retirement checks is often referred to as "double-dipping." Public debate has flourished on both sides of this issue (see, for example, Munnell and Connolly, 1979).

Development

In 1857 the first public pension program was designed to cover the New York City police force. It was not, however, until the turn of the century that pension systems became widely adopted in either the public or private sector (Bleakney, 1972).

While pension systems are not uniformly structured, a 1976 survey conducted by the U.S. House of Representatives showed that federal, state, and local governments administer approximately 6,700 pension plans. At the federal level alone, over 65 plans were recorded, the two largest being the Civil Service Retirement System and the Military Retirement System, together accounting for almost 95 percent of all active members participating (U.S. House of Representatives, 1978a).

In the same study, locally administered plans accounted for 80 percent of the state and local total. Two-thirds of the local plans covered fire and police workers exclusively but accounted for only 7 percent of all local participants. Thus pension plans are fragmented, especially at the local level.

Administration

Administration of a public pension system exhibits fundamental differences from administration of a private program (McCollum and Mundt, 1976). A private system is managed according to company policy standards established by statute or case law (Winklevoss and McGill, 1979). In contrast, legislative policymakers generally have direct control over a public pension system. Legislative control often implies that benefits, funding, investment and other pension management issues depend on politically inspired change, often without due consideration of the consequences (Bleakney, 1972). For example, granting police officers liberalized vesting privileges might be followed by demands for comparable features for other occupational groups. This phenomenon, called "leapfrogging," often occurs without adequate fiscal analysis of even the first benefit expansion.

While most public pension systems are locally administered, there is a movement towards centralized, state-administered management (Winklevoss and McGill, 1979; Jarrett and Hicks, 1976). Cost efficiencies, uniform benefits, maximum investment yield, and effective management and control serve as rationale for consolidation (Tax Foundation, Inc., 1976).

Consolidation also creates problems. For example, since extensive locally administered plans can lead to varying benefit levels across a state, such programs encourage increases in employee salaries in low paying jurisdictions prior to consolidation to allow those employees to achieve a level of comparability with all other jurisdictions following consolidation. Costs are therefore spread across the entire "consolidated" membership. The effort to gain uniformity through consolidation results in smaller-plan members actually receiving more benefits than before (Tilove, 1976), a plus for smaller-plan members but with greatly increased budget demands on their employers.

Under what conditions should a state-administered plan be chosen? Although there is no single test, several criteria seem reasonable. First, when the size of the employee group is small and relatively stable in a community with limited growth and resource potential, arguments favor consolidation. Basic requirements of a pension system include an ability to spread the liability across as large a work force as possible (Athearn, 1977). When a work force is small and unlikely to grow, members could not gain the benefits found, perhaps, in larger plans.

Second, when locally administered plans develop financial problems, attention usually turns to the particular state government for relief. In an effort to bring some systematic disclosure or resolution of financial problems, state-administered plans or general monitoring programs might be appropriate (U.S. Advisory Commission on Intergovernmental Relations, 1973).

Given the above conditions conducive to consolidated pension programs, what factors prolong fragmentation? First, members of a locally administered pension system usually have an interest in retaining control over their own program (Present, 1975). While members might not have a major impact on particular benefits, a locally administered plan theoretically allows more individuals to influence decision making. In addition, local policymakers fear the loss of local autonomy to state legislatures.

Even under statewide consolidation, proliferation of plans according to occupational group occurs (Tilove, 1976). For example, fire and police groups typically press for continued segregation of their plans from other groups' programs. By so doing, occupational groups can pinpoint their demands for benefit changes without having to worry about extending similar benefits to other work groups.

Benefits

Consideration of a plan's objective and its design raises profound issues for pension system operations.

Objective

Disputes rage over the objective of a retirement program. One view holds that retirement benefits should not total more than full pay at retirement. The public sector, in general, is very close to achieving this wage replacement objective (Tilove, 1976). Another objective is the constant-standard-of-living concept (Winklevoss and McGill, 1979). To maintain approximately the same standard of living that beneficiaries had immediately preceding their retirement, benefits must be indexed to increases in the cost-of-living, usually to the consumer price index (McGill, 1979). Grants of post-retirement income indexed to changes in the cost of living are widely sought by employees. Indexing, however, results in a dramatic increase in benefit costs (Jump, 1978, 1976; Present, 1975).

While public employee pension programs might adhere to the above objectives, many private sector employees receive less protection from economic insecurity. Observers then ask why taxpayers, who receive little or no protection against retirement, should subsidize government workers. While the topic provokes controversy among observers, voters may express less concern. Tilove (1976) recounts one example in which disadvantaged blacks in Los Angeles wards voted in favor of a pension-related measure giving "fair and desirable" pension benefits to public workers.

Design

Benefit designs vary from the systematic to the haphazard (Tilove, 1976). Model plans can guide pension plan administrators in systematic policy management (Winklevoss and McGill, 1979). However, since public plans are designed by politically motivated policymakers, benefits often lack a coherent pattern (U.S. House of Representatives, 1978a). Four design problems often encountered involve the use of employee contributions, the salary basis, vesting concerns, and social security issues.

1. Contributions

Public pension benefits result from employer as well as employee contributions. Public pension plans enjoy generally about one-third higher benefits than their private sector counterparts. Once employee contributions are accounted for, however, public and private plans are often approximately equal (Tilove, 1976). The reason for this equivalency is that private sector employees do not contribute to their pension program to the extent found in the public sector. There are calls for holding down public benefits to conform more nearly to private plans. But even if one discounts the impact of employee contributions, should one, Jump (1978) questions, use private sector benefit levels as a decision guide? Jump asks what is so inherently correct about the private sector standard? Regardless, comparisons between public and private benefit levels will continue.

2. Compensation Base

Most public employee retirement systems compute benefit levels based upon the final salary, averaged over the last couple of years, with the actual method depending upon the particular plan (U.S. House of Representatives, 1978a). Using a three-year average tends to be a favorite approach. New York City at one time used income levels "on the very last day of employment" to determine benefit levels but stopped this approach because it fostered the use of overtime as a way to boost pay levels on the last day (Winklevoss and McGill, 1979). New York City was by no means unique in the use of last-day pay or in experiencing the problems with overtime policy, especially with fire and police service plans. Unless tightly controlled, such systems provide major incentives to abuse overtime; programs become less controllable and inflate benefit levels (Jump, 1976).

3. Vesting

Public pension systems, like private plans, establish a date on which the employee acquires rights to the plan's stated benefits, although benefits will be claimed at a later, agreed-upon retirement age. Military pensions "vest" after 20 years, for example.

Pension plan decision makers usually give

major consideration to appropriate vesting dates and their consequences. For example, vesting policy can adversely limit employee movement (Rubin, 1965; U.S. Advisory Commission on Intergovernmental Relations, 1963). If employees perceive an overriding financial disadvantage in leaving a job only because they will not receive all the benefits of contributing to their pension plan, they will certainly experience frustration, loss of commitment, and other problems with which managers must deal. Several observers have recommended statewide, uniform vesting privileges to encourage at least intrastate portability of pensions and, therefore, employee mobility (Munnell and Connolly, 1979).

4. Social Security and Public Pensions

State and local governments can generally elect whether or not to join the federal Old Age, Survivors and Disability Insurance or the social security program (Patterson, 1982). While withdrawal is also an option, a majority of public employees having pension plans also have social security coverage, resulting in double coverage (Tilove, 1976). Benefit overlap becomes a major area of contention. Moreover, even when the government withdraws from social security coverage, some employees can still qualify for social security benefits. For instance, fire fighters enjoy work schedules that allow them to "moonlight" in a second career, assuring their social security benefits. Many advocate closer coordination and even mandatory social security coverage (Tilove, 1976; Munnell and Connolly, 1979).

Financing Policies

Pension programs can follow an actuarial-based reserve funding approach or use a pay-as-you-go method. A reserve funding program involves use of an actuarial plan to provide a systematic schedule of contributions based on long-term needs (Tilove, 1976). On the other hand, a pension program financed by existing members and employer appropriations to cover current expenses (such as benefits, refunds, and administrative expenditures) is referred to as a pay-as-you-go plan (Munnell and Connolly, 1980). Pay-as-you-go programs are generally in disfavor (U.S. General Accounting Office, 1979). Tilove (1976) notes:

> Pay-as-you-go arrangements encourage irresponsibility—the grant of benefits without recognition of the cost—and expose employees to the hazards of disappointment if the jurisdiction financing the system loses its ability to pay or if the taxpayers revolt against the ultimately high costs. (p. 348)

Despite such analyses, pay-as-you-go is the dominant means of financing public pension plans, including the U.S. military retirement system (Friend and Perreca, 1978; Munnell and Connolly, 1979; Tilove, 1976).

What accounts for the staying power of pay-as-you-go plans? One probable cause is the low level of annual appropriations typically required in a pay-as-you-go plan as contrasted to the contribution requirements of a fully funded plan.

Private plans illustrate full funding. The Employees Retirement Insurance and Security Act (or ERISA) requires a fully funded system for private pensions systems. This law was designed to keep private employers from abandoning businesses, and thus pension systems, leaving pension plan members without recourse or economic security (U.S. House of Representatives, 1978b).

Several commentators have advanced the idea that a fully funded system for government is questionable (Bacon, 1980; Tilove, 1976). The argument holds that governmental units enjoy seemingly perpetual life and access to tax resources (Public Service Laboratory, 1975). In fact, taxpayers might be concerned if current tax receipts were put into a funded reserve and not used for the benefit of current taxpayers. Besides, according to the U.S. General Accounting Office (1979), annual contributions would have to increase over 100 percent in order to get state and local public employee pension funds into compliance with ERISA standards.

Budget Issues

The budgetary impact of retirement programs in the public sector is enormous. Roughly one-half of the budgeted benefit dollar is comprised of employer payments for employee pension and social security programs.

Public employers' contributions to the pension funds of their employees are mostly funded from general taxes, not earmarked ones (U.S. House of Representatives, 1978a). Since numerous public services are also funded from these taxes, pension contributions have to compete with other spending programs for tax dollars. Pension contributions have been funded by other arrangements, however. Earmarked property tax receipts sometimes partially cover pension plan contributions

(Present, 1975). The state of Delaware, for example, used federal revenue sharing entitlements to cover contribution costs (U.S. House of Representatives, 1978a).

Can pension contributions be cut during austerity efforts? In many instances, pension funding is a mandatory appropriation (March, 1980; Jump, 1978). As a contractual obligation embodied in some state constitutions, arbitrary cutbacks in pension benefits are not possible.

However, the obligation has often been overlooked. Several jurisdictions actually have used pension system receipts to finance other annual operations (U.S. Advisory Commission on Intergovernmental Relations, 1973; Tax Foundation, Inc., 1976). Policymakers have extended public pension benefits in times when salary increases have been politically unappealing (Wellington and Winter, 1971). Some government jurisdictions facing severe financial crises have resorted to negotiations with plan members and unions to try to "call back" some of the most costly, liberalized benefits. Efforts to scale back existing benefit levels raise questions about the keeping of explicit or implied contractual obligations to employees about pension programs (U.S. General Accounting Office, 1980).

Investment

The most promising alternative to "cut-back threats" may be pension fund investment policy. Approximately one-fourth of state and local pension fund receipts result from investment yields (Tilove, 1976). Thus high investment yields reduce the need for increases in contribution levels.

Public sector pension programs have typically operated with limits on investment opportunities. That is, money could only be placed in fixed income securities, mainly federal and state-local investments. Certain types of more speculative investments have only recently gained acceptance (Tilove, 1976).

Recently, portfolio management has confronted demands for socially beneficial investment (Smart, 1979). These investments, their advocates say, achieve both important public policy goals and employees' economic security. Certainly the magnitude of pension fund assets prompts some commentators to argue pension funds' multiple uses (Rifkin and Barber, 1978; Drucker, 1976).

Social investments defy pat characterization. One example of a socially beneficial investment would be a policy that required a pension system to invest in local mortgage projects or other things that would help the community even if the investment yield would be much lower than might be received by going to the national investment market (Taylor, Webb and Parker, 1979).

While socially beneficial investment is politically appealing, questions arise about adopting such policy. Members and beneficiaries of the plan might question the reasonableness of buying the government bonds of a city such as New York City even if it would help the local community (Friend and Perreca, 1978). Thus the risk involved in any single investment and the risk to members of a loss in expected levels of benefits have to be examined (Smart, 1979).

Control

There are three types of controls that are important when considering public employee retirement systems: administrative, accounting, and political. First, administrative control involves the administrative apparatus constructed to foster efficient management of an employees' retirement system. This structure involves handling investments, constructing appropriate accounting systems, and processing claims effectively (Mandolini and Findlay, 1977).

The financial accounting systems for a public employees' retirement system serve not only to ensure a soundly financed system but also to increase the entity's financial reputation. Many public pension plans fail in both regards. Nearly all public pension plans, first, fail to follow generally accepted accounting principles in handling funds (U.S. House of Representatives, 1978a). Further, pension liabilities directly affect municipal bond ratings, helping or hindering the jurisdiction's capital investment program. For example, official statements for prospective bond issues that do not disclose pension funding conditions such as unfunded accrued liability lead to investor suspicion that the issuer has something to hide or does not understand the pension plan. The result of such management inattention is likely to be adverse (Fish, 1979).

Political control also affects pension plans, as we have already discussed. Budgets of local governments have been affected adversely by state legislators liberalizing benefits at the expense of local taxpayers. This results from having benefit-setting policy separated from the responsibility to implement such policies (Bleakney, 1972).

Regulation and Reform

As noted earlier, ERISA dictates private sector pension management practices. Attempts have been made to construct a federal regulatory framework for public employee pension systems (U.S. House of Representatives, 1978b; Gordon, 1976). Constitutional questions have thus far hindered enactment of such a scheme (U.S. House of Representatives, 1978a). Governors and legislators tend to push for state-level control over local plans rather than federal (see National Governors' Association, 1978). In fact, several states have centralized plan administration (Jarrett and Hicks, 1976). Also, state oversight commissions have been proposed to monitor local pension plans in lieu of direct state-administration (see Stakes, 1982; Denero and Stakes, 1978; Butler, 1976). Despite these efforts, calls continue for more effective "fail-safe" monitoring systems (Munnell and Connolly, 1979; U.S. Advisory Commission on Intergovernmental Relations, 1973).

Summary

This essay has outlined the key features and challenges facing pension administration and policy. An understanding of the purposes and design of pension programs helps the manager assess the consequences of benefit changes, for instance. In contrast, pension *mis*management results from inadequate attention to the interrelationships among and between the pension system and the government's financial and management needs.

Selected Bibliography

Athearn, J.L. *Risk and Insurance.* St. Paul, Minnesota: West Publishing Co., 1977.

Bacon, A.R. "A Note on Selecting the Appropriate Pension Funding Method for Localities." *Public Administration Review* 40 (1980): 265-69.

Bahl, R.W., and Jump, B. "The Budgetary Implications of Rising Employee Retirement System Costs." *National Tax Journal* 27 (1975): 479-93.

Bleakney, T.P. *Retirement Systems for Public Employees.* Homewood, Illinois: Richard D. Irwin, Inc., 1972.

Bleakney, T.P., and Maule, R.G. "Disability Benefits under Public Employee Retirement Systems." *Governmental Finance* 7 (1978): 17-23.

Butler, D.K. *Federal Regulation of Public Employee Retirement Systems: The Probable Impact on Major Texas Plans.* Austin, Texas: Texas Advisory Commission on Intergovernmental Relations, 1976.

Denero, W.A., and Stakes, M.E. *Public Pension Plans: State and National Issues.* Athens, Georgia: University of Georgia, Institute of Government, 1978.

Drucker, P.F. "Pension Fund Socialism." *The Public Interest* 42 (1976): 3-46.

Fish, W.W. "Perceptions of Pension Liabilities." *Governmental Finance* 8 (1979): 29-32.

Friend, E.H., and Perreca, J.S. "Proposition 13's Impact on Financing Public Employee Pension and Medical Plans: Something/Someone Has to Give." *The International Foundation of Employee Benefit Plans Digest* (1978): 3-7.

Gordon, M.S. "The Politics and Perils of Reforming Public Employee Pension Plans." *Employee Benefits Journal* 2 (1976): 2-7, 32-33.

Jarrett, J., and Hicks, J.E. *Retirement System Consolidation: The South Dakota Experience.* Lexington, Kentucky: The Council of State Governments, 1976.

Jump, B. "Compensating City Government Employees: Pension Benefit Objectives, Cost Measurement and Financing." *National Tax Journal* 29 (1976): 240-56.

———. "Public Employee Pensions and the Fiscal Crisis of States and Local Governments." *1978 Public Employees Conference Proceedings,* Brookfield, Wisconsin: The International Foundation of Employee Benefit Plans, 1978, pp. 1-9.

McCollum, W.J., and Mundt, B.M. "Philosophy and Equity of Municipal Pension Plans." *Management Controls* 23 (1976): 101-104.

McGill, D.M. *Fundamentals of Private Pensions,* 4th ed. Homewood, Illinois: Richard D. Irwin, Inc., 1979.

Mandolini, A.M., and Findlay, G.W. (Eds.) *Public Employee Retirement Administration.* Chicago, Illinois: Municipal Finance Officers Association, 1977.

March, M.S. "Pensions for Public Employees Present National Problems." Paper presented at the annual meeting of the American Society for Public Administration, April 1980.

Munnell, A.H., and Connolly, A.M. *Pensions for Public Employees.* Washington, D.C.: National Planning Association, 1979.

———. Financing Public Pensions. *New England Economic Review* (1980): 30-42.

National Governors' Association. *Public Pension Reform: An Overview.* Washington, D.C.: National Governors' Association, 1978.

Patterson, Archibald L. *Public Pension Administration.* Athens, Georgia: Institute of Government, University of Georgia, 1982.

Present, P.E. "Policy Decision and Administration of Local Government Pension Plans." *Governmental Finance* 4 (1975): 44-48.

Public Service Laboratory. *Do Retirement Programs Improve the Quality of Municipal Personnel?* Washington, D.C.: Georgetown University, 1975.

Rifkin, J., and Barber, R. *The North Will Rise Again.* Boston, Massachusetts: Beacon Press, 1978.

Rubin, H. *Pensions and Employee Mobility in the Public Service.* New York: The Twentieth Century Fund, 1965.

Smart, D.A. *Investment Targeting—A Wisconsin Case Study.* Madison, Wisconsin: Wisconsin Center for Public Policy, 1979.

Stakes, M.E. *Controlling Public Pensions.* Athens, Georgia: Institute of Government, University of Georgia, 1982.

Tax Foundation, Inc. *Employee Pension Systems in State and Local Government.* New York, New York: Tax Foundation, Inc., 1976.

Taylor, T.; Webb, L.; and Parker, R. "Public Employee Pension Funds: Their Potential for Neighborhood Development." *Public Employee Pension Funds: New Strategies for Investment,* L. Webb and W. Schweke (Eds.), Washington, D.C.: Conference on Alternative State and Local Policies, 1979.

Tilove, R. *Public Employee Pension Funds.* New York, New York: Columbia University Press, 1976.

U.S. Advisory Commission on Intergovernmental Relations. *Transferability of Public Employee Retirement Credits among Units of Government.* Washington, D.C.: Government Printing Office, 1963.

———. *City Financial Emergencies.* Washington, D.C.: Government Printing Office, 1973.

U.S. General Accounting Office. *An Actuarial and Economic Analysis of State and Local Government Pension Plans.* Washington, D.C.: Government Printing Office, 1980.

———. *Funding of State and Local Government Pension Plans: A National Problem.* Washington, D.C.: Government Printing Office, 1979.

U.S. House of Representatives, Committee on Education and Labor. *Pension Task Force Report on Public Employee Retirement Systems.* Washington, D.C.: Government Printing Office, 1978a.

———. *Public Employee Retirement Income Security Act of 1978, Hearings,* 95th Congress, 2d Session. Washington, D.C.: Government Printing Office, 1978b.

Wellington, H.H., and Winter, R.K. *The Unions and the Cities.* Washington, D.C.: Brookings Institution, 1971.

Winklevoss, H.E., and McGill, D.M. *Public Pension Plans: Standards of Design, Funding and Reporting.* Homewood, Illinois: Dow Jones-Irwin, 1979.

21 Public Purchasing
Principles and Recommended Practices

David Neuman and Paul M. Carren

The principles, concepts, conclusions, and recommended practices pertaining to public purchasing delineated in this article are focused mainly on purchasing of goods and services by state and local governments, and are related only indirectly to the area of construction and public works contracting. While improvement in purchasing programs and practices is preeminent as a pragmatic concern throughout our discussion, a detailed listing of recommended practices is presented as a separate supplement for convenient reference.

Issues and Challenges

There is much interest in improving procurement programs, an interest stemming from a variety of issues and challenges. The wave of technology that has characterized the national economy for the past decade or more has brought with it increasingly complex equipment, materials, and systems. Items with a high degree of technology frequently become obsolete in a short period of time by the rapid introduction of new and more refined products. As items become more highly developed, it becomes progressively more difficult to separate the "frills" from actual requirements and, consequently, to determine the best buy for the money.

The magnitude of public purchasing expenditures brings into focus the principle of accountability. A basic tenet of our society is that public officials having the authority to use and manage public resources also have a responsibility to give a full accounting of their actions. This accountability relates to the manner in which resources are applied and to the effect of their application, as well as to the specific objects for which public funds are spent. Effective and efficient purchasing programs based on sound principles are needed to give a proper accounting for purchasing activities. Public record and openness are also necessary features which not only act as controls in the system but also help foster public confidence in government itself.

Governments are faced with the need to provide more and better services to an ever-changing population. Different life styles, attitudes, and levels of sophistication result in different demands to be satisfied. Demands for more and better services by governments cannot be met merely by increasing the already heavy tax burden of the public. Government must stretch its funds and increase its productivity. The challenge of advanced technology and need for increased economy require that public purchasing officials continually update their technical knowledge, information systems, and purchasing techniques.

These conditions impact severely on budgets, the economy, and the marketplace. Until recently, public purchasing functioned in a market where supply and demand were balanced, or where a buyer's market existed. Now, market conditions change rapidly and drastically. Basic commodities are in short supply, and purchasing often finds itself trying to satisfy increasing demands within the constraints of a tight seller's market. The task

Reprinted from Management Controls 23 *(January-February 1976): 8-13. By permission of Peat, Marwick, Mitchell & Co.*

of obtaining products when needed, at competitive prices, is a major assignment.

In addition to the challenges of technology, public demands, and the market, purchasing officials must often cope with social, political, and business influences that seek preferred treatment. There is a need for strong statutory or regulatory safeguards to preserve the integrity of the purchasing process and to protect the government against loss caused by the misfeasance or malfeasance of its employees. However, while good safeguards and controls must exist, they should not be so restrictive as to stifle the professional judgment and personal initiative necessary for purchasing officials to function effectively in the public interest. One of the unique features of centralized public purchasing is the complete openness of its operations, which distinguishes it from private purchasing. But despite this general openness, there have been cases where favoritism has occurred in the awarding of contracts, and favoritism invariably reflects negatively on all public purchasing activities. Public purchasing officials must recognize and resist the pressures of those who attempt improperly to influence purchasing practices.

These many challenges demand professionalism at its best. Yet, the formal education that is the core of most professions does not exist to any degree in purchasing. Experience has been not only the best teacher, but sometimes the only one. Although attention to detail is necessary in this as in any activity, the professional must structure his approach to concentrate on managing assigned functions and detailed activities (e.g., formulating policies, supervising personnel, and directing programs). Developing a professional staff requires a systematic program encompassing education, experience, and continuous training which permits progression to a professional level.

Over the years, state and local governments have individually adopted a variety of public contracting laws, rules, policies, and practices representing whatever was deemed acceptable and expedient at the time. In some cases, these laws and policies have remained virtually unchanged for years; in other cases, they have been changed piecemeal or in response to a particular problem. As a result, state and local government statutes, regulations, and procedures generally have not developed in terms of any overall understanding, knowledge, or data, and they vary widely among state and local governments.

Many improvements, however, have been made by state and local governments in their purchasing operations. Perhaps the most significant of these has been the growth of more centralized purchasing, motivated largely by the recognition of the economies that could be realized. As with the laws, rules, and policies, however, the application of the concept of centralization varies widely. In adopting centralization, primary attention is given to specific types of commodities and to the types of activities which are traditionally associated with the buying function.

But it is important to recognize that variations among purchasing programs in terms of size, resources, and complexity of operations do in fact exist, and that no attempt should be made to dictate a single set of procedures. Purchasing philosophy and principles provide the foundations for public purchasing operations at all levels and for all types, but local conditions necessarily give rise to differing details in their application.

Organizational Structure

Regardless of the size of the governmental unit or the purchasing program, there should be a single central authority that is responsible for ensuring the integrity and effectiveness of the purchasing program. Yet despite the considerable progress made in centralizing purchasing operations, many major types of purchases are still made outside the umbrella of central purchasing, and statutory exemptions and exceptions still exist. Conditions such as these result in a division of responsibilities, diffusion of control, and loss of accountability. The centralization of purchasing authority also implies the centralization of responsibility and accountability, and the central purchasing authority has the perspective of the commonweal, not the special program interests of individual departments.

Delegation can and should still be made when using agencies that can more appropriately or better perform certain functions or activities. Such delegation of authority, however, should be made formally by central purchasing. Since the responsibility for delegated functions remains with the central authority, proper controls can thereby be established and accountability maintained.

The concept of a central purchasing authority fits almost every organizational structure or form of government. It can be applied by the largest of the states and by the smallest of the cities and towns. It relates to governments having boards of control over purchasing, as well as to those having very small purchasing operations. Although the concept of central purchasing may be applied by means of various organizational forms, it is best established at a sufficiently high level of government to permit independent and authoritative functioning with both suppliers and using agencies. Further, to be effective, this authority requires proper recognition and support from officials responsible for total government operations, such as governors, mayors, councilmen, and commissioners.

The central purchasing authority should establish the goals and objectives of the purchasing program, and these should reflect the spirit of the statutes and clearly set forth the intended results of the purchasing program. Similarly, a code of ethics should be prepared and published so that all persons, government buyers and suppliers alike, are aware of the professional behavior expected of them.

Planning and Scheduling

There is a growing need for good planning by all governmental elements if their operations are to meet the increasingly rigorous standards of efficiency and economy. Purchasing should participate in both the management and the operational functions of planning and scheduling.

Government leaders and managers should make use of the capabilities and expertise of central purchasing in the early stages of the planning process. Purchasing can provide valuable information on forecasted costs, market conditions, product availability, and changes in technology which could affect government decisions. Purchasing should also participate in budget review, facilities planning, and economic analyses. The benefits from early and constant participation in planning and scheduling accrue equally to purchasing and management.

Purchasing's involvement in planning and scheduling on an operational level is concerned primarily with consolidating needs and reducing costs through volume buying. Competent planning and scheduling can also reduce the effects of market fluctuations and supply shortages.

To provide for orderly procurement and to perform effectively in planning and scheduling operations, central purchasing needs a broad base of information. Much information is available in purchasing and using agency files, but it is frequently scattered and unstructured. Consequently, there is a need to develop information systems that will provide data in a format that is useful to purchasing management. Budgets and surveys of both using agencies and suppliers can add to the data base.

Bidders List

Establishing and maintaining a current list of qualified suppliers is an important part of a good public purchasing program.

There are differing viewpoints regarding bidders lists. One view is that any supplier should be included on the list, upon request. The other is that some form of prequalification is necessary to establish at the least that potential vendors are responsible. While all state and local governments have some form of bidders list, these two viewpoints have caused widely varying criteria for inclusion. In some cases, suppliers must provide only their name, address, and commodity category. In other cases, detailed questionnaires must be completed.

In our view, some type of prequalification is needed because it is impractical and uneconomical to include every applicant on the list, regardless of whether or not he is capable of performing satisfactorily. The prequalification program should promote fairness and impartiality and provide for exceptions, such as for new or small businesses. The procedures, evaluation criteria, and forms used should be set forth in writing.

The bidders list should be properly organized and maintained, including systematic updating to reflect accurately the current status of competition. The use of a commodity coding system which lists item classification groupings and, as necessary, product functions should be considered.

Responsibility for identifying potential suppliers rests with central purchasing. Methods and techniques to be used should be defined and developed into a regular program. Similarly, policies should be established which address the circumstances under which bidders may be removed or debarred from the bidders list, as well as reinstated after removal. The objective is to maintain an optimum base of qualified competitors. All policies for inclusion on and deletion from the bidders list should be set forth in writing and made part of the public record.

Competitive Bidding

Most state and local government laws require formal sealed competitive bids for purchases expected to exceed specified dollar amounts. There are historic prerequisites for using the formal sealed bid process. While purchasing officials and vendors alike are generally quite comfortable with the conventional bidding process, some do not realize that the absence or altered circumstances of one or more of the historic requisites do not preclude competitive bidding. Rather, it calls for purchasing officials to exercise initiative, innovation, and judgment to maintain an impartial environment for competition. Consequently, stress must be placed on the requirement that competition exist at all levels of purchases. All too often, expediency and convenience override the principle of competition where purchases are below the statutory amounts requiring sealed bidding. Where competition is lacking, purchasing officials must have sufficient authority to use their judgment in carrying out their responsibilities. However, there should be consistency in policies that provide for waivers of competition. Close scrutiny and a well-documented file are also essential.

As a general rule, all bidders on the bidders list for a particular commodity should be solicited. Written guidelines should describe the circumstances under which exceptions may be made. The central purchasing authority, moreover, should be responsible for the final review and approval of Invitations for Bids before they are issued.

At present, most state and local purchasing laws do not provide for competitive negotiation, which is a relatively new concept at these levels of government. Contrary to some beliefs, the use of negotiation is not intended to preclude competition and is not synonymous with single-source procurement. It is averred that competitive negotiation can be advantageously used in certain situations, and that it is in the best interests of the government to so use it.

Impediments to competitive bidding may be inherent in the purchasing operation, or originate as a result of legislation or suppliers' limitations. Purchasing activities should be reviewed periodically to eliminate features which give rise to impediments to competitive bidding, such as restrictive specifications, requirements for "most favored customer" clauses, or practices that are partial toward some bidders.

Existing laws should be reviewed, and those which adversely affect free and open competition, such as preference laws, should be amended or repealed. Proposed legislation which can be expected to have an impact on purchasing should be carefully reviewed to ensure that it does not impede purchasing's ability to uphold the requirements and principles of competition. Impediments stemming from suppliers can only be detected through vigilance, good records, and a program for analyzing periodically the record for unusual bidding or award patterns. Bid-award history files should be maintained to permit such analyses. Policies need to be established to deal effectively with identical bids and dictated contracts, and close liaison should be maintained with the Attorney General in all such matters. Many state and local governments require bidders to submit signed statements that their bids were prepared independently and without collusion. This practice should be encouraged.

Unusual conditions which affect competition can and do occur, and it is best to provide for these in advance. Typical examples are markets in which items are in short supply, and markets in which demand exceeds supply. There are ways to cope with such conditions, but purchasing officials need the authority to adjust and modify their procedures as necessary, lest they violate the law or find themselves unable to proceed.

Processing and Evaluation of Bids

Formal bids, correctly identified, should remain sealed until the time set for bid opening. The controlling and safeguarding of bids are important to vendors, the general public and, clearly, to purchasing authorities. Procedures relating to these activities should be established and monitored by central purchasing.

Bid openings should be open to vendors and to the general public. This practice fosters confidence in the integrity of the process and discourages collusion and favoritism. While informal bids are not subject to the same requirements, the informal bid process should still be an open one. Records should be maintained that are available to all interested parties, so that the entire spectrum of purchasing is open to public scrutiny.

It is best to prepare a tabulation at the bid opening, but when this is not feasible, alternative procedures should be followed. In any case, the public should have the right to witness bid openings and, as for all public records and documentation, the vendors and public should have access to the prepared tabulations.

Good practice requires that factors in addition to price be considered in determining the successful bidder. Consequently, bids should be carefully reviewed and evaluated. By statute, state and local governments require that awards be made to the "lowest responsible," "lowest and best," "lowest responsible meeting specifications," or other similarly described bidder. The phrase "lowest responsible bidder who submits a responsive bid which is most advantageous to the government" has evolved as the most suitable description of the successful bidder.

Guidelines should be established for determining which bidder is responsible and which bid is responsive and most advantageous. The standards of openness and impartiality are outlined in the statutes, but they should be further detailed in written policies. Although professional judgment must always be used, written guidelines will bring rationale, consistency, and documentation into the process.

Providing Adequate Safeguards

The principles, procedures, and structure of an effective public purchasing program should not only promote efficiency and economy, but also provide adequate safeguards against improper and unethical conduct. The best safeguards are the requirements for written procedures, complete records, and public access to these records. Documentation of each step of the process reveals the basis of any deviation and assists in keeping the process open. The openness of the process, moreover, should be supplemented by legislative deterrents to specific situations that can destroy the integrity of the purchasing process.

Conflict of interest statutes prohibit all concerned personnel from being in positions where self-interest and integrity may come in conflict. Such statutes should be inclusive enough to cover all government officers and employees, as well as their spouses, who could act to influence contract awards.

Obtaining particular brands, making unjustified emergency purchases, and other such practices can nullify good purchasing principles. Even if they are not overtly criminal, the potential damage to the integrity of the purchasing system can be great. Effective procedures require that the responsibility for such actions be placed squarely on the shoulders of those persons who made or authorized such purchases, and appropriate measures should be taken.

Technical Specifications

The preparation of proper technical specifications is one of the most important and difficult functions in the purchasing process. Specifications describe what is required or desired, and thus are the communication media between buyer and seller. The great variety of items that are purchased complicates specification writing, as does the fact that state and local governments can seldom dictate the exact characteristics of the products they buy and use. This vast and difficult field challenges every purchasing program, and all purchasing officials share the feeling that improved techniques and capabilities are needed.

Specifications should set out the essential characteristics of items being purchased, so that bidders can accurately compute their bids. This requirement relates directly to the suitability of the product for its intended use, and rules out both under- and over-specification of requirements. Specifications also should be nonrestrictive; that is, they must not unnecessarily limit competition.

Specifications take many forms, including brand names, qualified products lists (also called approved products lists, approved brand lists, or qualified brand lists), comparison of actual samples, designation for a special use, design, performance, and cost of operation analysis. While specifications based on performance are preferred, and some specifications are better than others, no one type is best for all types of products. There are situations where the use of a certain form of specification is necessary or expedient. Written guidelines should describe each type of specification, its advantages, and its limitations. Appropriate safeguards should also be specified, such as with brand name specifications. These should always include a statement that the brand name is used only to establish a quality level, and that equivalent items will be acceptable. Wherever possible, several brand names should be listed.

Regardless of where specifications originate or are prepared, the central purchasing authority should be responsible for final review and approval. The review process should determine whether or not the specifications are adequate for competition, and whether or not they call for a quality level which is suitable for the item's intended use. To preclude misunderstanding, the authorities, responsibilities, and procedures related to the specification process should be set forth in writing.

Standardization is another significant aspect of the specification process. Most states and many local governments have established programs to develop standard specifications for most or all purchases of a given item. These programs permit more efficient operations and result in lower prices because of volume purchases.

Much more needs to be done in exchanging specifications and related data among state and local governments. A basic rule in specification writing is to "look for and use whatever reasonable aids are already available." These aids include specifications already developed by other state or local governments, by the federal government, or by professional organizations. In this area, the most potentially significant program is a cooperative program to write performance standards under the aegis of the Council of State Governments and the National Association of State Purchasing Officials, with funding from the National Bureau of Standards. The impact of this program, if successful, will be tremendous.

Inspection and Testing

There should be assurance that the government gets the types and quantities of items called for in the purchase order or contract. Inspection and testing of items delivered by suppliers are important elements of the purchasing system. These practices cannot be left to an informal procedure that lacks direction and control. They should be formally established and centrally administered by purchasing, even though some of the activities may be properly delegated to using agencies.

The inspection-testing program should, therefore, be set forth in writing, preferably in a manual. The procedures should include a mechanism for reporting to purchasing, which should maintain the central files and be responsible for taking the necessary action, including contacts with suppliers. Central purchasing should also identify the outside facilities (e.g., local colleges or universities) that are available for testing as appropriate, as well as any available in-house facilities. Where appropriate, suppliers can be asked to furnish certificates of compliance or certified test results on items delivered.

Disposition of Miscellaneous Items

The disposition of surplus items and scrap is closely tied to the acquisition program and to inventory management, and is an important element of an overall materials management concept. Timely identification of surplus and scrap is essential. Although using agencies generally are in the best position to identify unneeded items, they often have little incentive to do so. Consequently, some governments give using agencies credit for the sales proceeds of items released.

While central purchasing should have overall policy and procedural control of the identification process, effective coordination between purchasing and using agencies is essential if a disposition program is to work. This coordination should take place within the framework of written procedures setting forth clear guidelines to be followed.

Central purchasing should be responsible for determining the most appropriate disposition method. Transferring items not needed by one agency to another that does need them is the best method of disposal.

Cooperative Purchasing

There is a variety of arrangements by which two or more government entities buy under the same contract or agreement. The major advantage is to obtain lower prices from volume buying, although this cannot always be achieved. Cooperative purchasing tends to encourage the manufacture of new or modified products which are not otherwise commercially available. The strongest cooperative purchasing programs require that all participants be actual parties to the contract. The weakest programs are permissive arrangements whereby third-party agencies can use a contract whenever and however they choose.

Cooperative purchasing programs have developed unevenly, and some sound principles of competitive bidding have been endangered through loose, optional types of arrangements. Recently, these dangers have been recognized so that commitments have been required of all parties. From a practical viewpoint, the largest participating jurisdiction normally should be the agreed focal point for contract administration because of its larger technically qualified staff.

Not all state and local governments have the same requirements and procedures governing purchasing. As a result, difficulties are frequently encountered in meeting the legal requirements of all participants. All state and local laws should provide authority to purchase cooperatively, but the laws should also require that cooperative purchasing will be permitted only when the purchasing jurisdiction assuming administrative responsibility conducts its purchasing operations according to the principles of open competition.

Professional Development

Statute and administrative law, policies, procedures, and organizational structure all mesh to provide the mechanism of public purchasing, but it takes people to put this mechanism into motion. Although purchasing cannot be called a profession in the strictest sense of the word—with implications of educational discipline, licensing, and professional standards or practice—public purchasers can and should nevertheless perform in a professional manner.

The educational needs and requirements of public purchasers have changed as purchasing has evolved through three identifiable phases. In the 1800s, laws largely concerned themselves with protecting taxpayers against favoritism and fraud, and were patterned after construction and public works contract law. The public purchaser was a technician. The need to get the most out of the tax dollar after World War I and the depression of the 1930s started the movement toward greater efficiency of more centralized purchasing operations. In turn, a need for more formal purchasing discipline became apparent, and it becomes more urgent as purchasing enters the third phase of its development, that of increasing the buying power of the tax dollar through a growing management orientation.

At the present time, there is no formal educational program to prepare the purchaser for this kind of role. Purchasing associations should assume the responsibility for formalizing the body of knowledge that supports good public purchasing practice, and state and local governments should commit themselves to training and professional development. Furthermore, purchasing associations should continue their efforts to promote the necessary structure of uniform principles and standards that will advance uniform application of this body of knowledge.

Some purchasing associations have already established professional certification programs to identify responsible purchasing performance among individuals who have attained a prescribed level of qualification. This is an excellent beginning, and their consolidation into one national program receiving full recognition by all associations in the field is a desirable goal. Such a national program, combined with a new commitment to communication with the publics served by public purchasing, is vital to the public confidence so necessary for effective purchasing programs.

Purchasing has evolved from a single buying function to one of management of public funds requiring knowledge of constantly changing technologies and market conditions, complex information systems, and new purchasing techniques. Without ongoing professional development, public purchasing cannot fulfill government's needs.

Controls

22 Accounting and Administrative Internal Controls

Price Waterhouse

Internal Control Objectives

How elaborate a system of internal controls needs to be depends on many factors as unique as one entity is from another. The diversity of operations, degree of centralization of financial and operating management, closeness of top government officials to day-to-day operations and numerous other factors all should be considered in concluding on the adequacy and appropriateness of an internal control system.

In its *Standards for Audit of Governmental Organizations, Programs, Activities and Functions,* the U.S. General Accounting Office defined internal control in government as "the plan of organization and all the coordinate methods and measures adopted to safeguard assets, check the accuracy and reliability of accounting data, promote operational efficiency, and encourage adherence to prescribed managerial policies."

The close resemblance of this definition to that applied in the private sector indicates the degree to which the broad purposes of internal controls in business and government are considered the same—namely, to alert senior officials to departures from established policies and procedures, and to detect activities which have not been properly authorized or which undermine the achievement of organizational goals and objectives.

Reprinted from Enhancing Government Accountability, *Washington, D.C.: Price Waterhouse & Co., State and Local Government Services Group, Edward J. Haller, chairman.*

The accounting profession has recognized, however, that this definition of internal control encompasses certain aspects of broad management control (e.g., operational efficiency) which are not reviewed or considered in any depth as a part of the traditional financial audit process. Consequently, the broader definition of internal control has been modified to recognize that there are two aspects of an overall control system: administrative controls and internal accounting controls.

- *Administrative controls* are the broad controls surrounding all activities carried out by officials to accomplish their objectives (e.g., planning, productivity improvement, quality control, economy, efficiency, effectiveness).
- *Internal accounting controls* are the controls surrounding the activities concerned with authorizing, processing, recording, and reporting transactions, and which operate within the broader control environment of administrative controls.

Objectives

Professional literature currently defines internal accounting controls as those controls which comprise "the plan of organization and the procedures and records that are concerned with the safeguarding of assets and the reliability of financial records and consequently are designed to provide reasonable assurance that:

a. Transactions are executed in accordance

with management's general or specific authorization.

b. Transactions are recorded as necessary: (1) to permit preparation of financial statements in conformity with generally accepted accounting principles or any other criteria applicable to such statements . . . and (2) to maintain accountability for assets.

c. Access to assets is permitted only in accordance with management's authorization.

d. The recorded accountability for assets is compared with the existing assets at reasonable intervals and appropriate action is taken with respect to any differences.

Limitations

It has been widely recognized that there are inherent limitations in any system of internal accounting controls. These limitations have been expressed as follows:

- In the performance of most control procedures, errors can result from misunderstanding of instructions, mistakes of judgment, carelessness, or other personal factors.
- Control procedures whose effectiveness depends upon segregation of duties can be circumvented by collusion.
- Control procedures with respect to the execution and recording of transactions may be ineffective against either errors or irregularities perpetrated by administrators or managers, or inappropriate estimates and judgments by them in the preparation of financial statements.
- Any projection of a current evaluation of internal accounting control to future periods is subject to the risk that the procedures may become inadequate because of changes in conditions and that the degree of compliance with the procedures may deteriorate.

These limiting factors should not dampen the zeal with which government officials pursue the development of an effective internal accounting control system. They are presented only to give recognition to the practical limitations of any control system.

Control Techniques

There are two important control techniques which are used in any internal accounting control system, i.e., the *segregation of duties* within the system, and *procedural controls* which govern the flow of transactions through the system. In other words, the internal accounting control achieved by a particular system depends on: (1) the way responsibility for transaction execution is segregated to create checks and balances, and (2) the actual activities and control procedures adopted, and the way they are executed.

Segregation of Duties

Assignment of duties to individuals should be segregated in such a fashion that no one individual controls all phases of the processing of a transaction, thereby creating a situation which permits errors of omission or commission to go undetected. Ideally, the flow of activities should be designed so that the work of one individual is either independent of, or serves as a check on, the work of another. For example, in most government organizations the property tax billing and collection functions should be segregated since combining these functions could permit concealment of an unauthorized diversion of collections.

Often a small unit of government will not find it possible to segregate duties to the extent considered most desirable because of its limited staff. An increase in the government officials' involvement in the monitoring of procedures then becomes essential.

As a practical matter, the principle of segregation of duties must be tempered by considering such variables as the volume, complexity and financial significance of differing types of transactions and the sequence of steps necessary to process them. These characteristics will, of course, vary widely from one unit of government to another. A continuing concern, as always, is the cost of maintaining controls in relation to the risk of loss due to error or fraud which might arise in their absence. Because of the cost of implementing segregation of duties control techniques, a unit of government may decide to accept certain risks by combining a number of responsibilities or functions. The implications of such combination should be thoroughly considered before implementation.

Procedural Controls

Identifying controls obtained through segregating duties is relatively easy compared to identifying controls obtained through the establishment of a network of procedures, documents and sequences of information flow. The almost unlimited variations in physical form, design, information content, number and flow of the documents, as well as degrees of mechanization used by different organizations to process transactions, further complicate any evaluation of the adequacy of procedural controls.

Although a wide choice may exist in the selection of systems and procedures used to process similar types of transactions, the specific procedures used should be evaluated based on whether or not they seem to reasonably accomplish their objectives. No one procedure, or combination thereof, is inherently more appropriate in all circumstances than another.

Our approach to administrative controls

As defined in professional literature, administrative control includes, but is not limited to, "the plan of organization and the procedures and records that are concerned with the decision processes leading to management's authorization of transactions."

Since administrative controls generally are designed with other than accounting activities in mind, there are only certain aspects of these controls which normally are considered when evaluating a system of internal accounting control. Specifically, consideration should be given to those aspects of administrative controls which:

Establish an Appropriate Control Environment

To establish an appropriate control environment, one requires those administrative controls which foster:

- Awareness through communication as to what procedures are expected to be followed.
- Attitude through creation of incentives to follow established procedures.
- Discipline through assurance that failures to follow established procedures will be detected and appropriate action taken.

Influence the Nature of Internal Accounting Control Procedures

Administrative control procedures may point to specific internal accounting control procedures required to achieve control objectives. For example, significantly different internal accounting control procedures would be used to control property tax or utility cash collections if a lockbox system were employed than if checks were received in the mailroom. The internal accounting control objectives in both situations are the same, but the internal accounting control procedures that are appropriate will differ considerably.

Help to Satisfy Internal Accounting Control Objectives

Administrative controls are designed primarily to facilitate planning, performance evaluation or to meet other organization objectives. Internal accounting control procedures are designed specifically to achieve accounting control objectives. However, at times administrative controls, when considered with other controls in a specific transaction system, will help to achieve internal accounting control objectives. For example, if monthly financial reports are used by the Superintendent of Schools to direct the remedial education program, then the reports are an administrative control. If, however, they are also used as a control to identify misclassification of charges to the wrong department (by the remedial education department head reviewing and calling for correction of inappropriate charges), they become an accounting control.

We believe that administrative controls may be divided into three groups: organization controls, operational controls, and information system controls.

Organization Controls

Organization controls are controls related to the manner in which the unit of government assigns responsibility and defines authority through the makeup of its organization structure and the delegation of authority within the structure.

The degree to which events and transactions are controlled by responsible individuals is often the key to well-managed and, therefore, well-controlled operations.

Some desirable characteristics of organization controls are:

- Organization structure supports management's overall goals.
- Framework for delegation and limitation of authority is well defined.
- Functional assignment of responsibilities is logical.
- Assignment of responsibilities is clear.
- Authority is delegated commensurate with responsibilities.
- Adequate and competent supervision and staffing are available with appropriate

coordination and communication among functions.

Because of diversity in size, objectives, programs, legal bases, and a host of other variables, there is no typical government organization structure which can be used as a standard of comparison to determine the strengths or weaknesses of any other government structure. Variety is to be expected among units of government in the extent to which organization structures are formalized and the degree of their sophistication.

Organization controls should have as their objective establishing a framework which:

- encourages adherence to policies and procedures, and
- provides for an orderly authorization process.

It is in the context of these key objectives that organization controls should be evaluated for their impact on internal accounting controls.

Operational Controls

Operational controls are those controls which provide assurances that the goals and objectives of a unit of government are met in an effective, economical and efficient manner, and that only authorized activities are carried out. Control is achieved through adherence to defined policies and procedures throughout the organization.

The operating policies and procedures of departments and agencies set the framework within which accounting activities take place. Operating controls determine how an organization implements its overall plan and how departments, offices and other units carry out their responsibilities. Operating controls should be:

- Suited to the organization structure and appropriate to carry out delegated responsibilities.
- Well defined, clear and documented.
- Well conceived and practical to carry out.
- Easy to interpret and apply.

The operating control system should serve as a means of communicating goals and objectives as established and authorized by senior elected or appointed officials. The existence of a civil service personnel system within the unit of government or the preparation of long-range capital budgets represent examples of operational controls which will enhance an accounting control environment. Most observers would agree that neither is essential to an adequate system of internal accounting controls surrounding payroll or capital asset expenditures. However, their presence fosters an attitude of accountability and provides assurances that payroll and capital asset transactions are entered into as intended by senior officials.

Where operating controls are well conceived and practical to carry out, they make internal accounting controls easier to apply and, thus, more effective. Where operating controls are lacking or are not conducive to systematic application, it is likely to be more difficult or impracticable to attain desired accounting control objectives.

Information System Controls

Information system controls are those controls which are achieved through providing properly summarized financial and operating data to appropriate levels of officials to assist them in identifying results, trends and opportunities for improvements.

In all organizations, planning and control over events and transactions depend on an official's knowledge of past, present and proposed activities and transactions. In all but the smallest government units, such knowledge is dependent to varying degrees on data provided through an information system.

Senior officials cannot be present to monitor each transaction nor be aware of each decision. They must rely on information systems as their "eyes and ears." One distinguishing characteristic of a successful agency or department will always be the quality of the data made available to its decision-makers.

Information systems will vary considerably between organizations. However, some of the characteristics that should be present are:

- Degree of detail is sufficient for a knowledgeable reader to identify out-of-line conditions.
- Contents are relevant to the user.
- Important information is highlighted.
- Information is reliable and timely.
- Distribution is at appropriate levels.
- Information provided is actually used to control the reported activities.

The information system is often dependent on the EDP [electronic data processing] system. As with any other function, guidance and control over the EDP function should be achieved by a network of administrative and accounting controls.

23 Municipal Accounting

Robert A. Reny

The purpose of accounting is to provide meaningful financial information that can be used to make decisions.

To be meaningful, the information should be as nearly complete, accurate, and up-to-date as possible. To be useful, the information must be relevant to the situation at hand, and presented in a format that is easily understood by the decision maker(s). Information should be gathered and recorded throughout the accounting cycle, be it monthly, quarterly, or yearly. The information is then reviewed, analyzed, and presented in the form of financial statements. Although there are some major differences between private firms and municipalities, including organization objectives, types of resources available, and legal constraints, *accounting in municipalities serves basically the same purpose as accounting in private industry*. The principles and procedures of accounting are not necessarily the same in the public sector as in the private; but the purposes are the same. Certain accounting principles are unique to municipalities. Nevertheless, an accounting system in the public sector, as in the private sector, exists to provide meaningful financial information, useful in making decisions. This chapter explains the principles and procedures of a municipal accounting system. . . .

Reprinted from "Municipal Accounting," in Robert A. Reny, Model Finance and Accounting Procedures *(Orono: Bureau of Public Administration, University of Maine, 1979).*

Principles of Municipal Accounting

Municipal accounting shares such basic concepts of commercial accounting as consistency, materiality, conservatism, and full disclosure. However, there are other distinct characteristics of municipal accounting that have evolved over the years. There exist basic principles of municipal accounting that have become a part of the whole body of *generally accepted accounting principles* dealing with government units. These principles can be summarized into eight areas:

1. Legal Compliance and Full Disclosure

The accounting system of a municipality should be able to reflect whether the municipality has complied with all applicable legal provisions, as well as fully disclosing the financial position along with the results of operations of all municipal financial activities. When a conflict between legal provisions and generally accepted accounting principles exists, legal provisions must take precedence.

2. Budgets and Budgetary Accounting

An annual budget should be adopted by every municipality, whether required by law or not, and the accounting system should provide budgetary control over governmental revenues and expenditures. It is recommended that the budget be prepared on the modified accrual basis (discussed later in this section) and that unspent appropriations be lapsed at year end to improve planning and control of expenditures.

3. Fund Accounting

Governmental accounting systems should be organized and operated on a fund basis. Each fund exists as an independent entity with a separate set of self-balancing accounts which consist of its assets, liabilities, fund balance or retained earnings, revenues, and expenditures or expenses. Separate funds are often required by law or sound financial administration because of the diverse nature of governmental operations and the necessity of determining legal compliance. However, only the minimum number of funds consistent with legal and operating requirements should be established to avoid unnecessary complexity. Eight different types of funds are recognized and are explained later in this section.

4. Fixed Asset Accounting

Fixed assets are assets of a long-term character which are intended to continue to be held or used, such as land, buildings, machinery, furniture, and other equipment. The fixed asset accounts should be maintained on the basis of original cost, or the estimated cost if the original cost is not available. In the case of gifts, the appraisal value at the time received should be used. Depreciation on general fixed assets should not be recorded in the general accounting records. Depreciation is taken, however, on assets of certain funds, such as those belonging to a municipal water utility enterprise fund. General fixed assets of a municipality should not be accounted for in the same fund with the current assets, but should be set up in a separate, self-balancing group of accounts called the General Fixed Assets Group of Accounts.

5. Long-Term Liabilities

All long-term general obligation debt issued by a municipality is an obligation of the governmental unit as a whole. This debt should be recorded in a separate, self-balancing group of accounts called the General Long-Term Debt Group of Accounts. Revenue bonds issued to finance operations in certain self-supporting funds would be obligations of that specific fund and would not be carried in the Long-Term Debt Group of Accounts.

6. Basis of Accounting

The basis of accounting is a method for matching revenues and expenditures during a specified period of time. There are several bases of accounting varying from a simple cash basis to the full accrual basis. The full accrual basis should be used whenever possible. The modified accrual basis is used where the nature of the governmental operation does not permit the use of the full accrual basis. The recommended bases of accounting for various types of funds are explained later in this section.

7. Common Terminology and Classification

A common and standard terminology and classification should be used consistently throughout the budget, accounting records, and the financial reports. Governmental revenues should be classified by fund as well as source. Expenditures should be classified by fund, function, activity, character, and classes of objects in accordance with standard recognized classification. . . .

8. Financial Reporting

Financial statements and reports, showing the current condition of budgetary and proprietary accounts, should be prepared periodically to control financial operations. At the close of each fiscal year, a comprehensive annual financial report covering all funds and financial operations of the governmental unit should be prepared and published. The principal financial statements required for adequate reporting of governmental finances are:

a. balance sheets,
b. statements analyzing changes in fund balances or retained earnings, and
c. operating statements.

Fund Structure

A *fund* is defined as an independent fiscal and accounting entity with a self-balancing set of accounts segregated for the purpose of carrying on specific activities or attaining certain objectives in accordance with special regulations, restrictions, or limitations. Each fund records its own particular cash and/or other resources together with all related liabilities, obligations, reserves, and equities. Funds are properly segregated when accounts are kept separate, and the resources from one fund are not used to meet obligations of another fund, unless the interfund transaction has been properly authorized and recorded.

Eight types of funds and two groups of accounts are explained on the following page. Each should be used for governmental financial operations only as needed. It is likely that most. . . municipalities would require only two or three separate funds.

1. The General Fund

The general fund is used to account for all revenues and expenditures of a governmental unit which are not accounted for in any other fund. It is usually the largest and most important fund in most municipalities. The general fund is an operating fund from which most of the current operations of a governmental unit is financed.

2. Special Revenue Funds

Special revenue funds are used to account for revenues derived from specific taxes or other earmarked revenue sources (except special assessments). They are usually required by statute, charter provision, or local ordinance to finance particular functions or activities of government. General Revenue Sharing, Anti-Recession Fiscal Assistance, and Community Development grants are good examples of special revenue funds.

3. Debt Service Funds

Debt service funds are used to account for the payment of interest and principal on long-term, general obligation debt other than special assessment and revenue bonds. Any notes or time warrants payable from general tax revenues over a period of time longer than one year require the use of debt service funds for their repayment.

4. Capital Projects Funds

Capital projects funds are created to account for all resources used for the acquisition of capital facilities other than those financed by special assessment and enterprise funds. Major capital facilities may be financed partially or entirely from proceeds of bond issues as well as other sources, such as federal or state grants, or transfers of current revenue from other funds within the municipality.

5. Enterprise Funds

Enterprise funds are established to account for the financing of self-supporting activities of governmental units which render services on a user charge basis to the general public. Water and sewer utilities are probably the most common examples. Commercial enterprise accounting is required for these funds and, therefore, fixed assets and revenue bond debt of an enterprise are both accounted for in the enterprise fund. Additionally, assets of an enterprise fund should be depreciated.

6. Trust and Agency Funds

Trust and agency funds are used to account for assets held by a governmental unit as trustee or agent for individuals, private organizations, or governmental units. Agency funds are primarily a clearing mechanism for assets held for a brief time, while trust funds usually exist over a longer period of time and usually involve more complex administrative and financial problems.

7. Internal Service Funds

Internal service funds, or intergovernmental service funds, are used to account for the financing of special activities or services performed by a designated organizational unit within a municipality for other organizational units within the same municipality. An example would be a central garage formed to handle vehicles for all departments of a municipality on a charge basis.

8. Special Assessment Funds

Special assessment funds are used to account for special assessments levied to finance public improvements, such as sidewalks or sewer lines, judged to be of benefit to the properties against which the assessments are levied.

General Fixed Assets Group of Accounts

The general fixed assets group of accounts is used to record those fixed assets of a governmental unit which are not accounted for in either the enterprise, internal service, or trust funds.

General Long-Term Debt Group of Accounts

The general long-term debt group of accounts is used to record general obligation bonds and other forms of long-term debt supported by the full faith and credit of the governmental unit.

Bases of Accounting

The basis of accounting to be followed in recording municipal transactions depends upon the purpose for which a fund has been established. Different types of funds require different bases of accounting.

The basis of accounting is a method for matching revenues and expenditures during a designated period of time. There exist three common bases of accounting in governmental operations:

1. Cash Basis of Accounting

Under the cash basis of accounting, revenues are recorded in the accounts when they are actually received in cash, and expenditures are recognized when the cash payment is actually made. Since services may be rendered in one fiscal period and the disbursements related to that service made in another fiscal period, the cash basis of accounting does not accurately present the complete financial picture at a given date.

2. Modified Accrual Basis of Accounting

The modified accrual basis of accounting is defined as that method of accounting in which expenditures (other than accrued interest on general long-term debt) are recorded at the time liabilities are incurred and revenues are recorded when received in cash (except for revenues susceptible to accrual and revenues of a material amount that have not been received at the normal time of receipt). Revenues considered susceptible to accrual consist of those revenues that are both measurable and available. Property taxes meet these criteria, and it is recommended that they be accrued when levied.

3. Full Accrual Basis of Accounting

Under the full accrual basis of accounting, revenues are recorded in the accounts at the time they are earned, and expenditures are recorded when the liability for them is incurred. The accrual basis is considered the superior method of accounting, since it provides a more accurate matching of expenditures with the associated revenues for a given fiscal period. The full accrual basis of accounting is recommended for use by Maine municipalities whenever possible. However, when the nature of the financial operation does not permit the use of the full accrual basis, the modified accrual basis of accounting is recommended.

Basis of Accounting and Fund Structure

Since the basis of accounting can vary with the nature and purpose of various funds, different bases of accounting are recommended for the fund structure described above. The modified accrual basis is recommended for all *budgetary funds* (those usually controlled through a current operating budget). The full accrual basis is recommended for all other funds. The bases of accounting for the eight recommended funds are listed below:

Modified Accrual Basis	*Full Accrual Basis*
General Fund	Capital Projects Funds
Special Revenue Funds	Enterprise Funds
Debt Service Funds	Trust and Agency Funds
	Internal Service Funds
	Special Assessment Funds

The Accounting System

An accounting system consists of an integrated structure of source documents, journals, ledgers, and procedures used to determine the financial position of an economic enterprise. It involves the composite activity of recording, summarizing, analyzing, and interpreting the financial transactions of any economic enterprise. It is the means by which to accomplish the goal of complete and accurate financial information that is of use to decision makers and the general public.

An accounting system is composed of four major components integrated into one unified structure:

1. Source Documents and Forms

Source documents and forms are the original documents that provide the necessary details of a financial transaction. Examples are invoices, checks, receipts, time cards, and purchase orders. Source documents and forms should be preprinted and prenumbered whenever possible. They should contain all data necessary to furnish an accurate record of each transaction. They often contain such additional data as proper authorizations and routing instructions.

2. Journals (Books of Original Entry)

Journals are used to make the first formal recording of a financial transaction. They organize and summarize transactions in an orderly manner such as chronologically, by type of transaction. The data recorded are usually taken directly from a source document. . . .

Four common types of journals are a cash receipts journal (Example 1), a cash disbursements journal, a payroll journal, and, finally, a general journal for all entries not recorded in one of the three specialized journals (Example 2).

3. Ledgers (Books of Final Entry)

Ledgers record the summary totals of transactions from the journals. They provide the balances which exist in any account at any given point in time. The general ledger consists of an individual account sheet for every asset, liability, revenue, expenditure, and capital account in use by a given municipality (Example 3).

Subsidiary ledgers are used when individual records are required in more detail than is practical to include in the general ledger. Subsidiary ledgers for current taxes receivable and delinquent taxes receivable are recommended for use by . . . Maine

Example 1: *Cash Receipts Journal*

Month					Page					
			REVENUE CONTROL ACCOUNT (A/C 172)		BALANCE SHEET ACCOUNTS		MULTI-COLUMN REVENUE DISTRIBUTION IF DESIRED			
DATE	EXPLANATION	CASH (A/C 101) DEBIT	A/C NO.	AMOUNT CREDIT	A/C NO.	AMOUNT CREDIT	A/C NO.	A/C NO.	A/C NO.
	A Cash Receipts Journal is used to record all cash receipts for a period of time and summarize them to form a basis for an entry to be recorded in the General Journal and then posted to the General Ledger.								
	EXAMPLE:								
6/30	*Total Receipts June*	*$4,500*	*A/C 172*	*$4,500*	*-0-*	*-0-*			

Example 2: *General Journal*

DATE		EXPLANATION	REF.	DEBIT	CREDIT
		This journal is used to record and describe all entries not recorded in a specialized journal or to record a summary from a specialized journal.			
		EXAMPLE: A summary entry to record all cash receipts for a month.			
6/30	*78*	*Cash*	*A/C 101*	*$4,500*	
		Revenues	*A/C 172*		*$4,500*
		To record cash receipts (in this case, all revenues) for the month of June from the Cash Receipts Journal.			
		This entry would then be posted to the above accounts in the General Ledger.			

Example 3: *General Ledger*

(Contains an account sheet for every type of account in the fund.)

ACCOUNT *CASH* **NUMBER** *101*

DATE	REFERENCE	DEBIT	CREDIT	ACCOUNT BALANCE DEBIT	ACCOUNT BALANCE CREDIT
6/30	*General Journal (p. 1)*	*$4,500*		*$4,500*	

ACCOUNT *TAXES RECEIVABLE–CURRENT* **NUMBER** *105*

DATE	REFERENCE	DEBIT	CREDIT	ACCOUNT BALANCE DEBIT	ACCOUNT BALANCE CREDIT

ACCOUNT *REVENUES* **NUMBER** *172*

DATE	REFERENCE	DEBIT	CREDIT	ACCOUNT BALANCE DEBIT	ACCOUNT BALANCE CREDIT
6/30	*General Journal (p. 1)*	*$4,500*			*$4,500*

ACCOUNT *FUND BALANCE* **NUMBER** *271*

DATE	REFERENCE	DEBIT	CREDIT	ACCOUNT BALANCE DEBIT	ACCOUNT BALANCE CREDIT

municipalities in order to control properly their major revenue source.

4. Procedures and Controls

Procedures are a sequence of instruction which govern the operation of a system. They help to ensure accurate and uniform handling of financial transactions. Procedures should be in writing, dated, and kept together in a detailed manual of all financial operations for a municipality.

A procedures manual should demonstrate the use of necessary forms and how to classify, record, summarize, control, and report information correctly in the accounting system. Standard procedures should be used by all personnel to avoid incomplete, misleading, and incorrect financial information.

Double Entry Accounting

The account is the basic means of providing information regarding each item for which a record must be kept. Accounts are used to record the amounts of money according to the things owned or owed by a municipality. The entire group of accounts used in an accounting system is called the general ledger. It exists to provide a record of the financial transactions of each fund over a period of time.

Accounts can be classified into three categories: balance sheet accounts, revenue accounts, and expenditure accounts.

Balance Sheet Accounts

Accounts that make up the balance sheet accounts appear in the balance sheet prepared at the end of a fiscal year. These are accounts which are not closed out to zero at the end of the year. Balance sheet accounts are classified into three types:

Asset Accounts: The things of value that are owned by the local government, such as cash and taxes receivable.

Liability Accounts: The debts owed to others by the local government, such as bills and notes payable.

Fund Balance: The accumulated value or net worth of the fund of the local government.

The relationship between these three different types of balance sheet accounts can be expressed as a simple equation:

Assets = Liabilities + Fund Balance

This equation is the essence of double entry accounting. Both sides of the equation must always balance. When one side of the equation is changed, the other side of the equation must be changed in the same amount to keep them in balance.

Revenue and Expenditure Accounts

Revenue and expenditure accounts do not appear on the balance sheet. These accounts are closed at the end of the fiscal year. Revenue accounts are used to explain the source of revenue earned by a local government. Expenditure accounts are used to explain the purpose for spending the money the local government has received.

Debits and Credits

Each ledger account is divided into two parts, known as the debit and credit sides. For every entry affecting the debit side (left-hand side) of an account, the corresponding amount must be entered on the credit side (right-hand side) of another account. In this manner, a balance is always maintained in the accounts with the total of all debit entries always equaling the total of all credit entries. This proof of accuracy is basic to the operation of a double entry accounting system.

When recording transactions, a decision must be made as to (1) which account is affected, and (2) whether the accounts are increased or decreased. *Debits* are increases in assets and expenditure accounts, but decreases in liability, revenue, and fund balance accounts. *Credits* are decreases in asset and expenditure accounts, but increases in liability, revenue, and fund balance accounts.

Learning the definitions of *debit* and *credit* along with the normal balances of the different classifications of accounts enables one to properly record a transaction in a double entry accounting system. Example 4 summarizes how to increase or decrease any type of account and should be learned carefully by an inexperienced person using this [chapter].

Internal Control

Municipal accounting systems must be structured, and procedures established, to ensure that accounting information is accurate and assets are safeguarded. Such structure and procedures promote efficiency and encourage adherence to municipal policies and all legal requirements.

Internal Control Defined

The term *internal control* describes those methods

Example 4: *How to Record Changes in Ledger Accounts*

TYPE OF ACCOUNT	CHART OF ACCOUNT NUMBERS	DEFINITION OF ACCOUNT	NORMAL ACCOUNT BALANCE	TO INCREASE ACCOUNT	TO DECREASE ACCOUNT
ASSETS	100-169	Things of value that are owned	Debit	Debit	Credit
OTHER DEBITS	170-199	Other accounts with debit balances	Debit	Debit	Credit
LIABILITIES	200-239	Things of value owed to others	Credit	Credit	Debit
OTHER CREDITS	240-299	Other accounts with credit balances	Credit	Credit	Debit
REVENUES	300-399	Sources of money	Credit	Credit	Debit
EXPENDITURES	400-499	Reasons for spending money	Debit	Debit	Credit
FUND BALANCE	271	Net worth	Credit	Credit	Debit

EXAMPLES: (1) Cash is received from State Revenue Sharing (a Revenue Account). Cash is increased (debited) and the Revenue Account is also increased (credited).
(2) Cash is paid out to pay outstanding Accounts Payable. Cash is decreased (credited) and Accounts Payable is also decreased (debited).
(3) Cash is received as payment of Taxes Receivable. Cash is increased (debited) and Taxes Receivable is decreased (credited).

adopted within an organization to safeguard cash and other assets, as well as to check the accuracy of the accounting to prevent and/or locate inaccuracies. An internal control system is not a separate or distinct system, but rather a set of methods that is an integral part of the accounting system.

There are many possible internal control procedures that can be introduced into an accounting system. Some are not always practical, since their costs often exceed their benefits. However, the basic procedures listed below can be introduced into most municipal accounting systems . . . .

Internal Control Procedures

1. All transactions should be recorded on an original (source) document.
2. Transactions should be approved and performed only by authorized personnel.
3. If possible, the original transaction should be checked or verified by someone other than the person who recorded it.
4. If possible, responsibilities for particular functions should be assigned to specific persons.
5. If possible, persons responsible for receiving or collecting assets should not have access to the accounting records of those assets.
6. The administrator should ensure that the initial recording of the transaction is entered into the accounting records correctly.
7. Mechanical devices, such as cash registers, check signers, validators, calculators, etc., should be used whenever possible.
8. A procedures manual should be prepared showing step-by-step instructions (who, when, where, what).
9. Preprinted, prenumbered forms, carefully designed for a specific purpose, should be used in numerical sequence.
10. If possible, a person should be made responsible for ensuring that all control procedures are working properly and are being adhered to by all personnel.
11. Outside auditors should be used whenever a problem arises; their expertise can resolve and avoid many financial and accounting problems.

It is important to keep in mind that these procedures and policies should not be looked upon as a nuisance, but as integral parts of an accounting system. They serve the important function of safeguarding public assets and ensuring the accuracy of data and financial reporting.

Summary

Municipal accounting is known as "fund accounting." It differs somewhat from commercial accounting. The primary interest is not on profit or loss, but on the "flow of money." Therefore, certain accounting principles have evolved that recognize the objectives of a governmental unit and the legal environment in which it operates. However, the basic objective of municipal accounting remains the same as in the private sector: the complete and accurate accountability of all financial transactions and the provision of meaningful information to all concerned parties. The only way to accomplish this objective is with a sound accounting system based upon generally accepted accounting principles.

24 Cost Accounting

Introduction

Cost accounting systems have long been used in business to measure productivity. In cost accounting systems, operating expenditures and certain allocated service costs are grouped together to measure the cost of a product or service. The theory and concept of cost accounting, which is to identify all the actual costs involved in producing a result, are transferable to government. Identifying the actual costs of delivering a particular service is growing more and more important for efficient, effective management.

This chapter introduces *direct cost accumulation* as a means to measure productivity in smaller local governments. Such an approach is acceptable and useful for management information purposes, since direct costs represent a large percentage of the costs of government and indirect costs require time and staff to monitor and allocate—which a smaller community may not have.

Without incurring significant additional administrative expenditures, a system can be established to collect, store and summarize actual costs of those activities or functions being measured. Costs are grouped under the designation of cost centers which segregate costs by service or function. Existing account structures whose purpose is to relate to budgeted line items or revenue funds cannot usually do this.

Reprinted from Performance Measurement and Cost Accounting for Small Local Governments *(Providence: Rhode Island Department of Community Affairs, n.d.).*

This material is intended primarily for the finance director and other members of the finance function of government. Exhibit 1 illustrates how financial functions are integrated into the entire productivity reporting system. With a reporting system established at the department level to measure workload and inputs such as labor hours by activity, finance directors can take the accumulated data and apply direct costing methods to determine the costs of activities. The costs are summarized into cost performance reports which indicate productivity and efficiency. These reports establish the foundation for decision making by management and the council.

The rest of the [chapter] discusses the components of cost and identifies each as either direct or indirect; it also discusses coding and recording costs. . . .

Identification and Classification of Costs

The costs of performing a service or completing an activity are usually classified as either direct or indirect. *Direct costs* generally include costs for materials, supplies, salaries and wages, services, etc., that can be readily measured and directly attributed to a particular activity or service being provided. For purposes of this [chapter], *indirect costs* are those elements of cost which are not readily identifiable with a particular service or activity, and must be distributed using some equitable method of allocation. Indirect costs are often referred to as "overhead" and include expenditures such as rent, utility charges, insurance, certain supplies, administrative expenses, etc.

Exhibit 1: *Financial Functions and Productivity Reporting*

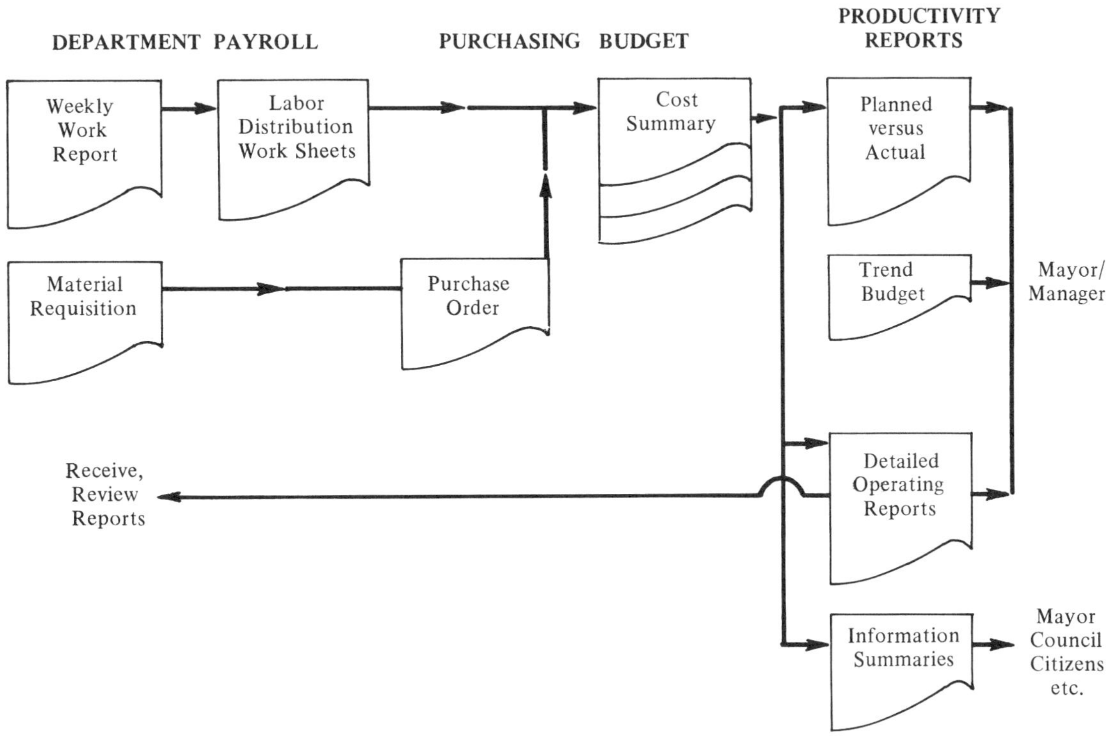

Fringe benefits, which are variously defined as either a direct or indirect cost, are considered an indirect cost.

Direct Cost Accumulation Defined

Direct cost accumulation is the process of assigning to a service, activity, or function of an operating unit of government all the costs that can be directly attributed to it. *Direct cost,* rather than total cost accumulation, is recommended for smaller local governments for the following reasons:

- Accumulating *only* direct costs is a relatively simple accounting operation.
- Direct costs can provide a very valuable *indicator* of productivity, since they represent a significant portion of governmental costs.
- Direct costs can be monitored without having to develop too complex a cost accounting system.

It is important to note, however, that accumulating *only* direct cost does *not* provide officials and managers with the actual total cost of providing services. Direct cost accumulation is, therefore, a valuable *indicator* of the actual cost of government services, although not the *complete* cost in an accounting sense which must include indirect costs as well.

Expenditure Accounts

When using costs as a measure of productivity, it is necessary to know which costs are included in the specific service, activity, or function that is being measured for output. It is equally important that the costs be classified consistently.

To ensure integrity and consistency in classifying expenditures, a systematic approach to recording costs should be established.

A chart of accounts should be developed and consistently followed in classifying and recording expenditures. It should be a detailed listing of expenditure accounts and be supported by account definitions. Smaller local governments should develop expenditure accounts that are responsive to their needs for cost information consistent with classification in *Governmental Accounting, Auditing and Financial Reporting* (*GAAFR*, or the "Blue Book").*

Governmental expenditures are usually classified on several bases:

- Classification by *Object*—commodity or service obtained from a specific type of expenditure such as supplies, insurance, etc.
- Classification by *Organization*—by department, division, bureau, or other administrative unit incurring the expenditure.
- Classification by *Character*—by the fiscal period(s) benefiting from the expenditure.

The following is a list of recommended expenditure accounts and definitions by *Object Classification* and includes identification of each as either a direct or indirect cost for purposes of the direct cost accumulation system being recommended. The structure of the accounts is consistent with the classification of expenditures in *GAAFR*. and that recommended for use by smaller local governments by the International MFOA Career Development Center in its manual on "Accounting for Smaller Governmental Units."**

Personal Services

Personal service costs include expenditures for salaries and wages (including expenditures for overtime, shift differential, holiday pay, hazardous duty pay, sick leave, military leave, bereavement, etc.), and employer's contribution to employee fringe benefits (such as insurance, retirement and pension fund, hospitalization, worker compensation, terminal pay, uniform and clothing allowances, unemployment insurance, and similar benefits).

The following personal service expenses should be classified as direct costs:

Salaries
Wages

The remaining personal service expenses are considered indirect costs.

Materials and Supplies

Materials and supplies include items and commodities which are consumed or used in providing the activity or service. Materials and supplies include office supplies; repair and maintenance (include building materials and supplies); and small tools and minor equipment having a limited life expectancy.

Materials and supplies may be classified as *direct* costs, if they can be specifically attributed to a service, activity, or function of the operating unit of government and are a significant cost element. Otherwise, they should be considered *indirect* costs.

Materials and supplies may be purchased in bulk and used over a period of time (inventoried) or acquired for a specific project. Only those materials and supplies actually *consumed* or used in providing a service, activity, or operation may be included as a cost of the project. Examples might be gas, sand, salt, patch mix, paint guns, hose, tires, parts, etc. The remaining materials and supplies in inventory are charged to a project when used.

Most office supplies, materials relating to repairs and maintenance, and tools are recorded as expenditures when acquired by a smaller local government. These materials and supplies are used in small quantities on many varied projects and often account for an insignificant portion of the total cost of a project. They are considered indirect costs.

Contractual Services

Contractual services include cost of utilities, insurance and bonding services, communications, rents and leases, and professional services.

Contractual services may be classified as *direct* or *indirect* depending upon the ability to assign the costs to a specific project. Smaller local governments often rely on service bureaus and special consultants, such as lawyers, for some functions of government normally carried out by larger local governments. Contractual services which can be directly attributed to a specific activity or operation are direct costs. If the contractual service is not directly in support of a specified activity or func-

*©1968 Municipal Finance Officers Association.

** © 1976 International MFOA Career Development Center, Inc.

tion (such as utilities), the costs must be allocated to multiple activities and are considered indirect.

Travel and Transportation

Travel and transportation costs are usually recorded on an individual basis. Expense reports are prepared by employees as the basis of reimbursement, or flat rate allowances are provided. Since these expenditures can be specifically identified, they should be considered *direct* costs. If specific identification is not possible, they should be allocated and treated as indirect costs.

Miscellaneous Charges

Miscellaneous charges include such expenses as memberships, dues, laundry services, and printing. These expenses usually cannot be associated with a specific individual activity. As such, they are considered *indirect* costs. When specific identification is possible, they should be treated as direct costs.

Capital Outlay

Capital outlays result in acquisition of or addition to fixed assets and include direct expenditures for construction of buildings, roads, and other improvements; purchase of equipment, land, and existing structures; additions; replacements and major alterations to fixed works and structures. *Excluded* from capital outlay is property and equipment with limited life and monetary value. Capital items usually have a useful life greater than one year. Assets will not be included as direct costs in most productivity studies since their useful life is extensive. However, a portion of the cost can be considered if the project warrants its inclusion and the community has sufficient staff to develop the computations.

Normally, a fixed asset depreciation schedule is prepared annually from an inventory of assets and based upon the useful life of each asset. It is included as part of the *indirect* costs distributed to measure activities, services, or projects. Depreciation expenses may be identified with a specific department or organizational subdivision if the asset records provide specific detail.

Most smaller communities do not have inventories or their records are inaccurate and incomplete, and specific identification may not be possible.

As an *alternative* to depreciation expense, an annual *"Usage Charge"* has been suggested in Federal Management Circular 74-4. On an annual basis, 2 percent of the cost of undepreciated buildings and 6 2/3 percent of equipment costs are used as the approximate annual expense.

Debt Service

Debt service includes principal and interest payments on loans, notes, and bonds. Principal and interest payments are generally not easily associated with a single activity or function and thus should be treated as *indirect* costs.

Account Codes

Account codes provide a structured method for accumulating costs. For productivity measurement, it is useful to be able to summarize costs organizationally by department, division, section, unit, etc., or by program, activity, element, etc.

As stated previously, in smaller communities many activities may be performed in one department, or they may be logically grouped by division (or bureaus). One approach that may be useful for smaller local governments in collecting costs relating to the various activities in each department is to maintain expenditure accounts by department and division. In this way, expenditures may be grouped by program, activity, or tasks and easily extracted for analysis.

The structure of account codes varies considerably in actual use. However, a typical coding structure that facilitates budgeting, accounting, and cost accumulation is illustrated.

X - XXX - XX - XX

FUND
EXPENDITURE
ORGANIZATION
PROGRAM

FUND
General
Special
Debt Service
Etc.

EXPENDITURE
Personal Services
Materials and Supplies
Contractual Services
Travel and Transportation
Miscellaneous Charges
Capital Outlays
Debt Service

ORGANIZATIONAL UNIT
General Administration
Finance Department
Police Department
Public Works
Etc.

PROGRAMS/SUBPROGRAMS
Community Protection
  Law Enforcement
Transportation
  Street and Sidewalk Maintenance
  Snow Removal
  Etc.

Work Codes

In order to know the cost of a particular activity, such as snow removal, garbage collection, etc., it is necessary to account for labor associated with these selected activities. Costs at this operating level are not normally recorded by smaller local governments using their accounting system.

A method which can accumulate this data fairly simply is the *Work Code*. Codes are assigned to each task, job, or project at the work unit level, usually a two or three digit code. Once developed and assigned, these work codes should be made readily available to all supervisors, who will most likely be responsible for keeping track of man-hours expended by task. The back of the weekly work report is a convenient place to have the work codes listed for easy access by the supervisor(s) completing this form.

A limited example of work codes for a solid waste collection activity is listed below.

WORK CODE	ACTIVITY
10	Solid Waste Collection & Disposal
10.1	Collect Refuse
10.2	Haul & Dump
10.3	Receive & Weigh
10.4	Clean Vehicles
41	Street & Highway Maintenance
41.1	Administration
41.2	Street Striping
41.3	Street Sweeping
41.4	Brush Cutting
41.5	Street Patching

Exhibit 2 lists additional categories of work codes that can be used for cost accumulation, including non-productive categories. It should be noted that when constructing the work code logic, it is desirable to create a universal set of codes for certain specific recurring activities. In this way, if the same activity is performed in more than one department, costs associated with it can be grouped and summarized using the activity code only. For example, mowing, if done in parks and in public works will have the same code, unless there is reason to analyze these costs separately.

The same nonproductive (indirect labor) codes should also be used by all departments. Costs associated with these charges can be readily identified and grouped for reporting by department, division, etc., or program, activity, or subactivity.

Exhibit 2: *Work Codes*

TIME WORKED

DIRECT LABOR	
10 Solid Waste Collection & Disposal	91 Holiday
.1 Collect Refuse	92 Vacation
.2 Haul & Dump	93 Sick
.3 Receive & Weigh	94 Bereavement
.4 Clean Vehicles	95 Military Leave
	96 Jury Duty
	97 Overtime Premium
INDIRECT LABOR	**ASSIGNMENT CODE**
61 Administration	11 Garbage Route 1
62 Union Meetings	12 Garbage Route 2
63 Training	13 Garbage Route 3
64 Etc.	14 Garbage Route 4
	15 Garbage Route 5

Example:

NONPRODUCTIVE CODE	
91	Holiday
92	Vacation
93	Sick
94	Bereavement
95	Military Leave
96	Jury Duty
97	Overtime Premium

The assignment code is a work designation code that can be utilized to accumulate costs associated with a particular project or work location. It is useful in determining efficiency of routing or particular work emphasis in a given area. . . . It allows for measuring the costs and work output for any given project area. It is possible that smaller local governments may not be able to immediately establish assignment codes, but they can provide added ability to gain a full knowledge of direct costs in a given area.

Expenditure Ledger

At whatever level of organization costs are to be accumulated, procedures must be developed to collect and summarize the data. The expenditure ledger, part of the accounting system, is usually the vehicle to accumulate expenditures for reporting the results of financial activities.

In smaller communities, a manual ledger is frequently maintained and is not very detailed. Operating expenditures are often recorded by object classification within departments, but they are not further subdivided by division and section, function and task.

For productivity analysis, the objective is to have a *cost* accounting system—a system which can support the performance data maintained by line departments with cost data at the same level of detail. Some alternatives for a smaller community to do this were discussed in the Account Codes section, but will be restated. If the accounting system is not, and cannot be, set up to maintain expenditure accounts by department, division and section, program and activity, and even task level in those instances where output is being measured at this level, the community can set up a system of subsidiary ledgers or a separate cost accounting system. This set of ledgers can group expenditures by program, activity, task or whatever level of detail is required by that community for measurement purposes. In other words, the community sets up cost centers which it wishes to monitor. These expenditure breakdowns could then be posted in summary by object classification to the expenditure ledger.

Exhibit 3 illustrates the productivity analysis flow that results after the cost accumulation to the operating department ledger accounts and to the expenditure ledger. All the direct costs associated with each activity, task, etc., being measured can be determined from the ledger subdivisions. Productivity can then be analyzed by applying these direct costs to the performance statistics which are generated by the various municipal functions such as police patrol, fire fighting, etc. If the municipality is also accumulating indirect costs and has determined methods to allocate these costs to departments, then productivity can be analyzed based on total costs.

As an alternative to manual collection and processing of data, automated systems are available for this purpose. Programs can be written to accommodate the summarization and allocation of costs to cost centers with ease and facility. Systems are available to satisfy the reporting needs of any size municipality and offer a viable alternative to manually processed data. Computer service cooperatives or some form of shared time can be a good approach for smaller communities.

Summary

In every instance of establishing a direct cost accumulation system, certain elements must be in place. These include:

- A chart of accounts
- An accounting system which can identify direct costs associated with individual departments and divisions
- A work code system which can accumulate labor hours for tasks in greater detail than the accounting system
- A reporting system, either automated or manual, to accumulate all direct costs by activity from the expenditure ledgers, subsidiary ledgers, work reports or other source documents

Exhibit 3: *Productivity Analysis Flow*

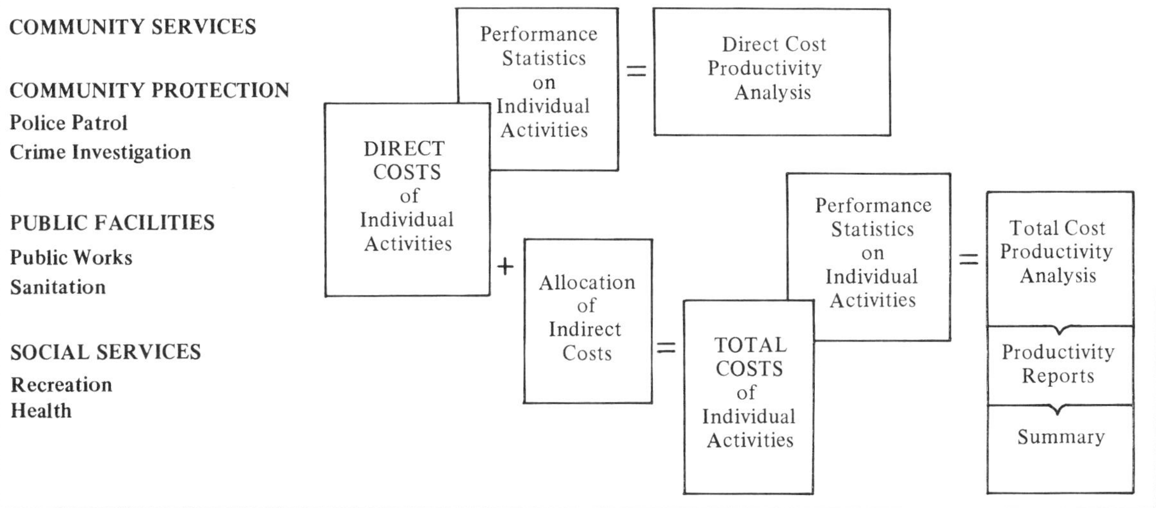

25 A Primer on Reading Local Government Financial Statements

Vincent Pivnicny

Summary

This primer highlights important concepts and topics associated with local government accounting. Virtually all local governments prepare financial statements in accordance with either "cash basis" or "modified accrual basis" accounting approaches. Section 1 briefly describes these two approaches and illustrates their differences with comparable model financial statements. Section 2 provides numerous practical suggestions on how an individual can analyze his or her own community's financial statements. Section 3 gives a quick overview of some lively topics of discussion among government accountants today.

Section 1: The Basic Financial Statements

It is generally understood and accepted by those who work with financial statements (and by the courts) that the responsibility for financial statements of both commercial enterprises and governmental units is in the hands of the issuer. In order to comply with the requirements of making a fair presentation of financial position and results of operations, a community should prepare a balance sheet, a statement of revenues and expenditures (and encumbrances, if appropriate), and a statement of changes in fund balance for each fund for the most recently closed fiscal year. General purpose units (counties, cities, towns, etc.) typically account for the major share of their financial activities within the so-called "General Fund" set of books. Figures 1, 2, and 3 present two sets of completed statements for the General Fund for the City of XXX; the dollar amounts on the right side of the page are prepared according to the modified accrual process required by generally accepted accounting principles; the dollar amounts on the left side of the page are prepared according to the widely used cash basis. In addition, Figures 4, 5, 6, 7, and 8 show the reader how the cash dollar amounts were transformed to modified accrual basis dollar amounts.

A Comparison of the Cash Basis and the Modified Accrual Basis

A major difference between the cash basis and the modified accrual basis is that the latter allows the recognition of certain taxes as revenues, even though they have not been physically received as cash; hence the asset "Property Taxes Receivable" in Set II of Figure 3. Also, this basis allows the recognition of expenditures before they are actually paid in cash; hence modified accrual accounting "payables" are listed as liabilities in Set II of Figure 3.

In Figure 1, Set I, the cash basis dollar amounts show actual revenues of $1,221,550, while in Set II, the modified accrual basis dollar amounts show

---

Reprinted from Vincent Pivnicny, "A Primer on Reading Local Government Financial Statements," Appendix B of Peter F. Rousmaniere, gen.ed., Local Government Auditing: A Manual for Public Officials *(New York: Council on Municipal Performance, 1979). The Council on Municipal Performance is preparing an updated book on auditing and financial statement analysis.*

actual revenues to be $1,174,500. The cash basis revenues are reduced when one converts the amounts to the modified accrual basis as shown in Figure 4. The current year's cash basis revenues include property taxes levied last year when they were levied and due. The cash basis would treat such taxes as revenues of the year in which they were collected. In any case, the net overstatement of cash basis actual revenues is only $47,000, a not very great or material amount when taken by itself.

In Figure 1, Set I, the cash basis dollar amounts show actual expenditures of $1,161,500, while in Set II, the modified accrual basis dollar amounts show actual expenditures to be $1,196,500. Contrary to the revenue side, one finds expenditures higher in the sample financial statements under the modified accrual basis than under the cash basis. This does not always occur when converting from one basis to another, but it is not at all improbable. Again, we find that the understatement of expenditures is a mere $35,000, not an overly great sum when compared, e.g., to overall expenditures of over one million dollars.

The overstatement of actual revenues and the understatement of actual expenditures, taken each by itself, do not appear to be excessive, but together they help to turn a cash basis budget surplus into a modified accrual basis budget deficit. Figure 2 shows a cash basis budget surplus of $60,000. The conversion to the modified accrual basis reveals a budget deficit of $62,000. Figure 8 shows how the surplus was converted to a deficit.

Suppose a particular local governmental unit finds itself confronted, near the end of a fiscal year, with a General Fund deficit. The law may not permit such a deficit. Better and more prudent management could have avoided the deficit. In order to avoid a breach of the law, local officials operating under the cash basis could arrange for "prepayments" of next year's revenues to be counted as this year's revenues. In addition, they can postpone the payment of expenditures chargeable against this year's budget. As a result, a cash basis budget deficit is converted to a cash basis budget surplus. The modified accrual basis would not have permitted such manipulations of the financial statements. Better and more prudent management would have been the answer to avoiding budget deficits rather than deceptive accounting manipulations.

Section 2: Analysis of Financial Statements

Changes in Fund Balance

What does the fund balance of the General Fund represent? The fund balance is defined as the excess of the assets of a fund over its liabilities. The fund balance indicates the resources available for expenditure in the next fiscal year even before taxes are levied. The only important qualification occurs in those cases in which portions of the fund balance are already reserved before entering the next fiscal year. In this case, the balance sheet may split the fund balance into restricted and unrestricted portions so that managers, the legislative branch, and the public get a true picture of the actual resources available for expenditure.

Figure 1

I. City of XXX			COMPARISON	II. City of XXX		
Analysis of Changes in Fund Balance Year Ending December 31, 19X8 (Cash Basis)			Actual revenues–see Figures 2 and 4	Analysis of Changes in Fund Balance Year Ending December 31, 19X8 (Cash Basis Converted to Modified Accrual Basis)		
Fund Balance January 1, 19X8		$15,000	Actual expenditures–see Figures 2 and 5	Fund Balance, Restricted and Unrestricted, January 1, 19X8		$85,000
Add:				Add or (Deficit):		
Excess of Revenues over Expenditures:			Encumbrances–see Figure 6	Excess of Revenues over Expenditures:		
Revenues	$1,221,500			Revenues	$1,174,500	
-Expenditures	(1,161,500)	$60,000		-Expenditures	(1,196,500)	(22,000)
Fund Balance December 31, 19X8		$75,000	Fund balances–see Figure 6	Fund Balance, Restricted and Unrestricted, December 31, 19X8		$63,000
				Reserve for Encumbrances, December 31, 19X8		$40,000
				Fund Balance, Unrestricted, December 31, 19X8		$23,000

Figure 2

I.
City of XXX
General Fund
Statement of Revenues and Expenditures
Compared with Estimated and Budgeted
for the Fiscal Year Ended December 31, 19X8

(CASH BASIS)

Revenue–Sources	*Estimated*	*Actual*	*Over (Under) Estimated*
Taxes	$ 800,500	$ 822,300	$ 21,800
Licenses & Permits	125,000	103,000	(22,000)
Intergovernmental	160,000	146,500	(13,500)
Charges for Services	70,000	91,000	21,000
Fines & Forfeits	32,500	39,200	6,700
Miscellaneous	12,000	19,500	7,500
Total Revenues	$1,200,000	$1,221,500	$ 21,500
Expenditures for	*Budget*	*Actual*	*Over (Under) Estimated*
General Government	$ 119,000	$ 115,305	$ (3,695)
Public Safety	251,300	242,795	(8,505)
Highways & Streets	88,500	84,000	(4,500)
Sanitation	45,000	44,900	(100)
Health	42,750	38,850	(3,900)
Welfare	45,000	44,000	(1,000)
Culture–Recreation	58,000	51,400	(6,600)
Education	550,450	540,250	(10,200)
Total Expenditures	$1,200,000	$1,161,500	$(38,500)
Excess (Deficit) of Revenues over Expenditures	-0-	$60,000	$60,000

COMPARISON

Total Estimated Revenues–see Figure 7

Total Actual Revenues–see Figure 4

Total Budgeted Expenditures are based on the assumption of a balanced budget

Actual Expenditures–see Figure 5

From a Budget Surplus to Deficit–Figure 8

II.
City of XXX
General Fund
Statement of Revenues, Expenditures and
Encumbrances Compared with Estimated
and Budgeted for the Fiscal Period
Ended December 31, 19X8

(CASH BASIS CONVERTED TO MODIFIED ACCRUAL BASIS)

Revenue–Sources	*Estimated*			*Actual*	*Over (Under) Estimate*
Taxes	$ 776,500			$ 770,300	$ (6,200)
Licenses & Permits	125,000			103,000	(22,000)
Intergovernmental	155,000			151,500	(3,500)
Charges for Services	70,000			91,000	21,000
Fines & Forfeits	32,500			39,200	6,700
Miscellaneous	12,000			19,500	7,500
Total Revenues	$1,171,000			$1,174,500	$ 3,500
		Actual			
Expenditures & Encumbrances for	*Budget*	*Expenditures*	*Encumbrances*	*Expenditures & Encumbrances*	*Actual Over (Under) Estimate*
General Government	$ 119,700	$ 120,305	$ 4,200	$ 124,505	$ 4,805
Public Safety	247,400	252,795	6,550	259,345	11,945
Highways & Streets	86,800	86,000	5,500	91,500	4,700
Sanitation	47,100	46,900	3,000	49,900	2,800
Health	43,600	40,850	4,600	45,450	1,850
Welfare	47,300	46,000	2,100	48,100	800
Culture–Recreation	55,200	53,400	3,850	57,250	2,050
Education	523,900	550,250	10,200	560,450	36,550
Total Expenditures	$1,171,000	$1,196,500	$40,000	$1,236,500	$65,500
Excess (Deficit) of Revenues over Expenditures & Encumbrances	$ -0-			$ 62,000	$(62,000)

Figure 3

I. City of XXX General Fund Balance Sheet, December 31, 19X8 (CASH BASIS)		COMPARISON	II. City of XXX General Fund Balance Sheet, December 31, 19X8 (CASH BASIS CONVERTED TO MODIFIED ACCRUAL BASIS)		
Assets			*Assets*		
Cash	$12,000	Receivables not reported on the cash basis	Cash		$12,000
Treasury Bills	38,000		Treasury Bills		38,000
Certificates of Deposit	25,000		Certificates of Deposit		25,000
			Property Taxes Receivable	$35,500	
			Loss: Allowance for Uncollectibles	(2,500)	33,000
			Due from Other Governments		10,000
Total	$75,000		Total		$118,000
Liabilities, Reserves, and Fund Balance		Payables not reported on the cash basis	*Liabilities, Reserves, and Fund Balance*		
			Liabilities		
			Vouchers Payable		$ 20,000
			Payroll Taxes Payable		20,000
			Due to Other Funds		15,000
		Fund balances See Figure 6	Fund Balance:		
			Restricted	$40,000	
			Unrestricted	23,000	63,000
Total	$75,000		Total		$118,000

Figure 4

How to Go from Cash Basis Actual Revenues to Modified Accrual Basis Actual Revenues

19X8 Cash Basis Actual Revenues		$1,221,500
Subtract:	Property Taxes Receivable, 12/31/X7 (net of estimated uncollectibles); this item represents property taxes levied last year and includable in last year's modified accrual basis budget, but were not collected until 19X8.	85,000
		$1,136,500
Subtract:	Due from Other Governments, 12/31/X7 (net of estimated uncollectibles);this item represents intergovernmental revenues includable in last year's modified accrual basis budget, but were not paid until 19X8.	5,000
		$1,131,500
Add:	Property Taxes Receivable, 12/31/X8 (net of estimated collectibles); this item represents property taxes levied for the current year and includable in the current year's modified accrual basis budget, but are unpaid at year end and are expected to be collected in the next fiscal year (see Figure 3).	33,000
		$1,164,500
Add:	Due from Other Governments, 12/31/X8 (net of estimated uncollectibles); this item represents intergovernmental revenues includable in the current year's modified accrual basis budget but are unpaid at year end and are expected to be collected in the next fiscal year (see Figure 3).	10,000
19X8 Modified Accrual Basis Actual Revenues		$1,174,500

The fund balance may increase from one year to the next; this is usually caused by revenues exceeding expenditures during that fiscal year, resulting in a net addition to the balance. One view of this situation is that this is a desirable strategy because it means that the government is building up a larger buffer to cover unexpected expenditures in the future. However, it is appropriate to ask a further question: "For what use are these new monies being accumulated?" Have the managers saved money by not expending resources on important or necessary investments for the community?

The fund balance may decrease from one year to the next; this is usually caused by current expenditures exceeding current revenues during the fiscal year, resulting in a net decrease in the balance. This may or may not forebode bad things for the community. The shortfall in revenues may be the result of a depressed economy in the community, or the overrun in expenditures may be the result of an unexpected binding arbitration award to municipal employees. Both of these developments are largely beyond control of the local managers. The decrease in the fund balance might also indicate an aggressive strategy by the community to apply its resources to important municipal services by using fund reserves rather than current revenue sources. In this case the questions are: "What did they spend the resources on?" and "Why did they spend them this year?"

CHECKPOINT ONE:
Did the fund balance increase or decrease?
What forces led to the increase or decrease?
Was the change within control of the municipal officials?
Was it the most appropriate use of municipal resources?

Analysis of Variances

The legal basis for public expenditures is the appropriate ordinance that legalizes the expenditure of public funds, and in most cases acts as a legal limit on these expenditures. The appropriate ordinances that are passed when the budget is enacted are also

Figure 5

How to Go from Cash Basis Actual Expenditures to Modified Accrual Basis Actual Expenditures

19X8 Cash Basis Actual Expenditures		$1,161,500
Subtract:	Vouchers Payable, 12/31/X7, represents expenditures chargeable to last year's modified accrual basis budget that were paid this year.	5,000
		$1,156,500
Subtract:	Payroll Taxes Payable 12/31/X7, represents expenditures chargeable to last year's modified accrual basis budget that were paid this year.	5,000
		$1,151,500
Subtract:	Due to Other Funds, 12/31/X7, represents expenditures chargeable to last year's modified accrual basis budget that were paid this year.	10,000
		$1,141,500
Add:	Vouchers Payable, 12/31/X8, represents expenditures chargeable to the current year's modified accrual basis budget that are unpaid liabilities at year end (Figure 3).	20,000
		$1,161,500
Add:	Payroll Taxes Payable, 12/31/X8, represents expenditures chargeable to the current year's modified accrual basis budget that are unpaid liabilities at year end (see Figure 3).	20,000
		$1,181,500
Add:	Due to Other Funds, 12/31/X8, represents expenditures chargeable to the current year's modified accrual basis budget that are unpaid liabilities at year end (see Figure 3).	15,000
19X8 Modified Accrual Basis Actual Expenditures		$1,196,500

Figure 6

How to Go from the Cash Basis Fund Balance to the Modified Accrual Basis Fund Balance

Cash Basis Fund Balance as of December 13, 19X8			$75,000
Add:	Property Taxes Receivable, 12/31/X7, not included in beginning Cash Basis Fund Balance.	$85,000	
Add:	Due from Other Governments, 12/31/X7, not included in beginning Cash Basis Fund Balance.	5,000	
Subtract:	Vouchers Payable, 12/31/X7, not deducted from beginning Cash Basis Fund Balance.	(5,000)	
Subtract:	Due to Other Funds, 12/31/X7, not deducted from beginning Cash Basis Fund Balance.	(10,000)	
Subtract:	Payroll Taxes Payable, 12/31/X7, not deducted from beginning Cash Basis Fund Balance.	(5,000)	70,000
Cash Basis Fund Balance, as of 12/31/X8, adjusted to reflect last year's Modified Accrual Basis Items			$145,000
Subtract:	Overstatement of Cash Basis Actual Revenues against Modified Accrual Basis Actual Revenues: Cash Basis Actual Revenues:	$1,221,500	
Less:	Modified Accrual Basis Actual Revenues	1,174,500	47,000
	Actual		$ 98,000
Subtract:	Understatement of Cash Basis Actual Expenditures as against Modified Accrual Basis Actual Expenditures:	$1,196,500	
Less:	Modified Accrual Basis Actual Expenditures	1,161,500	35,000
Modified Accrual Basis Restricted and Unrestricted Fund Balance as of 12/31/X8			$ 63,000
Subtract:	Reserve for Encumbrances, 12/31/X8		40,000
Modified Accrual Basis Unrestricted Fund Balance, 12/31/X8			$ 23,000

known as *estimated expenditures.* These expenditure estimates should be the result of the best efforts of the executive and legislative branch to estimate costs for the upcoming fiscal year. Department managers are expected to live within the budget appropriations unless uncontrollable problems occur.

To balance a budget for a fiscal year, estimated revenues must equal estimated expenditures. If estimated revenues are intentionally overstated, the tax rates are kept artificially low, and often the result is an end-of-the-year deficit in the budget. The statement of revenues, expenditures, and encumbrances can be used to assess the efficiency of managers in living within budget appropriations and the accuracy of the community's revenue estimating process.

For example, in Figure 2, Set I, two of the six revenue sources had actual collections that were less than the budgetary estimates. There are two alternative causes for such a discrepancy: either the estimates were unreasonably high, or the actual collections fell short of reasonable estimates because of adverse economic conditions or an inefficient revenue collection system. In the case of Charges for Services, Figure 2, Set I, indicates that actual collections exceeded budgeted collections by $21,000. The case of actual collections exceeding budget collections may be caused by either of two factors: the revenue estimate was low, or a combination of economic forces and collection efficiency led to higher than anticipated collections.

The same two perspectives can be applied to the analysis of expenditure behavior. In Figure 2, Set I, all classes of the cash basis actual expenditures were less than budgeted expenditures. These differences may be due to intentional padding of expenditure estimates, diverting of expenditures from agreed upon activities to save funds, or to actual managerial efficiencies. If actual expenditures had exceeded budgeted expenditures in one of the departments, it would not necessarily indicate inefficient management. Spending in excess of budgets often occurs, even in the face of legal prohibitions. The difference between actual and budgeted expenditures might be caused by artificially low budgeted amounts, uncontrollable economic or legal complications leading to higher expenditures, or, possibly, managerial inefficiencies.

A cost accountant would by analogy call these variances between actual and budgeted expenditures *budget variances.* In the private sector, especially in manufacturing operations, there are sophisticated and detailed methods for trying to isolate the causes of budget variances; however, it is more difficult to do an exact job in the public sector. The annual statement of revenues, expenditures, and encumbrances is a starting point. Look at the report and note any large discrepancies between budgeted and actual amounts. It is as important to look at large "good" variances (e.g., actual revenues exceeding budgeted revenues) as it is to look at large "bad" variances (e.g., actual expenditures exceeding budgeted expenditures).

After large variances have been noted, the next step is to attempt to isolate the cause of the variances (i.e., poor forecasting, uncontrollable factors, good or bad management, etc.). This step cannot be exact, but one useful starting point is to compare actual amounts with budgeted amounts for the same activity over a period of years. If actual figures always seem to be significantly *lower*

Figure 7

How to Go from Cash Basis Estimated Revenues to Modified Accrual Basis Estimated Revenues

19X8 Cash Basis Estimated Revenues		$1,200,000
Subtract:	Anticipated Collection in 19X8 of 19X7 Receivables	90,000
		$1,110,000
Add:	Anticipated 19X8 Receivables	61,000
		$1,171,000

Figure 8

How a Cash Basis Budget Surplus Can Become a Modified Accrual Basis Budget Deficit

19X8 Cash Budget Surplus		$ 60,000
Add:	19X7 Modified Accrual Basis Actual Expenditures paid in 19X8 (Figure 5)	20,000
		$ 80,000
Add:	19X8 Modified Accrual Basis Actual Revenues not collected in 19X8 (Figure 4)	43,000
		123,000
Subtract:	19X8 Modified Accrual Basis Actual Expenditures not paid in 19X8 (Figure 5)	55,000
		$ 68,000
Subtract:	19X7 Modified Accrual Basis Actual Revenues collected in 19X8 (Figure 4)	90,000
		$ (22,000)
Subtract:	19X8 Encumbrances Outstanding at Fiscal Year End (Figure 6)	40,000
19X8 Modified Accrual Basis Budget Deficit		$ (62,000)

than budgeted figures, it is possible that budget estimates for revenues and expenditures are being intentionally padded. If actual revenues are always *higher* than budgeted revenues, the estimates may be made intentionally low to make the revenue collection process look efficient. If actual expenditures are always *higher* than budgeted expenditures, it is possible that estimates are being kept artificially low to hide the actual cost of operations in the budget process.

Of course, there are other possible causes for consistent differences between actual amounts and budgeted amounts, and those causes cannot be identified by simply looking at a presentation of revenues, expenditures, and encumbrances. If a pattern is uncovered and the magnitude is sufficiently large to concern managers and policy makers, the only way to determine the cause in a more exact fashion is to order a special performance audit of the activity. The objective of the performance audit will be to determine the efficiency of the unit's managers and the accuracy of their revenue or expenditure estimating process.

CHECKPOINT TWO:
Are there significant differences between actual revenues and expenditures and the budgeted amounts?
Do these differences seem to occur annually to the same degree?
What appears to be the cause of the differences: poor estimating, uncontrollable factors, or efficient/inefficient management?
Do they warrant closer study?

Analyzing Encumbrances

An encumbrance reserves part of an appropriation. It is quite reasonable to assume that occasionally there will be commitments outstanding at the end of a fiscal year. Many accounting systems allow these appropriation commitments to stay in effect into the next fiscal year to be paid when the goods or services are delivered. Under such a system, a portion of the Fund Balance must be set aside to pay these future bills. *Reserve for Encumbrances* is the method used in modified accrual accounting, and is illustrated in Figure 1. This indicates that $40,000 in unfilled orders are outstanding at the end of 19X8.

It is important to note that, from an accounting point of view, an encumbrance is not an expenditure, but simply a reservation of funds. If the commitments made at the end of a year are large, yet not reported as in Figure 2, Set I, they may have an adverse affect on the cash flow in the following fiscal year and may indicate a policy of "hiding" actual expenditures. Figure 2, Set I, includes a cash basis positive balance of Actual Revenues Over Expenditures of $60,000; there appears to be no financial problem. However, City XXX's financial performance as reported on the modified accrual basis results in a negative balance of only $62,000. The reversal from a cash basis surplus to a modified accrual basis deficit, analyzed in Figure 8, is made possible in part by accounting for $40,000 in encumbrances at year end.

CHECKPOINT THREE:
What is the balance in the reserve for encumbrances?
Have total revenues exceeded the total of expenditures and encumbrances?
What impact, if any, will outstanding commitments have on the following year's cash flow or expenditure requirements?

Intergovernmental Revenues

Intergovernmental revenues are becoming an increasingly important portion of the revenue structure of all municipalities. The use of nonlocal sources of revenue tends to understate the actual potential financial burden services can place on a local revenue system. It is important to monitor the importance of intergovernmental revenue in the total revenue structure. Figure 2 indicates that for 19X8 the City of XXX estimates 13 percent of its revenue comes from intergovernmental sources. This percentage indicates, at least in an elementary fashion, that percentage of total revenue which would have to be replaced with local taxes or fees if intergovernmental aid should disappear. This may indicate the value of a policy of using the less certain intergovernmental revenues for other than everyday expenditures.

Section 3: Issues in Financial Reporting

Professional organizations, public accountants, and municipal managers do not totally agree on what should be included in all financial reports, and how certain types of financial information should be presented. This section discusses several important issues in the reporting of financial information.

The first issue is whether a government unit should prepare a *combined* balance sheet (which presents all funds but keeps them separate, including appropriate interfund balances) or a *consolidated* balance sheet (which factors out all interfund balances and presents one balance sheet with one "superfund balance"). At present, GAAP does not require a balance sheet from local governments.

Proponents of consolidated balance sheets argue that the multitude of interfund balances and the multiplicity of funds tend to obscure the true financial position of a community and fail to present the true "net worth" of the city or town. They go on to argue that a consolidated fund balance will represent the true balance of resources available to the municipality.

The definition of a fund includes, "An independent fiscal and accounting entity with a self-balancing set of accounts. . . . " Separate funds are established when legal or administrative necessity requires that revenues and expenditures be isolated in a separate fund in order to monitor responsibility and to analyze annual results of operations. Opponents of consolidated statements argue that lumping the fund balances of many independent funds together might give a false impression of the resources available to be appropriated in the following fiscal year.

Another issue, upon which there is increasing agreement, is the reporting of normally undisclosed costs. The most common undisclosed costs in the public sector are *rentals* or *leases, pensions, fringe benefits,* and *depreciation. Leases* are legal commitments of the municipality which must be met in the future. It would be neither inappropriate nor difficult to disclose the total of these future costs in a footnote to financial statements.

The Municipal Finance Officers Association and other groups concerned with improving municipal financial disclosure have stated that greater disclosure should be made of *accrued pension liabilities.* Accrued pension liabilities are similar to debts and leases in that they are financial commitments that municipalities must meet in the future and fund from revenue sources. One common way of accounting for pensions is to report pension payments in the year in which the payments are made into a reserve fund or directly to pensioners. This method ignores the often significant amount of future pension benefits "earned" by current employees during the fiscal year which have not been reserved.

The financial impact of pension plans can be substantial—even catastrophic. In one city, the administration brought about a local property tax reduction between 1973 and 1977 of about 2 percent. Yet during the same period it allowed pension obligations to grow without fully reserving for them. In 1978 the city's auditors reported that placing the annual pension funding plan on an "actuarially sound" basis would require raising pension appropriations to approximately 25 percent of the entire city budget.

Ideally, pension benefits should be reported in full in the year they are earned, even if they are not fully matched by contributions to a reserve fund. Many communities cannot or will not fund their pensions currently. In this case, the principle of full financial disclosure requires that, as a minimum, all accrued pension liabilities be reported separately in a note to the financial statements.

Employee fringe benefits such as sick and vacation leave raise similar problems but are less significant financially. They constitute costs incurred today that must be met in future years when employees exercise their rights to these benefits. Some accountants recommend that they should be funded and reported as expenditures or be reported separately as accrued liabilities of the municipality.

The depreciation of fixed assets in the public sector is an issue upon which no consensus has ever been reached. Depreciation is not reported for general fund assets, such as streets and office buildings.

The AICPA's *Audits of State and Local Government Units* and GAAFR recommend that a municipality maintain records on a General Fixed Assets Group for the fixed assets of the general fund. This group would be the repository of the value of all fixed assets at purchase price, so that a municipality would have a general indicator of the value of its assets. Neither association argues on behalf of depreciating this asset group as in the private sector and calling the annual depreciation an expense.

Proponents of public sector depreciation argue that the lack of annual depreciation computations disguises the true cost of maintaining and replacing municipal assets. They argue that full disclosure of costs requires depreciation of fixed assets.

All participants in the debate argue that it is important that a municipality be aware of the value of its fixed costs. This type of information is useful in making capital budgeting and repair decisions and for programming the future uses of public lands, buildings, and equipment, and there is virtually universal agreement that assets owned by public enterprises—businesslike operations such as utilities and hospitals—should be depreciated.

Concluding Remarks

At present, the field of local government accounting is in a state of flux. It is hoped that the end product of current efforts to upgrade local government accounting will be, for many communities, improved financial reporting to serve local officials, their constituents, oversight and grantor agencies, and creditors. This primer has summarized some of the more important concepts and topics regarding accounting standards and practice. The picture presented here is highly simplified and leaves out many features of this complex subject. Individuals wishing to learn more should consult individuals who are knowledgeable about local government accounting.

26 Financial Communications

Coopers and Lybrand

Adequate financial communications to users warrant at least three types of documents: (1) an annual report; (2) interim reports; and (3) official statements prepared in connection with proposed offerings of debt securities.

Annual Reports

A municipal annual report should be the key communications tool. If the needs of taxpayers and investors are to be met, it should, in addition to historical financial statements, include predictive financial data and statistical and interpretive information.

The following information should appear in the annual report:

- General information, including:
  a. Name of the municipality and other organizations included in the reporting entity.
  b. List of the principal officials, of both the municipality and the other organizations included in the report, who are responsible for financial affairs; an explanation of the process by which they are chosen; their remaining terms of office; and a description of their backgrounds and powers.
  c. Description of the powers and responsibilities of each branch of government of the municipality and the other organizations included in the reporting entity.
  d. Reference to the availability of detailed financial reports of the municipality and other entities included and how they may be obtained.

- Additional financial information:
  a. Description of the principal facilities of the municipality, and the capital improvements plan for the next five years, showing proposed expenditures for each year by type of asset, intended use and source of funding. A similar disclosure for the other organizations as a whole should also be made. The aggregate original cost and estimated replacement cost of fully depreciated assets and assets that will become fully depreciated during the next five years, together with a brief description of intentions regarding replacement, should also be disclosed.
  b. Comparison of planned and actual operating results and debt service on a budgetary basis for the current year with actual results for the preceding four years and projected results for the ensuing year, and explanations of material changes of observable trends.
  c. Commentary by public management on results for the year and progress toward objectives, and statement of objectives for the ensuing period together with any

Reprinted from Financial Disclosure Practices of the American Cities II: Closing the Communications Gap *(New York, Coopers & Lybrand, 1978.)*

other comments deemed appropriate by management.

d. Description of nature and availability of city reports on efficiency and effectiveness.

e. Bond ratings, if applicable, and any changes in them during the year.

- Comparative demographic data:

a. Average change in population.

b. Per capita income, per capita tax burden (for operations vs. debt service) and average changes in them.

c. Description of principal industries, their economic stability and the economic effects of major additions or losses of business.

d. Growth rate in local source revenue vs. that in expenditures vs. that in per capita income.

e. Fair value of taxable and non-taxable property.

f. Average change in per capita long-term liabilities (i.e., bonds, pension and lease obligations, etc.) vs. average change in liabilities as a percentage of fair value of taxable property, and changes in these.

g. Analysis of population and changes in its age, educational attainment, school enrollment, ethnic background, employment (manufacturing vs. service; private enterprise vs. government), income levels and rates of unemployment.

h. The total number of local government employees; number of employees funded directly by intergovernmental resources; number of employees who belong to collective bargaining units; expiration dates of significant union contracts; compulsory arbitration requirements; and a characterization of labor relations.

i. Changes in the consumer price index vs. changes in per capita income.

j. Other data, as circumstances warrant, deemed useful.

The above list of demographic data is not intended to be exhaustive or representative of some minimum standard. Rather, it illustrates the type of information useful in interpreting and analyzing municipal financial statements. We believe the communications process is significantly enhanced when statistical data is integrated with a commentary on operating results and future prospects.

Interim Reports

Interim financial reports provide necessary links between annual reports. Though material events presumably are disclosed through the news media, municipalities also have a responsibility to put those events in perspective and make disclosures available to users outside the community.

Interim financial information released by private business varies from condensed financial and operating data and comments about significant events to more extensive financial information comparable to that in annual reports. Regular issuance of financial information on an annual and interim basis, usually quarterly, permits updated evaluations. This information would probably be already available in reports public management has prepared to monitor adherence to budgetary limitations and for other purposes, which need only be summarized.

Because an objective of interim reports is to furnish information about significant events and transactions since the latest annual report, the reports normally may be limited to:

- Data concerning financial position and changes in cash position for the interim period and for the year to date. Data on the flow of funds should include a comparison of actual results vs. allotments and a description of amendments to the previously adopted budget.
- Description of any significant changes in the judgments made in preparing historical financial statements, the assumptions underlying predictive data and any other factors affecting statistical or interpretive information.
- Disclosure of significant events occurring during the interim period.

Interim financial information should also be included in official statements.

Official Statements

Official statements are disclosure documents prepared for new offerings of debt securities to enable potential investors to assess the municipality and the investment risks. They contain: (1) information about the organization of the municipality, its management, the services it provides and its economic environment; (2) financial information; and (3) specific information on the securities being offered.

An official statement, although it includes data of interest to a variety of users, is directed primarily to potential investors. Present investors, however, faced with a decision to hold or sell their municipal obligations, have the same information needs as prospective investors. The relative risks of an initial offering are substantially the same as those in the secondary market. Thus, except for specific information about the offering, the official statement's disclosures should be of the same scope and depth as the annual report's.

An official statement, then, should consist of the municipality's latest annual report supplemented with information pertinent to the offering of securities, such as:

- Statement of the legal authority for issuance of the obligations.
- A complete description of the offering including terms, rights of holders, redemption or advance refunding features, tax status, registration provisions, restrictive covenants and sinking fund requirements, if any.
- Description of the expected source of funds to repay the obligations, or resources or assets pledged as collateral, if any.
- Disclosure of the amounts and anticipated sources of any additional funds necessary to achieve the stated purpose of the offering, together with an explanation of the status of actions taken to acquire such additional funds.
- Description of the priority of holders of the securities offered in relation to holders of other securities of the municipality.
- Identification of the circumstances in which the municipality may issue additional obligations, including debt obligations with rights precedent to or on a par with the securities being offered.
- Pro forma calculations of compliance with restrictive covenants, assuming the offering is completed and the proceeds expended for the intended purpose.
- Description of the third party trustee, if any, the temporary uses of proceeds and the circumstances under which the proceeds will be disbursed.
- Bond ratings for the issue of securities being offered and other market-acceptability data. If applicable, explain reasons for different ratings for other outstanding issues.
- Other disclosures necessary to prevent the official statement from being misleading.

Special-Purpose Reports

Special-purpose reports often provide more information about specific aspects of an entity's financial affairs than is practical to present in a general-purpose financial report. They are prepared, for example, to demonstrate compliance with the terms of a grant, establish the basis for changes in user charges, determine the cost of operating a specific department or evaluate the potential consequences of decisions. Investors in revenue bonds are interested in the financial condition of the enterprise activity that constitutes the only or primary source of repayment. Taxpayers may also want such information to evaluate user charges—as in the case of a city-run housing project whose objective is to recover all operating costs and debt service requirements from tenants. If project operating costs are expected to rise substantially, the increased rents necessary to achieve this objective may exceed tenants' capacity to pay. This could reduce occupancy and, hence, the funds available to repay bondholders. In extreme cases, public management may deem it appropriate to subsidize a portion of the housing project's operating costs from funds derived from the tax base as a whole. Another reason for preparing special-purpose reports would be to permit an evaluation of a supposedly self-supporting government activity, such as fire inspections, for which a fee is charged. That evaluation requires more information than is available in general-purpose reports.

The activities of other units of government are interrelated with the city's. A city's decision to levy additional ad valorem taxes may affect the ability of, say, a water authority to increase user charges. Thus, users of some special-purpose reports should also be interested in summarized financial information for the economic entity providing local government services.

Because special-purpose reports concerning specific aspects of government operations may be best understood when viewed from the perspective of the reporting entity as a whole, we recommend they make reference to the availability of the municipality's general-purpose annual and interim financial reports.

27 The Needs of Users of Governmental Financial Statements

Sidney Davidson, David O. Green, Walter Hellerstein, Albert Madansky, and Roman L. Weil

Financial statements of state and local governmental units are designed to serve a broad audience of potential users. That audience could be classified in a variety of ways. We suggest attention be centered on the needs of four groups:

1. the general public, made up largely of the taxpayers of the governmental unit preparing the report;
2. investors and creditors (and their advisors), both present and potential, of the governmental unit;
3. employees and potential employees of the governmental unit; and
4. officials, both elective and appointive, of the governmental unit.

The General Public

The largest group of potential readers of governmental financial statements are the interested and informed taxpayers. They are concerned with the impact of government activities on their daily lives. They are interested in (1) whether the level and quality of services being rendered by the governmental unit is what they want and (2) whether they are able to purchase services through the tax system. The informed public is concerned with how much of the service is being paid for currently and how much will require future tax levies or other revenues. Taxpayers are also interested in the rate at which existing resources of the governmental unit are being consumed.

Potential taxpayers comprise a subset of the general public. Business firms and potential homeowners choosing a location for activity or purchase are interested in the financial position and prospects of the governmental unit in which they may locate. There are many factors that will enter into their final decision, but knowledge of the financial standing of the community will certainly be one of them.

The informed citizens in the general public are neither expert accountants nor trained financial analysts. However, many of them in their business activities, in their private investment decisions, and in various other ways have developed some understanding of the terminology and meaning of the financial statements of commercial enterprises. Financial statements of governmental units are far more likely to be understandable to the general public if they are couched in the same language, presented in the same general form, and largely use the same accounting concepts that business does. There is a danger, of course, of obscuring the important differences between government and commercial units by presenting government reports in commercial terms. The primary goal of commercial enterprises is to make a profit. That is not the primary function of a governmental unit. Government attempts to provide the type and quantity of services deemed appropriate by its citizens. The power to levy taxes is one of the most important, if not the most important, resources of a governmental unit, yet such tax-levying power is

---

Reprinted from Financial Reporting by State and Local Government Units *(Chicago, Ill.: Center for Management of Public and Nonprofit Enterprise, Graduate School of Business, n.d.).*

difficult to portray within the format of commercial-type financial statements. Careful choice of statement captions and proper narrative in the footnotes to the statements can, however, overcome much of the difficulty and result in meaningful governmental statements prepared in the commercial form.

For informed citizens who seek a composite overview of the governmental unit, statements which present overall position and results using familiar terms and forms would be most desirable. Through such statements, the impact of government activities on the daily lives of the citizens and the implications of those activities for their future may be better understood.

Investors and Creditors

Investors and creditors are those who buy government securities and those who provide goods and services to government on a credit basis. The volume of state and local government securities being issued is steadily growing and represents a substantial segment of the capital market. As Exhibit 1 indicates, the volume grew steadily in the decade from 1966 to 1975 from almost $18 billion in 1966 to over $58 billion in 1975. Total government obligations of this type issued in the decade exceeded $380 billion. Since interest on these obligations is exempt from federal income taxes (and, frequently, from state income taxes as well), and since inflation helped many taxpayers move into higher tax brackets, governmental securities have become more attractive to larger groups of investors and could continue to grow in appeal.

Data on the amount of credit extended to state and local government units by suppliers of goods and services are not available, but the amount of such credit clearly represents a very large sum at any given moment.

Investors and creditors must choose among a variety of investment and credit-granting opportunities. While some investors and creditors limit themselves either to commercial or to government investments, there is a large group who must decide among the competing alternatives in the broader market of both classes of security issuers. Investors must compare the risks and potential rewards in both markets. Since the securities market for commercial enterprises is much larger, most investors are accustomed to analyzing financial statements in that framework. The same may also be said of credit grantors. Both groups place initial, and probably primary, reliance on the financial statements to inform them of the position and prospects of the entity in which they are investing or to which they are granting credit.

Exhibit 1: *Volume of State and Municipal Borrowing 1966-1975 (in Millions)*

Year	Par Amount Long-term Issues	Short-term Issues	All Issues	Number of All Issues
1966	$11,089	$ 6,524	$17,613	7,430
1967	14,288	8,025	22,313	7,964
1968	16,374	8,659	25,033	7,887
1969	11,460	11,783	23,243	6,395
1970	17,762	17,880	35,642	7,604
1971	24,369	26,281	50,650	8,811
1972	22,941	25,222	48,163	8,420
1973	22,953	24,667	47,620	8,147
1974	22,824	29,041	51,865	7,701
1975	29,326	28,973	58,299	8,107
Total	$193,386	$187,055	$380,441	78,466

Source: *The Weekly Bond Buyer,* Vol. 202, No. 4324, page 25, "Volume of State and Municipal Borrowing 1900-1975.

State and local governmental units may be paying a substantial price in higher interest costs for their failure to provide financial statements that are meaningful to a broader group of investors and analysts. The present group of specialists in state and local financial obligations generally do a good job of working with data that are frequently inadequate, but more complete and more understandable financial statements might expand the market, thus resulting in lower interest costs.

Employees

Both present and prospective employees are concerned with the fiscal soundness of their employers and the present and likely future scope of the employer's activities. This is, of course, true of employees of both commercial and governmental enterprises, but it is only one of the many factors they consider in selecting job opportunities and in assessing the desirability of job changes. Society as a whole is best served by free labor markets with informed participants who make initial and subsequent location decisions on the basis of meaningful, comparable data. To the extent that an employer's financial status is important, reports that are more easily understood, and that facilitate comparison with other potential employers, are clearly desirable.

Of special interest to employees, present and prospective, is the financial soundness of an employer's pension and retirement plans. As pensions and other fringe benefits become more important features of the compensation package, understanding their financing becomes more significant to employees. A clear statement of the financial condition and of changes in the condition of the pension plan is an important and desirable attribute of financial reporting for employees.

As far as employees are concerned, understandability and comparability with other governmental and nongovernmental potential employers are probably the most important and desirable attributes of financial reports.

Government Officials

Officials of state and local governments, both elected and appointed, need detailed data about the past and planned operations of the many subunits of the government. They need information on the demand for various types of services and the effectiveness with which those services are delivered. Detailed financial summaries and nonfinancial reports are required if the officials are to perform effectively. But these officials also need an effective way of assessing (1) how decisions on specific topics will fit into the overall financial picture of the governmental unit and (2) how they will affect the unit's present and future flexibility on financial matters.

Governmental officials, with few exceptions, understand the intricacies of contemporary fund reporting. Even with many years of experience, however, it is difficult to comprehend the interfund relationships resulting from many legislative actions. The availability of a single set of consolidated statements which strives to capture a composite view of financial position and operations should be helpful. Detailed reports stressing compliance with legal requirements would continue to be essential, but they would complement the composite view.

The preceding survey of the needs of users of governmental financial statements underlines the need for a set of consolidated statements treating the government unit as a whole, expressed as nearly as possible in commercial accounting terms and format. Such a set of statements would marshall the vast amount of available financial data about the government unit into a single composite picture facilitating an understanding of the size and scope of its activities. The statements should help the reader understand where the unit stands and how it got there, what services it has rendered at what cost, and how efficiently. Such statements should provide a common base for the general public, investors and creditors, employees, and officials to develop the analyses that may lead to sound decisions about government activities.

28 Understanding Municipal Financial Audits

Harold I. Steinberg

If auditing procedures were the same in every state, understanding the financial reports of a municipality would be much easier. But there are 50 different states, and the approach to accounting and auditing for local governments varies drastically.

In New York the law requires that school districts be audited by independent certified public accountants each year. But for cities and counties, there is no such requirement. Instead the State Auditor comes in every two or three years and performs an audit.

Next door in New Jersey the State requires that local governments be audited by what are called RMAs–registered municipal accountants. On the other side of New York, Connecticut is one of the few states to require audits by independent public accountants, for the most part CPAs. Illinois follows the same practice.

The scope of the audits also varies from state to state. In New York school districts, for example, not only financial statements but financial and statistical data are audited. The data are used by the New York State Education Department to analyze the educational function and recommend policy to the State Legislature. The municipalities are audited for compliance with state law and for operational efficiency.

In New Jersey the purpose of the audit report appears to be to uncover irregularities. In Illinois and Connecticut the objective is to see that there are financial statements and that they fairly present the municipality's financial condition and results of operations in conformance with generally accepted accounting principles (GAAP).

Although these differences in requirements are merely illustrative, they do point up the need for standardization in several respects: (1) presentation of municipal financial statements; (2) the scope and purpose of audits; and (3) qualifications of the auditors.

The main reason for an independent audit of a government entity is to provide an objective opinion of the reported results. Furthermore, well-executed audits guide management and reveal opportunities for improving operational efficiency. A uniform requirement that audits be made by appropriately qualified independent public accountants (generally CPAs) would be a boon to people who scrutinize municipal financial reports for various reasons, including evaluation of municipal securities.

Accounting Principles Develop

A CPA is concerned primarily with whether a financial report is fairly presented in accordance with GAAP. His role calls for him to review and furnish an opinion as to the financial statements. As he bases this opinion on widely known and utilized principles, people who read the report should understand both the background and the content of the principles.

Fund accounting, which is the basis of accounting for local governments, has a long history. In 1934, the Municipal Finance Officers Association of the United States and Canada (MFOA) organized a committee on governmental accounting in order

Reprinted from Management Controls *24 (January-February, 1977): 15-18. By permission of Peat, Marwick, Mitchell & Co.*

to define more clearly and codify the principles of fund accounting as they applied to municipal accounting. Subsequently, the National Committee on Governmental Accounting (NCGA) issued a variety of publications, of which the latest and most significant is *Governmental Accounting, Auditing, and Financial Reporting* (GAAFR)–sometimes referred to as the "Blue Book."

While CPAs recognized the existence of the NCGA list of recommended accounting principles, they did not universally accept GAAFR as the final word. But in 1974 the AICPA published an authoritative professional guide: *Audits of State and Local Government Units,* which except for a few modifications recognized and endorsed GAAFR.

Seven Principles for Municipal Accounting

For the purpose of accounting and reporting, both GAAFR and the AICPA guide define eight specific funds and two groups of accounts that a government unit should use. They are: general fund, special revenue funds, debt service funds, capital projects funds, enterprise funds, trust and agency funds, [internal] service funds, and special assessment funds; and the general fixed assets group of accounts and the general long-term debt group of accounts.

The second principle discussed in the AICPA guide deals with budgetary accounting, which is a key element in governmental accounting. The aim of government is not to make a profit but to provide services efficiently and within the parameters of the law. Reporting the budget allows the financial statement reader to compare actual revenues and actual expenditures with planned revenues and planned expenditures, and thus evaluate the government's financial results in relation to its initial objectives.

The third principle deals with legal compliance. Compliance with the law would not provide a presentation be consistent with GAAP in circumstances where legal requirements impose accounting standards different from GAAP. If legal requirements result in something other than GAAP, and legal requirements are the basis on which the financial statements are prepared, the municipality or a reader of the statements cannot expect a CPA to state, in rendering his opinion, that the statements conform to GAAP.

The fourth principle states that the basis for governmental accounting is either the modified accrual or, in some instances, the accrual method of accounting. Modified accrual has much in common with accrual accounting. With a few minor exceptions, expenditures are recorded when incurred. Revenues are recorded to the extent that they are measurable and available to finance expenditures. It is this "susceptible to accrual" concept for revenues that differentiates modified accrual from full accrual.

The fifth principle deals with fixed assets accounting. General fixed assets are not reported upon in individual funds but in a separate group of accounts. But because historical cost information often is not available for such fixed assets, many municipalities fail to account for them. GAAFR treated this problem by stating that estimated historical cost is an acceptable basis for recording fixed assets. The 1974 AICPA guide dealt further with the problem by stating that certain non-movable types of fixed assets need not be capitalized–e.g., roads, bridges, sidewalks, drainage systems, etc. Furthermore, depreciation is generally not required in governmental accounting, except in the enterprise funds–funds in which government's business-type activities are recorded. The guide states that the recording of an allowance for depreciation in the general fixed assets group of accounts would be acceptable.

The sixth principle covers long-term liabilities which are reflected in the general long-term debt group of accounts. According to the guide, they should not be reported in the general fund or any other fund since they are obligations of the entire community and will be supported by the general credit and tax-raising power of the community.

The seventh and final principle concerns the types of financial statements required for a governmental entity. The guide states that for each fund there should be a balance sheet; a statement of revenues, expenditures, and transfers, including the comparison of actual and estimated revenues and actual and budgeted expenditures; and a statement of changes in fund balance, or retained earnings in the case of the enterprise fund. In addition, there should be a statement of changes in financial position for any enterprise funds.

Every Auditor Seeks Special Knowledge

These, then, are the principles that a municipality should follow in conducting its accounting and preparing its financial report. They are the same principles an auditor will look for in the conduct of a municipal audit. In order to perform an audit that results in an opinion on whether a municipality's financial report adheres to these principles, and meets the standards set by the AICPA, an auditor undertakes several tasks.

First, he devotes considerable time and effort to obtaining a comprehensive understanding of the municipality. More specifically, he looks at state statutes, particularly those affecting financing and accounting. He studies the city's charter to learn the powers and duties of the city and its officials.

He goes over local ordinances, especially those that define how the city raises its monies and the authority it has to spend them. He looks at the budget to see what the budgeting process is, to note where the city gets its resources and where it spends them. He reviews the minutes of the city council meetings to learn what the council is deliberating on or planning. He checks on the federal and state grants to ascertain the unique activities in which the city is involved.

The auditor examines the city's bond indentures because these very often have unique accounting and auditing implications. And he checks other matters such as the funds the city maintains, its accounting system and personnel, its internal reporting system, and its relationship with other governmental units.

Systems Evaluation Approach

The audit itself has two objectives: ascertaining the reliability of the data, and ensuring that it is presented in a manner which will provide a fair picture of financial condition and results of operations. In undertaking the audit, some use what is called a "systems evaluation approach," which focuses on transaction cycles, organizational objectives, and internal control features. This approach is particularly appropriate for municipal government audits because organizational objectives and internal control features are the very matters with which a city council and the taxpayers are most concerned.

In other words, by looking at the internal control features, the auditor is determining the extent of the examination necessary to determine the reliability of the financial data. At the same time, however, he is looking at operating considerations, and these, too, are of major concern to the municipality, its taxpayers, and the investment community.

How the Auditor Expresses His Judgments

With this approach to the municipal financial audit, there can be three types of output: the management letter, the financial report, and supplementary data—all equally important in analyzing a municipality's financial situation.

The management letter is the vehicle the auditor uses to comment on significant strengths and weaknesses in the system of internal controls and to submit pertinent recommendations for improvements. Often required by law in a municipal audit, the management letter is usually a public document. Underwriters, attorneys, credit-rating agencies, and others involved in the municipal bond market should have a considerable interest in the management letter, since in many ways it can be more revealing than the financial statements. They should ask for it; they should read it carefully; and they should delve into it, particularly in critical areas.

For example, a municipality can be overexpending its budget in several categories. Reading the management letter may reveal whether this condition is the result of poor budgeting control or a casual regard for the law.

The Financial Report

The second item to come out of an audit is the financial report. It is important to bear in mind that the municipal financial report is not really a report on the city, but on individual funds established to operate the city.

The report frequently has an introductory section consisting of a letter from the municipality's director of finance. This letter is often extremely important. Following the letter should be a set of combined statements, which give the reader an overall look at the municipality's finances. The combined statements present data from the statements of all funds. But combined statements not accompanied by detail can be misleading. The detail follows, therefore, in statements for each of the different funds. Indeed, the MFOA's suggested disclosure guidelines advise that a local government include the "appropriate financial statements" reviewed by a CPA, with an opinion as to their conformance to GAAP or state standards, in any disclosure document.

The debt service fund financial statements should also be of value. For each bond issue outstanding, there would be a balance sheet. The key figure here is the fund balance, which is the money on hand to pay the debt for that particular issue.

There would also be an operating statement for each issue. This tells the reader where the municipality is obtaining the revenues to service the debt. It also shows what the debt service actually is during the year.

The statement in which the city's general long-term debt payable is reported is also crucial. It shows where the city expects to get the money to pay its debt. Report readers should note that there is an item here not normally found in commercial statements called "amount to be provided." When the reader sees this caption in the statement of general long-term debt, it means that the city obtained a referendum or passed a bond ordinance and, as a result, there is a lien or obligation on the city to raise the monies in future years to pay this debt. This is the only place in a government's financial statements that such a caption should be seen. If it appears anywhere else, what the government may be doing, in effect, is recording and recognizing revenue in advance or avoiding reporting a deficit. And that is not acceptable under GAAP.

Financial statement readers should note carefully whether the auditor refers to conformance of the statements with GAAP or with state law. There is a difference and it should not be disregarded.

Something else financial report readers might look for is a certificate of conformance, awarded by the MFOA. The certificate means that the city has submitted its financial statements for review by a qualified panel and that the statements have met certain prescribed standards of excellence for financial reporting. More important, perhaps, it means that the statements contain information necessary for a reasoned, studied analysis of the city's finances.

Supplementary Data as Early Warnings

The final products of a financial audit are the financial and statistical data that are not set forth, at least explicitly, in the financial report. Some of these data relate to the property base, debt structure and economic indices—the kinds of things that indicate a city's capacity to pay its bonds.

Meaningful supplementary data should go beyond the issue of the capacity to redeem bonds and take in such factors as the quality and stability of the city's other revenues. For example, municipalities get a good bit of money from intergovernmental grants and from user charges. What are these? How large a proportion of a city's revenues are they? How stable are they?

Supplementary data should also show how monies are used for purposes other than debt service. How much does the city pay for social services versus recreation? How much for public safety versus economic development? How much on capital outlay?

This type of data can be an adjunct to an audit, since most of the data are collected in the course of the audit. A good analyst would then use the data to determine if trends exist. For instance, data might reveal an increasing excess of expenditures over local revenues. And this should be a cue to start asking such questions as: Is there an expanding reliance on outside revenues? Is the excess due to poor budgeting practices? In short, supplementary data can be used as the basis for a set of financial warning indicators that, in turn, can be used to evaluate the strength and stability of a municipality.

The municipal financial audit then, in essence, is a three-pronged approach to understanding a municipality's fiscal health. It provides a management letter dealing with, among other things, the control strengths and weaknesses of a government's financial machinery. It provides an independent attestation on a set of financial statements that conform to GAAP or the state's requirements. It provides financial and statistical data that can be used to establish trends. All are increasingly vital to the public and, specifically, to municipal bond offerings as investors look for reliable information on the financial condition of issuers.

[This article is adapted from one published by *The Daily Bond Buyer,* to which *Management Controls* extends thanks.]

29 Standards for Audit of Governmental Organizations, Programs, Activities and Functions

Part I–Introduction

Purpose

This [selection] contains a body of audit standards that are intended for application to audits of all government organizations, programs, activities, and functions–whether they are performed by auditors employed by federal, state, or local governments; independent public accountants; or others qualified to perform parts of the audit work contemplated under these standards. These standards are also intended to apply to both internal audits and audits of contractors, grantees, and other external organizations performed by or for a governmental entity. These audit standards relate to the scope and quality of audit effort and to the characteristics of a professional and meaningful audit report.

The American Institute of Certified Public Accountants (AICPA) has adopted standards and procedures that are applicable to audits performed to express opinions on the fairness with which financial statements present the financial position and results of operations.[1] These standards are generally accepted for such audits and have been incorporated into this [selection]. However, the interests of many users of reports on government audits are broader than those that can be satisfied by audits performed to establish the credibility of financial reports. To provide for audits that will fulfill these broader interests, the standards in this [selection] include the essence of those prescribed by the American Institute of Certified Public Accountants and additional standards for audits of a broader scope as will be explained subsequently.

Reprinted from Standards for Audit of Governmental Organizations, Programs, Activities and Functions *(Washington, D.C.: U.S. General Accounting Office, 1972).*

Scope

A fundamental tenet of a democratic society holds that governments and agencies entrusted with public resources and the authority for applying them have a responsibility to render a full accounting of their activities. This accountability is inherent in the governmental process and is not always specifically identified by legislative provision. This governmental accountability should identify not only the objects for which the public resources have been devoted but also the manner and effect of their application.

This concept of accountability is woven into the basic premises supporting these standards. These standards provide for a scope of audit that includes not only financial and compliance auditing but also auditing for economy, efficiency, and achievement of desired results. Provision for such a scope of audit is not intended to imply that all audits are presently being conducted this way or that such an extensive scope is always desirable. However, an audit that would include provision for the interests of all potential users of government audits would ordinarily include provision for auditing all the above elements of the accountability of the responsible officials.

Definitions of the three elements of such an audit follow.

1. *Financial and compliance*–determines (a) whether financial operations are properly conducted, (b) whether the financial reports of an audited entity are presented fairly, and (c) whether the entity has complied with applicable laws and regulations.
2. *Economy and efficiency*–determines whether the entity is managing or utilizing its resources (personnel, property, space, and so forth) in an economical and effi-

cient manner and the causes of any inefficiencies or uneconomical practices, including inadequacies in management information systems, administrative procedures, or organizational structure.

3. *Program results*—determines whether the desired results or benefits are being achieved, whether the objectives established by the legislature or other authorizing body are being met, and whether the agency has considered alternatives which might yield desired results at a lower cost.

The audit standards are intended to be more than the mere codification of current practices, tailored to existing audit capabilities. Purposely forward-looking, these standards include some concepts and areas of audit coverage which are still evolving in practice but which are vital to the accountability objectives sought in the audit of governments and of intergovernmental programs. Therefore the audit standards have been structured so that each of the three elements of audit can be performed separately if this is deemed desirable.

It should be recognized that a concurrent audit of all three parts would probably be the most economical manner of audit, but often this may not be practical. Furthermore, it may not be practical or necessary to perform all three elements of the audit in particular circumstances. For most government programs or activities, however, the interests of many potential government users will not be satisfied unless all three elements are performed.

In memorandums of engagements between governments and independent public accountants or other audit organizations, the arrangements should specifically identify whether all, or specifically which, of the three elements of the audit are to be conducted. Such agreements are needed to ensure that the scope of audit to be made is understood by all concerned.

Basic Premises

The following certain basic premises underlie these standards and were considered in their development.

1. The term "audit" is used to describe not only work done by accountants in examining financial reports but also work done in reviewing (a) compliance with applicable laws and regulations, (b) efficiency and economy of operations, and (c) effectiveness in achieving program results.
2. Public office carries with it the responsibility to apply resources in an efficient, economical, and effective manner to achieve the purposes for which the resources were furnished. This responsibility applies to all resources, whether entrusted to the public officials by their own constituency or by other levels of government.
3. A public official is accountable to those who provide the resources he uses to carry out governmental programs. He is accountable both to other levels of government for the resources such levels have provided and to the electorate, the ultimate source of all governmental funds. Consequently he should be providing appropriate reports to those to whom he is accountable. Unless legal restrictions or other valid reasons prevent him from doing so, the auditor should make the results of audits available to other levels of government that have supplied resources and to the electorate.
4. Auditing is an important part of the accountability process since it provides independent judgments of the credibility of public officials' statements about the manner in which they have carried out their responsibilities. Auditing also can help decisionmakers improve the efficiency, economy, and effectiveness of governmental operations by identifying where improvements are needed.
5. The interests of individual governments in many financially assisted programs often cannot be isolated because the resources applied have been commingled. Different levels of government share common interests in many programs. Therefore an audit should be designed to satisfy both the common and discrete accountability interests of each contributing government.
6. Cooperation by federal, state, and local governments in auditing programs of common interest with a minimum of duplication is of mutual benefit to all concerned and is a practical method of auditing intergovernmental operations.
7. Auditors may rely upon the work of auditors at other levels of government if they satisfy themselves as to the other auditors' capabilities by appropriate tests to their work or by other acceptable methods.

An inherent assumption that underlies all the standards is that governments will cooperate in making audits in which they have mutual interests. For many programs that are federally assisted, it would be neither practical nor economical to have every auditor at every level of government do his own background research on the laws, regulations, objectives, and goals of his segment of the program. Therefore, to provide the auditor with the necessary background information and to guide his judgment in the application of the accompanying standards, federal or state agencies that request state, local, or other levels to make audits are expected to prepare broad, comprehensive audit instructions, tailored to particular programs or program areas.

The content of such audit guidance should include a digest of, or as a minimum, citations to applicable statutes, regulations, instructions, manuals, grant agreements, and other program documents; identification of specific audit objectives and reporting requirements in terms of matters of primary interest in such areas as program compliance, economy, and effectiveness; and other audit guidelines covering specific areas in which the auditor is expected to perform.

Part II—Summary

Part II is a summary of the standards. Parts III, IV, and V explain the standards more fully.

Part III—General Standards

1. The full scope of an audit of a governmental program, function, activity, or organization should encompass:
   a. An examination of financial transactions, accounts, and reports, including an evaluation of compliance with applicable laws and regulations.
   b. A review of efficiency and economy in the use of resources.
   c. A review to determine whether desired results are effectively achieved.

   In determining the scope for a particular audit, responsible officials should give consideration to the needs of the potential users of the results of that audit.
2. The auditors assigned to perform the audit must collectively possess adequate professional proficiency for the tasks required.
3. In all matters relating to the audit work, the audit organization and the individual auditors shall maintain an independent attitude.
4. Due professional care is to be used in conducting the audit and in preparing related reports.

Part IV—Examination and Evaluation Standards

1. Work is to be adequately planned.
2. Assistants are to be properly supervised.
3. A review is to be made of compliance with legal and regulatory requirements.
4. An evaluation is to be made of the system of internal control to assess the extent it can be relied upon to ensure accurate information, to ensure compliance with laws and regulations, and to provide for efficient and effective operations.
5. Sufficient, competent, and relevant evidence is to be obtained to afford a reasonable basis for the auditor's opinions, judgments, conclusions, and recommendations.

Part V—Reporting Standards

1. Written audit reports are to be submitted to the appropriate officials of the organizations requiring or arranging for the audits. Copies of the reports should be sent to other officials who may be responsible for taking action on audit findings and recommendations and to others responsible or authorized to receive such reports. Unless restricted by law or regulation, copies should also be made available for public inspection.
2. Reports are to be issued on or before the dates specified by law, regulation, or other arrangement and, in any event, as promptly as possible so as to make the information available for timely use by management and by legislative officials.
3. Each report shall:
   a. Be as concise as possible but, at the same time, clear and complete enough to be understood by the users.
   b. Present factual matter accurately, completely, and fairly.
   c. Present findings and conclusions objectively and in language as clear and simple as the subject matter permits.
   d. Include only factual information, find-

ings, and conclusions that are adequately supported by enough evidence in the auditor's working papers to demonstrate or prove, when called upon, the bases for the matters reported and their correctness and reasonableness. Detailed supporting information should be included in the report to the extent necessary to make a convincing presentation.

e. Include, when possible, the auditor's recommendations for actions to effect improvements in problem areas noted in his audit and to otherwise make improvements in operations. Information on underlying causes of problems reported should be included to assist in implementing or devising corrective actions.
f. Place primary emphasis on improvement rather than on criticism of the past; critical comments should be presented in balanced perspective, recognizing any unusual difficulties or circumstances faced by the operating officials concerned.
g. Identify and explain issues and questions needing further study and consideration by the auditor or others.
h. Include recognition of noteworthy accomplishments, particularly when management improvements in one program or activity may be applicable elsewhere.
i. Include recognition of the views of responsible officials of the organization, program, function, or activity audited on the auditor's findings, conclusions, and recommendations. Except where the possibility of fraud or other compelling reason may require different treatment, the auditor's tentative findings and conclusions should be reviewed with such officials. When possible, without undue delay, their views should be obtained in writing and objectively considered and presented in preparing the final report.
j. Clearly explain the scope and objectives of the audit.
k. State whether any significant, pertinent information has been omitted because it is deemed privileged or confidential. The nature of such information should be described, and the law or other basis under which it is withheld should be stated.

4. Each audit report containing financial reports shall:
   a. Contain an expression of the auditor's opinion as to whether the information in the financial reports is presented fairly in accordance with generally accepted accounting principles (or with other specified accounting principles applicable to the organization, program, function, or activity audited), applied on a basis consistent with that of the preceding reporting period. If the auditor cannot express an opinion, the reasons therefore should be stated in the audit report.
   b. Contain appropriate, supplementary, explanatory information about the contents of the financial reports as may be necessary for full and informative disclosure about the financial operations of the organization, program, function, or activity audited. Violations of legal or other regulatory requirements, including instances of noncompliance, and material changes in accounting policies and procedures, along with their effect on the financial reports, shall be explained in the audit report.

[The following sections provide further elaboration of selected standards, including:

III.1. Scope of Audit Work
IV.3. Legal and Regulatory Requirements
IV.4. Internal Control
V.3. Content
V.4. Financial Reports]

III.1. Scope of Audit Work

The first general standard for governmental auditing is:

The full scope of an audit of a governmental program, function, activity, or organization should encompass:

1. An examination of financial transactions, accounts, and reports, including an evaluation of compliance with applicable laws and regulations.
2. A review of efficiency and economy in the use of resources.
3. A review to determine whether desired results are effectively achieved.

In determining the scope for a particular audit, responsible officials should give consideration to the needs of the potential users of the results of the audit.

This standard places on officials who authorize and prescribe the scope of governmental audits the responsibility for providing for audit work that is broad enough to fulfill the needs of all potential users of the results of such audits. The standard is not intended to prevent such officials from authorizing specific assignments of parts of the total scope of the audit work required by the standard or from authorizing special audits, nor is it intended to prevent auditors from performing such audits. However, those responsible for authorizing governmental audits are charged with the knowledge that, for most governmental programs, their full responsibility for obtaining audit work is not discharged unless the full scope of audit work set forth in the standard is performed.

The general objectives of the above categories of audit work are as follows:

1. Examinations of financial transactions, accounts, and reports and compliance with applicable laws and regulations shall include sufficient audit work to determine whether:
   a. The audited entity is maintaining effective control over revenues, expenditures, assets, and liabilities.
   b. The audited entity is properly accounting for resources, liabilities, and operations.
   c. The financial reports contain accurate, reliable, and useful financial data and are fairly presented.
   d. The entity is complying with the requirements of applicable laws and regulations.
2. A review of efficiency and economy shall include inquiry into whether, in carrying out its responsibilities, the audited entity is giving due consideration to conservation of its resources and minimum expenditure of effort. Examples of uneconomical practices or inefficiencies the auditor should be alert to include:
   a. Procedures, whether officially prescribed or merely followed, which are ineffective or more costly than justified.
   b. Duplication of effort by employees or between organizational units.
   c. Performance of work which serves little or no useful purpose.
   d. Inefficient or uneconomical use of equipment.
   e. Overstaffing in relation to work to be done.
   f. Faulty buying practices and accumulation of unneeded or excess quantities of property, materials, or supplies.
   g. Wasteful use of resources.

   Efficiency and economy are both relative terms and it is virtually impossible to give an opinion as to whether an organization has reached the maximum practicable level of either. Therefore it is not contemplated in these standards that the auditor will be called upon to give such an opinion.
3. A review of the results of programs or activities shall include inquiry into the results or benefits achieved and whether the programs or activities are meeting established objectives. The auditor should consider:
   a. The relevance and validity of the criteria used by the audited entity to judge effectiveness in achieving program results.
   b. The appropriateness of the methods followed by the entity to evaluate effectiveness in achieving program results.
   c. The accuracy of the data accumulated.
   d. The reliability of the results obtained.

In some cases an auditor may be asked to participate in a program evaluation effort by accumulating data himself for evaluation of a program or activity under audit. When such work is to be done on a coordinated basis, the evaluation techniques should be uniformly prescribed for the whole program at some central level. The auditors at the various program sites should only be required to accumulate data and compare it with the prescribed measures. To do otherwise would be economically unfeasible and would lead to wide variations in the measurements applied to similar projects by different auditors. . . .

IV.3. Legal and Regulatory Requirements

The third examination and evaluation standard for governmental auditing is:

> A review is to be made of compliance with legal and regulatory requirements.

In governmental auditing, compliance with pertinent laws and regulations is particularly significant because government organizations, functions, programs, or activities are creatures of law and have more specific rules and regulations than are usually applicable to private organizations.

This standard places upon the auditor the responsibility for determining whether the organization, program, function, or activity under audit has complied with the requirements placed upon it by pertinent laws and regulations. In reviewing compliance with pertinent laws and regulations, the auditor should consider not only statutes and implementing regulations but also the related legislative history, legal opinions, court cases, and regulatory requirements, including such documents as grant or loan agreements.

When the auditor is at the central-agency level, he should ordinarily take the responsibility for determining the laws and regulations which should be considered in the audit. When grants from another level of government are involved, legal and regulatory requirements should ordinarily be obtained from that level and should be made available through audit guides to the grantee's auditor. To do otherwise would result in substantial duplicate work in cases in which there are two or more entities to be audited. Furthermore, the grantor is familiar with these statutes and requirements and can provide them and the related supporting data with far less effort than would be required by the grantee's auditor.

In making his review, the auditor at the central-agency level should select and review those laws and regulations which have a direct bearing or a significant impact upon the entity to be audited or its operations. The laws and regulations which may apply to a specific government organization, program, function, or activity are often very extensive, and the auditor cannot be expected to review every law or regulation which may in some way impact on the entity. Consequently, this type of review requires considerable judgment. As a general rule, the auditor first should find out from the audited entity's management the legal and regulatory requirements it is required to follow. He then should make his own tests to determine whether any requirements are being overlooked by the entity. Some sources of information on legal and regulatory requirements follow.

1. Legal or legislative data, including:
   a. Basic legislation.
   b. Reports of hearings.
   c. Legislature committee reports.
   d. Annotated references from reference services covering related court decisions and legal opinions.
   e. Historical data relating to the movements to achieve the legislation and similar prior legislation.
   f. State constitutions, statutes, resolutions, and legislative orders.
   g. Local charters, ordinances, and resolutions.
2. External administrative requirements, including:
   a. Memorandums from federal, state, or local administrative agencies.
   b. Guidelines and other administrative regulations affecting program operations from federal, state, or local agencies.
3. Grant arrangements, when grants are involved, including:
   a. Proposals from grantees.
   b. Pertinent correspondence from grantors and grantees.
   c. Memorandums of meetings held to discuss the grants.
   d. The grant documents, including amendments.
   e. Grant regulations.
   f. Grant budgets and supporting schedules.

The nature and purpose of the review of legal and administrative requirements will tend to vary with the element of auditing being performed.

Financial and compliance–The auditor is to test the financial transactions and operations of the audited organization, program, function, or activity to determine whether that entity is in compliance with pertinent laws or regulations. The auditor also is to make a review to satisfy himself that the audited entity has not incurred significant unrecorded liabilities (contingent or actual) through failure to comply with, or through violation of, pertinent laws and regulations.

Economy and efficiency–The auditor is to make a review of the laws and regulations applying to any aspect of the audited organization, program, function, or activity in which he attempts to make a judgment regarding whether existing practices can be made significantly more efficient or economical. Such a review is needed because determinations of how the entity's tasks can be accomplished more efficiently and economically cannot be done properly without an understanding of the purpose of the entity and what it is legally required to do. Such a review is needed also to provide the auditor with information on constraints on the entity's authority to change its practices to make them more efficient and economical.

Program results–The auditor is to review the laws and regulations pertaining to the goals and objectives of the audited entity's programs or activities in sufficient depth to gain a working understanding of the results that are expected from the programs or activities. He must also do sufficient testing to determine whether the program or activities are being performed in conformity with applicable laws and regulations.

IV.4. Internal Control

The fourth examination and evaluation standard for governmental auditing is:

> An evaluation is to be made of the system of internal control to assess the extent it can be relied upon to ensure accurate information, to ensure compliance with laws and regulations, and to provide for efficient and effective operations.

This standard places upon the auditor the responsibility for determining how much reliance he can place on the audited entity's internal controls to ensure accurate information, ensure compliance with applicable laws and regulations, promote efficiency and economy, and produce effective results. His findings will help him determine the extent of detailed examination work he must perform to achieve the objectives of the audit.

Internal control comprises the plan of organization and all the coordinate methods and measures adopted to safeguard assets, check the accuracy and reliability of accounting data, promote operational efficiency, and encourage adherence to prescribed managerial policies. The term embraces the policies, procedures, and practices established or encouraged by management as well as the plan of organization and other measures intended to carry them out.

The characteristics of a satisfactory system of internal control would include:

1. A plan of organization that provides segregation of duties appropriate for proper safeguarding of the entity's resources.
2. A system of authorization and record procedures adequate to provide effective accounting control over assets, liabilities, revenues, and expenses.
3. An established system of practices to be followed in performance of duties and functions of each of the organizational departments.
4. Personnel of a quality commensurate with their responsibilities.
5. An effective system of internal review.

These elements, as important as each is in its own right, are mutually reinforcing and all are so basic to adequate internal control that serious deficiencies in any one normally would preclude effective operation of the system.

A complete review of internal controls as a specific requirement would often be prohibitive in terms of available resources. Examining all such controls would not be efficient auditing because of the irrelevance of some controls to the basic issues which are the subject of the audit effort. Therefore the auditor should concentrate his attention on those controls which are important to the issues being audited.

The extent of work required to adequately review internal control will vary with the element of an audit being performed.

Financial and compliance–A sufficient review is to be made of internal controls to permit the auditor to determine how much reliance he can place upon the accounting records and reports to accurately portray the financial condition of the organization, program, function, or activity and to safeguard its resources. The extent of his own tests of the accounting data should be based upon his assessment of the reliability of an audited entity's internal control. The review should be sufficient to permit the auditor to determine whether policies, procedures, and practices are consistent with the applicable laws and regulations and whether the system of internal control can be relied upon to provide reasonable assurance that such policies and practices are being followed.

Efficiency and economy–The review is to include a review of policies, procedures, practices, and internal controls applicable to any aspect of the activities in which the auditor attempts to make a judgment regarding whether existing practices can be made significantly more efficient or economical.

Program results—The auditor is to review those policies, procedures, practices, and controls which have a specific bearing on the attainment of the goals and objectives specified by the law or regulations that created the program, activity, function, or organization under audit.

Internal review is an important part of internal control, and the auditor should look into such work in performing any of the three audit elements listed above. The auditor should consider the extent of the internal review work and the extent to which that work can be relied upon to ensure that other aspects of internal control are functioning properly. The auditor should take full advantage of the products of the internal review in making his audit.

In view of the wide range in the size, variety, and nature of governmental organizations, programs, activities, and functions, and in view of their organizational concepts and operating methods, no single pattern for internal review activities can be specified. Many governmental entities have internal review activities identified by other names, such as inspection, appraisal, investigation, organization and methods, and management analysis. These activities are often in the nature of management services, and in varied ways they assist management in currently supervising, advising, and reviewing designated functions. To prevent duplication of effort, all auditors—regardless of their level of government—should use, to the maximum practical extent, the work that other auditors or internal review personnel have previously performed.

V.3. Content

The third reporting standard for governmental auditing is:

All reports shall:

1. Be as concise as possible but, at the same time, clear and complete enough to be understood by the users.
2. Present factual matter accurately, completely, and fairly.
3. Present findings and conclusions objectively and in language as clear and simple as the subject matter permits.
4. Include only factual information, findings and conclusions that are adequately supported by enough evidence in the auditor's working papers to demonstrate or prove, when called upon, the bases for the matters reported and their correctness and reasonableness. Detailed supporting information should be included in the report to the extent necessary to make a convincing presentation.
5. Include, when possible, the auditor's recommendations for actions to effect improvements in problem areas noted in his audit and to otherwise make improvements in operations. Information on underlying causes of problems reported should be included to assist in implementing or devising corrective actions.
6. Place primary emphasis on improvement rather than on criticism of the past; critical, but balanced, comments should be presented of any unusual difficulties or circumstances faced by the operating officials concerned.
7. Identify and explain issues and questions needing further study and consideration by the auditor or others.
8. Include recognition of noteworthy accomplishments, particularly when management improvements in one program or activity may be applicable elsewhere.
9. Include recognition of the views of responsible officials of the organization, program, function, or activity audited on the auditor's findings, conclusions, and recommendations. Except where the possibility of fraud or other compelling reason may require different treatment, the auditor's tentative findings and conclusions should be reviewed with such officials. When possible, without undue delay, their views should be obtained in writing and objectively considered and presented in preparing the final report.
10. Clearly explain the scope and objectives of the audit.
11. State whether any significant, pertinent information has been omitted because it is deemed privileged or confidential. The nature of such information should be described, and the law or other basis under which it is withheld should be stated.

This standard places upon the auditor the responsibility for preparing a report that will be easy to understand, will present the scope of the audit and the auditor's findings and conclusions in an objective and complete manner with appropriate support for positions taken, and will provide recommendations for improvement whenever feasible and appropriate.

Conciseness

The reports should be no longer than necessary to communicate the information the auditor is reporting. Reports should not be mired down with too much detail—words, sentences, paragraphs, or sections that do not clearly tie in with the report messages. Too much detail detracts from the reports, may even conceal the real messages and may confuse or discourage readers.

Although there is room for considerable judgment in determining the content of reports, it should be kept in mind that reports which are complete, but still concise, are more likely to receive attention.

Accuracy, Completeness, and Fairness

Report preparation, review, and processing procedures should be applied to produce reports that contain no errors of fact, logic, or reasoning.

The need for accuracy is based on the need to be fair and impartial in reporting and to assure users and readers of reports that what is reported is reliable. One inaccuracy in a report can cast doubt on the validity of an entire report and can divert attention from the substance of the report.

Although reports should be concise, they should not be so concise that they do not fully inform the user. Reports should contain sufficient information about findings, conclusions, and recommendations to promote adequate understanding of the matters reported and to provide convincing, but fair, presentations in proper perspective. Sufficient amounts of background information should also be included.

Readers should not be expected to possess all the same facts that the auditor has, and therefore reports should not be written on the bases that the bare recitals of facts make the conclusions reached obvious or inescapable. If the auditor has conclusions or opinions that he wants the readers to know about, he should state them specifically rather than leave them to be inferred by the readers.

Objectivity

Findings should be presented in an objective and unbiased manner and should include sufficient information on the subject matter to provide readers with proper perspective. The objective is to produce reports which are fair and not misleading and which, at the same time, place primary emphasis on matters needing attention. The auditor should guard against the tendency to exaggerate or overemphasize deficient performance noted during his review.

The information needed to provide proper report balance and perspective should include:

1. Appropriate information as to why the examination was made.
2. Information about the size and nature of the activities or programs to which findings relate so as to provide perspective against which the significance of the findings can be judged.
3. Correct and fair descriptions of findings so as to avoid misinterpretation and misunderstanding. Information should be included on the size of tests and the methods of selecting items to test so that readers may relate such information to the total activity and to the findings.

Adequate Support

All factual data, findings, and conclusions in reports should be supported by enough objective evidence to demonstrate or prove the bases for the matters reported and their accuracy or reasonableness. Except as necessary to make convincing presentations, detailed supporting data need not be included in reports.

Opinions and conclusions in reports should be clearly identified as such and should be based on enough audit work to warrant them. In most cases one example of a deficiency cannot support a broad conclusion and a related recommendation for corrective action. All that it supports is the findings of the fact that there was a deviation, error, or weakness.

Recommendations

The auditor's report should contain appropriate recommendations whenever his review discloses that significant improvement in the audited entity is possible. He should also make recommendations to effect compliance with legal or regulatory requirements when significant instances of noncompliance are noted.

If the auditor cannot make appropriate recommendations because of limited audit scope or other reasons, he should state in his report the reason that he is unable to recommend appropriate corrective measures and what additional work would need to be done to formulate recommendations.

Constructiveness of Tone

The tone of reports should be designed to encourage favorable reaction to findings and recommendations. The titles, captions, and texts of reports should be stated in constructive terms. Although findings should be presented in clear, forthright terms, the auditor should keep in mind that his objective is to obtain favorable reaction and that this can best be accomplished by avoiding language which unnecessarily generates defensiveness and opposition. Although criticism of past performance often is necessary to demonstrate the need for some management improvements, the emphasis in reports should be on the needed improvements rather than on criticism.

Issues Needing Further Study

If the scope of the audit or other factors limit the auditor's ability to inquire into certain matters which he believes should be studied, the auditor should include in his report such matters, if of sufficient importance, and the reasons why he believes these matters merit further study.

Recognition of Noteworthy Accomplishments

Information as to the satisfactory aspects, not just the deficient aspects, of operations examined, when significant and when warranted by the extent of the work, should be included in the auditor's report. Such information is often necessary to fairly present the situation which the auditor finds and to provide appropriate balance to his report. In addition, when such accomplishment may be emulated by others, the inclusion in the auditor's report may result in improved performance by other government organizations that read the report.

Views of Responsible Officials

One of the most effective ways of ensuring that reports are fair, complete, and objective is through advance reviews and comments by persons or by officials of the organizations, programs, functions, or activities whose operations are discussed in the reports. This produces a report which shows not only what was found and what the auditor thinks about it but also what the responsible persons think about it, and what, if anything, they are going to do about it. This kind of report is more useful to the recipient.

Comments on report drafts should be objectively considered and evaluated, and the report presentation and conclusions should give appropriate recognition to them. The advance comments and analyses of them should be fairly presented in the text of reports. An agency promise of corrective action should be noted in proper context but should not be accepted as justification for dropping a significant point or a related recommendation.

When the advance comments oppose the auditor's findings or conclusions and are not, in his opinion, meritorious, the auditor should state his reasons for rejecting them. Conversely, he should drop a point or modify a position if he finds the argumentation to be meritorious.

Scope and Objectives

The scope of the audit should be stated in all reports. Some audits are more limited in scope than others, e.g., those confined to specific functions, activities, or locations. Such limitations of scope should be clearly and explicitly identified. When successive audits vary in scope, the auditor should explain why particular work was or was not performed and also should use individually tailored language in the scope section of the report to define the limited nature or special aspects considered in performing the audit. The time period covered in the audit should be indicated.

The scope of the audit should clearly indicate whether each of the three elements of audit examinations—financial and compliance, efficiency and economy, and program results—were made and the extent of each element.

The audit report should include a summary statement of the objectives of the audit as identified in the audit guide or engagement memorandum. This statement is essential to provide the reader with the proper perspective, i.e., a background against which any reported findings may be considered. Management may request special coverage; this too should be provided in the audit instructions.

Privileged and Confidential Information

Certain financial or operating information is prohibited from general disclosure by management or by federal, state, or local laws or regulations. Such information is usually provided only to persons authorized by law or regulation on a need-to-know basis.

If the auditor is prohibited by such requirements from including some pertinent data in his report, he should describe what has been omitted and the requirement that makes the omission necessary. The auditor should obtain assurance that a valid requirement for the omission exists and that the doctrine of privilege or confidentiality is not applied to information that would reflect unfavorably on management but for which there is no valid reason for withholding.

V.4. Financial Reports

The fourth reporting standard for governmental auditing is:

> Each audit report containing financial reports shall:
>
> 1. Contain an expression of the auditor's opinion as to whether the information in the financial reports is presented fairly in accordance with generally accepted accounting principles (or with other specified accounting principles applicable to the organization, program, function, or activity audited), applied on a basis consistent with that of the preceding reporting period. If the auditor cannot express an opinion, the reasons therefor should be stated in the audit report.
> 2. Contain appropriate, supplementary, explanatory information about the contents of the financial reports as may be necessary for full and informative disclosure about the financial operations of the organization, program, function, or activity audited. Violations of legal or other regulatory requirements, including instances of noncompliance, and material changes in accounting policies and procedures, along with their effect on the financial reports, shall be explained in the audit report.

This standard places upon the auditor the responsibility the auditor assumes for the financial data presented and for providing appropriate explanatory comments on significant financial issues affecting the reports and compliance with legal or other regulatory requirements.

Opinions on Financial Reports

When financial reports of federal departments, states, cities, counties, and other units of government and their programs, functions, or activities are being examined, the auditor should give his opinion as to whether the reports have been prepared in accordance with appropriate principles of accounting, applied on a basis consistent with that of the preceding period, and whether the auditor's examination was made in accordance with the accompanying auditing standards. Illustrative opinions are included in federal audit guides and in pronouncements of the American Institute of Certified Public Accountants.[2] When conformity with special accounting principles is required instead of with generally accepted accounting principles, the special accounting principles followed by the audited organization, program, function, or activity should be specified in the opinion.

Accounting Principles

Accounting principles are guides or rules developed from experience or from research. Their purpose is to provide assurance that the information presented in the financial statements is valid, useful, and reliable. The auditor should make sufficient examination into the accounting principles used to permit a professional opinion as to whether the accounting system and the representations of management evidenced by financial reports are in conformity with such principles. Material changes and the reasons for them, if ascertainable, should be identified and their effect upon the financial reports, both historically and prospectively, should be explained. The auditor should also state his opinion as to the propriety of the change. Accounting principles on which the auditor's opinion is based should be identified in his report, as should statutory or administrative provisions adversely affecting the accounting principles in use by the organization, program, or activity.

Consistency

The auditor should state whether the entity under audit has consistently followed the same accounting principles from one reporting period to another. This standard applies not only to data shown in statements of financial condition and operating reports but also to budgetary or statistical data which may be covered by the auditor's report.

When a qualification is required because of a lack of consistency that is material to the financial report, the qualification statement should describe (1) the reasons for the qualification, (2) the effect upon the financial reports of the audited entity, and (3) the auditor's opinion of the acceptability of the change.

Disclosure

A governmental entity's reports and statements, both financial and operational, ideally should contain the information necessary for users—management, the electorate, creditors, grantors, and others—to form an opinion on the effectiveness of the stewardship exercised by the responsible public officials. The responsibility for providing such information is that of management. However, the auditor should comment if the data provided is insufficient to disclose any matters which may have a material effect upon the financial reports.

Adequate disclosure does not imply or require that an excessive amount of information be furnished. Disclosure should, however, be fair and reasonably complete—but not so complex as to confuse or impede understanding. Information should be reduced to manageable and understandable proportions, yet it should avoid summarization to such an extent that needed background or relationships are omitted or blurred.

Weight should be given to materiality, which is the relative importance or relevance of an item included in or omitted from a financial or operating report. There are no universal ratios or percentages that can be used as standards of materiality for financial or operational processes or transactions. Materiality should be based on judgment.

Six specific indicators of materiality which can be used individually or in combinations are:

1. Absolute dollar amount.
2. Ratio of amount of an item to an appropriate base figure.
3. Length of life of an asset.
4. Importance of the item to the accomplishment of the mission.
5. Importance to the maintenance of adequate controls, such as a pattern of small discrepancies.
6. The characteristic of the items involved, such as indications of malfeasance or misfeasance.

Events that occur subsequent to the end of the period under audit may have a material effect on the operations of the entity or on its operational or financial reports. Such events may affect financial reports directly, may affect the entity with indirect effects on financial reports, or may affect conditions under which the operations take place. If such events occur they should be disclosed in the audit report either by revision of the financial reports or by commentary in the auditor's report.

Legal or Regulatory Requirements

In any governmental audit in which the auditor is expected to give an opinion on the fairness of the presentations in financial reports, compliance with applicable laws and regulatory requirements is a matter of importance because noncompliance might result in liabilities not disclosed in the financial reports. Compliance with laws and regulatory requirements, in many instances, assumes an even greater importance since the recipients of the financial reports and the audit reports also want to know whether funds designated for certain purposes were spent for those purposes.

The standards for examination and evaluation require consideration of applicable laws and regulations in the auditor's examination. The standards for reporting require a statement in his report regarding any significant instances of noncompliance disclosed by his examination and evaluation work. What is to be included in this statement requires judgment. Significant instances of noncompliance, even those not resulting in legal liability to the audited entity, should be included. Minor procedural noncompliance need not be disclosed.

Although the reporting standard is generally on an exception basis—that only noncompliance need be reported—it should be recognized that governmental entities often want positive statements regarding whether or not the auditor's tests disclosed instances of noncompliance. This is particularly true in grant programs where authorizing agencies frequently want assurance in the auditor's report that this matter has been considered. For such audits auditors should obtain an understanding with the authorizing agency as to the extent to which such positive comments on compliance are desired. When coordinated audits are involved, the audit program should specify the extent of comments that the auditor is to make regarding compliance.

When noncompliance is reported, the auditor should place his findings in proper perspective. The extent of instances of noncompliance should be related to the number of cases examined to provide the reader with a basis for judging the prevalence of noncompliance.

Notes

1. The basic standards are included in "Statements on Auditing Standards," issued by the American Institute of Certified Public Accountants.
2. See "Statements on Auditing Procedure," particularly Statement 33.

30 The Expanded Scope of Government Auditing

Alfred Cancellieri and Darryl Enstrom

Preface

In August 1972, the General Accounting Office (GAO) issued a publication entitled *Standards for Audit of Governmental Organizations, Programs, Activities and Functions.* The standards are intended to apply to all government levels. One of the underlying objectives is to stimulate state, local, and federal government organizations to improve the quality of their auditing functions; an additional goal is to facilitate control and evaluation of federally assisted programs.

The GAO standards, as they relate to financial audits, endorse the generally accepted auditing standards of the American Institute of Certified Public Accountants. The GAO standards, however, have expanded the definition of auditing to comprise compliance with applicable laws and regulations, efficiency and economy of operations, and effectiveness of program results.

The standards apply to all government organizations, programs, activities, and functions; in addition, they apply to internal audits and to those audits performed by or for a government entity of contractors, grantees, and other external organizations. Adoption of the standards by various government agencies is required, although each of the three audit components, as described later, can be performed individually. The GAO indicates that all three elements do not always have to be included in the scope of every audit if their inclusion is not deemed desirable or practical, but that the scope and objectives of an audit should be clearly explained in the auditor's report.

Application to commercial and industrial usage of the kind of auditing called for in the GAO standards would appear to warrant consideration. Uneconomical practices are among the basic concerns of both business management and government officials. This attitude is reflected in the following comments of Ellsworth H. Morse, Jr., Assistant Comptroller General of the United States, quoted from his article "Performance and Operational Auditing":

> . . . achieving efficient, economical and effective operations is a basic management responsibility. That responsibility must be discharged in the light of each organization's duties and authority. The entire structure of the management system of organization, operation and control should be designed to achieve this objective.[1]

As stated in *Auditing by Perception,*[2] Coopers & Lybrand ". . . believes that it is the responsibility of the accounting profession to aid in the development and dissemination of techniques and enhance efficiency." One such technique is an operational controls review. Our method for integrating this investigative approach into the Firm's approach to auditing is concisely described in that report.

This [selection] is designed to furnish auditors with broad guidelines for applying the GAO standards as they relate to determining whether or not the government organization being audited is

Reprinted from The Expanded Scope of Government Auditing, *1976, with permission of Coopers & Lybrand (U.S.A.).*

(1) complying with applicable laws and regulations, (2) managing and utilizing its resources in an economical and efficient manner, and (3) achieving desired results or benefits. Examples of findings and recommendations included here are based on audits conducted by Coopers & Lybrand.

This [selection] has been published as part of an overall commitment by Coopers & Lybrand to help auditors in the public sector raise the level of disclosure to the public. As part of this same program, the Firm sponsored a joint study with the University of Michigan on *Disclosure Practices of the Major American Cities: A Public Report.*

GAO's Expanded Definition of Auditing

The expanded audit scope called for by the GAO encompasses compliance with applicable laws and regulations, efficiency, economy, and evaluation of program results. The GAO defines these audit elements as follows:

1. *Financial and compliance*—determines (a) whether financial operations are properly conducted, (b) whether the financial reports of an audited entity are presented fairly, and (c) whether the entity has complied with applicable laws and regulations.
2. *Economy and efficiency*—determines whether the entity is managing or utilizing its resources (personnel, property, space, and so forth) in an economical and efficient manner and the causes of any inefficiencies in management information systems, administrative procedures, or organizational structure.
3. *Program results*—determines whether the desired results or benefits are being achieved, whether the objectives established by the legislature or other authorizing body are being met, and whether the agency has considered alternatives which might yield desired results at a lower cost.

The GAO has structured the standards so that each of the three components can be executed separately. The standards place on those who authorize and determine the audit scope the responsibility for obtaining audit work that is broad enough to fulfill all the needs of potential report users. It is understood that, in certain circumstances, it may not be necessary or feasible to carry out all three elements, but it is essential that arrangements be made specifically indicating which ones will be performed and to what extent before the audit work is begun.

Compliance with Applicable Laws and Regulations

Auditing compliance with applicable laws and regulations requires professional judgment on the auditor's part. Otherwise, the time that it would take the auditor to obtain and review all necessary data might make that review uneconomical or even prohibitive. In addition, there would not be sufficient assurance that all applicable laws and regulations had been considered. The AICPA committee on relations with the General Accounting Office, in its publication entitled *Auditing Standards Established by the GAO—Their Meaning and Significance for CPAs,* states:

> In the absence of established criteria, it will be extremely difficult for an independent public accountant to render a report on compliance which does not include a disclaimer [of opinion] concerning the entity's overall compliance with appropriate laws, rules, and regulations.

To guide the auditor on a compliance audit, those organizations requesting the audits should summarize the various citations to applicable statutes, regulations, instructions, manuals, grant agreements, and other program documents. Furthermore, the organization should identify specific audit objectives and reporting requirements.

If the laws and regulations against which compliance is to be measured are not clear and could, therefore, be misinterpreted, unintentional noncompliance might result. The failure to adhere to applicable laws and regulations can significantly affect a client's operations.

For example, when we were reviewing the various bond ordinances during the audit of a particular city, we noted that certain provisions were ambiguous. One bond ordinance required the city to charge "such rates and amounts for such services and facilities adequate to provide *net water and sewer revenues* equal to not less than 125 percent of the maximum amount for account of requirements on all revenue obligations then outstanding." In performing our compliance tests, we could not find any clarifying language describing which accounts made up "net water and sewer revenue." One interpretation of the provision was that net water and sewer revenues included *all* revenues less *operating* expenses; another interpretation, that only *operating* revenues less *operating* expenses equalled net water and sewer revenues. Under the latter interpretation, the city was in default for the fiscal year being examined.

In another instance, when we were analyzing the various sinking funds required by the bond ordinances, the finance department brought to our attention the fact that the funds deposited monthly towards the semiannual principal and interest payments were being maintained in noninterest-bearing accounts and were not being invested on a short-term basis. The finance department explained that this was a result of the bank's interpretation of the bond ordinances. We suggested that the city negotiate with the bank and place the funds in short-term investments. It did, and interest revenues on the sinking funds climbed by approximately $25,000 annually.

In another case involving revenues, a city government implemented the Firm's suggestion to extend its sewer service surcharges to all industrial customers covered by the ordinance authorizing the surcharge. This action increased ninefold the number of customers being billed and raised sewer service revenues substantially.

To assist the auditor in administering the audit requirements that help detect a client's failure to comply with appropriate laws and regulations, comprehensive audit programs, tailored to particular activities, are required.

Efficiency and Economy

"Operational controls review" is Coopers & Lybrand's term for what is commonly referred to as "operational" or "management" auditing. The Firm's operational controls review is performed in connection with the normal financial audit; the significance of control deficiencies (measured in dollars whenever practical) is discussed in a letter to management. Our approach to the identification of uneconomical practices and inefficiencies in the commercial and industrial sectors applies equally to government organizations.

A key aspect of the operational controls review is the degree to which clients adhere to preferred practices. A preferred practice is one that we have found successful (or a criterion that we have found optimal) through experience with, and study of, many clients over a period of years. There are specific operational auditing procedures for testing conformity with each practice. Failure to follow a preferred practice is one of several signals that a client's procedures may be inefficient or uneconomical. . . .

The use of the preferred practice technique has enabled us to suggest changes that have significantly improved operations in the municipalities the Firm has audited. For example, several local governments have bettered their procurement methods by acting on comments incorporated into management letters. Recommendations have included (1) standardization of similar articles bought for various city departments, (2) establishment of a centralized procurement function to improve a city's buying leverage, and (3) establishment of economic order quantities.

In several cities, we found that the EDP department was not adequately planning and scheduling operations, bringing about both excessive operating costs and deficiencies in meeting the information needs of user departments. For these particular cities our recommendations included:

1. Developing comprehensive long-range data processing plans that would encompass the requirements of each city department, in terms of relative priorities, hardware and systems needs, and level of staff training and experience.
2. Establishing control procedures to enable city councils to properly review and make informed decisions about carrying out EDP plans. These procedures would allow the councils to monitor progress against plans and to decide on the commitment of future funds.
3. Developing hardware and software compatibility with neighboring government units to disperse the development costs and promote processing flexibility.
4. Delegating the responsibility to the internal audit function for reviewing proposed new applications for cost effectiveness before implementation. Involvement during the development phase also helps to ensure that appropriate accounting and operational controls are built into the new systems, thereby preventing later costly revisions.

During an audit of a state's department of education (DOE), we observed that the purchasing policies specified that one of the departmental purchasing office's duties was to "fix standards of quality and quantity and develop standard specifications after consultation with the proper authorities." There were no standards, however, for educational equipment. In their absence, individual schools and offices bought their own equipment on the basis of individual preferences as to make and model. Consider, for example, the following sample of equipment purchases made by 30 schools and their district office.

Equipment Description	No. of Schools & Office Making Purchases	Quantity Purchased	Cost	No. of Makes & Models Purchased
Tape recorders:				
Cassette	30	300	$15,000	20
Reel to reel	10	15	2,500	5
Projectors:				
Movie	30	40	20,000	15
Film/slide	15	40	5,000	15
Slide	10	15	2,000	14
Overhead	15	35	6,500	10
Typewriters	15	75	19,000	12
Television sets	5	25	3,000	3
Phonographs	15	60	5,500	15
Duplicators	15	25	20,000	12
Cameras	5	15	1,300	10

As shown in the table, numerous makes and models of each kind of equipment were purchased. The most extreme example is the purchase of 15 slide projectors, which represent 14 different makes and models. We recognize that variations in the makes and models purchased would necessarily occur, to some degree, because of differences in equipment demands. Accommodating individual preferences and needs in equipment purchases, however, should be balanced against the economics of that practice.

With the expanding use of educational equipment, it was evident that standardization was essential. Standardization makes it possible to consolidate equipment purchases and buy in bulk. In one year, this DOE's equipment purchases totaled approximately $2.3 million. Clearly, bulk purchases make favorable purchase discounts and bid prices feasible, thus reducing equipment costs.

Bulk purchases usually also make it easier to get service contracts because bulk buying generally means fewer brands of equipment are bought; the DOE had been having difficulty in securing service contracts. In addition, many products are also sold with attached warranty service, or warranty availability, and the vendors frequently obligate themselves to perform inspections or adjustments as part of that service. It is desirable that performance of these services be monitored to assure their performance within a realistic period of time. Obviously, the monitoring would be facilitated if fewer and more qualified vendors were selected.

In this particular case, we understood that vendors were generally reluctant to provide repair and maintenance service under all-inclusive service contracts because of the wide range of equipment brands used by the schools. For the fiscal year, the DOE's expenditures for equipment repairs and maintenance were approximately $336,000, of which only $58,000 was covered by service contracts. While, in some instances, service contracts are more expensive than ad hoc repairs, the DOE would almost certainly benefit from the favorable prices for repairs under these contracts.

Bulk purchasing would also offer the DOE the opportunity to obtain time-price contracts. These allow the purchaser to buy required equipment over a period of time at the bid price established in the contract, provided that a specified minimum number of items are purchased. Thus, equipment can be replaced at convenient intervals within the contract period at a fixed price. The purchase of fewer brands could enable the department to determine equipment life on a more uniform basis, making it easier to plan equipment replacements.

We recommended that the department of education develop standards for specifications so that it could (1) purchase school equipment in bulk (we emphasized that the department should continue to press for the necessary information from the various school districts to enable the department to implement a volume purchasing program) and (2) secure repair and maintenance service contracts on a wider scale.

Effective Cash Collections at the County Level

An examination of a county's financial statements revealed duplications of check receipt listings and delays in depositing these checks, thus curtailing the amount of available cash for investment.

The cash application division received certain cash collections, prepared lists of the checks received, and sent lists and checks to the cashier's office. The cashier's office held the checks while awaiting notification from the cash application division of the proper account to be credited. After the cash application division had checked out all the receipts on the list of checks, a second listing, showing the proper account identification, was dispatched to the cashier's office. The receipts were then posted and included with that day's deposits.

We noticed that the elapsed time between preparation of the list of checks and their actual deposit ran from five to seven days; the average dollar amount of a day's mail receipts ranged from $55,000 to $65,000. Therefore, undeposited checks on hand at all times approximated $235,000. Had the county treasurer invested that money at current rates, the county coffers would have been enriched by about $26,000 in yearly interest income.

We recommended that the cashier deposit the cash collection as soon as it was received from the cash application division so that the treasurer could invest the money immediately. If necessary, the revenue could be temporarily posted to a suspense account until the proper coding had been determined.

Program Results

As envisaged by the GAO, the audit of program results comprehends an evaluation of the effectiveness with which established program or activity objectives are being fulfilled. This represents a significant expansion of the traditional audit scope, and is probably best described in the following quote from the American Institute of CPAs' *Auditing Standards Established by the GAO–Their Meaning and Significance for CPAs:*

> Reviewing and reporting on program results, or effectiveness, is on the leading edge of what has been done in auditing. The state of the art is such that little has been established for auditors in the way of precedent, evaluation guidelines, or measurement criteria although information developed in other disciplines may be useful.

This aspect of the GAO's expanded definition of auditing also challenges the auditor in that neither clearly defined goals and objectives nor established and acceptable measurement criteria may have been specified. To judge whether or not a program is effective, results have to be measured against *clearly defined* goals and objectives.

In the absence of clearly defined goals and objectives or prescribed measurement criteria, it may not be feasible for the auditor to ascertain whether a program is accomplishing its desired results or to what extent. Poorly defined goals or objectives may make it impractical to review program effectiveness because others may have differing conclusions about a particular program's effectiveness when measured against inadequately defined goals or objectives. Therefore, to enable the auditor to perform a useful review, standards on which judgments can be based are crucial.

In developing objectives, those responsible (e.g., the body authorizing the audit, legislature, etc.) should consider the following steps:

1. *Define major functions for the program involved.* This requires analysis of the role of a "unit" in relation to the program's overall mission. Functions should cover all of the "unit's" major responsibilities. For example, the main responsibilities of a procurement unit can be expressed in terms of three major functions, namely, provision of materials and supplies (1) of proper quality, (2) on time, and (3) economically.
2. *Derive the objectives from the major functions.* The objectives for each period should represent improved performance for that function compared with the prior period. For example, buying materials and supplies of proper quality leads to the objective of a lower rejection rate, whereas furnishing materials and supplies on time and economically leads to the objectives of fewer late deliveries and reduced operating costs, respectively.
3. *Establish a work plan and a timetable for achieving the desired results.* This entails (1) identifying the procedures that must be completed to carry out the objectives, (2) estimating the time requirements for completing each procedure, and (3) establishing the deadlines for each procedure.
4. *Establish monitoring devices.* These are essential so that the people responsible can be alerted to deviations from plans and targets early enough to take suitable action.
5. *Establish appraisal devices.* These can be used to assess the plan after its completion with a view towards formulating improved future plans.

After the objectives have been defined, evaluation of progress towards the achievement of the desired results may be measured by preparing periodic reports that record actual performance in relation to the established goals, preferably on the basis of accomplishments completed as well as costs incurred.

When requested to perform an audit of program

Exhibit 1: *Flowchart Illustrating Decision Table for Program Results*

DESCRIPTION

1 Does the client have definitive objectives/goals?

2 Objectives must be developed by organization authorizing the audit.

3 Auditor should ascertain the clarity of objectives/goals against which results can be effectively measured.

4 Have quantified and measurable criteria been identified?

5 Agency must identify criteria for use in judging effectiveness.

6 Auditor should determine relevance and validity of criteria used to judge effectiveness in achieving desired results.

7 Has data been accumulated with which to measure identified criteria?

8 Agency should accumulate data on:
(1) resources used
(2) results achieved

9 Auditor must review appropriateness of methods followed and accuracy of data accumulated.

FLOWCHART

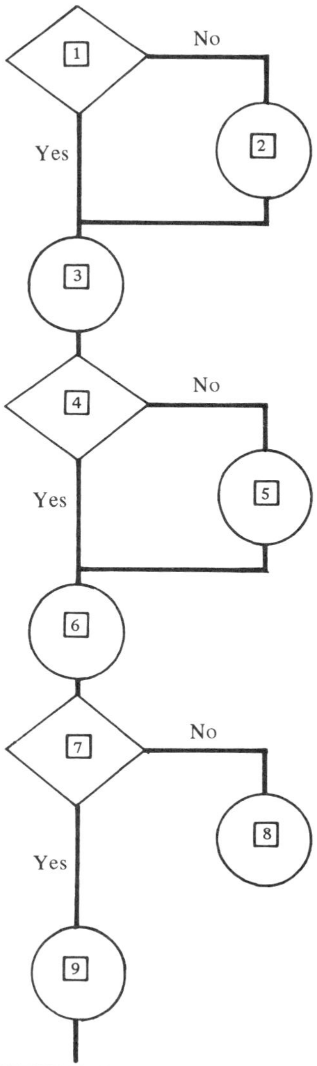

DESCRIPTION

10 Is work to be done on a coordinated basis (i.e., where there are various program sites)?

11 Are evaluation techniques uniformly prescribed?*

12 Agency should prescribe uniform evaluation techniques.

13 Agency personnel at various sites should accumulate data for auditor review and comparison to prescribed measures.

14 Auditor should analyze and evaluate all data in relation to objectives.

15 Auditor should review findings with client personnel.

16 Auditor should prepare his report.

*In the absence of uniform evaluation techniques, wide variations in the measurements applied to similar projects by different auditors may result in inefficiencies in determining the effectiveness of the program as a whole.

FLOWCHART

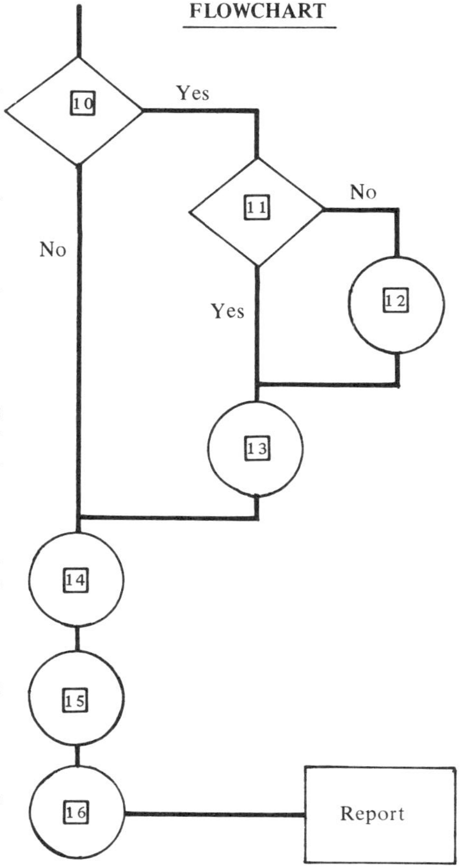

results, the auditor should consider: (1) the relevance and validity of the criteria used by the audited entity to judge effectiveness in achieving program results; (2) the appropriateness of the methods the entity follows to evaluate effectiveness in achieving program results; (3) the accuracy of the data accumulated; and (4) the reliability of the results obtained.[3]

Exhibit 1 illustrates a systematic outline approach the auditor might use in performing an audit of program results.

Summary

Many state and local governments are being crunched in a financial nutcracker, caught between the necessity of offering an expanding number of services that their citizens expect and the problem of paying for those services. By implementing programs based on the GAO guidelines, municipal administrators will have better tools at hand with which to plan, control, and evaluate their operations. They will also find it easier to inform the public where their tax dollars are going and to what effect.[4]

Notes

1. *The Journal of Accountancy,* June 1971.
2. The booklet, *Auditing by Perception,* one of the C&L Reports to Management series, may be obtained by writing to the Coopers & Lybrand *Newsletter,* P.O. Box 682, Times Square Station, New York, N.Y. 10036.
3. Based on *Standards for Audit of Governmental Organizations, Programs, Activities and Functions.*
4. [See] Coopers & Lybrand and the University of Michigan, *Disclosure Practices of the Major American Cities: A Public Report.*

31 The Municipal Audit Choice and Opportunity

What Is the Purpose of Municipal Audits?

Municipal audits are a valuable management tool in evaluating the performance of cities and towns. If municipal officials are to use this tool to maximum advantage, however, they must understand what audits are and must participate actively in the process. The purpose of this [chapter] is to help municipal officials understand auditing and the audit process so they may effectively use independent audits to the maximum advantage of the community and its citizens.

The [chapter] also aims to help local officials plan and organize the auditor selection process. An audit can only yield its maximum benefits if the municipality's non-financial officials, both elected and appointed, are involved in and understand the audit process, and are not inhibited from asking important questions. This [chapter] is designed to enhance their understanding.

What Is an Audit?

An audit is an examination—of systems, procedures, programs, and financial data. The product, or result, of an audit is a report; the most common example of which is the report rendered by an independent auditor of how appropriately an organization's financial statements depict its financial condition and results of its operations. To be able to render a report in which the public, investors, local officials and other users may be confident, the auditor must gain a full understanding of the municipality being examined. An *independent* audit is one performed by persons not affiliated with the organization being audited—the relevant example here being the independent, or "outside," auditor engaged to audit a municipality's financial statements.

Why Is an Audit Required?

In this era, there is increased scrutiny of all levels of government spending. Citizens are demanding better explanations of how government spends tax money. Audit requirements are increasing for all levels of government. One example is federal revenue sharing regulations, which require every recipient of $25,000 or more of revenue sharing funds to have an independent audit of its annual financial statements (including *all* funds) at least once every three years. . . .

Who May Perform Financial Audits?

Financial audits may be performed by certified public accountants, [or others as provided by state or local laws]. . . . Compliance audits for federal revenue sharing purposes must conform to the formally established professional standards known as *Generally Accepted Auditing Standards.*

Reprinted from "Summary of the Audit Process," in The Municipal Audit: Choice and Opportunity, *prepared jointly by the accounting firm of Coopers & Lybrand and the Massachusetts Department of Community Affairs, Office of Local Assistance. By permission of the Massachusetts Executive Office of Communities and Development.*

Why Shouldn't Municipal Financial Officials Select Auditors?

The audit focuses on the municipality's financial systems, and so is necessarily an evaluation of those responsible for the systems' operation. This includes not only the financial officials but all the municipality's departments, because they are all engaged in financial activities. To date, the selection of auditors has often been delegated to financial officials (collectors, treasurers, auditors, and accountants).

Why Should Elected Officials Get Involved in the Audit Process?

Elected officials should get involved in the audit process because their involvement significantly benefits them and their communities. Governing a municipality requires management of its financial affairs; and so it is vital that municipal decision-makers participate in the audit process, which is a key ingredient in overall management. This involvement is important because:

1. The municipality's financial operations and internal controls may be substantially improved as a result of an audit, since auditors are required to report in writing any significant control weaknesses they find, and would normally make recommendations for needed improvements—particularly if their attention is directed to areas of concern by municipal officials at the outset.
2. Precisely because the public's demand for understandable financial information is growing, it is highly desirable—for both the public *and* municipal officials—that this information is supported by the credibility of the professional opinion of an independent auditor intelligently chosen.
3. By participating in the audit process and gaining insight into the financial operations of the municipality, the municipal officials render an important public service, and enhance their ability—and visibility—as public servants.

Financial auditing is an evaluative process performed in accordance with well-developed professional standards. To accomplish an audit, trained auditors must obtain a thorough understanding of the municipality's operations. This in-depth, objective evaluation may result in positive recommendations for revenue increases and expenditure reductions which may save the municipality substantial sums. For example, as a result of audits, Massachusetts municipalities have achieved significant savings from recommendations for improved cash management, centralized purchasing and reductions in fringe benefit costs.

Any in-depth evaluation of a municipality's activities has political implications. For example, if an independent auditor concluded that the municipality's financial records were in such disarray that they could not be audited, people might question what had been happening to public funds over the years, and be concerned with a possible loss in federal or state aid. Even a benefit such as the savings mentioned previously may have political implications because the public might then ask why financial officials hadn't saved money on their own.

Public officials who do not involve themselves in this process will miss an opportunity to gain additional insight into their government's operations and to effect constructive change.

The selection of an auditor can be a challenge. Auditors' capabilities vary, and their differences can be important to the municipality and its officials. As municipal officials who have involved themselves in the selection process have discovered, perceiving these distinctions may be difficult. However, if the municipality is going to realize the maximum benefit of the audit, they must be perceived and evaluated in terms of the municipality's needs.

Who Should Select the Auditors?

It is recommended that the auditors be selected by an audit committee of elected officials who have overall responsibility to the public for the departments to be audited. In addition, it is advisable to include . . . the chief administrative officer and informed citizens as well.

The audit committee should seek the advice of anyone it believes can help—particularly individuals knowledgeable about audits and auditors.

What's Involved in Determining the Municipality's Audit Needs?

Once the committee has been established, it should determine the municipality's particular needs. The needs may include the financial and compliance audit for revenue sharing requirements, any other grant programs which require financial and compliance audits and any specific evaluations the municipality may require.

The committee should also consider other factors in assessing their municipality's needs such as:

- The need for accounting and financial advice.
- The adequacy of controls exercised by the municipality's computer service bureau.
- The need for technical assistance in planning computer applications.

How Specific Should the Request for Proposal Be?

All too often, proposal requests include terms calling for "operational," "performance," "economy or efficiency" audits or combinations of them. If such requests are made, they must specifically identify the types of audits sought and the areas they will cover. Otherwise, the proposing auditors' responses to these requests may be general or lack comparability, thus making it difficult to evaluate them. If the municipality cannot define its requirements for such specialized audits, it may be best not to include them in the initial request for proposal, but rather to discuss the potential for these types of audits with the auditors after they have completed the initial financial and compliance audit and issued their report of comments and recommendations.

Should the Committee Establish Selection Criteria?

Once the committee has determined the audit requirements, it should determine the procedures it will follow in soliciting and evaluating the proposals. Comprehensive definitive selection criteria should be established, and their relative importance assigned by the committee. The criteria are:

- Skill, experience and the amount of time of the specific persons committed to perform the services requested.
- Auditor's demonstrated understanding of the municipality's requirements and plan for meeting them.
- Prior experience and reputation of the auditor in auditing municipalities.
- Price.

Once the municipality's needs—commonly called the scope of the examination—and the selection criteria have been established, the committee should then write its request for proposal and send it to prospective auditors. The proposing auditors' written proposals, oral presentations and references should be judged against the criteria. Checking references is particularly important.

Each committee member's evaluation of the prospective auditors will necessarily be subjective. This should not be of concern. Once the selection has been made, the reasons should be documented and communicated to the appropriate municipal body that has the legal authority to authorize the contract. All the auditors that proposed should be notified who has been selected and the reasons for the selection.

Should the Committee Continue to Be Involved after an Auditor Has Been Selected?

Once the selection has been made, the audit committee should stay involved. It should oversee the preparation and signing of the contract or other agreement, and it should review drafts of the audit reports prior to issuance. A member of the committee or its representative should be designated to maintain day-to-day liaison with the auditors. If the audit is not properly planned and coordinated, it may disrupt the municipality's operations and its benefits will not be realized. At the conclusion of the audit, the committee should determine if another audit should be performed, if so, what type, when and who should perform it (the current auditor or one newly selected by starting the process outlined here again).

What Will the Auditor Expect?

Generally, auditors will expect the following unless stipulated otherwise:

- An organized, timely and well-documented closing of the municipality's books, including adequate supporting documentation and reconciliations of accounts.
- Clerical assistance in typing requests for confirmation and obtaining documents from the files.
- Availability of key personnel to obtain an understanding of the municipality's operations and systems.
- Professional treatment of their staff.
- Adequate working conditions.

What Should the Municipality Reasonably Expect of the Auditors?

The municipality should expect the following from its auditors (whose ability to fulfill these expectations should have been established by the selection process):

- They should communicate what they are going to do and what they have done.
- The individuals involved in the audit should be trained and well-supervised.
- They should plan the timing of the audit procedures to minimize any disruption of the municipality's activities and ensure timely completion of the audit.
- They should immediately communicate any problems they encounter. (The audit committee would be an appropriate recipient of such communications.)
- They should issue a report of comments and recommendations in which weaknesses in financial controls and opportunities to reduce costs and enhance revenues are identified, and suggestions for improvements are made.

The atmosphere in which the audit is conducted should be positive. This is possible only if the auditors and municipal officials fully understand one another's expectations and communicate often and freely.

Should We Have an Audit Every Year?

Because of its benefits, many municipalities which have had an audit [not required by law] intend to continue the audit process on an annual basis. Some of the benefits cited are:

- Auditors' recommendations to improve financial systems have resulted in significant savings through revenue increases and expenditure reductions.
- Recommendations for improvements from an objective, independent auditor are easier to sell and implement.
- The independent audit is a way of evaluating the performance of key elected and appointed public officials.
- The auditor is a resource which may be used throughout the year to provide advice and help you solve problems.
- An audit and the presentation of financial statements with an auditor's report enhances the municipality's credibility in the investment community. It may increase the number of bidders for municipal securities and affect the interest rates which must be paid.